CALL ME BY MY NAME

WOLDE TEWOLDE AKA
OBO ARADA SHAWL

Call Me By My Name
Copyright © 2024 by Wolde Tewolde

All rights reserved. No part of this publication may be reproduced, distributed, or transmitted in any form or by any means, including photocopying, recording, or other electronic or mechanical methods, without the prior written permission of the author, except in the case of brief quotations embodied in critical reviews and certain other non-commercial uses permitted by copyright law.

Library of Congress Control Number: 2024923927

ISBN
979-8-89641-000-3 (Paperback)
979-8-89641-001-0 (eBook)

CALL ME BY MY NAME

By Way of Introduction

It is gratifying that the current Prime Minister of Ethiopia has one name but many titles, such as colonel, doctor and Christian with muslim background and I might add a guerrilla fighter. What a title!!! Congratulations Mr. Prime Minister.

According to the Ethiopian Orthodox astrological calendar, Mr. Abiy belongs to the leadership category, Arbatu Ens'sat. I hope he can join with the others of his type.

The question is does Mr. Abiy know the root causes of the Ethiopian Revolution. If he does not, his rhetorical promises would remain rhetorical. For this reason, I would like to offer him some conceptual historical phenomena that galvanized the Ethiopian Revolution. The true Ethiopian Revolution has not yet been consummated. Everything we had were slogans of one type or another.

The current Prime Minister seems to repeat what Aman Andom and Endalkatchew Makonnen has done before. Mr. Abiy's call for peaceful resolution for Eritrea is not different than that of Aman Andom. The release of prisoners and press freedom is a repeat of what the then Prime Minister Endalkatchew Makonnon has done for ninety days. I hope Abiy's drama will last for one hundred days.

For my readers of "call me by my name" which was regularly written on every month of 13, this sequel will come out on 23rd of each month. I hope, this is a progress of a decade forward.

The causes of the Ethiopian Revolution

Now let us move to the root causes of the Ethiopian Revolution and its accomplishments. There is no dispute that the Ethiopian ancient regime, represented by the Monarchy, the Clergy and Nobility have existed side by side for Millenia. And there was little doubt that ordinary Ethiopians needed change, whether we call it revolution or reform. The following organizations or liberation movements have taken the task to change the ancient regime.

- ELF/EPLF both from Eritrea
- TPLF/EPRDF
- OLF/Mieson
- EPRP

What were the issues of the day? There were three of them. These were: -

1. Land to the tiller aka Feudalism
2. Reactionary Bureaucracy and
3. Imperialism both East and West

Which organization or movement become champion of the above issues? The answer is depicted as follows: -

- The Oromo Liberation Front took the issues of land to the tiller as they were best suited for their territorial conditions. With the help of the Derg, they have accomplished their mission.
- The TPLF with the help of its prisoners of war has accomplished to dismantle what it calls the Shewa Amhara Bureaucracy.
- ELF/EPLF have taken Imperialism by the horn.
- EPRP single handedly is still striving to implement all three issues of FBI (Feudalism, Bureaucracy and Imperialism. It is a daunting task to accomplish.

Can we have undone what is done?

The physical geography of Ethiopia cannot be changed for it is demarcated by Natural phenomena. The political geography can be changed by the will of the people but not by politicians or organizations. The example between Eritrea and Ethiopia is a clear example of noncompliance by the people. In Ethiopia or Eritrea, flags and visas can be issued but the Environment does not allow the Bureaucratic adherents, be it of Karl Marx or Max Weber. Ethiopia is a unique country.

The possible way forward for all politicians and revolutionaries of Ethiopia would be to take heed of the two WW, i.e. Wellega and Wollo provinces. Wellega is in the west representing conservatism and Wollo is in the east representing liberalism. In my opinion, the Oromo and the

Amhara issues are entrenched in these provinces. The North represented by Eritrea's understanding of Imperialism and the South depicted by Socialist Revolution seem outdated.

As to the TPLF, it has immersed itself as an enemy of all the Amharas. It has created its own destruction by targeting the Amhara as the ruling class and now the boomerang came to its own house as another ruling class. What a tragedy!!! As to the people of Tigrai and land, there is not going to be any change. The Tigrians and their land is a bridge to the entire nation of what we call Ethiopia.

Concluding Remarks

EPRP both of Ethiopia and Eritrea has done a wonderful beginning to bring change to all peace-loving nations. EPRP's initial slogan was "Democracia in Ethiopia" and "Peace in Eritrea." To put this into practice, the political party is still holding to the values mediation, arbitration and negotiation (MAN).

Now, it seems that EPRP has a tempo for breathing oxygen from all parties. Everybody seems to collude with Ethiopia, with all people, demand for change and ally to form political parties. All this was enshrined and entitled to the existence of EPRP. Mr. Abiy would benefit from the history of EPRP.

TRUTH WILL PREVAIL
For questions or concerns mail to: woldetewolde87@outlook.com

AADWA TWO: Call me by my name

Obo Arada Shawl

April 13, 2010

A Short Commentary on the recent conferences held on the so-called Horn of Africa

Why the Horn? The Horn looks like a peninsula and it juts into the Arabian Sea and it lies along the southern side of the Gulf of Aden. Physically it stretches to 2 million sq. km and demographically houses app one hundred million people.

According to the classification by the State Department of USA, the Horn of Africa comprises, Ethiopia, Somalia, and Djibouti and currently it includes Eritrea but not the Sudan.

The Horn of Africa is defined by geography and by geopolitics that was why President Bush has established OEF-HOA (Operation Enduring Freedom for the Horn of Africa).

The recent past two conferences on the Horn of Africa - one was held in Arlington Virginia and the other - in San Jose, California were meant to deal with the pure and localized politics of Eathiopia. Whereas, ሙሁር አካል the M"hur Akal of Eathiopians define the Horn in terms of Africa"s wholeness, the ጽን ሐተ ሙሁር Tsin"hattee Muhur Akal class of Eathiopia refers to the politics of Ecountries - the base of our Ethiopian Revolution.

Why is the M"hur Akal class is interested in the so-called Horn countries? I believe because they see the map of Africa protruding into the sea of Somaliland. Ironically, by doing so they seem to symbolize all of us in a country with a non-working government. Their inner feelings reflect in physical geography as opposed to political geography, which is fundamental to our understanding for the success of the two conferences.

The choice of Eathiopia"s Tsin"hattee Muhur Akal ጽን ሐተ ሙሁር አካል depends on the political geography of SEEDS (Sudan, Eritrea,

Ethiopia, Djibouti and Somalia). An honest and correct step for people's integration could follow. For no one in his right mind plant seeds without soil preparation, and this preparation we call it a la DEMOCRACIA.

The conference on the Horn of Africa that was held in San Jose was beneficial in the sense that different alternatives have been presented. They were as follows:

- Federation by Prof. Daniel Kinde – meaning -„we are all equal"
- Confederation by Professor Tesfazion Medhanie – meaning – "separate but equal"
- "Undemocratic atmosphere" prevails in Eritrea emphasizes Prof. Mesfin Araya
- "Under these dictatorial regimes, neither confederation nor federation can be viable alternatives" says Aregawi Berhe (PhD.)
- "Non-violence struggle" as an alternative by Obo Jawar Mohammed
- "Healing and embracing one another" preaches Ato Obang Metho
- "Healing and reconciliation" as a process says Ato Abebe Gellaw

It is true that the above alternatives are beneficial and viable but the question is how.

First things first, let us have a proper name for our country, then let us delimit boundaries and then address one another by Ato or Weizero. Ethiopia and Eritrea do not represent the Horn, rather they represent themselves, are not creation of men. In order to do these we all need to understand the rudimentary concept of democracy if not DEMOCRACIA.

Democracy in two countries but one system

In our case, the first ADWA has happened 104 years ago. The educated muhur Akal has yet to settle the issue of ADWA First in order to move on. Most of them are stuck with it.

For one, ADWA I became a cause for Eritrean nationalist separation and Somalia's claim on Ogaden, Oromia's claim based on Minilik's victory, and above all – the Shewans glory of Minilik in the name of Ethiopia camouflaged also in Minilik first name.

To settle these issues of claim and counter claim, the second AADWA II came into play not to add fuel to the nationalist contest but to move on the path of development of governance, stability and prosperity via DEMOCRACIA.

AADWA II, was genuinely embarked by the University students of Eathiopia not only to heal the rifts between the victims and victors but also to initiate, develop and transfer the positive aspects of ADWA I.

Unfortunately, despite the huge sacrifice of human, destruction of animals and plants (HAP). The Eway Revolution has been damaged and arrested thanks to the vicious leaders who came from the same place of controversy.

What is to be done?

The first step is to take sides. There are three alternatives if and when good governance, development, peace and security are to prevail.

- Those who want to move on with the concept AADWA II, stay and continue the struggle for justice and the rest of freedoms
- Those who want to stick with ADWA I go and enjoy conferences – it is not a new phenomenon we did it before
- Those who want to follow the current leaders whose leaders were born in the same village but not associated with both ADWA AADWA II and I – please go and vote to be voted out. No excuses. We had enough of it.

In other words, ADWA ONE depicted the past; AADWA TWO reflects the future while the TPLF leadership represents the present moment - make a CHOICE.

TRUTH WILL PREVAIL
For comments and questions: woldetewolde@yahoo.com

An Open letter to Ato Mersha Yoseph - BREAKING NEWS OR BREAKING EPRP?

By Obo Arada Shawl

*The crocodile group is dead The animal group is imprisoned
The oak is burning Shaebia and Woyane, give us a break*

~Anonymous

BREAKING NEWS OR BREAKING EPRP?

Was this communicant Political, Intellectual or Ideological? We demand answers.

VOA (voice of America) on June 13 - a day of reckoning - broadcasted an interview with two veteran members of EPRP leadership.

The interview by Tizta Belechew was poignantly straightforward. Here are the two main points of contention.

First: *Why should you have the same name of EPRP, Mr. Mersha?*

Mersha's answer was that no one could have the same name, legally.

If legally, you cannot have the name of EPRP, then what is the point of having the same name? If we cannot accept the rule of law then are you going to fight with guns in order to retain the name of EPRP? I think it is a lesson that we all should learn to accept defeat. It should be an honorable task to hold on to the true name of EPRP. It is one thing to hold on to a true name but altogether a different matter to live by EPRP's values and principles. But tacking a small **d** will not do the trick. EPRP is not a corporation. It is a political party. It is not a separate entity as in „corporation'. EPRP is a human name with emotions and feelings.

Second: *Mersha claims that Iyassou has gone to Asmara to meet Issayas.*

You should have told your audience <u>why</u>, <u>when</u> and <u>how</u> Ato Iyassou met Ato Issayas. If you were doing this just to counter the allegation of signing an "affidavit" for working with Mr. Mellese, this would not work for you but against you.

For me personally, both claims do not only make sense but they are absurd to the core. EPRP since its inception has been struggling

- Politically
- Intellectually
- Militarily and
- Legally in that order

Why this disruption and confusion of the long and arduous pattern of leadership and follower ship suddenly become news for a lot of people? Are we done with the first three areas of struggle of political revolution, intellectual discussion and military operation to move on to the legal (loyal) aspect of struggle? I am sure succumbing to a tyrant and to a dictator while DEBTERAW AND HIS COMRADES ARE IN PRISON will disappoint many people.

That would be my first point.

The second point is that EPRP was well known for working among workers, intellectuals, students, peasants, women and the military. Working among or with them did not in any way mean to spy on them but rather to EDUCATE and if possible to organize them so that they can protect themselves from oppression or exploitation. This is a unique style of EPRP mission and vision, unlike many organizations that infiltrate for spying and policing purposes.

In EPRP's political culture, there was no polarizing figure nor should there be but there were and are issues that polarize and they were resolved democratically.

1. Take the issue of comrades' ሀ እና ለ (Ha and Le),

2. Take the issue of assessment and evaluation of the past struggle in order to continue or to abandon the struggle both inside and outside, which was dubbed as run-away (ብተና)
3. Take the issue of walk- away because of dictators in the leadership,

Are they not all ended up democratically? I believe they were.

But this one – altering name with no legitimacy and no moral aspects will be the first of its kind in the history of four decades of struggle. Mr. Mersha you seem to forget that ዴሞክራሲያ was/is the soul and heart of EPRP. It is the raison d'etre of its existence as one intellectual put it and its asset as one politician has said it to be.

In today's world – a digital age has this to offer: MMT

- My space
- My face
- Twitter

Do these mean anything to you Ato Mersha? I know you are an old guard like me but hey we should adjust to the generation at hand. I advise you to consider the pro and cons of pal talk, radio talk, text messages and many other harmful and useful means of technology.

EPRP from the beginning was denied space – Politically Speaking

EPRP members were denied to show up their faces – Intellectually Speaking

And now are we to twitter of the military?

Where is DEBTERAW, Ato Mersah, answer us, please?

Were you not the last person to inform me about the military operation? Ato Iyassou has outsmarted you even politically when he said "ወያኔ በእኛ ሬሳ ላይ ተረማምዶ ነው ያለፈው" I clearly remember that you were my first hand witness of the so-called final operation to destroy EPRP once and for all. That was then, what about now? Any change?

Please, reconsider your position. You have _walked away_ on the pretext of some dictatorship in the leadership. Promise us that you can **walk-in** when you have promoted your small d to Capital D. But no more confusion, please, enough is enough. Thanks.

CALL ME BY MY ADDRESS:

Solutions with DEBTERAW, II

Obo Arada Shawl alias Wolde Tewolde

The EPRDF led by TPLF stands for Biological relation
The Eway Revolution led by EPRP stands for Ideological Relationships
The EPLF led by PFDJ stands for physical Geography
What do you stand for?

BIOLOGY, IDEOLOGY AND GEOGRAPHY (<B>I<G>)

That the Ethiopian government is biologically organized is an open book.

That the Eritrean government is based on physical geography has become a fact. That EPRP is based on Ideas is well established.

So, what is yours, opposition groups?

BIOLOGY

Since their last emperor of Yohannes who was deeply involved in religious matters was killed, the Aristocracy of Tigrai, on the one hand, began searching for connection to the Aristocracy of Shewa via marriage (blood). The Church, on the other hand, was deeply involved in teaching the masses of Tigrai to be faithful to Orthodox Christianity hoping to live a good life after death.

Leaders of TPLF were emerged and embarked against the Monarchy, the Aristocracy and against the Clergy, hoping that Enver Hoxha will lead them into the worldly Tigrai. Contrary to their expectations, however, their worldly power was fulfilled by the West especially by America. But America is about ideas and investment that the TPLF leaders lack.

The easy outlet for TPLF leaders is to connect with their kin's and kiths of Highland Eritrea. Thanks to the Badme war, they broke the kin relationship. And so, the TPLF embarked, true to the level of understanding, upon biology/ethnicity. Will this ethnic level of consciousness help them to stay in power? The majority of liberated or conscious politicians do not think so. I predicted that they would be toppled by the year 2013 of Pope's year.

The feudal King Yohannes of Tigrai must have infuriated the TPLF leaders for he was deeply a religious man an 'Orthodox Christian' at that. Now that the TPLF seems to be bent on revenge of their king's religious wars, if at all they are confused on what Christianity versus Muslim means. For safety reasons, the leaders of TPLF aspire to lead Ethiopia by dividing on biological terms. But this division is very dangerous. It did not work for Hitler with all his capability and ideology.

Blood is thicker than water, is an outdated and out of line concept in the modern world.

IDEOLOGY

EPRP from day one embarked on concepts and ideas for transforming Ethiopia and its people.

EPRP leaders boldly came out that neither biology nor physical geography should be a panacea for Ethiopia and Ethiopians. Instead, they taught its members and associates members about ideas (ideology) that will solve the cultural oppression and economic exploitation by a method known as DEMOCRACIA and Revolution. As most of my readers remember, the land question, the labor question and the capital question have been and still are in the agenda of EPRP despite the Monarchy's surrender, the disarray of Military Dictatorship and the capitalists' confusion. EPRP's demands were clear then and clear now. They are land to the owner! Employment for the urban dwellers and a debt free nation should be the ultimate desire of our people. No more no less.

Let us ask ourselves now. What happened to the land? Who owns it? What about employment, education? And what about national debt? These are questions to be answered by many of us in the Diaspora and elsewhere.

In other words, EPRP is demanding justice for political prisoners as well as for private individuals and food for the entire populace. Can EPRP collective leadership deliver *justice and food? One has to search and* *find their liberal politics and social conservative history, along with their balanced values of Kolegna, Weina and Degegna (***KWD**)*,* in order to answer this question. Peace with their enemies and democracies within their own party was and is the hallmark of EPRP, regardless of some dissenters in the party apparatus.

What is not accepted is the struggle of EPRP's powerful ideas and methodology. It is one thing to research and establish for what EPRP stands and another matter to lump together TPLF, EPLF and EPRP together. It is true, three of them have similarities in organizational principle but they had very dissimilar ideas and concepts of **Modernization**, **Unity**, Religion and **Education** (Mu-Re ሙሬ).

GEOGRAPHY

The Eritrean Liberation Front (ELF), the precursor of EPLF had clarity in its goal and objectives.

It wanted to demarcate Eritrea from Italian colonial boundary. EPLF had no clear contention of the boundary other than separating Eritrea from Haile Sellasie's Ethiopian rule, having labeled itself as a progressive front. The emphasis of EPLF was on the concept of self-reliance. This self-reliance neither fits with Ethiopian Fronts nor with foreign nations. In fact, a mixture of fear, confusion, outrage and nervous hope has reigned among Eritreans. In other words, EPLF leadership did not seek for a political geography despite the Eway Revolution of Ethiopia. EPLF is still based its agenda for itself and others on physical geography devoid of political geography.

Where and Why is DEBTERAW is in prison?

It is to be recalled that on July 3, 2008, a one-day event was held to memorialize or to immortalize DEBTERAW Tsegeye G. Medhin. The participants and the attendees have almost agreed that DEBTERAW has three personalities, that of a Prisoner of conscience, that of an Artist as poet/literary and that of revolutionary Politician.

The three dimensional nature of DEBTERAW as a Prisoner, as an Artist, as a Politician has been explained to the full house capacity of attendees.

Since the Eway Revolution of 1974, until 1991, DEBTERAW was deeply involved in Revolution. As the AEthiopian majority live in rural peasant areas without economic infrastructure, DEBTERAW and his political party thought, it was proper to educate the majority of people in the countryside, first and foremost. At the time, 95% of the population was using traditional modes of transport such as mules, horses and walking on foot. Also, 90% of the goods in Ethiopia were being transported either by camels, donkeys or on human backs. Not only transportation and communication were missing in AEthiopia but also Mass Media such as newspaper, radio and telephone were either in short supply or they were banned. This scenario did not create any doubt among student body and professionals in Ethiopia and Eritrea at the time. In fact, this scenario has led to initiate the Revolution from the countryside. As a result, an armed revolution was launched in the countryside.

Power, according to historical contexts has three elements that of a coup d'etat, insurrection and protracted guerrilla Revolutionary war. DEBTERAW did not believe in coup d'etat, EPRP did not support insurrection although some EPRP leadership members have knacks for it.

DEBTERAW's EPRA is a revolutionary army or what we call ANKI (አንቂ) army. MANKAT (ማንቃት) means to identify your enemy on class basis. Scientific knowledge and religious knowledge are not contradictory. They are complementary for DEBTERAW and his party of EPRP. Herein lies the basic difference between the army of TPLF, EPLF and EPRA. This should be the main focal point of discussion among professors and doctors if they want to solve the problem of AEthiopia.

DEBTERAW was captured alive when the TPLF with its allies attacked EPRA's liberated zones during the 1990. Where is he now? For 17 years, he is held incommunicado somewhere in Tigrai province or state (note that Tigrai is an isolated Killil, it is neither a province nor a state of AEthiopia). That means he has no address, for Tigrai is inaccessible to any Ethiopian. Compare this cruelty to the DERG's era of holding prisoners. During the DERG's time, every prisoner was allowed to see or to be visited by friends or family members. My mother in law was permitted to visit her daughter in Makalle prison. I used to be visited by my family members every week and supplied with food everyday while in Alem Bekegne prison. In this sense, the DERG was better than the Woyane and Shaebia's way of handling prisoners. Too many literatures have been written and anecdotal stories have been told and retold about the cruelties of the current governments of Ethiopia and Eritrea.

Conclusion

Belief of a system of government where the *rule of law* and *rule by law* simultaneously prevails regardless of biology or geography is EPRP's mantra. EPRP did not have role models neither for religion for it is a private matter nor for politics for it is public domain. EPRP follows the zonal dimension of Degegna, Weinegna or Kolegna in terms of geography. It is about natural settings of demarcation regarding of geography and orthodox system of religious belief. EPRP members and associates respect all the five places of worship, i.e. The Church, the Cathedral, the Mosque, the Synagogue and the Board Room. I believe that is why DEBTERAW and his party have transcended into the Fifth Dimension.

I do not know whether, the EPLF or TPLF leaders accept these places of worship or seeking a place in Hinduism, Taoism, Buddhism or Atheism.

For comments and critics woldetewolde@yahoo.com

CALL ME BY MY NAME & ADDRESS;

A Commentary Solutions with DEBTERAW

The Burning Issue or the Entertaining issue!

November 23, 2008

- One was born in Eritrea's village dominated by Catholics and the other was born in Gonder town dominated by Orthodox Christian
- Both were Revolutionaries one in political science the other in artistic songs
- One is a professor by profession and the other a singer by trade
- Both individuals are Arada and from Arada – if you know what I mean!
- One lives in NY, where anything goes and the other lives in Addis, where everything fails.

The professor is Mesfin Araya (PhD) and the singer is Tamrat Molla (Ato). Why are you comparing these two individuals, one may ask. One of them is my friend and the other is from my Kebele. Although I have personal knowledge about them, I do not wish to write something of a personal nature. My interest in writing this article is about issues that concern all of us, old, adult or young, male or female, literate or illiterate. I believe there is a missing link between what singers grasp and what theoreticians or Revolutionaries were supposed to understand and apply.

A week ago, two events have happened, one Online Web and the other on Radio Wave. My comments might help to educate *readers and listeners. Please, read the speech and listen to the interview.*

A commentary on the Professor's speech

Professor Mesfin gave a speech on the occasion of EPRP's 36th anniversary. It was true that EPRP was a vanguard for the Ethiopian Revolution, because revolution by definition was anti establishment. Notice, It was not about *change!!!* For that reason too many progressive student leaders, workers, trade leaders, teachers and progressive bureaucrats had joined the EPRP and of course, thousands if not millions had followed what EPRP was doing, saying and writing in the publication of DEMOCRACIA.

What about now? How do literate people like the professor show or lead EPRP members or supporters to get going, especially at a time when there is a rift or confusion in issues of names and addresses? A slogan to call that EPRP is the sole political leader for Ethiopia is not tenable. We do not have to be an EPRP apologist to feel a twinge of pity for the insult condemnation of the party. The Revolutionary Party had and has to tolerate all names and abuses. EPRP was and is not about leadership per se. It was about the burning issues of peace in Eritrea and dismantling the land tenure system in the rest of the country. Since all our bets were on democracy, EPRP since its inception to the current DEBTERAW's dungeon prison and beyond has not yet to be fulfilled.

What is democracy? Call me by my name and address.

"There is no river that you did not cross, no mountain that you did not climb and there is no blood that you did not split."

The above may be a figurative statement but it does not beat to the tune. The statement sounds very militaristic. It has no democratic tone.

But EPRP was and is about democracy. It is about capital D not M. In fact, the infamous slogan coined against the works of EPRP was. Those who became enemies of EPRP were not only the DERG, the EPLF or the TPLF but it was and is WE – the civil society that had difficulty in understanding FREEDOM OF CHOICE. Is this not the same thing what the current opposition groups are portraying? Democracy is not embedded in our culture. It is a cultural thing – political at that. What is democracy and what is leadership?

Suffice to say at this time that Tesfaye Debessay (PhD), a Catholic, Tsegeye G.M. aka DEBTERAW, (an Aethiopian scholar) and Osman

Ahmed (Engineer), a Muslim have worked together hand in glove with the understanding of common bond, balance and boundary (CBBB).

I do not want to go on commenting on professor Mesfin's message at this time. There are too many flaws open for argument.

"EPRP had plenty of educators and Revolutionaries but not plenty of business leaders – least political leaders. AEthiopia needs high-profile politicians, intellectuals and business leaders collectively what I call.

Professionals do not wear masks, however, history and politics is their witness.

Is the professor seeing miracle or mirage? All post discussions about EPRP centered on diversity of thought and vigorous debate on issues and being able to surround oneself with people with whom you disagree without being disagreeable, because we feel that it is going to lead to a better answer. What is the better answer? That is the burning question of the time. One possible answer is how to organize. If I were the professor, I would train and organize many EPRP members and supporters in his University, which would not be difficult for him.

A commentary on the singer's speech

Although the purpose of the interview was meant to get financial and moral support for Tamrat's deteriorating health conditions, Abebe Belaw, the radio monitor, raised issues of political nature. The singer was hailed as a hero for fighting against feudal titles or feudalism.

What is Feudalism anyway?

Feudalism is a term used in the early modern 12th Century long before Gondar was founded. It has legal as well as military obligation where lords tenants (and kings live not in the political system we know today. In feudal system, on the one hand, the status of a person depended in everyway on his position on *the land,* while on the other hand, land-tenure) determined political rights and duties.

For almost 400 years, several Neighborhoods or Quarters have traditionally divided Gondarians. Those who claim power from the dynasty of king Solomon such as the Hamasiens and the Shewans usually had no fixed capital. By 1635 FASSILIDES had founded his rule at Gondar. Gondar became an old imperial capital of the historic BEGEMDIR (the land of the Beja tribe). For a singer as Tamrat feudalism may be difficult to define precisely as a working definition. I have no doubt though that Tamrat knew the social aspect of feudalism.

EPRP has defined feudalism by analogy as Semi-Feudal where there were (aristocrats erfs in practically in all northern Ethiopia and landlords and tenants in the rest of the country. In short, oppression ( ) and exploitation (has become the norm in Tamrat's days. He has seen it in Gondar and he has seen it in Addis Ababa being practiced.

In order to alleviate the political oppression and the economic exploitation, EPRP with its committed and dedicated members and supporters had gone into a territory where no man has gone before so to speak. The liberated and the conscious Gondarians fought Melaku Teffera to the bitter end.

Singer Tamrat – though technically rebelled against his father, he did not rebel against *the root causes of the problem*. His song was just a reflection of the popular demand of the time, after all art is the reflection of the populace.

I have attended the ratification of the DERG's Constitution in our Kebele. The meeting was scheduled to last for four hours. The Kebele cadres spoke for half of the time only on and Tamrat was the top speaker on the issue of DIKALa. No wonder the DERG has to collapse on its own merit. Later on, we have learnt why the issue had become important as Menghistu Haile Mariam begotten a child out of wedlock. One wonders where this child is today.

The point I am trying to make is that the singer did not or could not have played a role model for eliminating feudalism. He was only an instrument who did not understand the feelings of his father let alone the source of feudalism. By the way EPRP has never fought a cultural war. It was very careful not to indulge on people's culture. On the contrary, many individuals assumed names of minorities to diffuse oppression. I believe the famous name Hama Tuma must have come to be something to do with it.

Concluding Remarks: One-Seven-Eleven

I have always believed in the process of democratization, which incorporates, conceptualizing- designing-planning-programming and budgeting (5 tasks).

In EPRP's lexicon, (5). Alternatively,

- Information officer
- Organizer
- Strategist
- Manager and
- Leader

And by slow accretion of small changes over long periods, EPRP's vision, mission and value has taken place as Professor Mesfin has pointed out in his speech. But it should be remembered that the contribution of EPRP was undoubtedly via DEMOCRACIA – the rule of the people, by the people for the people. Democracy is not about division; it is about Unity in a unique way.

Neither the type of call by the professor nor the claim of the singer is warranted.

DEBTERAW has shown us all those Revolutionary steps progressively for almost 40 years and we should continue to uphold if we so desire to unite the whole country known as AETHIOPIA. DEMOCRACIA is the way and let us choose to pick one or two tasks as specified above but not grapping all of them at the same time.

For comments and questions: woldetewolde@yahoo.com

Call me by my Name, Address or Title ...

NAT

By Obo Arada Shawl

June 7, 2009

I am ignorant, please educate me

On Ferenji

I am ignorant
Answer me why the C.I.A. aspire to **yoke** the Blue & Red of Aethiopia
Answer me, if you know
Why the European Parliament wish to **untie** the yoke
Tell me, if you know
Why the Asians penetrate unto us

On Nationality

I am ignorant,
Educate me why Mr. Afeworki wants me to be an Eritrean
Tell me also why Mr. Zenawi, his ally don't want me to be an Eritrean
Answer me why the Oromos want me to be an Oromian, If and when they become Independent
Not from Eathiopia but from Abyssinia
Educate me why I cannot be a Somalian
Do I have the right to be a citizen of any country?
Please tell me if I can't be

On Religion

I am ignorant,
Educate me why the Pentecostal Christian wants me to join them
Tell me if you know, why the Catholics want my misery Tell me again why the Protestants dearly love me Answer me, why the Muslims find interest in me
Educate me, why the Jewish Community admire my company
How ignorant can I be?

On Language

I am ignorant,
Answer me, if I am qualified to be an Amharic speaker
Please, tell me if I am an Amhara Answer me, what an Amhara is For I know many languages Based on languages
Where does one belong?
In America, Asia or Europe
Tell me if you know

On Politics

Strange as it may sound,
I love the sound of BR (ብር)
Than the BR itself (Blue and Red states)
I love EE countries, in fact everything about E Strange as it may sound, I don't like the Asian mix For I am Yoga
Connected to by land and Rainfall Connected to History and Culture (ሀር) I am an Eathiopian

CALL ME BY MY ADDRESS:

A commentary on Marathon and Sprint

By Obo Arada Shawl alias Wolde Tewolde - August 27, 2008

> *"In America, if you have a name, an address and a phone, they say you are in business; in Ethiopia, if you have a title, a family and a community, we say that you are an entity."*
>
> ~Anonymous

In America, there are over 60, 000 baby names while in Ethiopia there are less than five thousand baby names averaging one name for 5,000 and 12,000 respectively. What about addresses and phones, I will leave these to my readers to figure it out. As for me, I have my name though I am still searching for my address. My address is where Debteraw and many others have disappeared.

Last two weeks, I have viewed two phenomenal events one in China and the other on Ethiopian websites. The Chinese, of course was about sports but the Ethiopian was about politics - of leadership.

The Beijing event was exceptionally phenomenal as it was watched by the sports fun and world leaders who were perhaps interested in the way China functions. The other phenomenal event was the proposal by a professor lawyer who went on rampage to nominating leaders for Ethiopia. The Chinese have displayed their past and their future using the number 8 i.e. E-3

The name of Obang Metho is familiar not in real Ethiopia but in the Ethiopian websites. I appreciate him for using his native name unsparingly.

He is one of the few individuals who are courageous enough to be addressed by given names. Call me by my name. What is in a name?

However, despite Ato/Mr Obang's effort to blend the past and the future, he has failed to show how to blend them. It would have been much simpler had he resorted to the past history of Gambella, where the Ethiopian tourist organization promoted the number 13 i.e. B. I hope Mr. Obang admits that Ethiopia is a country of the 13th months of sunshine. I believe that the number 13 is the solution for Ethiopia's past and future, in spite of the incident that happened on

December 13, 2003 – the cause for the Anuak massacre.

Although I do not know how Ato Obang thinks about the use or abuse of Gambella as a tourist center during the Monarchy time, or how he sees the Bridge of Gambella that was built foe no economic value. Menghistu Haile Mariam personally supervised to build a bridge – the longest bridge at that - with 210 m. in length. The Gambella bridge was not only the longest bridge in Ethiopia but it also the only bridge flooded by neon lights. I do not know much about Ato Obang except via the Internet but I know way too much about his birthplace. Does Mr. Obang know that his birthplace is the Center of Africa as studied by the Russians?

I am not writing to demean the lawyer professor but to remind him that he is unintentionally assisting to destroy the bridge that is intended to connect the Afar, to Gambella via the highlands of Ethiopia, i.e. the beginning to the future (A-G). This is the Marathon political struggle of Ethiopia. Mr. Obang seems to prefer a struggle of Sprint.

At the Olympics, the sprinters of America (both men and women) have failed but the Marathons of south of Ethiopia have prevailed. So the wind is not coming from the west as in Gambella, it is coming from Kenya, to the south of Ethiopia. A big O is coming from the south too. In the name of harmony, I advise Ato Obang to follow the spirit of Baro and Sobat rivers. They just flow smoothly. We have had enough resistance from the North. But the Northern have history, some positive others negative. I am not sure the use and abuse of Ethiopia's name in Obang's literature. Is Mr. Bang referring to the Biblical Ethiopia, Minilik's Ethiopia, Haile Sellasie's Ethiopia, Menghistu's Ethiopia, Zenawi's Ethiopia or the citizens of Ethiopia? Which address is he interested in? Ato Obang writes about Anjuak justice. What about others justice? If there is no moral or legal law in the entire country of Ethiopia, how is it possible to acquire justice for the Anjuaks? Mr. Obang by implication is accepting the dictatorship of the ethnic minority. What is normally or internationally norms of justice is through the recognition of the rule of the majority and the rights of the minority. If I am wrong, please, Mr. Obang I am ready to listen and learn.

The main reason I am attempting to remind Mr. Obang is to challenge his article on nominating or suggesting the would be Ethiopian leaders at the disposal of those who spent their lives to solve problems of Ethiopia be it oppression or exploitation. What kind of leaders is Ethiopia looking for, Mr. Obang? Moral leaders, business leaders, social leaders, religious leaders, military leaders and so on and so forth, who are you looking for? I think you were referring to political leaders or national leaders. I also think Mr. Obang wanted to build a bridge, a bridge of reconciliation and harmony. As Mr. Obang knows the physical bridge of Gambella did not bring harmony between Menghistu and citizens of Ethiopia. Was that why Mr. Obang was unable to nominate leaders from the Menghistu era, from the aristocracy, from the Fronts, from political parties and from the military veterans? Mr. Obang's reasoning seems to me that he does not like those people who struggled to change the feudal, bureaucratic and the imperial (both socialist and capitalist) systems. Mr. Obang should focus on his pastor Christians not meddling in politics, economics, sociology, engineering etc. etc. Or is there something Mr. Obang is after. Let us hear from his side, particularly we want to know how Mr. Obang Metho understands the word

Debtera least to know the whereabouts of DEBTERAW.

I hope the professor will read the following article, which might help him to connect the past to the future. The article is on the nature of Ethiopian marathon of political struggle in the hope that Mr. Obang might revise his nominations for political power or abstains from it.

NB:

This article was written on the eve of the London talk before the TPLF and the EPLF were handed or assumed political power. It was submitted to IMBLTA magazine but the editors never published it. Some revisions have been made to reflect to the current condition.

It is to be recalled that the Imblta groups were advocating that democracy was a fait accompli with the coming of EPLF and TPLF. Currently the then editors of Imblta have become president of Addis Ababa University and the ambassador of the Ethiopia to the United States of America. With their appointments, democracy is halted. Indeed a fait a accompli! This is a lesson for Mr. Obang and others. The Imblta group was minority in the community of Ethiopian intellectuals and they could not bring justice but injustice.

Demo a fait accompli too?

Points of Departure: Myth/Reality

- Zonal habitation – occupational territory
- Multinational – museum of people
- Oldest nation – first man's settlement
- Christian Island – tolerance of religion
- Colonialism - Democratization

Societal Change: The means justifies the end

- Coup d"etat (classical style)
- Insurrection (Russian/French style)
- Protracted War (Chinese style)
- Rose/velvet/yellow/Ginbot 7 Revolutions (untested style)
- DEMOCRACIA (Ethiopian style)

The new World Order: The end justifies the means

- Truth
- Faith
- Peace
- Democracy
- Prosperity

Concluding Remarks

Demo a fait accompli too?

Without comparison to make, the mind does not know how to proceed

-Alexis de Tocqueville

Introduction

Nothing is more common these days than the idea that the people living in Ethiopia are eminently sane given the fact that a great number of individuals in the midst suffered from severe form of hunger, revenge and desperation. Is this because of AEthiopian societies have become politically conscious as a result of their bitter struggle for revolutionary change or because of their human conscience deeply rooted in their long **history** and **culture** (²`)?

For whatever reason, the Ethiopian societies have proven themselves in a time-honored manner to be saner than was expected of them. Some displayed extreme discipline for not fighting over the distribution of food aid, a probable result of a philosophy deeply ingrained in „man does not live by bread alone". Others showed mercy for not shooting their fellow men. Further, the soldiers turned their guns against their rulers who became unruly arrogant. In short, the AEthiopian ∀ populace showed restraint and magnanimity towards their fellow men. To the present day, all acts of provocation of ethnicity, regionalism or religiosity are being rejected.

In this article, an attempt will be made as to how AEthiopian intellectuals, particularly Revolutionaries, have theorized to seize political power. After all it is in the area of politics and economics that the AEthiopian people need clarification, as they are well aware of their cultural, historical, linguistic and religious differences.

Points of Departure: Myth/Reality

AEthiopians because of their heavy dependence on oral tradition have been subjected to oral myth/reality syndrome, particularly since the onset of the revolution. Many points of departure prominent among them are an issue of colonialism vis-à-vis democratization. As a result individuals and groups have varied facts and opinions on the following issues:

1. That AEthiopian society live in three distinct zones of climate, DEGA (2400 m above sea level), WEINA (1700-2400 a.s.l.) KOLA (below 1700 m a.s.l.)
2. That their country is inhabited by many nationalities making it a museum of people
3. That their society is as old as the Bible dating back to the creation of AE (Adam-Eve)
4. That their country is a Christian Island surrounded by Islam making it a nation of religious tolerance.
5. That an alien concept of colonialism and national self-determination has deeply wounded them.

For the common people of Ethiopia, the above points are simply a matter of observation and belief. However, on the part of the intellectuals, the above assertions require thorough research and study especially the fifth dimension of colonialism and self-determination.

What about the émigrés intellectuals at large? Why do we keep repeating social blunder? Is it because of a false step (faux pas) in the idea of progress that is implicit in the myth of the left – which feeds on the idea of a continuous movement or is it because the new world order including its philosophy is in catastrophe?

Was Ethiopia a nation of immigrants melted in a traditional way? Is it as old as Japan and Iran? If so could it have been as rich as Japan or as independent as Iran? Or is AEthiopia as old as any African country? Do AEthiopian people live along religious lines or climatic zones? Without fully answering these questions can we be so sure that by claiming part of these societies we are not deceiving ourselves? It is therefore unnecessary and unwarranted for the intellectuals to try to conclude about the myth/reality of AEthiopia before they can answer the previous questions satisfactorily.

Many a neurotic believes that his/her compulsive rituals, or his hysterical outbursts are normal reactions to somewhat abnormal circumstances that occurred in Ethiopia. How do we view ourselves? Have we shown any wisdom in keeping the equilibrium of Ethiopia? The balance between politics and religion; between names and address; between transport and communication and the marathon and sprint and of myth/reality is still hanging on a tight rope.

Broadly, the intellectuals are of two kinds: One group is that which follows the wish of the people and the other which became if not inconsiderate of its peoples" misery and its country's degradation, at least, inconsistent with its actions.

For fifty years now, our intellectuals have seem to be saying "give us problems, we can create enemies". Without knowing what AEthiopians actually want, or what is essential to them; whether it is money-sex-pride; whether psychoanalysis or Marxism: whether to live individually or collectively, our intellectuals" chose categorically either of Marxism or confusion.

Why? Daily humiliation of the colonized Eritrean, Oromian, Somalian or Tigrian, his/her objective subjugation is not merely economic. Even the poorest colonizer thought himself to be – and actually was superior to the colonized? That too is part of the colonial privilege. May be this is true, but isn't the motivating force of the colonization economic? Deprivations of the colonized are the direct result of the advantages secured to the colonizer. The Eritrean, the Oromian, the Somalian and the Tigrian nationalist have all claims that colonial privilege is not solely economic. However, EPRP has taught tirelessly the difference between *oppression* and *exploitation*.

SOCIETAL CHANGE: The means justifies the end

At the onset of the Ethiopian Revolution of 1974, by and large, the majority of Ethiopians aspired for a societal change, perhaps for a revolutionary one. This can be testified by the fact that only few people stood by the side of the collapsing Imperial rule. It is safe to assume therefore, that the majority of AEthiopians had supported the revolutionary change. What fascinated me most was the line-up of the domestic forces, organizations in overt and covert forms to follow the direction and instructions of DEBTERAW's DEMOCRACIA calling for a REVOLUTION and the present outcome of the effort for a second round of change.

What are revolutions and why do they occur? Why do some succeed and others fail? Are they necessarily violent upheavals, or can there be non-violent revolutions? Why do people rebel? What motivates them to risk their lives for such a cause? For centuries, the main question in revolution has perplexed social scientists, philosophers and even rulers. No one can answer these questions satisfactorily. A revolution may succeed or fail-the emphasis is on the effort – on the part of the revolutionaries and may choose as its object of a political/social transformation, or simply a change of rulers.

Perhaps the most useful definition of it is that which combines questions of success, violence and the object of revolutionary change." A revolution is any attempt by subordinate groups through the use of violence to bring about (1) a change of government or its policy (2) a change of regime, or (3) a change of society, whether this attempt is justified by reference to past conditions or to an as yet unattained future ideal."

What then, is a revolution in the AEthiopian context? The AEthiopian Revolution is a mixture of all three and it has both a success and a failure story. It was not only purposive but also developed ideological justifications and invariably entailed violence. Although the outcomes are not yet documented, the anti-feudalistic rule as reflected in the "land to the tiller" and the bureaucratic rule as portrayed in the "Amharanization" process seem to be over. The socio- economic inequality as proclaimed in the fight against "both imperialist" has yet to be redefined.

The national/nationalities question was ill conceived and poorly debated. Most of us were inclined towards optimism that once our people are enlightened (agitated), the natural order of things would assert itself. That is, the old tradition, prejudice and fanaticism that were prevalent in Ethiopia would be put aside. The problem was how to enlighten (inform), organize and arm the Ethiopian nationals/nationalities.

It is in this process of politics/economics (T"n*f*& TÅ^Ë*f* ሃ "Tc ፥ Öp mankat, mastatek ena mastatek) that AEthiopian intellectuals have failed to spell out to the Ethiopian people. Political/social transformation or a simple change of ruler was at the cornerstone of each struggle. Undeniably though, all agents of change have adopted the three classical (historical) method of taking power by means of: -

1. Coup d"etat
2. Insurrection and
3. Protracted war
4. Ginbot 7

I will deal with each of them in the manner of my observation, experience and judgment.

Coup d'etat (Sð"pK S"Ócƒ mefenkle mengst)

A coup d"etat is an attempt to change a government by a sudden attack against the actual machinery of administration. Under proper condition, a comparatively small number of determined men can capture the state. It is for men who could never hope to raise or equip armies for a civil war, or with no chance of calling forth or controlling the wave of a revolution. Normally, a coup d"etat is considered in three stages; the preparatory stage; the attack phase and the consolidation phase. The preparatory phase begins with the first tentative plotting against the existing regime and continues until the first shot is fired on the day of the coup. The attack phase, beginning with that of the first shot, lasts until the old government has been overthrown and the new one installed. After the violence of the coup is over, the consolidation phase continues until the rebel regime is firmly established in power, with its opponents neutralized and the country pacified. A classical example of a coup in Ethiopia was the attempt to topple the imperial rule by the Neway brothers during December 1960.

We have witnessed many coup d"etat plots initiated from within and outside of Ethiopia. Ethiopian repressive circumstance forced the leading conspirators to plan and exile, but there were also many disadvantages to this. The coup d"etat émigré leaders of Ethiopia have drifted out of touch with political realities in Ethiopia and so miss the moment of opportunity. It is also true that when leaders are separated from their followers by national and international boundaries, problem of liaison and communication often became acute, effective control is hared to maintain, and the intelligence available to them is usually out-of-touch. Another failure of our émigré leadership is that friction and jealousies have developed between those who break the dangers of underground work at home and those who live in the comparative comfort and safety of exile. Even though, a coup possesses decisive advantage over the civil war and revolution, in the Ethiopian case it did not succeed (though some sources have registered three successful coups in Ethiopia. Could the source of failure emanated from the Ethiopian proverb Ñ<M‰ u=kÁ¾`

¨Ø ›ÁxōØU (gultcha bikeyaer wet ayataftim). I.e. the use of different ovens will not change the taste of food.

As the peak of the Revolution, there was a story of the DERG's dream that it wished that all Ethiopians functioned via a unitary throat so as to chop easily with its "Revolutionary Sword" when the need arises. All those who hope to overthrow a government by a sudden violence of coup d"etat may take this dream for a motto. The techniques of a coup d"etat is not new, it is as old as government itself. It seemed not to work in the Ethiopian societies though despite its unpopularity there are some people residing abroad willing to initiate and perpetuate it.

Insurrection (u¯Sî am'ez)

The second type of taking power is through insurrection. It is a rapid mobilization of military force, accompanied by mass action. The Paris Commune and the Russian Revolution of 1917 usually epitomize it. This is different from a coup d"etat in which a select and restricted band of conspirators seize power without mass participation. In the Ethiopian case, insurrection has never taken place despite some people's claim of EPRP's brief attempt of it so as to supplement to its guerrilla rural warfare. What about TPLF's power taking in Addis Ababa? Could it be classified as insurrection or a coup d"etat or what?

Urban guerrilla war is possible only if the strength of the establishment has deteriorated to the point where armed bands can move about in the city. Such a state of affairs has occurred only on very rare occasions and it has never lasted for any length of time, leading within a few days either to the victory of insurgents or the incumbents. A normal use of "urban guerrilla" is a euphemism for urban terrorism, which has a negative public relations image. Because of this,

EPRP always advised its members to dissociate themselves from "traditional terrorism" although a few fringe groups openly advocated terrorism solely against their true enemies. True urban terrorism can undermine a weak government, or even act as a catalyst of a general insurgency but it is not an instrument for the seizure of power. Urban terrorists cannot normally establish "liberated zones", their operations may catch headlines but they cannot conduct mass propaganda nor build up a political organization. Despite the fact that modern society has become more vulnerable than in the past to attacks and disruptions of this kind, urban terrorism is politically ineffective except when carried out in the framework of the overall strategy of a political movement, usually sectarian or separatist in character, within an already existing mass basis.

It is believed that EPRP unlike many other guerrilla movements did not regard itself as urban guerrillas; its assassinations were largely symbolic acts of "punishment" meted out to individual members of the forces of oppression – they were not usually part of an overall strategy.

Initially EPLF and TPLF guerrilla operations were mainly directed against the armed forces of the enemy and the security services, as well as installations of strategic importance. At a later stage, however, modern urban terror became less discriminate in the choice of its targets. Operations such as bank robberies, hijacking, kidnapping, and of course, assassinations were expected to create a general climate of insecurity. Such actions were always carried out by small groups of EPLF/EPRDF people; EPLF and EPRDF units of an urban guerrilla groups could not grow beyond a certain limit as the risk of detection increased with the growth in numbers.

Protracted Armed Struggle (¾}^²S ¾ƒØp ƒÓM yeterazeme ye'ttk tigl)

The methodology applied to usurp political power in almost all Ethiopian cases was through a protracted armed struggle. Their basis of claim, however, was radically different from each other.

EPLF has waged protracted war on the basis of a „colonial theory".
TPLF is waging wars for power on the theory of „ethno-nationalism"
EPRP is struggling for politics on the theory of „multinationalism"
OLF is waging war for democracy on the theory of „ethno-colonialism"

Guerrilla warfare has consistently been the choice of the weak that oppose the strong, for it enables them to avoid direct decisive confrontations and rely on harassment and surprise. It is different though in that it is a military tactic aimed at harassing an adversary, whereas revolutionary war is a military means whereby to overthrow a political regime.

In revolutionary war any guerrilla action that needs explaining to the people is politically useless; it should be meaningful and convincing by itself. To kill an ordinary soldier in reprisal for the assassination of guerrilla is to descend to the same political level as a reactionary army. Far better is to create a martyr and thereby attract mass sympathy than to lose or neutralize popular support by senseless killings without an evident political goal. To be victorious in a peoples' war one has to act in conformity with the interests, sentiments and will of the people. A military victory is worthless if it fails to be politically convincing. Only time will tell whether the Ethipian Fronts have played their cards well.

Following are some of the tenets that I believe were used in their guidelines, which perhaps have heavily influenced them in their struggle to bring a societal change in Ethiopia.

- "The object of war is to preserve oneself and annihilate the enemy" as preached by Mao Zedong and practiced by EPLF
- "The Chinese communist party claimed to power through its military arm, political power grows out of the barrel of the gun" as practiced by TPLF
- "We must emphasize politics. Our army is an army in the service of politics and politics must guide the military in its day to day work" as preached by Lin Piao and practiced by EPRP
- "A hundred victories in a hundred battles is not the best of the best; the best of the best is to subdue the enemy without having to fight" Chinese proverb as practiced by OLF.
- Let us demonstrate to the world and seize political power as has happened during the Soviet collapse (Kinjit style)

On the basis of these strategies of struggle for liberation and the means to achieve their objectives, which one is the right choice for AEthiopia and AEthiopians? The reader should take a pick and discuss its merits and demerits as for me; DEBTERAW's EPRP was the right path.

Many readers will raise their eyebrow because so far EPRP has failed to seize political power. But the fact of the matter is that tactical victory is not equal to strategic defeat. The tactical victory in AEthiopia is kept by the use of combatants instead of peacekeepers.

The new world order: The end justifies the means

The majority of Ethiopian revolutionaries had emphasized on the means of a struggle rather than on the end. Even the DERG initially had accepted the motto (ÁKU"U ÅU ßq" Ä"<ÅU yale m"n"m dem chikona ywdem). But it proved futile that it resorted to the end product rather than the means. Is it not true that we greet one another by saying(cLU peace)? It may show that we love peace. Somebody has to come up with an insight why we love peace in words but not in deeds. The catchword these days is peace. The choice between the gun and the platform must be spelled out. War does not end unless it immediately follows by communication and dialogue. May be the bridge of Gambella will help provided that Ato Obang is wise to incorporate the number 13 in his quest for political power.

Unlike many AEthiopian understandings, politics at its best is a civilized activity. Politics can preserve the peace, protect human rights, advance economic well being and encourage excellence in the arts and science. Politics at its worst though, leads to war, tyranny, economic ruin and barbarism particularly for those on the losing side of the struggle for power. No one should assume that EPRP is a loser. EPRP was and is on the side of justice be it for Anuak, Darfur or Agame.

Politics according to EPRP is a process, within or among political communities whereby Ethiopian

- Values are articulated, debated, and prescribed.
- Diverse political actors as individuals, interest groups, regional or local governments cooperate and struggle for power in order to protect their fundamental interest and advance their personal desires and
- To advance public policy for the entire national interest of a nation called AEthiopia.

The history of EPRP according to DEBTERAW, as written in DEMOCRACIA is as follows: -

- To identify the problem and pick the question to be solved
- EPRP's main questions were political injustice and poverty

- Identify the necessary conditions of justice and prosperity
- EPRP had/has a target to shoot and a goal to achieve
- EPRP made a conscious choice to adopt DEMOCRACIA

DEMOCRACIA, according to DEBTERAW, is the government of the poor and the free. The choice of EPRP was a polity of democracy from the beginning while others had/have a choice to by lead by one Monarchy or a Tyranny, by a few Aristocracy or Oligarchy. Everyone and everybody should have a choice in promoting his ideas but to have ideas one has to be free to be creative. In Ethiopia, there were and are still killers of ideas. The new world order cannot be new to EPRP. Checking in hindsight and foresight, it is of paramount importance to consolidate the search for DEBTERAW's whereabouts because with him lies justice for all including for the Anuaks.

Concluding Remarks

In the past, nationalism, ideology, ethnic had dominated the life history of AEthiopians. Today in the global strife, we seem to be lost in the rank of prioritizing to listen to or to follow the Priest- Evangelist-Imam-Rabbi (PIER) teachings. What an aberration? What has happened to the leaders and managers of the Eway Revolution?

For comments and criticism: woldetewolde@yahoo.com

$\forall$ *A+E = Ethiopia plus Eritrea (¿?)*

CALL ME BY MY ADDRESS:

Solutions with DEBTERAW, A commentary

Obo Arada Shawl alias Wolde Tewolde -

November 1, 2008

What: Intellectual gathering
Where: along the golden gate to the White House in a place called Ethical Society
Why: To celebrate 36 years of ideological and political struggle

There is neither ONE Ethiopia nor Ethical Society as at to date. I am of course, speaking ideologically and politically not intellectually.

When Walleligne Makonnen was writing about nations and nationalities, he was writing ideologically about the oppressed nations and nationalities of Ethiopia that were dominated by the elite TAGS's political power i.e. Tigrai, Amhara, Godjam and Shewa. In other words, Walleligne was referring to the century old modes of thinking and governance namely of the kings of Yohannes of Tigrai, Tewodros of Gondar, Tekle Haimanot of Godajm and Shewa's Minilik.

Nations and nationalities of Ethiopia duped by the propaganda of their own so-called liberators were fighting ideologically to become independent from what their liberators call Amhara domination (notice Amhara implies to Gonder). In Marxist terminology, however, it was referred to as the oppression and exploitation of nations and nationalities. Alternatively, the Eritreans were seeking for Employment, The Oromos were seeking for Opportunity, while the rest of nationalities including all Amharas were seeking for Equality (EOE). These concepts of equality, opportunity and gainful employment had galvanized the so-called nations and nationalities.

Walleligne and his party EPRP broke with the ranks of the majority of Ethiopian elites not only ideologically but as well as politically speaking. For Walleligne and DEBTERAW both Amharas could not stand against the plea of all nations, nationalities or internationally for that matter.

And so with a single idea of self-determination including secession as written by Walleligne as and an impeccable **Theory of Organization by DEBTERAW** led us to the current state of affairs. For their principled stand both individuals were labeled as agents of either of EPLF or foreign countries. Both were agents of their own party, EPRP and conversely EPRP has supported their principled position.

In order to bolster EPRP's existence and to show solidarity with the outside world, Walleligne had coordinated a group of Revolutionaries to hijack an Ethiopian plane. The objective and history of all the hijackings including that of Walleligne's group will be known in due course and it is not the purpose of this commentary. The confusion in relation to self-determination, secession and association with Woyanes' policy of path to separation and Shaebia's association of struggle has blurred the real EPRP's belief and path for an Eway Revolution via DEMOCRACIA – the antithesis for all nationalists.

Those who blame Walleligne and his EPRP see things through the prism of mechanical and ideological connections. Take the simple case of importing a bomb and a gun from Asmara! Take the case of the sole survivor from from Adua! Take the name of Tadeletch whoever or wherever she is! Take the case of Emmanuel who is an economist not a student of medicine as claimed by the "so-called know it all"! Take the case of the current Eritrean implementation for self-determination camouflaged in self-reliance! Take the case of Woyane's policy on secession! These and other claims are all outside the realm of EPRP's circle. Let us put the blame where it belongs. Call it whatever and however you like; this is an irony, a paradox or an aberration.

I believe it is very essential to tell the whole truth and understand of the origin and destination (O-D) of EPRP by simply reviewing the political history of (TTsW). ▬▬▬▬ while focusing on the current EPRP's struggle for finishing the Marathon of struggle.

Having this in the background let me go back to the meeting of October 25, 2008, which is relevant for all people in the region.

The gathering, first of all, was a well coordinated and ethical at the same time. Coordinated because, there was no lack of attendance despite of the heavy rain. Secondly because many activities have been conducted despite limited time constraint.

Besides, various support letters and poems were read to the audience and groups and organizations such as Representative from Ethiopian woman's association

Were all represented in this eventful event.

The most amazing thing was the Recognition of an Ethiopian woman dubbed as the "mother of EPRP" who joined EPRP leaving her 13 children to pursue the Eway Revolution. What an amazing dedication and belief. It is a role model to be emulated by so many of us who claim that we love our country and people.

While on dedication, the other person many of us should respect and dignify is Ato Fassika Bellette who has been in the ups and downs of the Ethiopian struggle for change. On a personal level, his background would not allow him to aspire for Revolution but he did for the sake of all AEthiopians. Ato Fassika, true to his name, wanted everyone and everybody to have every week if not every day.

Ato Fassika Bellette, one of the Tsinhate Muhuran elites of Ethiopia have finally spoke up on political and intellectual terms. It is better to listen or read his speech as posted in www.Ethiox.com. He ultimately reached the peak of Ras Dashen having traveled the long march from Mercato-Assimba-Tselemt – Ras Dashen, an arduous journey to bring democracy (the rule of the people, by the people and for the people) by means of DEMOCRACIA - an Ethiopian version.

This person is a dedicated man who kept the party of EPRP intact. He was not an ideological man, he was all throughout an intellectual man and he has kept his intellectual integrity and party ideology intact for 36 years. What an amazing man.

Ato Fassika, however, laments in the following that "the ease with which all Ethiopians are distracted by the petty and trivial, our chronic avoidance of tough decisions, our preference for scoring cheap political points instead of rolling up our sleeves and building a working consensus to tackle the big problems of Ethiopia".

His only drawback is that he is ahead of his time for F comes after E i.e. 6 > 5. Besides F has one missing leg F = E i.e. 5 < 6. In addition his father's name as in B has yet is to be deciphered to be 13. This is part of my entertainment with Latin alphabets and Ge'ez Fidels.

As far as I am concerned, the letter F is ahead of me and the letter B is not my forte unless it is deciphered.

Concluding Remarks

Although I have met individuals who were labor leaders in Ethiopia and ESUNA (Ethiopian students in north America), none of them were represented in the event.

The role of these two organizations before and during the Revolution was highly significant. It is somewhat ironic that the labor union leaders of Ethiopia who actually led to the demise of the ancient regime and Esuna leaders who were at the forefront for the supply and provision for EPRP financial and foreign literature did not have a say in this forum. It is unimaginable that the downfall of the Monarchy, the dictatorship of the Military known as the DERG would collapse without these two giant Organizations.

For the surrender of Woyane or Shaebia's leadership, these two organizations should be re-established again. For without the working class and the intellectuals, nothing will happen in either Ethiopia or Eritrea.

At this meeting, I have sensed a hunger for new ideas and new kind of politics that favors common sense of ideology, and one that focuses on those values and ideals that hold common as AEthiopians. The common bond between the Red and the Blue state of Ethiopia must be coordinated. It's time for all of us to learn from the American way of Red and Blue political system of classification.

Lastly, I am very proud on the organizing committee whose courtesy and bond of friendship were easily discernable. Thanks to Ato Ayna Alem of Radio Finote for inviting me and thanks to Ato Bellette Yemane who constantly and relentlessly informs me about all the activities of EPRP around Washington Metropolitan Region.

It is all-important for all of us to cope up with the digital age for an individual person has presented the evils of Pal Talk by a means of a poem. I think the first step for democracy is free speech. Pal Talk discussions is crucial for understanding the nature of democracy. Pal Talk discussions whether online or print largely depends on the moderators like any other low - tech meetings. For this I have an admiration for the Assimba Pal Talk moderators. Truth will prevail

For comments and criticism: <u>woldetewolde@yahoo.com</u>

CALL ME BY MY ADDRESS:

Solutions with DEBTERAW

Obo Arada Shawl alias Wolde Tewolde

MESKEREM 1, 2001 alias

September 11, 2008

Of Introduction

These days we are witnessing articles written by real names more than pen names. I hope it is a step foreword towards freedom of using one's given name. What is in a name? By now everybody and everyone in Ethiopia seems to decipher what his/her name means. Call me by my name is past due and so I move to "call me by my address".

History and Culture are the two culprits for most of our problems. What is history and what is culture? These are two fundamental questions to be answered by each and every one of us if our perceived problems of social, political and economic are to be resolved.

There are many histories and cultures (HC). I cannot discuss them here.

Today, on the beginning of our AEthiopian Millennium new year, I want to present personal histories of struggle (ጋድል) of three individuals in the hope that their experience will lead to some lessons to be learned from their Education and Experience (EE).

Of Encounter

Forty years ago, to be exact forty-three years, the three of them met in college. All three of them had respect for Religion, for the Emperor and for Wealth. At the same time, they had fear of the Clergy, of the Government and of the Rich. It was DEBTERAW, however, who revealed to them the secrets of the Clergy vs. religion: of the Emperor vs. his government and of the Aristocracy vs. the intelligentsias. In other words, these three individuals came face to face with _freedom of faith_, _political choice_, and _economic opportunity._

Today, after 36 years, the three of them once again met in Washington, DC with their freedom of religion, political choice and economic opportunity in unison and intact. What a wonderful encounter! Many thanks to DEBTERAW TSEGEYE G. MEDHIN'S enlightened and mentoring.

The thing that surprised them most is that none of them has changed name in as much as the place they met. It was in a restaurant where the names of Addis Ababa communal communities are displayed on the walls of the restaurant. The hostess invited them to sit between WUBE SEFER and ERI BEKENTU! One of them said to himself, "am I still crying for nothing?" for he used to live in Eri Bekentu neighborhood.

As one of the trio has been recently to Addis Ababa, (the other two have never been either to Ethiopia or Eritrea since 1972), the two asked him whether these places of WUBE and IRI still carry the same names and same surroundings. He himself was surprised by their inquiries. He said, "People like you „developers" are outside the country, what do you expect?" he posed a rhetorical question. "Everything is in the same condition but with subdued people", he concluded.

Most people who have been to Addis Ababa remember that Wube Sefer and Eri Bekentu were full of vibrant people. Their colleague briefed them about the current Ethiopian practice of religion, politics and economic development in the country. "There is so much a sad story and history to tell to people in the Diaspora", he said. Could this be a result of their mentor DEBTERAW's prolonged imprisonment and disappearance?

Who knows? Call me by my address! Where am I?

Of Background

After graduation, all three were employed in the ministry of communication and transport authority (though all three graduated in economics with special emphasis in International trade). However, right after their employment, like most of their colleagues, these three individuals have been in the shadows of death since the DERG assumed political power.

Despite fear of the Clergy, the Emperor or the Bureaucracy, the majority of graduates of the 1970s have embarked upon the positive work of Minilik's Development Programs, Haile Sellasie's Education effort, Tewodros' concept of Unity and Yohannes's Religious beliefs. However, the Military and its mentors as well as the Nationalists rejected everything that these kings stood for and instead emulated foreign models of development.

But these three had quickly realized that the ministry they had joined, though critical, was in an infant stage. At the time, out of the population of Ethiopia, 95% of the passengers were using traditional mode of transport whereas over 90% of the goods and services were being transported by pack animals. This realization from their work place accompanied by their education and Debteraw's mentoring had convinced them to alleviate the Ethiopian transportation and communication system via Planning. It was in this area of planning that the then government of Ethiopia and subsequent regimes failed to convince these individuals to bring them to their side. Instead, these individuals have chosen a different path of struggle to bring change (the Eway Revolution led by EPRP).

Here is a review of their religious, political and economic values in concordance with the past and the future.

Of Religion

The history of AEthiopian religion is based on the symbol of the flag of red, yellow and green. This flag with a primary color was perceived as a bond between the Creator and the AEthiopians. Emperor Minilik II, had embraced it as a country national flag for Ethiopia. However, the narrow nationalists of Tigrai, the humble nationalists of Oromia and the arrogant nationalists of Hamasien have rejected this Flag of sacrifice, peace and prosperity. One has to look closely at what has been added to the current TPLF flag, to OLF flag and to Eritrean government flag. As far as color is concerned, there is no difference. The difference is that the leaders have their own design of stamp of passion to rule or desired to be. Their common factor is their enmity towards Emperor Minilik who adopted it as a national flag. Were the Nationalists against the color of the flag or faith upon which the flag was based? I cannot tell. As far as I can decipher, it is not the color but the faith. If so, let them reveal their faith, whatever it is.

Minilik was not a fervent religious man. In fact when he was deep in economic and social development plans, there was opposition towards his implementation program. For example, he wanted to install telephone lines. There was stiff opposition, but just for implementation purposes, he threatened the pope that he was going to change his religion.

Of Politics

The system of government was the centerpiece for the Eway Revolution as proposed by EPRP. It is appropriate to quote Minilik's plea for establishing a modern system of government.

European government consuls have arrived in our country, Ethiopia. This is uncommon in our Ethiopian system of government. They cajole us by saying that without a rule of law, there cannot be a country worthy of a government. You also know that they want us to surrender to them. Even though Ethiopia had system of rules and regulations, in a few days, we will have new system of government based on Europeans, I have written rules upon which you will carry your duties and responsibilities without quarrels, without jealousy thereby fully cooperating to strengthen our government.

If we carry on to serve our people, it will be beneficial to our government and our country. No one will envy our country. Even though I have tried and tried tirelessly, without minister, council or consul, it is a

one-man show resulting in discrediting my efforts.

Now with less sleep, less drinks, less love for money but more love for people, I hope you will accomplish the tasks I have assigned to you. In as much as I have trusted you, you should also appoint those whom

you trust, those who don't love money, those who do not abuse the poor but really can help them.

As far as money is concerned, I will give you salary so that you will never solicit money from the poor except the required tax. If you go beyond the rules of love set and exploit the poor, I will have to hate you. You will be abused. In the name of your Soul, the Bible and the Cross-, you will be excommunicated.

(Atse Minilik II, Paulos Gnogno, and P: 360)

And so Minilik in the spirit of implementation for his programs, he had appointed ministers in the following ministries appointed in order of their importance.

1. አፈ ንጉስ (Afe Nigus) For ministry of Justice
2. ፊት አውራሪ (Fit Awrari) For ministry of Defense
3. ጸሃፈ ትእዛዝ (Tsehafe Tazaz) For ministry of Pen
4. በጅሮንድ (Bejrond) For Finance and Home affairs
5. ሊቀ መካስ (Like Meqas) For ministry of Interior
6. ነጋድራስ (Negadras) For the ministry of Trade & Foreign Affairs
7. ከንቲባ (Kentiba) For the ministry of Agriculture

The current regimes of Shaebia and Woyane don't understand the power of *justice* and *food* in the way Minilik understood it. What a travesty!

Of Economics

There is and was no economic thinking in Ethiopia. The current leaders of Ethiopia do not seem to differentiate between Needs and Wants, a basic premise for economic theory. Previously, they had the Albanian model of development and now they seem to be caught between the Chinese and American model of development.

Of Conclusions

The trio individuals has concluded that the TPLF/EPRDF government don't seem to embrace any works of Haile Sellassie I, Tewodros, Minilik or of Yohannes IV. They also, do not follow the Eway Revolution of Ethiopia as spearheaded by EPRP. Instead they are operating in the footprints of the DERG. The DERG collapsed on its weight and this one is no exception. Without vision and planning (tools for development in political system, religious mechanism for love and peace and above all economic development) the regime of Zenawi cannot survive. It is predicted that it will collapse on 2013 Julian calendar and it is also predicted that Eritrea and Ethiopia will merge into one **E** on 2013 Gregorian calendar.

Happy New Year to all AEthiopians.
Let it be the beginning of our true Millennium
For comments and criticism: woldetewolde@yahoo.com

CALL ME BY MY NAME:

After the symposium

Obo Arada Shawl alias Wolde Tewolde -

July 13, 2008

TPLF seeks Light where there is none
EPLF seeks Victory where there was once
OLF seeks Democracy on the ground
EPRP seeks Knowledge above ground

Ten days ago, on July 3, 2008, a symposium was held in Washington, DC. The main purpose of the symposium according to Assimba Forum was to reach a consensus on how to fight for the release of TSEGEYE GEBRE MEDHIN alias popularly known as DEBTERAW.

On the agenda of Assimba forum, it was stated that DEBTERAW was to be seen from three dimensions, that of human, professional and public. In other words, DEBTERAW is a prisoner of conscience, an educator and a political figure.

Debteraw as a prisoner

Although the organizers of the event did invited many representative organizations and institutions that are related to the Human Rights aspects of DEBTERAW, few have come to participate in the one-day event. As at now, it is not definitely determined why many of the invited speakers did not show up. But among those who showed up include the following: -

- Mesfin Mekonnen representing, Human Rights Council (HR2003)
- Captain engineer Fantahun Kahsay representing Solidarity committee for Ethiopian political prisoners (SOCEPP) and
- Dr. Mankelklot representing one of the Ethiopian Mass Media

The representative of Human Rights appealed to all the attendees of the symposium that as Ethiopians, we should be aware of at least, the fate of our human aspects if not for the animals and plants of Ethiopia. He said that there are tons of human right abuses in Ethiopia among them the abuse on DEBTERAW who has been imprisoned in incommunicado by the TPLF regime since 1991. It is time that we campaign for the implementation of the HR2003 so that our problems could be resolved peacefully. Ato Mesfin spoke on the current progress of H.R. 2003. He promised that if the Senate passes the legislation on H.R. 2003, it would have enormous impact on the Ethiopian societies as a whole.

Engineer Fantahun has spoken at length about what it means to be imprisoned for so many years as he was a victim himself. He was forced to abandon his profession to dwell on the rights of prisoners of Ethiopia.

Dr. Mankelklot has advocated for a change in his own words "to carry out a revolution".

However, he neither elaborates on what kind of revolution nor the methods of revolution. He elaborated on a lot of issues of concern to all Ethiopians.

Debteraw As An Educator

Many individuals, young and old, have presented DEBTERAW's works of non-visual arts. He was presented as one of the best of Ethiopian artists, educators in democracy and revolution. DEBTERAW's acumen of struggle and change for all peoples of Ethiopia was par excellence. He was depicted as the alpha omega of One Flag, One Fidel and many Freedoms. In order to testify this, a well-known person from Sweden was scheduled to be a guest speaker for the occasion.

Unfortunately, this person by the name of Hailu G. Yohannes alias known as GOMERAW could not make it. It is sad that Ato Hailu is in what is known as in G"ZOT.

DEBTERAW & GOMERAW. What do they have in common? Both are revolutionaries, educators, artists and democrats. The only difference is that one is imprisoned INSIDE the country while the other is held ABROAD. **Let us free them to free ourselves.**

Debteraw and Gomeraw are twins in terms of Ethiopian, Arts and Literature with the background of Orthodox religion. Both did not believe in an organized religion. In the Orthodox Church, religion is relatively connected to DEMOCRACIA. The true knowledge and wisdom emanates from the monasteries of Ethiopia and Eritrea and not from the Board Rooms of Corporation or from the Vatican of Rome. Whatever the case since both are held in prison, we cannot discuss the issue of Ethiopian Orthodox Christianity. I had planned to discuss the issue of religion vis-à-vis politics during the symposium, but for technical and for lack of speakers on the subject of religion, we were forced to abandon the topic altogether.

Debteraw As A Public Figure

What makes Debteraw's case as special is that DEBTERAW is an icon of a well-known political party organization popularly known as EPRP that became a target for harassment and banishment since its inception. DEBTERAW was number one target of the DERG era and still remain number one enemy of the TPLF regime.

On the one hand, EPRP was and is represented by the concept of one Flag, one Fidel and many freedoms. Because of many disinformation and propaganda towards the Ethiopian rainbow and the Geez script, even its own supporters wrongly condemned EPRP.

On the other hand, as freedom is precious, it is also costly. Many Ethiopians and Eritreans either afraid of its cost or its practicality, they do not stand with EPRP at least in the open forum. Because of these fears and tribulations, people from ERHCO and the Mass Media of Ethiopians did not show up in the one-day event for DEBTERAW. What a travesty!

The symposium was both a success and a sad story. This day and date was a day of special importance to hundreds of Ethiopians, Eritreans and to thousands of EPRP members, supporters and sympathizers. This day was meant to be the beginning of the end. The beginning of what and the end of what, one might ask?

We are living in a time akin to the Roman Empire when people stopped believing in what might call the main organizing principle of their society and instead pioneered new forms of community in which to live out of the realm of moral life. EPRP should be judged by posterity, as all of us should be ultimately. The DERG, EPLF and the TPLF are dictated and justified in the first instance not by political principles but by an extra-ideological perception (correct or incorrect) of imminent benefit or threat. EPRP's stand was correct.

Even today, unlike EPRP's mainstream political party, in Ethiopia and Eritrea, expediency rule and principles are expendable. It is time that a new beginning should be on the horizon. People had enough of „blood is thicker than water" as espoused by EPLF and OLF and „what is in it for me" as espoused by TPLF.

Concluding Remarks

Debteraw Tsegeye's revolutionary struggle is about courage and faith. It was not about dethroning the king, deposing the DERG or eliminating EPRDF per se. It is about **fighting for** not fighting back. EPRP owns a piece of Ethiopian and Eritrean political history. These days" arguments abound. There are 10 sides to every story and very little agreement from one version to the next.

However, EPRP only negotiate with those who have something to gain by giving EPRP what it wants. EPRP see a clear way to take revenge on someone who wronged it. Of course, the best revenge is always to be so fabulously over the whole thing that EPRP couldn't careless. EPRP's internal coping mechanism is getting a workout healing and then forgiveness. If members of EPRP are feeling sore, at least they can take solace in the knowledge that is good for EPRP.

The one-day event symposium as expected had audience who listened to the divergent point of view, found common ground and willing to embrace new visionary ideas. Thanks to Assimba forum, especially to the balanced conduct of Ato Sewyew and Ato Elias. It was a wonderful event for a change based on a human cause.

For comments and criticism: woldetewolde@yahoo.com

CALL ME BY MY NAME:

A debate with Debteraw, extra 13

Wolde Tewolde alias Obo Arada Shawl

13 July 2007

DECIPHER THE LETTER **B**
SPIN THE
LETTER E PUT
THEM
TOGETHER
AND BE
WHATEVER YOU WANT TO **BE**

My sister and I were born on Paguame 3, during the 13th Month of Sunshine countries of Ethiopia and Eritrea. How many of us were born if not on the 3rd, at least during the month of Paguemen? If you know, please assist me in figuring it out. In Eritrea, there are 33,000 of us. In Ethiopia, there would be approximately about 430,000 (33 x 13).

Are these minorities denied of their religious rights? Can't these sections of population be both Ethiopians and Eritreans at the same time? Is there a <u>*relationship*</u> between those who claim to be born during the 13th (month of no pay no bill), ID (Income-Debt) free generations, and the tenth nationalities (Jeberti) of Eritrea? I think there is in terms language and religion in both countries. Ethiopia is deep in combating religious concept while Eritrea is anti-language. A third party is highly involved in politics. Thus Religion, Language and Politics are at the center of our struggle for change. This is just a thought and not a sermon. Call me by my name.

In Eritrea 13 individuals have met in Cairo during the 1960s in order to start a liberation movement for Eritrea. Almost simultaneously, seven individuals or cells were gathered inside Eritrea also to start a liberation movement. Is there a common factor for number 7 and 13? The sum of course is twenty but the difference is plus or minus depending, which comes first, Harnet or Naznet? 13:20 ratio expresses the frequencies and cycles of **Creation,** now scientifically verifiable through the latest discovery "solving the greatest mystery of our time" (The Mayan Calendar: by C.J. Cal leman).

In Ethiopia, JC = 13, i.e. Jesus =10 and Christ =3. The Apostles were 12 plus Christ they were thirteen.

Today is Friday 13, a bad name for a lot of non-Ethiopians just like some Ethiopians fear the coincidence of Monday and June (Segno & Sene). What is that the number 13 is both revered and feared?

In America, the number 13 is behind every important value. The 13 stripes in the National Flag, in the "E pluribus Unum" and in the great Seal of the USA are few examples. And even the City Council of DC government the number 13 along with its channel is relevant.

The Egyptians were the first to develop a superstition for the number 13. For the Egyptians the number 13 was for Immortality. For the Romans it is associated with ill omen that will bring death and destruction. But present day Italians frequently play Toto Calcio by using the luck of 13.

Number 13 is a secret and sacred power. This number though has been shunned for centuries. Some architects omit the 13th floor from office buildings to this very day. It is usually considered to be a superstition. Triskaidekaphobia from the Greek is Tris = three Kai= and Deka = ten

So what is wrong with number 13? We know the saying that one man's meat is another man's poison. For various reasons 13 is considered a number carrying special significance in many cultures. There is Lucky 13 and there is Unlucky 13. Which one is ours? Tell me Ethiopians or Eritreans!

Washingtonians including Ethiopians love to travel on the 13th street in Washington DC. I do not know why. May be for its convenience.

Debteraw is missing in Action, or to be precise, he is missing because it looks as if he got some action to carry out. EPRP is missing in part or in whole?

Is it a coincidence that G WE W, who is the 5th African American with four-star rank in the Army, has been tapped to lead the Pentagon's new U. S. AFRICAN COMMAND?

Concluding Remarks

The purpose of this article was to provoke the hearts and minds of all Ethiopians and Eritreans alike to think outside and inside of their boxes at the same time. The tools of alphabets or numbers are of secondary importance to the physical, political and social geography's of Ethiopia and Eritrea. It is a well-known fact that TPLF thrives on division based on ethnic languages instead of national language. EPLF, on the other hand, promotes unity based on mixed economy by suppressing religion, language and culture. EPRP survives on ideological theme. Call me by my name. What is my name?

History taught us that in confusion like those of PFDJ's way of doing business in Eritrea and in Woyane's diversity of ethnic languages have not solved any major problem. Both Ethiopia and Eritrea are way back before the Millennium came into existence. Both the national liberators (Shaebia) and the ethnic liberators (Woyane) are acting like the Athenians and Spartans of ancient history.

Debteraw once wrote to me as follows" Tequeraquso, Tequeraquso, AND qKen D'r-Drrr yemibal yimetal, tesfa atquretu", roughly this means having struggled for so long, there will come a time for a **negotiation."** Both groups have forsaken our traditional culture of mediation, they do not trust in arbitration. I hope they will heed to Debteraw's position of Negotiation. What a wonderful prediction once again by the **true Debteraw. You are the MAN (Mediation-Arbitration-Negotiation) Debu. Thank you for your advice.**

For comments and criticism: woldetewolde@yahoo.com

CALL ME BY MY NAME:

A small talk with Debteraw

By wolde tewolde alias Obo Arada Shawl

Background: In the 1970s, a Symposium on Ethiopian Holidays was conducted in the auditorium of Haile Sellasse I University. In this auditorium, two leading Artists were listening carefully to what was being discussed. They were Tsegaye Gebre Medhin, the Revolutionary and Tsegaye Gabre Medhin, the Evolutionary.

Long aware of each other's work, they have never met until they air their view in the auditorium on how to change Ethiopia and the Ethiopians. Debteraw had ignited a provocative thought that would escalate the leading Revolutionaries in the Intellectual University Community. He asserted that KINET (ኪነት) is the domain of the majority of Ethiopians known as the "Masses" whereas Tsegaye, the "Laureate" indicated that KINET (ኪነት) belonged to the Elites. According to Debteraw's Political philosophy, the Ethiopian traditional values included

1. *Tolerance in Democracy*
2. *Unity in Diversity and*
3. *Freedom in Religion*

According to the "laureate's" political understanding, the Ethiopian traditional values were embedded in

1. *Gratitude*
2. *Respect and*
3. *Love*

From the above line of thinking, our intellectual capacity still persists in our current differences. Where are we now? Whose idea was correct? And whose methodology are we to follow? Are we in the same wavelength about KINET? What is the current issue? Is it political or apolitical? I leave the answer to readers?

My relationship with Debteraw is perpetual. I contacted him on Christmas day of this year and I posed some important questions. Here is how he responded?

Question: In order to make it current, can you decipher your name for me as you decipher once to distinguish yourself from the Artist "laureate" Tsegaye GM?

"G" = government of the people by the people for the people = Democracy. JC = Jesus Christ is equal to 13. I remember you were trying to discuss something along those lines.

Answer: Your remember that very well? OK. As you know, we were attempting to <u>explain</u> the Ethiopian <u>situation</u> and how to <u>change</u> Ethiopia and the Ethiopians. My proposal at the time was how to proceed from Q = 17ᵗʰ century to T =
20ᵗʰ Century via R = Revolution
S = Conspiracy + Secrecy = 19ᵗʰ Century = Gabriel
🙂 = Cross = T = ø = 20 = Hintseta (☻"i✠☬)
The letters of T and S should contribute to the Ethiopian Revolution. Putting them together will sound my real name. Other than Ethiopians, no one can pronounce this sound çì. A case in point about the disaster Tsunami (èìಠ"☹) in Asia. Ask small kids where you live, they cannot say my name. Teach your kids to say my name. That will help.
Back to your question, my name is deciphered in numerical like this.
Tsegeye = 79
GM = 20
E ===== one
Tsegeye + GM + E = 100 is equal to a Century

Question: What is the significance of this number?

Answer: You may remember when we embarked on the Ethiopian path of Revolution, we recognized the Kedada, (ኢሮፕ) in the letter R and we allowed the letter B to be deciphered. **Feudalism** expressed in the "land to the tiller", **Bureaucracy** expressed in "Ishi Nege" and **Imperialism** expressed in terms of "paper tiger" as labeled by EPRP, "airless tire" labeled by MIESON and "man eater" as labeled by the DERG were our tri enemies. I cannot tell you where we are now in terms of ideology. Personally, I am in a messed up Amara-Tigre bureaucracy worst than Ishi Nege. At least, during the Minlik era of Ishi Nege it was balanced by No (Embyew) concept. Today, there is no embyew to any of the FBI (Feudalism, Bureaucracy and Imperialism) pressure. Let alone to combat Imperialism, nobody dares to label or to say no. I assume you have a better understanding about Imperialism since you live within it. I hope you will expound it to me when we meet next time. Be a connecter of 18th c to the 22nd century. We are still embarked upon 18th going on to the 21st Century, a long way to catch up but still we are making it, though at a high cost. That is the significance of my name ie. a Centruy. By the way are you coping up with your people? I mean the Eritreans?

Question: Can you assess the Ethiopian situation now?

Answer: Oh yes! The Ethiopian Revolution is going fast, probably if not at the speed of light, at the speed of sound. Creation according to theology, Adam was born in today's Eritrea and Eve was born in today's Ethiopia. Archaeologists and Historians confirm that too by discovering bones and artifacts and they named them as **Lucy and Innocent**. We in turn baptized them in our own languages as ኤ"ዐኔ(ሰሰ) Dinknesh) and ኛአቶ (Gherhi) respectively. They claim they found them in the lands of the Afar and the land of Hamasien.

So what is happening now is that all eyes are in present Eritrea and Ethiopia. They need an answer from Mother Ethiopia as *identity crisis* of humanity abound. Be careful in identifying between those who are in search of true identity and those who want to destroy identity. I call it the **ME** and the **WE** crisis. I advise you to go on pursuing to differentiate between the true Revolution and the fake revolution.

Remember your deceased friend WM. I tell you to tell your friends that we should aim to the 22nd century. That is one day at a time (ME) and eye balling into the future (WE). You know what I mean?

Question: Do you mean Wallelign Makonnen?
Answer: Yes that is him.

Question: Is he not discredited for dismembering the Ethiopian nation?
Answer: Oh no! He united the Ethiopians. But Ethiopia did not get it yet. In fact he did what exactly God would have done. The Lord loves diversity and so Walle, the Makk (the name of Ethiopia & Eritrea) connector. I know this because of my scholarship to God.

Question: Where are you located now?
Answer: You know me, I belong to the "Animal" force of EPRP. I am in my kingdom. I roam everywhere. By the way, do you meet with your old friends the "Crocodile" Group?

Question: What is your proposed solution for Ethiopia?

Answer: (ዐፀቶ) AGMELAGO.

Question: What is that?

For comments and criticism: woldetewolde@yahoo.com

CALL ME BY MY NAME:

A small talk with Debteraw, Part II

Wolde Tewolde alias Obo Arada Shawl

February 23, 2007

On January 9, 2007, the above topic was posted on Debteraw.com. Comments and inquiries were forwarded to the writer of the topic as well as to the Editor of Debteraw's Website. Some of the salient points were as follows: -

1. Please write more on Tsegeye's
2. Why is Dbeteraw is in prison while other's are in political power?
3. You are confusing us but still thank you
4. Who would replace Debteraw?
5. Did you say you talked to Debteraw this X-mass?

If you check with the previous talk with Debteraw, the connection was disrupted when the interviewer asked Debteraw about the solving Ethiopia's political dilemma. Debteraw responded as "ÅÅGMELAGO" ("ÓSLÔ). But then, our communication was disrupted. It was something like climbing a mountain. Until I get the full sense of it, I feel obligated to answer what the readers of Debteraw Website have asked me. Here lies my answer to your questions and curiosities. Thank you for asking.

Please say or write more on Debteraw?

There are so many things to write about Tsegeye Debteraw. Since the question is not specific, I assume the question emanated from a person who knew Debteraw in person or at least he knows there were two prominent personalities by that name. I will dwell on Debteraw's political philosophy and methods of struggle.

Many Ethiopian educators prescribed an all panacea for Ethiopia based on what they learned in London, Paris, Moscow and America. Though not openly, but tacitly they ascribed the Ethiopian poverty due to the prevalence of Orthodox holidays. Debteraw was opposed to this line of thinking. He believed that both religion and politics were at work not only for poverty but also for progress. He argued that neither the Board Room, nor the Cathedral, nor the Central Planning nor the Monastery would alleviate poverty.

<u>*Physical geography as well as political geography*</u> was the two main culprits, Debteraw used to argue. He desperately wanted to struggle along these lines. That was why he wanted to contact a prominent Geographer, a well-known Artist and a famous Journalist.

"Laureate" Tsegaye was supposed to promote Ki'NET (Ÿ='ƒ). Debteraw put his wages on his Mokshe (V¡g) for breaking the political barrier in Ethiopia. He also hoped against hopes that Professor MWM (mesfin wolde mariam) would lead to kill the physical distance among Ethiopians. Debteraw worked hard to develop awareness and appreciation of Ki'NET for the purpose of breaking the political and physical barrier in the country. The Arts, according to Debteraw, "are the cultural fabric that hold the Ethiopian societies together and that give meanings to the very existence of Ethiopia." Ethiopia evolved as a nation and developed its own identity when its people began to celebrate their cultural and artistic heritage and learned how to express in their own languages.

The National Theatre of Haile Sellassie I and Hager Fikr Theatre were established to promote art on a higher level. They were meant to promote music, dance, theatre, food, clothing, the way Ethiopians celebrate marriage, the way they live and the whole package. It is a matter of finding the truth what the "laureate" Tsegaye have done to the progress of Arts in Ethiopia, especially Ha Hu (GG<) in six months and Enat Alem Tenu. The revolutionary arts have turned to be prostitution for arts. It is also important to watch out what the Hager Fikre in Diaspora is being carried out by NWM. I leave this aspect to the readers to find out by themselves.

We have to look elsewhere if one has to find out the true progressive promoters of Ethiopian cultural arts, The two outstanding personalities who contributed much to the promotion of Arts are Tesfaye Lemma and Tsegeye GM, alias Debteraw. They both wrote poems and short stories. Their role was to inspire Ethiopians to believe in themselves as well as in their country.

For Debteraw, he aspired to work on nation building and empower individual identity. He wanted to give new meaning to Ethiopian culture because culture is life. Ethiopian culture is the tradition, the values we have to build on and pass to our children. But at the same time, he did not forget that culture is dynamic and subject to change. The cultural change though should come voluntarily. "The Ethiopian culture has to be strong enough to feel that it has something to protect and something to offer", Debteraw argued. With that clarity in mind, Ethiopians are able to accept people, give part of their culture and accept part of foreign culture. That was Debteraw's vision for Ethiopia, a rich legacy to bequeath to Ethiopian Youth (›=Ḋ¨K=) if not in the country, in the whole wide world.

Why is Debteraw is in prison while other's are in political power?

During the 1960-70, Debteraw's main objective was to replace the rule of Monarchy in Ethiopia by the Dictatorship of the Working class alias known as proletariat. For this he was labeled as a teacher who poisons school children. Showing light to Ethiopian children was considered as poisonous by the Haile Selassie's ancien regime. Even after graduation, he was assigned to teach grade II level. When the military junta in lieu of the working class of Ethiopia took power, many intellectuals supported the take over by the DERG, but Debteraw insisted that the Provisional Military Administrative Council

(PMAC) could only become a Fascist Dictatorship. "By any means", Debteraw argued, "The PMAC would not be a Revolutionary council but a fake one, pure and simple". What a visionary personality!!! For some of us it took seventeen years to grasp it. Menghistu hunted him down, but true to his name Debteraw was elusive and the Junta could not catch him.

The present government led by the TPLF was exposed by Debteraw as follows: - "'"Ëa" "Å vQ` ¯d"

"Å}^^" (Zinjeron wede bahr asan wede terara). That is the way TPLF leadership operate, Debteraw wrote. Another infallible prediction by Debteraw!!! So you can see why Debteraw is in prison. Unless and otherwise there is justice based on the rule of law or Tabot, there will be no amnesty for him nor his life will be spared. Debteraw will only be happy or stop predicting/ prophesizing if Ethiopian kept their health, happiness and freedom. Debteraw is the true scholar and role model for Democracy in Ethiopia and Eritrea.

You are confusing us but anyway thank you

I have been using to explain Debteraw's concept of problem solving by deciphering letters and numbers. He was a humorist par excellence.

Some say that Debteraw is dead, but I have my doubts. The last time Debteraw was dying, I was a witness, to his reliving. For most of us dying is a milestone. For Debteraw, it is fresh material. But suppose for a moment that he is really dead this time, we have lost a great, great and great Ethiopian dreamer, self-invented and self-made Revolutionary that Ethiopia holds onto. Every one of us who knew him understands his revolutionary zeal and method of struggle are fresh with us and it is up to us to tell the next generation to follow him wherever and whenever he is.

Debteraw is also a political satirist. We should all remind now and then the whereabouts of every individual Ethiopian. SÓðŏ ›G<"U SÑðŏ (detention and disappearance) should not be an accepted norm. Obituaries must be our point of struggle. I know we do not care about killing animals and plants but should we not care about killing people. Think about this, is this confusing. Where is Debteraw? Ask that question until you get the full account. We don't have to be accountants. It is a simple self- respect for human life.

Who would replace Debteraw?

There are tens of thousands if not millions who have _common cause_ and _common bond_ with those of Debteraw. Debteraw was not only a leader but he was also a follower. No one can lead unless he/she knows how to follow, that is the dictum of his Democracy.

Did you say you talked to Debteraw on this X-mass day?

Yes, I did. But I do not know whether I was connected to his soul or mind. That will be coming soon with the help of the Almighty, God.

For comments and criticism: woldetewolde@yahoo.com

CALL ME BY MY NAME:

A small talk with Debteraw, part III

Wolde Tewolde alias Obo Arada Shawl,

February 23, 2007

"What's in a name? That which we call a rose by any other name would smell as sweet."

- Romeo and Juliet," Act 2, scene 2

Perhaps Shakespeare wasn't right when he wrote the question for Juliet. There are so many Tsegeye's among us - prominent ones - the late "laureate" who translated Shakespeare's work into Amharic. Another is the living Mulugheta Lule who calls himself Tsegaye GM Araya and many more tsegayes. Are these names weird coincidences or deliberate attempts to emulate somebody else? Isn't it true that Ethiopians have religious names and popular names and no family names? We normally address one another with adjectives or what many wrongly call feudal titles. These days, it is common practice to address people as Doctors. Why don't we ask ourselves what our fathers' occupation? I like to practice with the acronym of **ACRM**. Are you the son/daughter of an Academic, a Civil, and a Religious or of a Military father/mother? I think it is better to ask this way instead of what is your ethnicity's background?

We are all alike in names. What about in deeds? For a start, let the living Tsegaye speak for himself and let's us leave the dead Tsegaye alone. Celebrating the deceased Tsegaye or speaking for the living Tsegayes is not appropriate. It is not only correct to speak about those whom we do not know their whereabouts /disappeared, like Debteraw but wise to inquire. We should also give credit to the DERG era where relatives were informed there whereabouts. We all remember the "Sink Makebel" tradition, it should continue. Let us fight for it.

Debu, we know you are out there - somewhere, everywhere - in the boundless eternity of cyberspace. The invasion of Debteraw's privacy and the shattered anonymity - all there for us not to complain but at least decipher Debteraw's history, vision and organizational skills. This week as I clicked on Debteraw's. Com, three pictures, one on the left, one in the middle and the other on the right hand side mesmerized my eyesight all in flash backs in memory. In the Haile Sellasie University all three pictures merged together in my memories. The good and the bad mixed up. Is it a coincidence or by design that

I came to view these pictures? That of a Revolutionary, of an Artist and of a student President, posted side by side. It is appropriate to tell their stories in relations to Ethiopia and its citizens. It may be a guide to political action in revealing their works and experiences. An independent body should make a thorough study of these three personalities.

To give the devil its due credit, the "laureate" translated many of Shakespeare's works. Many Ethiopians assisted him while in bed and admired him for his **elitist work.** I understand they are still trying to celebrate his death. What about Haile Sellassie I and Menghistu's contribution to society, for sure, they cannot all be all irrelevant and useless. There should be some good things to celebrate. Tsegaye the "laureate" has celebrated his 50th year (1957) when he wrote his first piece Ye Dem Azmera. You can decipher for was not creative. He was a copycat. As far as I am concerned, he let people live in an artificial and hollow world. He. Debteraw, Tsegeye on the other hand, was creative, looking forward to solve problems. Teaching by example is Debteraw's mantra. Tsegeye (without an A vowel) GM is the natural scholar for Ethiopia. He was chosen or Destined to bring the country into *the human electoral process.* That means a complete transformation of legitimacy of governance (legitimacy from God claimed by Haile Sellassie I, Dictatorship of working Class professed by the DERG but practiced otherwise; legitimacy from the Electoral Process but rigged by ethnicity) or by the peoples' will i.e. Democracy as was proposed by Debteraw's Political Party. How was he and his comrades proposed to meet the objectives and goals?

Debteraw told us by *Naturalization*. He used to tell us through **openness and acting natural.** That was the reason why he labeled some of us as "The Animal Group" as opposed to the "Crocodile Group". Debteraw did not meant to divide and conquer the CCBE (Common Cause, Bond and Experience) sections of Ethiopians. All he was saying it is natural to fear and conquer fear. Both are revolutionary struggle. If we demean one over the other, that is considered arrogant or cowardice. What Debteraw could not stand though was to be an opportunist especially where there is no opportunity. On the one hand, going underground or being "crocodile" as Tekalegne Wolde Emmanuel (teacher), Gebru Gebre Wolde (social scientist), and Zeru Kihshen (economist) were not considered cowards. It just meant that they were comfortable to carry out their mission of Revolution while in underground. On the other hand, it was acceptable for Debteraw to see people such as Yohannes Berhane (geographer & geologist), Wallelegne Makonnen (Administrator), and Tecle Gebru (pharmacist) to act naturally in the open so as to pursue the Revolution in Ethiopia.

Debteraw's mission and vision in the countryside

Debteraw wrote a letter to me while I was in Ethiopia. He asked me about the erection of the statue of Dilachin. He was curious to know whether the statue was flat -Duldum or pointed sharp? He continued to write, if it is sharp at the top just like the Washington Monument, we are finished, if not we will survive from the onslaught of the DERG. And he was right; we are relived from the terror of the military junta. What a visionary personality!Once again we exchange letters. This time, I wrote to Debteraw to confirm whether he has lost one of his fingers in the fighting with TPLF. Actually, I was hoping that it would be one of the bad fingers that provoked literally the CCBE Community. As true to his usual sense of humor, he wrote me back, "I think you need it now than ever while in America." I was a bit surprised, but hay, don't we all need it? What a visionary and clarion! But to his credit, Debteraw never left the Ethiopian soil not even to the Sudan where the TPLF claimed that they had a meeting with Debteraw and his delegation. But it was not true; as usual it was a lie.

So, what was Debteraw doing in the countryside of Ethiopia? As I indicated last time in my article, Menghistu desperately needed to catch at least one leader of a "Demos" as they were popularly known to bring him down to his knees; Debteraw went to the countryside to join the Long March of EPRA.

Let us see what happened to him after the Bitena? (Let us disband and go home). Debteraw insisted that the Revolution would continue but those who want to disband can go home. They are welcome to go home. Mockingly, to some he said, you are homesick (Yenate Enjera Tayegne) like those (Ye Dem zemen, Chkona Yiwdem Yaleminm dem). To make more dramatic, he challenged them to climb a hill, he said, "if we can climb this hill without stopping - we will overcome, otherwise we will be disbanded." A certain Ayalew Kebede witnessed this challenge by …Debteraw. What a teaching by example!

What happened after 1991 when the TPLF + EPLF with the support of the "Sudanese" government with the blessing of the Department of State (DOS) to take over the cities of Asmara and Addis? What happened to Debteraw? Whenever the trough of a Revolution climaxes, it is natural that an alignment and realignment occurs. When these huge combined armies rolled over the countryside of Ethiopia and Eritrea, no one claims to be even Pontius Pilate. We have seen this during the collapse of Haile Sellasssie I, we have seen betrays of great proportion during the collapse of the DERG. Opportunists change sides now and then. This is what Debteraw used to tell the intellectual community. Debteraw was not against those who want to take advantage of a situation. In fact, he gives due credit to those who looks for an opportune moment provided a major shift in idea and core value takes place.

From what I have learned from people who where in the Heart of Ethiopia (Godjam province) somewhere in Belaya Terrar where Debteraw was located, he was betrayed just like Peter/Judas did to Jesus. Debteraw commented about the betrayal like these. "These are people who cannot differentiate between Tekle Haimanot and Giorgis or Marx and Max. Let us leave them alone." That was an outstanding comment.

Proposal

The community of Debteraw aka CCBE should come together and do first things first. That is to write a memoir of CCBE community with special emphasis on Debteraw, a scholar of Ethiopia. Deciphering the word Debtera in the speller check will give us a debt era that is exactly why I am getting a message from Debteraw. We are deeply indebted to the CCBE community and the country known as Ethiopia. With debt, there is no freedom whatsoever. If there is please, challenge or educate us.

For comments and criticism: woldetewolde@yahoo.com

Debteraw Blog
Just another WordPress.com weblog

CALL ME BY MY NAME:

A small talk wit Debteraw, Part IV

Wolde Tewolde alias Obo Arada Shawl,

March 3, 2007

A profile of a Revolutionary poet alias Debteraw, of a Poet/playwright alias "Laureate" and of a student President were shown on Debteraw.com website during the month of February, the month of cleaning. In my previous articles, I suggested that a study would be appropriate to compare and contrast these three personalities. It may be a guide to a political action by revealing their <u>works and experiences</u>. Two of them are deceased and the third has disappeared into thin air! I am more interested in the one who was made to disappear. The dead will be in the hand of the Almighty. While we will write about them, Allah will speak for them. We need to speak for those who were made to disappear and imprisoned.

On the left side of the Web Page, a portrait of the Revolutionary poet is displayed. We see Debteraw in academic gown and in a uniform of guerrilla fighter with no machine guns, indicating that he was representing the party of EPRP and not of the army, EPRA. In the middle, we see a picture of the "laureate" Poet in his office pondering what to write or what to translate. To the right of the Web Page, we see a profile of a one-time college student President and Secretary of various Organizations posing in non-relaxed mood.

Prosecution of a Geographer; Burial for a President; Memorial for a Poet and a Search for a Revolutionary and an Event for a Journalist to start Mass Media Production to Ethiopia!!! What coincidences? Since all five careers are very important for our communities, the month of March should be dedicated to all of them.

We will label them as PR-J-PG Associates. Together, they formed a formidable alliance of change in their professional careers. They were partners in the pursuit of Health, Happiness and Life (HHL) for Ethiopians. All Five personalities did not had/have panoramic vision of Ethiopian Culture and Politics. The two Tsegayes or POETS aspired to bring change and positioned themselves as liberal leftist, the Journalist would remain neutral - only writing the truth, and the two professors of Geography and Social Work respectively would aspire to educate Ethiopians to know their country's physical and social aspects of life. I am not trying to glorify or demean the group. I am not also interested to pass judgment on their past history. What I am attempting to portray is that, all of them have done their useful work albeit following different paths – the path of Sympathy (halyot) and Empathy (skfta). According to the Dictionary.com the words are explained as follows: -

Both empathy and sympathy are feelings concerning other people. Sympathy is literally 'feeling with'-compassion for or commiseration with another person. Empathy, by contrast, is literally 'feeling into' - the ability to project one's personality into another person and more fully understand that person. Sympathy derives from Latin and Greek words meaning 'having a fellow feeling'. The term empathy originated in psychology (translation of a German term, c. 1903) and has now come to mean the ability to imagine or project oneself into another person's position and experience all the sensations involved in than position. You feel empathy when you've "been there", and sympathy when you haven't. Examples: We felt sympathy for the team members who tried hard but were not appreciated. /We felt empathy for children with asthma because their parents won't remove pets from the household.

In other words, the following equation applies to each of the five personalities in pursuit of leading Ethiopians.

P = Poet aiming at the heart

R = Revolutionary aiming at the head

J = Journalist aims at truth

P = President aiming at respect and

G = Geographer aiming at a country Now we know the names and the whereabouts of Poet "laureate" Tsegaye Gebre-Medhin; of Revolutionary Tsegeye G-Medhin; of Journalist, Mulugheta Lule alias (aka Tsegaye

Gebre-Medhin Araya); of student President Makonnen Bishaw and of Geographer Mesfin Wolde Mariam; it is time to profile them according to the positive contributions they have made to the societies of Ethiopia. I can testify that Debteraw's strength lies on empathy. I do not know about the other partners; let other witnesses testify about the other associates practice in terms of sympathy or empathy. It is to be noted that Debteraw's knowledge transcends beyond Latin, Greek or German. So whose method/vision are we to follow?

Vision

Vision is everything for a leader as it is indispensable. Why? Because vision leads the leader and the leader in turn leads the followers. As the saying goes – show me a leader without a vision, and I'll show you someone who isn't going anywhere. At best, he is traveling in circles. I know Debteraw is traveling in five (Pentagon) shapes.

Vision could not be acquired through buying, begging or borrowing. It has to come from the inside. Debteraw never had a problem with vision because of his creativity and desire for excellence; he always saw what could be as I explained in my previous articles. Vision isn't some mystical quality that comes out of a vacuum, as some Ethiopians seem to believe. It grows from a leader's past and the history of the people around him. Debu did not follow the Devil's way but the Eway.

Let us say that every one of us wanted to be empowered or empower our citizens. Just about every one of us has the potential to become or empower others by following four steps. They are: -

Commitment
Relationship
Position and
Respect

We need to assess these concepts with reference to how the PRJPG Associates have conducted themselves in leading the Ethiopians. And we also need to test ourselves how we behave in the following three sectors of communities if given the opportunity to lead or follow. I may be wrong to assess these five intellectuals nevertheless; here is my own assessment of each leader and educator.

- Tsegaye, the Poet led by <u>Commitment</u> and was appealing to the Ethiopian Heart.
- Tsegeye, Debteraw was/is leading with <u>Relationship</u> and was appealing to the Ethiopian Head.
- Makonnen, the student President was leading by <u>Position</u> and was appealing to Authority.
- Mesfin, the Geographer is leading by <u>Respect</u> and is appealing to the physical Body of Ethiopia.
- Mulugheta, the Journalist is leading via all of the above and is appealing to the true condition of Ethiopia.

Today, it is well known that there are problems in Ethiopia if not in the whole world. Moral decay in the Haile Sellasie University, crisis of mission in the Churches of Ethiopia and crisis of commitment in the civil communities among Ethiopians are well documented. As a prelude, a brief history is presented for reference purposes.

ACADEMIC Community

During the time of Makonnen Bishaw, there was no lack of morality. The student population was conscious about Education. In 1969, demand for education was a focal issue for students. Students adopted a slogan "education for all." The Emperor, though a minister for education since 1944, abdicated the post in 1966 after students became restless. The student body was motivated to serve his/her country and his/her countrymen. It was highly disciplined student population. But the Freedom of Speech, Expression and Assembly (SEA) were curtailed. When MB won the election, Debteraw congratulated him personally, but told him up front that he cannot continue to survive with the knowledge he acquired from London. I believe Debteraw was telling him to acquire Ethiopian local knowledge i.e. to be in the shoes of the oppressed and exploited. President Makonnen believed in the power of Position. MB believed that one couldn't empower people if he/she does not lead by decree. Who can give you permission for another person to succeed? A person in authority, a parent, boss or pastor was the only ones to empower people, seems of President Makonnen's mantra in life. What about now, it is everybody's guess that immoral officials are running the University? The University of Addis Ababa has become a place of immorality. We are all sorry for his death. But MB died without knowing, even the true nature of his spouse. He should have acquired the indigenous knowledge of Ethiopia before running for presidency. If there is no SEA, there could not be any functional presidency, Debteraw used to warn and teach. MB repeated the same mistake during May 2005, election.

CHURCH Community: As to the religious part of contribution by Debteraw, it was invaluable. Debteraw has the required education of all types of Christian religion, that of Orthodox, Catholic and Protestant. He had no problem with any religion. I do not know how he calls himself, an Orthodox Xian, a Catholic Xian or a Protestant Xian, a Muslim or a Jew. After all, he used to say jokingly, they are all brothers with a different brand name. What is in a name? Call me by my name. But Debteraw for sure, he used to agree unconditionally that the State and the Church should be separated. He is a son of a head of a Monastery, and I am a son of a high priest. We both rebel but I am not a scholar, I am ignorant of any theology. But we believe in Freedom of Religion. In voluntary organizations such as the church, the only thing that works is leadership only in its purest form. Followers in voluntary organizations such as the Orthodox cannot be forced to get on Board. If the leader has no influence over them, they won't follow. There is a crisis in our churches because of the lack of separating the State from the Church.

COMMUNITY (Civic)

The nationalists were labeled by the Haile Sellassie government as bandits and were bend to sell their territories to foreign powers. They proved His Majesty and the DERG wrong. Or are they doing exactly as they were accused of? Leaving aside the foreign powers clout on the nationalists, they seem to destroy the purpose of communal Ethiopia of the past, of the present and for the future.

Debteraw was tolerating, the laureate, in terms of Democracy. They used to talk and discuss about KINET (property of the Ethiopian populace). Both poets had languages we did not understand, but they usually tolerate each other. Debteraw appealed to the laurels of laureate to "differentiate his name from his name". What is in a name if you cannot differentiate, Debteraw used to tease the laureate. But the laureate could not call a spade a spade. Debteraw was one of the critics to oppose the show of HAHU in six months and Mother Courage (Enat Alem Tenu).

Debteraw, on the eve of the Revolution, concluded that conditions of the Arts, the economy, employment opportunity and above all Education – the main concern of Debteraw, could only be realized by changing the system of government. He believed it then and he believed it now. And I fully support him because we are not having tolerance in Democracy (SEA), Unity in Diversity and Freedom of Religion. These three issues are the hallmarks of Debtera's proposition for both Ethiopia and Eritrea.

For comments and criticism: woldetewolde@yahoo.com

CALL ME BY MY NAME:

A small talk with Debteraw, Part V

Wolde Tewolde alias Obo Arada Shawl

March 13, 2007

Debteraw, SS is a person who knows the purpose of health, happiness in life here on Earth and after death. He also understands that progress can be achieved via *information*, *knowledge* and *wisdom*. For that, he graduated from college to acquire information, he taught in classrooms as well as in the fields to possess knowledge and he went to the Monastery to enrich his wisdom from the Almighty, God.

In other words, Debterw has studied the law of three and functioned in squares and rectangles among Ethiopians. Now he is operating from the four corners of Ethiopia while studying the Pentagon, the language of five. It is a little bit complex to understand the nature of his position, at this time.

It is to be recalled that I have contacted and interviewed him around X-mass of this year (See Part I of this article). However, I lost contact when I asked him about his proposed solutions for Ethiopia's ills when he responded "AAGNMELAGO). Today on the 13th of March, I have contacted him and posed some relevant questions of the day. Here are his answers: -

Question: What is AAGMELAGO?
Answer: It is "an access to the RED SEA, Religious Freedom; Cultural-Civilization and Governances all working in unison."

Question: Are you up-to-date with the current conditions of Ethiopia?
Answer: Oh yes, the land question issue is not yet resolved.

Question: Are you talking about BADME demarcation?
Answer: No, that was not an issue in the first place.

Question: What was the issue then?
Answer: The proclamation says that all lands belong to the government. And who is the government? And what kind of government do we have? A government that does not accept defeat, a government that does not believe in unity-in-diversity and a government that does not tolerate opposition are totally alien to the Ethiopian way of life. We have a government that is bent on revenge, disunity and cheat.

As long as the government cannot solve the land ownership, conflicts on unfair seizure of land cannot be avoided. As long as the government owns the land, any developer can bribe any official who in turn can seize the land in the name of government. The slogan "land to the tiller" in February 1965 that was led by Gebru Gebre Wolde, social philosopher and the then President of UCU (University College Union) got a response by the DERG in February 1975. Inform me if the then President who is still alive is happy with the way of the present land holding system. In short, there is no concordance between the Public Opinion versus the Public Policy.

Question: Is it not true that the current government have many diversified parties based on ethnicity?
Answer: First of all, they do not have political parties. **They have all kinds of parties but political**. I am not speaking of diversity based on philology, languages and dialects. Look at the diversity of Ethiopia - the mountains of Sahel, Dashen, Tulu and Batu, look at the Rift valleys, the Danakil plains, The Blue Nile Basin and the Ogaden deserts. We used to call them in three dimensions, i.e. DEGA, WEINA and KOLA. Human, Animal and Plant lives on diversified lands. Diversity in ideas and thought, freedom of religion and diversified in cultures should have been the primary criteria for unity. The major political goal of EPRP was and is to form a democratic state based on popular participation. Respect for human as well as civil rights was supposed to be guaranteed for all nationalities. Democracy and Independence from foreign powers should have been asserted. Tell me in the history of Ethiopia with the possible exception of the 18th and 19th centuries that the kings were not united with the people. Our current leaders and educators (the Doctors and Generals) speak only in terms of Haile Sellassie, Minilik, Yohannes and Tewodros. What has happened to the Ethiopian Revolution? I need an answer from you guys who are not physically in prison

like us but mentally in prison in foreign countries. Don't you understand what a true Revolution means - a Revolution that was conceived in the University, initiated by EPLO, proposed by EPRP and still burning among all Ethiopians and Eritreans? It is called the *Eway Ethiopian Revolution*.

Question: Can you explain to us briefly what the Eway Ethiopian Revolution means?

Answer: If you did not get it let me briefly explain. There are no scholarly debates what is/was not a revolution that took place in Ethiopia and Eritrea. The etymology of Revolution is strictly turning or rolling back to its original place. The difference in definitions and explanations arise because of definitions and approaches. The "Animal" of EPRP differentiates between Revolution and Rebellion. For instance, the TPLF believes in the barrel of the gun and aims at toppling the Amhara elites. The EPLF believed in Independence from colonialism that was overdue from Western Powers but aimed wrongly at the Ethiopians. The OLF believes in Democracy, which is its natural habitat. So you can see the struggle between rolling backwards and moving forward.

A Revolution is derived from Latin and it means turning around. Something significant that usually happens in a relatively short time of span or long period of time. Human history has passed through various stages defining Revolutions in various ways. They differ in the duration of the Revolution, the motivating ideological factor, and the number of participating revolutionaries and in the means they employ. All of these result in a socio-political change in the socio-political institutions or in a change of culture or economy. What happened to Ethiopians and other Revolutionaries? You tell me!!!

The Revolution of the Celestial spheres, which overthrew the official cosmology decreed by the Catholic Church, the word acquired its subversive political connotation. The Ethiopian Revolution should be seen in socio-political change in the socio-political institutions. Political and socioeconomic revolutions have been studied by many social scientists in the realm of sociology, history and political science. Many generation theorists have attempted to develop detailed theories of why and when revolutions arise in three approaches of psychological, sociological and political. Our Eway Revolution was not in all three approaches. It was neither psychological nor sociological. It was only *political* and we have to keep it that way until we get it right in the process.

Many studies of revolution refer only to four classical "Great Revolutions". All four were famous and uncontroversial examples that fit almost all definition of revolution. They are as follows: -

The Glorious Revolution (1688) the Biblical Way – followed by Haile Sellassie I The French Revolution (1789) The ELF Way - followed by Melese

The Russian Revolution (1917) The Lenin Way –followed by Menghstu The Chinse Revolution (1927-1949) the Mao Way – followed by Essayas EPRP has its own model of Revolution, The Eway Revolution. I plead with you to follow that way.

Question: What is your stand on the role of unity, love and peace?
Answer: Unity-in-diversity, Let hundred thoughts contend and let hundred flowers blossom. We should have access to the SEA (freedom of Speech, Expression and Assembly).

Question: What about love?
Answer: Love is the domain of religion. It should be an orthodox (original) where an individual chooses to love or hate.

Question: Does this contradict with the thesis of Reconciliation or Democratization that prevails in Ethiopia's holidays?
Answer: No, No, I am not talking of national or public holidays. I know you have holidays of X-mass, the birth of prophet Mohammed, Ramadan and Easter, Meskeram and Meskel.

Question: What about peace?
Answer: There is no peace if you are not prepared for war!

Question: I do not understand.
Answer: You will understand in due course.

For comments and criticism: woldetewolde@yahoo.com

CALL ME BY NAME:

A small talk with Debteraw, VI

Wolde Tewolde alias Obo Arada Shawl

March 23, 2007

So far, we have formed a glimpse of who Debteraw is, what he stands for and where he is currently roaming. I hope we have all agreed that Debteraw professional acronym is READ. That is he is a Revolutionary, an Educator, an Artist and a Democrat. I have attempted to describe him vis-à-vis with known personalities such as Mesfin W. Mariam (Geographer) and Makonnen Bishaw (Social scientist) with his Mokshe the "laureate" Tsegaye GM. and also with the Journalist, Mulugheta Lule who adopted his name.

Now it is time, *Why and How* he and his political Party, EPRP still persists despite all odds. It is time to debate with him about the future of Ethiopia and Ethiopians? However, before we do that, we have to grasp why Debteraw was involved in the Eway Revolution – a Revolution that took place both in Ethiopia and Eritrea.

Debteraw used to tease me that Eritreans lack the poverty of philosophy while Ethiopians love the philosophy of poverty. Now the reverse seems to happen.

On the one hand, actually the Eritrean/Ethiopian individual does not differ in rank in this extreme manner. It is quite impossible to grade them in a mental hierarchy, which will be demonstrably and objectively correct. Consequently, for political and social purposes (even though they vary in social usefulness), Eritreans/Ethiopians should be treated as though all were equally capable of mental fulfillment, as having equal claims to the consideration of society and equal rights to express their will about the conduct of society, and in the end to determine their own policies and governments.

On the other hand, we must not fall into the mistakes of individualism and crude sort of democracy. Debteraw used to argue that the mass of individuals in a society, nurtured in unfavorable conditions, doomed to crippling activities and educated not for *responsibility* and *integrity* but for mechanical service and docility, may be quite unable to recognize what is readily best for them as individuals capable of mental development and quite incapable of judging public policy. Further Debteraw argued that we must recognize, that a policy based on the expressed demands of the majority of individuals may fail to satisfy the deeper needs of those individuals themselves.

This fact must not be made an excuse for authoritarianism on the part of the enlightened minority. We have today plenty of evidence of tyranny (Ethiopia and Eritrea) to which this inevitably led us to. Instead, the enlightened minority must have worked by reasonable persuasion and the example of its own personal integrity and responsibility, till the masses recognize them as appropriate democratic leaders. **Unfortunately it is always easier to gain recognition and power by deceitful and emotional propaganda, and to secure it by coercion.** This style has to change Debteraw used to argue. Probably this line of discussion is the first main reason why I developed an appreciation for Debteraw's work.

A second reason for our common cause, bond and experience (CCBE) lie in the other most golden question of **How?**

History has taught us that there were three methods of changing governments, of course, excluding the recent yellow or velvet revolution. They were, Coup D'etat, Insurrection and Guerrilla Encirclement. Debteraw and his party EPRP did not endorse the first two means of struggle. Instead they have chosen the Guerrilla encirclement type of change. It was anticipated to be a long and arduous struggle to get hold of a genuine revolution that would benefit all Ethiopians including Eritreans. A Guerrilla type of warfare similar to that of China but with a local Ethiopiann" culture/nature which takes into account the following five tasks.

- To support a peasant who identify with the people of Ethiopia and Eritrea in spite of (Race- Class-Religion)
- To organize workers and peasants on Class basis (have and have not)

- To teach young adult to be Readers, disciplined and responsible citizens
- To arm those who know their class enemies and use their ammunition for defensive purposes only and
- To educate Party members that the Party i.e. EPRP will always lead EPRA and not the other way round.

In other words, teaching by example similar to that of Paul and Peter was the hallmark of Debteraw and his colleagues. Inasmuch as Paul and Peter have shortcoming not only in their background but also in their way of approach to teaching, Debteraw and his comrades were short of perfection.

Despite Debteraw's quest for satisfactory answers for the 5W questions, he and his followers were labeled in such a way as: -

Troublemaker instead of **opinionated**
Provocateur instead of **talented**
Polemicist instead of **impossible**
Opportunist instead of **flawed** and
Iconoclast instead of **idiosyncratic**

Although I am not a journalist in the true sense of it, I always follow the principles that apply to all journalists. Most of the time I tamper spinning around _the five Ws of what, where, when, who and why_. For our inquisitive minds and maybe for many other unknown perceptions, we may be liked and disliked at the same time. Here is how we reason out the Eway Revolution.

The What	*Question:* A Revolution in Ethiopia changing a 16th -18th centuries feudal system to Democratic Party System.
The When	*Question*: 1960 -?
The Where	*Question:* From Moyale to Karora and From Kurmuk to Assab
The Who	*Question:* E Party of Vision and Mission
The Why	*Question:* To catch up to the 21st Century
The How	*Question:* By Combining **Visual, Print and Internet.**

At this juncture, let us see how Debteraw operated in his acronym of READ (Revolutionary, Educator, Artist and Democrat).

The Word: Debteraw as an *Artist"*

To give credit to the devil, I am one of those who pursued education and learning in boarding schools. Haile Sellassie I was a reformer of a modern education. He was recognized as a champion for education for he was acting as a minister of education (1944-1966). Haile Sellassie I was also the chancellor of the University and all graduates used to receive their degrees directly from his hands.

But in reality, the Emperor was illiterate, a very bad role model for higher Education. According to Kapuscinski, in his book entitled the "Emperor", His Majesty was acting illiterate or unwilling to write or sign. Kapuscinski reiterates that the Emperor did not like reading and writing. This means that the King had enormous problem in running the modern government let alone the whole country. No wonder Debteraw wrote poems after poems regarding His Majesty's abdication of power.

A bottleneck against creativity for positive change- a pretender Emperor- can only allow people like him to run the affairs of all Ethiopians.

Then came Essayas (head of EPLF) who is reported to **read and listen** with no written documentation. He has focused on learning and speaking many languages. It's not known his love for the written word.

Later came a military man by the name of Menghistu (head of PMAC) who was not trained in anything except in explosives. He lived by his training in exploding the country in the name of Revolution – creating a massive havoc among true Revolutionaries. Menghistu's skill of communication was through **listening** and a good part of talking.

Now Mellesse (head of EPRDF) survives with identity crisis on being a revolutionary and/or a democrat, an Eritrean or/and an Ethiopian. It is known that he prefers **talking** to reading despite his claim of having a lot of books instead of wealth.

Debu abhors illiteracy that is why he became Debteraw par excellence. Call me by my name, a decipherer of letters. But don't take me wrong he does not demean illiterate only he dislikes illiteracy.

- Debteraw's does not demean illiterate people
- He does not praise educated merely for being educated.
- He tells it as is – objectively. That is, he is vocal-speaking out loud what is in his mind regardless of political power, religious, education or any other status.

The Written Word: "Debteraw As Educator"

Debteraw was a graduate of Education Department and true to his education and experience; he always propagates on **Learning and Education.** He did not advocate education per se. From the Student Movement days, the learned and the educated communicated via

Reading and Writing, discussed and argued like civilized societies should do. It is to be noted that Ethiopians and Eritreans have Geez alphabets ranking among two dozens countries who have alphabets of their own. As a result they agreed to disagree on the methods of struggle. Every thing they wrote has been documented. That is the advantage of the written word. The saying that Bekal Yale Yiresal

Bezhuf Yale Yiweresal is very true to the core.

Each side of the Student Movements has created a coalition and has put its arguments into struggle and now into cyberspace. Let us see what those who were communicating with the written words have written: Kiflu Tadesse in his book, the Generation, writes

"Convinced that the student movement had exhausted it political potential and that the next phase of the struggle required a different organizational basis, hundreds of radicals went abroad."

Kiflu continued to write in the same page as "The absence of a tradition of political parties and the prevailing climate of repression, made many feel they had to organize abroad within a relatively peaceful environment."(The Generation, Kiflu Tadesse: The departure of the Radicals p.71)

It is a well-established fact that Debteraw and his followers never left Ethiopia. Those who left went back not through Bole but Bale. They have been following the ATM and HLC trails traveling in physical and mental capacities. Assimba-Tselemti-Mercato is the physical trail and

Unity-Love-Choice is the mental trail a long march. And as they say, the rest is history.

Of equally important written document from the Haile Fida group asserted that

"There has never been a political party in Ethiopia, no sector of the society or any class or any mass organization was ever coordinated by a political party, never stopped work or forwarded petitions, or made demonstrations. The conclusion we draw from this is that the subjective condition is lagging behind"(Teglatchen, No. 4, 1973 quoted in the Generation p.79)

The above statement was totally wrong especially when it relates to Eritrea.

The E Word "Debteraw as a Revolutionary"

Currently, many coalitions have their own arguments and discussion into cyberspace. Is there a common issue for all of them apart from the HE & SHE pattern of debates? I think we can take lessons from the PM of Ethiopia and the President of Eritrea who fights over WE or ME concepts. Carl Von Clausewitz, a military theorist said: "war is a continuation of politics by other means". In our case, mediation and arbitration do not seem to work but negotiation appears to be a continuation of struggle by other means.

Debteraw having planned and programmed for solving Ethiopia's problems by a project named AAGMELAGO- a concept deep in languages, theory and applications, is outlined here for discussion purposes only. I shall attempt to explain what he has in mind.

The Project

AAGMELAGO: It is a road map from the RED SEA (below sea level) to RAS DASHEN (highest Mountain). Specifically, it is about Economy, History, Social, Cultural and Political Landscape. The nodes along this Road Map incorporate the Philosophy, the Religion and Living style of all Ethiopians. Since Ethiopia's physical, political and religious Centers are vital concern to many who claim Interfaith or Pluralism, the significance of this AAGMELAGO concept should be carefully understood. Debteraw radical thinking is not radical per se but meant for the happiness of his people what he calls Ethiopians. As long as every individual is **happy** and **healthy** the way our forefather designed it to be, Debteraw's pleasure will be infinitesimal.

Concurrently, Debteraw expressed the following opinion.

America has an interest in the **BLUE NILE BASIN** for control Europe has an interest in Gondar Region for purposes of contact or revenge.

Asia (represented by China) has an interest in cheap Market. Arabs have an interest in the **RED SEA CORRIDOR.** Israel has an interest in the flow of the Abay River, ethnic languages and common history. Last but not least, Debteraw for all practical purposes wished to accommodate all of the above interests. The question is **HOW?** I will find out when he contacts me next time.

Concluding Remarks

The power of five in terms of pentagonal dimension seems complete. That is the interests of AAAEI should be incorporated and prioritized. Debteraw seems to have the answers to these complicated situational questions. He can do it by the Power of God and E5.

For comments and criticism: woldetewolde@yahoo.com

CALL ME BY MY NAME:

A small talk with Debteraw, VII

Wolde Tewolde alias Obo Arada Shaw

April 5, 2007

The Crocodile is dead, The Animal is imprisoned The Oak is burning
Let EPRP start rolling
To arrest TPLF & Shaebia from stonewalling

Will The Real EPRP leaders and members, stand up, please!

Last week, Debteraw's Website displayed three items of concern to all EPRP members and supporters. The picture of real Debteraw himself dressed in academic gown in Ethiopian "learned" fashion and as a peasant fighter. In the middle of the Website, an invitation by ASSIMBA.ORG for Pal talks discussions. The discussants were leaders such as Eyasu Alemayehu (Revolutionary/writer), Fassika Bellette (Leader/Economist), Ghenet Girma (Female leader), Asnake (colonel) and Aselefecth (Revolutionary Mother). On the third column, two ex-leaders of EPRP but returnee ready to discuss issues of the past and present.

Also an article on Debteraw's continuous struggle plus a book of Hama Tuma narrating the African cannibalism of Democracy was posted on the same page.

What a wonderful scene and coincidence.

"The EPRP was a clandestine organization where the identity of the members, including the leadership, was little known to the public. Very little is known about their history and how they operated, let alone outsiders, very few of the members knew or cared to know about the leadership, contrasting to the Ethiopian cultural setting where the leader is considered an important figure." (The Generation: Kiflu Tadesse p.2)

EPRP was and is not a secretive organization though for tactical reasons, some of its leaders and members were working clandestinely for fear of retribution. But Most are open with the public and with their Party's agenda. The writer knows the crocodile group but he would have done disservice to the Animal group if he did not tell their stories that sacrificed their lives, their properties, their careers and everything including their families in order to respond to Debteraw's vision and mission.

Now that every individual, organization or political party is coming out in the open, it is time to call me by my name. What is my name? 35 years ago, April 1972 (Miazia 1965) a new political party of its kind headed by the crocodile Group was formed in underground; 32 years ago, April 11, 1975 (Nhassie 5, 1967), the clandestine EPRP, headed by the Animal Groups came out in the open to lead the struggle of the Eway Revolution. 33 years ago, September 11, 1975 (Meskerem 2, 1966), the rule of the Monarchy was terminated. 40 years ago September 1967, I met Debteraw who encouraged me to fight for freedom of speech, expression and assembly (SEA).

I have 3 more years (2010) to touch and speak to Debteraw in person. Why celebrate when we cannot even call him by his name? A number by itself has no meaning unless it is related to an object. **32** years, **33** years, **35** years **40** years or even **2000** years have no validity if we do not relate to EPRP as a real political Party that played a major role in the lives of a self-less youth Generation who followed the path of Christ.

As for me, the Eway Revolution is the one I am interested in. We should not gloat over, let historians explore the question who was right. EPRP is not the one who brought about the current situation in Ethiopia or Eritrea, but we do want to pitch in to bring about a resolution of the bad situation. As far as EPRP is concerned, it can afford to tell the truth and suggest specific viable alternatives, which to our mind will pave the way for cooperation. But first, EPRP has to have a project for the fallen comrade's feeling and to those who have been held incommunicado. But what about the living comrades feeling? History should be interpreted not told and retold.

EPRP has nothing to be ashamed of. Unbiased image rather than about improving its image is the task at hand. When EPRP put its cards on the table, about why and how, it does business with United Democratic Front, Coalition Forces, OLF, or any force for that matter, people have no problems with any of that. I see nothing wrong in having our lives and actions covered with a pinch of salt, our natural talent and history. What can be done? Just call me by my name!!! Just use visual, Internet and print (VIP) and say more and more frankly what, why and how EPRP as a whole did it to bring the fundamental change in Ethiopia and Eritrea.

Celebrating for unhappiness and celebrating for happiness are totally different things. In politics as in business, the way to create enduring advantage is not by beating the competition at its game but changing the nature of the game. The real key to success is self-discipline. The current leadership of EPRP has it all as far as discipline but not the initiative to invest time with people instead of spending time with people. Their calendar should be filled by priorities not to fill the calendar by request. As to the members, the opposite is true, they seem to have lost the self-discipline and they spend their time in living day-to-day reacting to current situations.

Many spoke and wrote about EPRP. But the majority described EPRP what it is not instead of what it is. The **Why** and **How** questions distinguish EPRP from other individuals, organizations and civic communities.

EPRP's five tasks:

- To teach, educate and persuade
- To assist in organizing various associations
- To arm in self defense
- To plan and manage its resources
- To lead and be lead

HAPPY EASTER FOR ALL OF YOU

For comments and criticism: woldetewolde@yahoo.com

CALL ME BY NAME:

A small talk with Debteraw, VIII

Wolde Tewolde, alias Obo Arada Shawl

April 13, 2007

A glimpse in Ethiopian Politics, Religion and Culture

Revolutionary phrase has killed the Russian Revolution, Lenin used to complain. Local fascism will definitely kill the Ethiopian Revolution was the prediction of Debteraw. How true, violence by the Military, Demagogue by some Ethiopian elites and untenable nationalism by the Nationalists have indeed killed the true Eway Revolution in Ethiopia and Eritrea.

In my article of Part VII, I have attempted to account the Revolutionary journey of EPRP's eventful years in its historical context. In the process, I have included the name of Christ and his Resurrection. My idea was to celebrate the survival of a _Selfless Generation_ who survived for 33 years in ordeal, and in the end to hope for EPRP's Resurrection. But some readers took me for a fool or lunatic. I appreciate for their expressed opinions. As for name-calling it is similar to how Debteraw was labeled in the 1960-70. Debteraw was not allowed to teach above grade 3 even with his college degree. Why because the officials believed he was poisonous and dangerous. Call me by my name; I was not called Debteraw without a reason.

Debteraw's Christian belief coincides with that of Juan Aries. Man's or women most precious possession is **Freedom**. What exactly do we mean by freedom? Are we, as the people of E-countriere free? It is not the concept –it is the terminology. The issue in Ethiopia is not the relationship between church & state but the relationship between dogma and rationality. The truth will make you free (John 8:32). Debteraw is a genuine hero whomever was anti-communists including those of Ethiopian Communist

Party known as E'K'OPA, against populists, nationalists and puritans in that order. Debteraw's courage, principle and perseverance (CPP) were not against democratic principles but against dogmatic teachings. Christ stood for the underdog so also Debteraw. Christ taught by parable and Debteraw is still teaching by example. So it goes.

Juan Aries in his book entitled the "the God I don't believe in" has commonality with that of Debteraw's. Here are some of the laws of freedom that might induce readers of Debteraw's Website concerning religion and freedom.

1. I am free when I believe in a God who has created everything in freedom
2. I am free when I accept the freedom of others
3. I am free when my freedom is worth more to me than money
4. I am free when I succeed in being a person
5. I am free when I accept the fact that my life should be ruled by conscience
6. I am free when my freedom is not for sale at any price
7. I am free when my voice contributes to shaping the course of history
8. I am free when I continue to proclaim my right to freedom even from behind prison bars.
9. I am free when I go on saying "No" to oppression even with a gun at my head
10. I am freed when I am able to say "No" even to God
11. I am free if I am able to give my life for a man rather for an idea
12. I am free when I believe in a God who will not respect of having created me free
13. I am free when, although I failed in something, I still believe that God and the sun and I are new each day and that there is always time to begin again.

Freedom for many Ethiopians comes either by **Reason or Grace,** but in the case of Debteraw, it is both, a Balancing Act. According to Debteraw, EPRP will set Ethiopians free in the political sense. God has created and set Ethiopia free in the religious sense. It is to be recalled that Adam is from Eritrea and Eve from Ethiopia (See Article Part I)

Culturally speaking, there is a silver lining between Ethiopia and Ethiopians. Because of fear from speaking the truth, too much damage has been done to all nationalities and nations of Ethiopia. The following is an example of confusion, which led to destruction and havoc of people and resources. The current hollow slogan Ethiopiawinet, Ethiopiannes or Hager Fikr or by any other name cannot bring a panacea for Ethiopians. It has to be synchronized Ethiopians with Ethiopia. How many Amara, Muslim, Oromo, Agame, Gurage Somali or Hamasien or Afar should be harassed, insulted or die before we all become Ethiopians. The way of Debteraw and the Eway Revolution is the salvation or the resolution to all our real and perceived conflicts. Let us take heed of the AAGMELAGO concept for solutions.

It should be noted that Debteraw is not a scientist or a philosopher. He is a scholar and a mentor for all Ethiopians, by being a revolutionary, an educator, an artist and a democrat (READ, see Part VI).

Theology, as a science, draws conclusions from principles that are given by God in revelation and are accepted on faith by man. Ethics is the study of human happiness and how to achieve it. Both areas of studies are within the domain of Debteraw. Friday the 13th and Sene Ena Segno are outside of Debteraw's realm of belief system.

It is time to change our attitude on cultural biases. The following misnomer in quotation is long overdue for serious consideration.

"Oromo is the name by which this large ethnic group refers to itself. Oromo pertains both to race and to language, Afan Oromo, whereas Galla, like the terms Amara and Muslim refers to faith and not to race. Therefore, an Ethiopian is traditionally called Amara if he is a Christian, Muslim if he is of the Islamic faith, and Galla if he practices the traditional Oromo faith or is an animist."(See ch. I, p.29, in Evangelical Pioneer in Ethiopia)

For comments and criticism: woldetewolde@yahoo.com

CALL ME BY MY NAME:

A small talk with Debteraw, IX

Wolde Tewolde alias Obo Arada Shawl,

April 23, 2007

Why have you forsaken me?

The Military ruler of Ethiopia aka DERG used to classify its arch enemy EPRP into 4 categories, **MEWAQ'REGNOTCH** (in reference to the leadership); Qitr Nebse Gedayotch (in reference to **MEDEGNOTCH** aka EPRA); **DISIPLEGNOTCH** (in reference to the regular members) and **JELEWOTCH** (in reference to associate members). The history of EPRP cannot be complete without the full account of these categories, though.

But who knows or who is responsible for the dead, the living, and the lost and/or for those coming of age? On the one hand, to give due credit to EPLF, but mostly to the family structure of Eritrea, all are accounted for, while on the other hand, be it under the DERG or the current regime of EPRDF, few has the ability or the gut to search for the dead, the lost or the living. What a terrible dilemma we all are facing?

What about EPRP's accountability for its members and supporters? Although I believe Debteraw is alive and well, we have to know what has happened or happening to his compatriots in the field of Struggle of ATM (referring to AAssimba: Past; Tselemt: Present; Mercato: future)? Where am I? Don't abandon me! Call me by my name!

Two decades ago, Debteraw had sent me a message from Quara via a personal delegation advising me to return home in his own words "Home is always Home, no matter what." On my part, I was projecting as to how to resettle Ethiopians or Eritreans in the Appalachian Mountains of America in contradiction to the government of Ethiopia which was resettling the

Abyssinians into the lowlands of Ethiopia. My view was that all Amharas or Hamassiens alias known as ABYSSinans could not live in low lands. They can only live in the natural setting of room temperatures. Debteraw's view concurs with me but it must be in Ethiopia. He is unappreciative to be neither immigrants nor emigrants. He loves the country of Gherhi (ADAM) and DInknesh (EVE). Debteraw said he will never exchange living outside Ethiopia for all Worldly WEALTH or POWER.

At the time, I was in Blacksburg, VA Tech University when he sent this important wisdom. A week ago, the world has seen what has happened in Blacksburg, Virginia, USA. Personally, I have failed to resettle either an émigré Eritrean or an émigré Ethiopian. Debteraw was right again. Call me by name! What is my name?

A decade ago, I have attended a funeral service for one of the DISIPLEGNA who was gunned down while working in a parking garage. He was new to America. He was in prison during the era of the DERG. He was also against the nationalists of Tigrai and Eritrea while in Ethiopia. Incidentally, he was from SEMEN ETHIOPIA.

About five years ago, I have also attended a funeral service for one of the MEWAQREGNA who committed suicide for unknown reasons. I am told his family members were glad for his passing away. He belonged to an Ethiopian aristocratic family. It was a kind of revenge for his involvement in EPRP. Incidentally, he was from MEHAL ETHIOPIA.

Last week, I have attended a funeral service for one of the MEDEGNA (rebel group).This time it was the service for the dead who became paralyzed for 11 years. Although a large number of people attended the funeral service and his corpse was placed in an expensive Casket, there was real sadness in the community. There was nobody who was related in blood. He was by himself. His only family was EPRP community. Full Stop.

Incidentally, he was from DEBUB Ethiopia. Surprisingly, all three services were conducted in the same funeral home, in Georgia Ave, NW, Washington, DC. I wonder whether EPRP owns the Funeral Home or could it be that we Ethiopians use the same place, product or service time and again. And I am wondering myself why I keep attending these services as I am not so keen in attending burials, weddings, or meetings. One thing, I like for sure is that I want to deal with the living, especially with the underdog. Why one might ask?

Let me briefly explain. The first was gunned down by an assailant, the 2nd was suicidal and the third was paralyzed for 11 years. EPRP was and is an immense and unparalleled political party, mainly as far as doing the right thing. Nevertheless, EPRP remains largely unappreciated by Ethiopians and Eritreans. Why because many negative comments and criticism have been launched for so long. But the fact of the matter is that there are very few negative figures in the entire history of EPRP. One should not forget that EPRP is a political party. Its personalities stand on Principle as opposed to Blood or Benefit (BPB).

EPRP will be the first legitimate Political Party rested on genuine popular support of the entire Ethiopian and Eritrean populace for it has brought public politics to a country where for thousand of years, politics had been confined to the kings and the aristocrat's court intrigues and Politburo who fight behind the back of all Ethiopians.

EPRP has a clear **vision** and a strong **sense of purpose.** It is trying to attain freedom for Ethiopia, whose people had always lived in fear of the State. EPRP has achieved both goals, at least for its members and supporters. Yet EPRP made many mistakes. Some were inevitable; some probably could have been avoided. But it took responsibility for all that its members did in its name. EPRP yearned to make Ethiopia a better place. And so nobody in his right mind would be interested in destroying the mission and the institution of EPRP.

EPRP, from the outset wanted to establish a multi party system, a representative government, an independent media, and a sound judiciary system, all of which are still missing in both Eritrea and Ethiopia. For now, two countries and one system may be the answer. Hellewe, Hellewe, Laba Sebertani is the current cry of all Ethiopians.

CALL ME BY MY NAME:

A small talk with Debteraw, X

Wolde Tewolde alias Obo Arada Shawl

May 13, 2007

This day is the 13th day of the month. Besides, the number 13 being the day for our salvation, it is the Mother's day. Happy Mothers' Day to all mothers of the country of 13 months of Sunshine! This month is also celebration of Jamestown, VA. The Catholic Pope in Latin America. Ethiopian woman was beheaded in Saudi Arabia. European promise grants money for Eritrea. The APERT of EPRP is in full swing.

THE PAST and THE PRESENT

What is missing in the history of EPRP? Summing-it-Up! Sum-Up! Sum-up! Here is the chronology.

1960-1972	Pre-EPRP – Student Movement
1972-1980	EPRP minus ANJA alias known as the Faction
1981-1991	EPRA minus Bitena
1991- Present	EPRP plus Allied Forces

I am sensing that Debteraw will appear in the next issue for a final sum-up of EPRP's history and a new guidance for the coming millennium.

For now, let me briefly comment on the current discussion of "Can Idiots be useful". The recent discussion on this topic is similar to that of 1991. *"Another Federation? An Eritrean perspective,"* written by Tewolde Medhin. It was an episode that was written in IMBYLTA, volume I, No. ¾: 1991.

"George Bernand Shaw once said 'the reasonable man adapts himself to the conditions which surround him. The unreasonable man persists in trying to adapt surrounding conditions to himself. All progress depends on the unreasonable man' In our region, the unreasonable have done their useful work; the reasonable can now reap the fruits of their efforts by adapting as best they can to the conditions created by rebellion." (Highlight mine)

The above quotation was tacked into my article without my knowledge and consent. However, it tells us what and how dishonest people such as the president of the University and Prime minister of Ethiopia are teaching and guiding the youth of Ethiopia. The editor is currently the president of the university in Ethiopia. As it turns out, Andrias Ashete is the rational and prime minister Legese Zenawi is the irrational. What a team!!! Are they in the same boat or what? Judgment is left to the readers. As for me, integrity and honesty is of paramount importance to the Ethiopian youth.

For balancing purposes, in any given EPRP's **collective** leadership composition, theoretically, there will be two conservatives, two liberals and one Independent. Politically I describe Hama Tuma as an Independent individual in EPRP's leadership history. In Friedrich Nietzsche's writing, there is a great line, which says: A thinking man can never be a party man. Like Debteraw, Mr. Hama Tuma is a thinking man. Once I asked Hama that he has moved from a fabled liberal to a centrist position. He said he doesn't know. He said that he does not use spatial metaphor. If Hama was an effective politician – he could have shifted ground when the ground he's on is collapsing under him. He never veered from his position. Hama Tuma wrote, the article on "can idiots be useful?" on a personal note not as a leader of EPRP. EPRP's view always comes with a consensus not only of leadership but also of its members. Besides, Hama uses his real name when it relates to EPRP, call me by my name. I believe he wrote this article for purposes of discussion and probably he has succeeded.

But the question is why supporting Hama or opposing Hama per se should be become an issue by itself? Are we trying to kill the message or the messenger? It is not EPRP's style of leadership to kill the messenger for the individual has always bear the responsibility. Nobody can control individuals. But they are encouraged to be governed by the rules of the game of politics. EPRP always teach its members to be Confident, Independent and Disciplined (CID). And the Party is aware that the human nature is composed of passion, emotion and compassion. The current discussion on Hama's article is a reflection of this PEC. I believe it is always better to express than to suppress. The freedom of SEA (speech, expression and assembly) should always be respected whether individually or collectively. The liberation for freedom should continue by any means necessary.

Once upon a time, when I did not know about Corporation - Debteraw in his usual sense of humor and rhetoric said the following: "In the corporate world, when you see two men battling each other, they call them gladiators. If they see two women competing, they call it catfight. But when we see two Ethiopians fight we call it a Love-fight. The fight between the blind supporters of Hama Tuma and the rest is an Ethiopian fight (Halyot). As a reminder, EPRP used to kill only the message provided it is in the interest of the **proletariat** nowadays known as the **consumers.** The issue of Idiots is not an Ethiopian phenomenon only. It is a global issue. It is about who controls the mind of the human race collectively. Adjectives and titles are dead with the feudal system but the idea and mission of EPRP is still alive.

THE PRESENT and THE FUTURE

Commenting on the previous article, ix, dated on April 28, 2007, Ato Tedla commented on April 29, 2007 at 6:19 AM, like this:

EPRP is dead. Leave it to rest in peace

As is, the above statement seems plausible. But it is obvious that one needs explanation. EPRP at one time was full of innovators, persuaders and entrepreneurs (PIE). The question was how to share the pie. What pie? The Ethiopian pie!

In the 1960-70, two interests were converged in Revolution and Reform. Debteraw chose Revolution. Ato Haddisu Alemayehu, author chose Reform by writing a booklet expounding the type of administration needed for Ethiopia –'Western Democracy or Eastern Dictatorship.' After a long debate and discussion, Debteraw and his comrades of EPRP convinced Ato Haddisu that it is not about either/or Democracy. There is only E democracy for Ethiopians. Debteraw expounded personally the Eway Revolution. Ato Haddisu Alemayehu who wrote F'KR ESKE MEKABR was so exalted by EPRP leadership and embraced their ideas of promoting politics of development in the entire country known as Ethiopia.

EPRP theoreticians have motivated its leaders and members by awaking themselves and recall where they come from. The simple explanation of the five systems of government did not exist in western or eastern. We could observe them in Ethiopia live and ugly. *Primitive society (dominated by Mothers) can be seen in Godjam, the slave type could be observed in Gonder Region, Feudalism in Tigrai Region, and Capitalism in Hamasien Region and Socialism in Arsi Region,* one article wrote. In one lifetime, EPRP made it clear to all. For EPRP, it is not about reading a history on Democracy from the Greeks alone. Reading only consolidated the perception of its members, associates and supporters they already possess.

Really good leaders, men and women, are storytellers. They can articulate the issues in a way that is quite understandable. They communicate issues in a way people understand. Debteraw has long been interested in government and business leadership and in the professional development of teachers and professor. But teachers and professors who would be leaders in government and business were hit hard by the enemy and fled or died in vain. Now nobody tells his or her story. Let it begin to tell their individual story.

In order to answer the missing link in EPRP's history, the 5 Ws should be answered fully.

Mr. Tedla is advised not to give up hope if he is a believer in the Eway Revolution or to participate if he is a scientist in shaping the future. For his own sanity, though, let Mr. Ato Tedla be a journalist for EPRP by trying to answer the 5 Ws (what, who, where, when and why) including the How if possible. What are we seeing now? Where are we going tomorrow? I for one believe in the solution that lies in the Heart of God Jam and the Red blood. The way to that path is called AAGMELAGO

For comments and criticism: woldetewolde@yahoo.com

CALL ME BY MY NAME:

A discussion with Debteraw,

Wolde Tewolde alias Obo Arada Shawl

June 13, 2007

Little Knowledge is dangerous (Anglican church) Silence is golden (Coptic church)
Too much information is lethal (Vatican)
Wisdom is everything (EPRP collective leadership) Balancing is an Ethiopian ACT

So far, the collective leadership and the Party of EPRP have survived many ups and downs. The AB (ANJA & b'TENA) story within EPRP is relegated to history. The concept of B'tena has been realized by almost everybody for its social and cultural havoc. ANJA belongs solely to the leadership style whereas B'TENA refers to the members or followers of the Party. Both leadership and follower ships should equally share accountability and responsibility Anja and Bitena respectively. However, before relegating them into archives, we need to put them in their proper perspectives.

Collective Leadership

The first test of the leadership style has happened as a result of the defection of the eight members from the small nucleus of the armed forces in Aassimba, immediately following the land reform proclamation. Among many of the main topics discussed by the central committee in preparation for the conference was the <u>issue of democracy within the Party</u> of EPRP. At the time, many Ethiopian student leaders were conscious of the role of a Secretary General in many Communist movements as an evil ground against its members. Kiflu Tadesse in his book "The Generation" put it in the following manner: -

> In many of the communist parties, the post of the Secretary General had produced very powerful and autocratic leaders. In some cases, the Secretary General replaced the party and became its embodiment. In the days of the student movement, those who seemed ambitious for office were regarded with suspicion. The nature of democracy was deemed important, especially for a clandestine organization where the membership had difficulty in controlling its leadership. The experience of the organization, coupled with that of the international communist movement, had enabled many of the central committee members to look for a remedy to the problem.

Kiflu continued to write,

> Some EPLO CC members had discovered that the role of the General Secretary could be quite detrimental to the internal democracy of the organization. Some of the leading central committee members had misgivings about Berhane Meskel's attitude and handling of issues as Secretary General. Working in Berhane's absence in Addis Ababa for almost a year, the other central committee members had developed a working relationship they felt was harmonious and effective, and saw no need for supervisory function performed by the Secretary General. The harm that the post caused to the internal democracy of an organization seemed to outweigh it benefits. After some discussion, it was decided to propose an amendment to the constitution abolishing this post as being incompatible with party democracy and to replace it with a central committee secretary with purely technical functions.
>
> ~(Kiflu P: 237)

Berhane Meskel Redda, the then Secretary General was furious about the power change. That was the basis of ANJA or Split within the EPRP leadership. The Party of EPRP along with its members and supporters has suffered in particular and the Ethiopian populace in general as a result of this split. As every body knows it, it was bloody and devastating experience to all Ethiopians. As it happened concurrently with the Red Terror, it did not only created confusion but also became an anomaly though professor Gebru Tareke unwittingly called it an aberration.

Have we learned from it? I hope so! I am sure had Berhane Meskel got his way, the Party of EPRP would have been in power a long, long time ago. I know thousands have joined EPRP for the simple reason because Berhane Meskel or others like him with impressive personalities were involved in EPRP. But hey, deep at heart all Ethiopians do not want powerful individuals. That is our culture. A collective culture, and I am proud to be one of it. Until we build a system of government like that of USA or some European countries, we cannot afford to have powerful individuals who will eventually be dictators in due course. It is human nature to abuse power unless one is governed by the Rule of Law or controlled by a Check and Balance System of government. For such a struggle, EPRP would be an asset for Ethiopia and a model for all Africa. Is my name compatible with my deeds? I am Debteraw of EPRP. Call me by my name. No individual dictatorship in Ethiopia!

Along this line of collective leadership, EPRP also designed a slogan "People's Provisional Government". Why because Ethiopians have to participate not to be led blindly. We are still at that demand after 33 years! What price for Democracia! Signing documents like that of Kinjit leaders in Diaspora is hardly a consolation. EPRP's leadership and followers are not bonded by signatures but by faith and noble cause. If the collective leadership and the followers at large were working hand in glove, why then B'tena took place? The following paragraphs will elucidate.

B'TENA (Disorganization)

After being informed or as was during those days, when one becomes conscious, the next step was to get organized. According to the study conducted by EUS (Ethiopian University Service), the northern part of highland Ethiopia was mostly organized on a village or AaDI basis. The rest of Ethiopian regions were largely sparsely inhabited and scattered.

The balance between freedom and control came into power play. The supporters of the DERG mainly MIESO have delimited the urban areas into Kebeles and the rural Ethiopia into Gebere (Peasants) Association. EPRP leadership was concerned with this type of delimitations as an infringement on the freedom of peoples' rights. EPRP followers also have sensed that MIESO's intension was not genuine. I, for instance knew Wondimu Desta, the French educated architectural engineer who was genuine enough to delimit Addis Ababa into economic zones. But it was abused by the DERG and it is still abused by the current government. This type of KiLiL zoning heavily paralyzes CUD. What a travesty - Zoning for development transformed into chaos and imprisonment!

To counter that attack or rather to overcome this obstacle of freedom of movements, EPRP formed a Zonal sector in the urban centers and a Regional sector in the rural areas.

The rest is history. Members of EPRP have been underground and aboveground for a long period of time with the difficulty of distinguishing the real enemy from the true comrade.

EPRP community was from the beginning a genuine community of individuals who really believe in "unity-in-diversity". The Party believed then and now, that the greater mental diversity of the members, it is better so long as each can recognize that others however, alien are sincerely loyal to the common enterprise of Eritrea and Ethiopia. As Olaf Stapledon, in his book of Philosophy and Living wrote:

> **Genuine community entails that the members of the community shall be bound together in mutual enrichment and mutual obligation either by direct personal contact or by the established will for community. It is impossible to have genuine community without a resolute will that all members of the community shall be treated with respect and kindliness which every individual desires to receive from his neighbors. Personal intercourse and the abstract will for community may be regarded as the two kind of cement which consolidate communities."**

~(Olaf P: 292)

As it was explained in previous articles in "civilized society", there is very little to deserve the name. Civilization is after all, is not a modern convenience or a mechanical power. It is only a process of advancing to more civil mode of behavior from a less mode of behavior. In other words, civilly is treating people as persons in services of immediate _social contact_ and in _social organizations_. The fabric of Ethiopian culture is congruent with these social relationships and organizations.

Back to the B'tena phenomenon, given the background of EPRP formation after a long movement of students, workers and teachers consolidation, it was natural, that the workplace, the home and the office (WHO) to be in consonance to move foreword to push Ethiopians for a better nation.

But many organizations, governments, Fronts and in particular TPLF was undermining EPRP. The main reason behind EPRP's failure was not as popularly propagated because of B'tena by its own members and followers or by the RED TERROR or by the work of ANJA. It was simply as a result of Woyane's evil doings. Here is why.

Firstly, *TPLF denied EPRP to operate in Tigrai province.*

Secondly, TPLF tipped the DERG in Makale to stop EPRP recruits from joining EPRA. It was both an act of sabotage and an act of selfishness'.

Thirdly, TPLF hoodwinked or duplicated EPRP in various forms disguised as EPRP similar to the Geek legend of the "Trojan Horse".

Fourthly, TPLF prevented EPRP's from participating in any forum in the country and outlawed EPRP since it came to power in Ethiopia.

Finally, the most devastating evil of all-evils was the assault on EPRP's base area of God jam and Gonder and still holding EPRP's leadership like Debteraw incommunicado for over 16 years.

So B'tena is a misnomer. It is neither the fault of members of EPRP leaving the Party nor the fault of the collective leadership for failing to regroup its members; it is the sophisticated work of the TPLF taking advantage of Ethiopian gullibility. It is that simple and obvious.

Conclusion

The enemy as in 9/11 did not come from outside, rather there was no enemy. We have been told that the Eritreans wanted to sell their country to foreign powers or nations. Sixteen years have passed, yet they have not cut the deal and they do not seem to do that in the near future or ever. The TPLF is an enemy within. It is controlling all aspects of economy and freedom. The concept of KiLiL and Free Market is anti-freedom of movement and anti-socioeconomic freedom respectively.

On the one hand, the leadership of ELF had the tendency of following the Baath Party, TPLF had the ideology of Enver Hoxha, EPLF's leadership were followers of Mao's ideology, Mieso story was about following Marxism-Leninism. While on the other hand, although many EPRP supporters like those of ESUNA, were contemplating to follow varied ideologies, Debteraw's EPRP was against pursuing foreign ideology of any sort. The collective leadership of EPRP aspired to find their own ideologies based on their history and culture- the issue of originality and practicality. It was true that some individual leaders were emulating Che Guevara, Ho Chi Mi and Kafka or from religious history some individuals were in the footprint of Jesus' or Mohammed's or Buddha's goodwill practice thus fulfilling the good will of their fellow men and to all human beings for that matter.

As a policy, EPRP collective leadership has always been inward looking. The previous regime had a policy of hospitality towards foreigners. None of the alumni of Haile Sellasie I University has the desire to work in the ministry of interior. Most of them wanted to be a minister for foreign affairs. What about now? I leave judgment to readers.

Q&A with READ

In all the past conversations with Debteraw, it was intended to spell out **Who** Debteraw is and **What** he stood for; I hope we have achieved something in return. We have come to the conclusion that Debteraw is equivalent to READ, i.e. a Revolutionary, an Educator, an Artist and a Democrat. Our core problem is the inability to READ. Those who read are in a single digit! Do you believe that? We better believe it! In addition, those illiterates have stopped to listening; instead they have resorted to talking. Our slogan or program should be "READ TO ME" DEBU!

For the time being, I have conducted an interview with Debteraw and here are his current thoughts and ideas.

Question: Can you tell us in simple words what distinguishes Haile Sellassie, Menghistu and Zenawi or between the Monarchy, the DERG or EPRDF/TPLF?

Debu: Haile enjoys mystery; Mengistu prides in false promise and Zenawi is insidious. Haile believes he is one of the chosen people even if he is not. Menghistu believes that he can control everybody including nature. Zenawi believes that he can be a copycat of Melese Tecle who was dedicated to the cause of Democratic Ethiopia. Zenawi wanted to be accepted both as an Eritrean and as an Ethiopian based on blood. But the question is not about biological; it is about an idea of history, culture and political value. It is a fact that he took what he though was his hero, Melese Tecle without understanding what he stood for. Call me by my name! That is the fallacy of the TPLF leadership who at the same time cannot operate in harmony with themselves. I am sorry to say that many who were born from both sides of parentage are still suffering. EPRP has solved this dilemma long before it started its revolutionary struggle. Unlike Kiflu who wrongly portrayed the ethnic background of EPRP leaders as from this ethnic or that ethnic background, EPRP has waged its struggle on the basis of **common cause, common bond and common experience**. Individuals like Obo Arada Shawl, for instance, have become both Eritrean and Ethiopian simultaneously based on their beliefs of Democracy and Justice.

Question: What does present EPRP stands for?
Debu: The letter E stands for both the country and its people. There is no one without the other. That is EP= Peoples of Ethiopia. R=Revolution and P= political party which replaces the line of Haile Selassie who was the 225th king of Ethiopia. That is how EPRP got its name. It was a difficult task but it will get there. If there is any letter to be left out, it is the letter R that may be replaced by Respect, Relationship and Rehabilitation.

Question: What is the solution for Ethiopia?
Debu: AAGMELAGO is an Ethiopian ideology of futuristic concept embodied in cultural, religious and politics of governance bundled up together. It is a roadmap for progress and stability for the whole of Ethiopia.

Question: It was easy for you to share what you believe in, because of your intuitive, but it is harder for us to back up everything with facts and figures?
Debu: Let my work speak for itself. Science and Technology has not touched Ethiopia. By this I do not mean about the science of Earth, Life and Space. I mean of cells, atoms and electromagnetism.

Question: Your sense of humor or organizational skill was exemplary. You were able to transform something from simple to fabulous in less than five minutes, for instance in organizing EPRP, how did you do it?
Debu: By becoming down-to-earth humble, open and honest!!!

Question: Who are the men and women behind the idea of EPRP leadership?
Debu: The mouthpiece for EPRP was and is the Weekly Publication of Democracia. At the beginning, Tesfaye Debessay, Yohannes Berhane and myself became the editors. All three of us showed what commitment means and what a showdown with oppressors of life, happiness or health. DEMOCRACIA is my name. Every man or woman whose thoughts and feeling is expressed or written in this Publication is already a leader. Decipher my name – it will also reveal my deeds.

Question: What is Earth – Life - Space means to you?
Debu: I have studied these mysteries in my father's monastery. All three are one and the same. The right question is what is politics and what is religion. EPRP's mission was to ask the questions of WHY and HOW. The question of Why belongs to politics or religion and the question of How is the realm of science.

Question: Some people say that EPRP is dead; it should be left in peace. What do you say?
Debu: Is this the Truth, Opinion or Fact? It is a TOF (tough) question? Let everybody answer it?

Question: Do you have energy leaks caused by judging others?
Debu: I spend my energy on creativity and on restoration. Judgment halts progress. When we as leaders judge others, we inhibit our own forward motion. Also, when we judge others, we are not doing our job because we are not in sync with the energy that moves us forward. Jesus said to Peter, "What business is it of yours what I say to John? Keep your eyes on your own forward motion". John. 21:21-22. *I say to you one day at a time while focusing on the future.* This should be the motto of EPRP.

Question: What advise do you give to leaders?
Debu: Leaders must have not only vision and communication skills but also tremendous personal resolve. While leaders attract followers, at any moment they must be able to walk away from them, lest they become followers themselves.

For comments and criticism: woldetewolde@yahoo.com

CALL ME BY MY NAME:

A discussion with Debteraw, XII

Wolde Tewolde, alias Obo Arada Shawl, June 23, 2007

REVOLUTIONARY INSPIRATION VS WOUNDS OF HOPE

The Past	The Present ***	The Future
No deal at Makdela	Unity at Adua	Debu's Release
Death at Metema	Peace at Adua	Peace in Agame (Assimba)
Flight to Harare	Bitena at Adua	Prosperity at Marcato Plea at the League of Nations Stability with Aagmelago

The three cornerstones upon which Ethiopia was built are FAITH, LOVE AND HOPE. Debteraw and his colleagues realized that the faith in the Ethiopian Church, the love from Monarchy/Aristocracy, and the hope from the modern schools would soon vanish as they have already failed. As an alternative, a vision and a mission to solidify the faith, to democratize the government and to reform the educational system were designed. Debteraw took the lead in organizing the clergy, the workers and the teachers. Debteraw was already empowered, unlike many of his would be comrades, by the inside information of the Imperial Palace, by the Wisdom of the Monastery and by the knowledge of the University for he studied in the three highest Institutions of Ethiopia that were powerful and relevant at the time.

As a result of Debu's high talent and capacity for change, Ethiopia has created a formidable Political Party Organization, called Ethiopian/Eritrean Peoples' Revolutionary Party otherwise known as EPRP. Thanks to Debteraw's indefatigable skill of organization. It is in par with Awate's single bullet shot heralding the long march of struggle for political change.

The rule of the Anbessa is gone; the rule by Choice (DEMOCRACIA) has arrived. Hoorah to Awate and Debteraw, that is to the bullet and the pen. What is mightier in present day of Ethiopia or Eritrea, I cannot say as both tools for change used by Shaebia and Woyane are imported.

But what went wrong if these two incidents were correct? What went wrong if both initiatives had vision and mission? Why the single bullet shot and the four letters of EPRP have failed to resolve the issue between Ethiopia and Eritrea? Is there an end in sight?

There is simple explanation but not single answer for these questions. The problem does not lie with those who started the struggle, rather it lies squarely on those individuals, groups or organizations who want quick response for questions of who, what, where and when instead of Why and How. Awate and Debteraw, on the one hand, had anticipated different conclusions. Their followers, on the other, did not like to pose the questions of why and how. They seem anemic to these two questions. So the simple thing to do would be for all of us to ask the why and how questions to find the answer because in here lie the correct and simple answer. How Awate answered these two questions will be discussed in one of my future articles. But for now let me go back as to how Debteraw instilled and spread Revolutionary Inspirations particularly in urban areas of Ethiopia.

Debteraw's Organization of EPRP analyzed the prevailing conditions of Ethiopia before its members and supporters embarked on the Revolutionary Path. Below is how it was explained:

FAITH: EPRP, the agent of change for Ethiopia and Ethiopians have failed to see the faith-the love- the hope under the ancient regime of Haile Sellassie I, under the auspices of the DERG, or under the TPLF/EPRDF, no matter how they claim the history of Ethiopia to be, a century; two millennium; five millennium or more. What matters for EPRP was that the old system did not work or cannot cope up with the modern world, unless a revolution would take place.

When we say faith, a lot of people associate this word with religion. That is one aspect of faith but the other aspect is related to science - A science of principle, a Natural Habitat for the Animals. According to Debteraw, the written word from God informed him that there is no vision without preparation. The human animals of EPRP have come in the open. It was not only naturally necessary, it was also scientifically correct. All faiths of religion, politics, poverty, social etc. have come to the public debate.

If one carefully examines Debteraw's picture in Debteraw's Website, he or she can see that Debu was prepared to topple the government by wearing khaki and a bag (mind you not a gun) and an academic gown in recognition to the power of knowledge. Of course, he accepted the label of Debteraw as a token for the desire to reform the Ethiopian Church. No one, though, can see his inner belief in the website, it is written in his heart of hearts. If this three dimensional of Debteraw is not inspirational leadership, what is it then? Call me by my name. Do you live by your name? Debteraw's faith is embedded in rocks not on sands. The faith in Principle whether in Nature (science) or in Human Service was and still is the passion for Debteraw and his associates. And so the struggle continues until the Big Debteraw is released. We have to have faith in all aspects of life.

Without faith, there is no hope. EPRP's faith is still intact.

LOVE: Love is a noble thing. It is not only human it is also Godly. Ethiopians have been practicing to love strangers for too long regardless of their guests' enmities or friendship. Ethiopians loved strangers probably more than the aliens loved themselves. But Debteraw observed or sensed that this type of love was not healthy. In fact, it demeans Ethiopians. Poverty was not a choice. When famine struck, the Tigrians and Wolloyes simply accept it as a noble task for getting assistance. (See how humble they were during "we are the world" in the musical event of 1984). Love, according to Debteraw is supposed to be a two way street.

In order to love, at least one has to be respected not only by the Almighty, at least by the donors be it foreigners or local givers. The bureaucrats of Ethiopia and the foreign businessmen or investors however we call them, all began to expropriate (take away peasants' land) and underpay workers below the minimum human living conditions. And so Debteraw and his comrades demanded for land to the tiller and minimum wage for workers of Ethiopia. If this is not love, what is it then? Call me by my name!

That was an Ethiopian Revolutionary Inspiration. As the old traditional belief of faith and love have been shattered to the core, thousands and millions of students, workers and peasants believed in EPRP inspirational leadership. As a result of this Revolutionary Inspiration, all Ethiopians regardless of their ethnic background and nationality shared not only love towards one another but also life itself. What is your name? Call me by my name!

HOPE: What about Hope? Having failed in the land issue, in reforming the Abyssinian Bureaucracy and to change the curriculum for education, for whatever reasons, practically every individual including the Emperor himself desired for a change – a change for reform or revolution. However, those who wanted reform could not change the supply side of economics. They were silent not because of fear but because they cannot deliver what Ethiopians want. Galvanized by the Ethiopian students, the clergy, the nobility, the bureaucrats and the intellectuals, supported the demand side of economics resulting in the Ethiopian Revolution. Below are how different organizations; groups or fronts structured their path to hope for themselves and for their countrymen.

NAME	*AGENDA*	*SLOGAN*	*PRACTICE*
Monarchy	Const. Reform	F'ATA (give us time)	Solo
DERG	Revolution	Revolution or Death	Kinet chifera
MIESO	M-L	Arm Us	Indoctrination
ELF	Independence	Liberal democracy	Armd struggle
EPLF	ditto	Awet n'Hafash	Organization
TPLF	separation	Down with Amhara	Hidden issues
OLF	Independence	Gada system	Single issue
CUD	Federalism	Victory	Election
EPRP	**Ethiopia**	**DEMOCRACIA**	**Unity in Diversity**

Hope is the single area where every body is still failing with the exception of EPRP's PARTY Collective Leadership. Specifically, the Wounds of Hope have emanated from the followings: -

- The Haile Sellassie regime tried to give Hope by reforming Land in the South and bring Peace in Eritrea. Too little too late.
- The DERG used Kinet as a weapon to give Hope mainly via Tilahun Gessese's song "Yitayegnal Biru'h Tesfa K'abyetu Beste Jerba". It was false Hope.
- MIESO, "Revolutionary Ethiopia or Death", through political indoctrination. They got both. Russian domination and their own death.
- ELF an Independent Eritrea via Armed struggle and a little bit of Democracy. They lost both issues to their rival.
- EPLF an Independent Eritrea and freedom in Democracy. They got one and lost the other. Harnet vs. Natsnet.
- TPLF a Separate State with the hope of Unity with Tigrai-Tigrigni population and domination over the Amhara and the Oromo. They seem to have lost all.
- OLF an Independent Oromia headed by Wellega elites and a Democratic Ethiopia taking Finfine as its seat. So far they have no control.
- EPRP simply Ethiopia/Athiopia/Othiopia/Abssynia or any name via DEMOCRACIA. They seem to have succeeded partially, for EPRP success is a journey.
- CUD Federal Ethiopia headed by "Direct Election". So far they have lost what they have gained.

As we can see, in today's world everybody is crying for DEMOCARACY. And who stood for Democracy all along – It is no other than EPRP. The hope for all Ethiopians and Eritreans was dashed because of the lack of understanding of Democracia! A process for decision-making. And so all the wounds of hope are blamed not on the wrong doers but on those who took or followed the right path towards HOPE. Call me by my name. What is my name?

What about now? Let us think twice before we become destructive once more. We had enough of Anjas and Bitenas. As I have indicated in my article of June 13, 2007, call me by my name: A debate with Debteraw, XI. Anja refers to leadership whereas Bitena refers to our way of life (Culture). At this juncture, it is wise to rethink lest we dash our hopes when we see Democracy in the Middle East and in Africa being implemented. And so it imperative to explain what EPRP means by DEMOCRACIA.

What does Democracy meant to Ethiopians or Eritreans? Democracy is the rule by the people. But this definition does not indicate how to put it into practice (remember the question of How). In general, there are three accepted ways of practicing democracy. The Eway is the fourth way and it is the Debteraw's way - ~**Unity in Diversity**~. **(Luynet Ylemlm)**.

Here are the three accepted ways,

- *Participatory Democracy: The people discuss options then agree on a decision.*
- *Representative Democracy: The people choose representatives to make decisions for them*
- *Direct democracy: The people vote on options presented to them*

The central theme is that there is great diversity in the ways in which the three models of democracy are put into practice. The question is how can a group make collective decisions? If we follow the democratic theory, the Ethiopian people are to rule, but how do we know what Ethiopians want. People, who need to make decisions that concern them as a group – all 77 million including Eritreans, use DEMOCRACIA or any member of individuals who must accept a collective decision. Since Participatory Democracy – give Ethiopians the power over decisions and discussions; EPRP preferred mainly this type of Democracy for its revolutionary struggle. The problem however is inherent in the decisions – making the structure of power vulnerable due to cultural biases as we have witnessed in the ANJA and BITENA cases. Otherwise, EPRP was practicing or supposed to follow these simple procedures as indicated below:

Components parts of EPRP's collective leadership

- **Setting the Agenda:** What is question?
- **Debate:** What are the possible answers?
- **Choice:** Which answer does the people prefer?
- **Implementation:** Putting the chosen solution into practice

CONCLUSION

It took about 13 years (1960-1973) for the student movement to set the agenda, seven years (1973-1980) to debate the issues, again 13 years (1980-1993) to make a choice and it is taking over the limit of 33 years (2007 - ?) for Implementation of EPRP's agenda.

In addition to their faith for political change and love for their country, EPRP Collective leaders and members have now gained an incredible Experience and Confidence. And the Hope is still alive and well.

EPRP leaders and their followers as a rule of thumb do consider the following necessary components of participatory democracy.

- All members can raise an issue, suggest solutions, take part in final decisions
- Face-to-face meetings
- Much discussion so that all who want to contribute can be able to do so
- Tendency to want consensus.

If all are to have a say, a part in ruling, then each voice must have equal weight. When a group in society to have their views counts for more than other groups then it would be an oligarchy masquerading as democracy. As DEMOCRACIA is about choices, the democratic decision-making involves people expressing a preference for one option over the others and the final decision, reflecting those preferences. So, for the Ethiopians to rule they must have a call to their preferences weighed equally when a final decision is made. The big question then is how to determine the opinion of the group as a whole. It is only via DEMOCRACIA, a way for every EPRP member to express.

In EPRP, decisions are arrived collectively by all members after some discussion of the alternative and without recourse to vote. When such methods are adopted by more formal group this is known as participatory democracy, alias known as a **Collective Leadership in EPRP's, vocabulary.**

What is wrong with this type of leadership and follower ship? EPRP is a model for this. Let us debate, before we indulge in making a choice of that group, organization or party. EPRP is about pursuing issues and interest for oneself, community and society at large.

***This is food for thought.
For comments and criticism: woldetewolde@yahoo.com

CALL ME BY MY NAME:

A debate with Debteraw, XIII

Wolde Tewolde alias Obo Arada Shawl,

07.07.07

What does Debteraw mean? A couple of months ago, someone bitterly but respectfully emailed me. Another individual who knows me personally and who believes in himself as a real Marxist came and attacked me verbally "why in the name of Debteraw- a Marxist like myself- portray him as a reactionary who has faith-love-hope. What is wrong with you?" I knew then he read my article call me by my name, XII.

Wow! I thought everybody knew what it means. I was wrong. Having conducted numerous inquires and interviews, it is clear to me that Debteraw means different things to different people. When I asked what it means, the answer ranges from the extreme concept of evil to the other extreme of the highest literary scholar. As an Eritrean, I used to be scared by Debteras. In my childhood, my sister told me that a certain Debtera had lived in our village specifically he was living with my family. I believe I never met him, though. However, as an Ethiopian, Debteraw has liberated me in all aspects of the concept.

Debtara according to Thomas Leiper Kane in his Amharic-English Dictionary defines as follows": unordained member of the clergy who is well-versed in traditional church learning and who performs the hymns and sacred dance during Mass." In Geez dabtara means the tent in which the Ark of the Covenant was kept in Moses' time. There you have it.

According to my own understanding, here is how I explained to the Marxist and the layman who wants to know what debteraw means.

I explained to the Marxist politely but sternly that there were typographical errors in my last article especially in the past and in the future tables and terms displayed. But in Debteraw's relationship to FLH i.e. Faith-Love-Hope, the middle letter is the most important for Debteraw. That is the balancing term and that is why Debteraw is known. He has a deep love for the people of Ethiopia including Eritrea. Faith and hope may be a good and important virtue for people but it is a matter of priority. I said to this individual Marxist, "may be you are full of faith in Marx but dead in love and hope. What I was explaining in the article was that Faith of the churches, Love of the Palace and Hope of the University have decayed and so Debteraw who was versed and well experienced in the operations of the Synods, the Palace and University believed in being revolutionized. Accordingly EPRP's priority was to the change the palace or the subsequent governments until the desired institutions of the church, the government and the university are relevant institutions to be loved and respected by all Ethiopians and Eritreans.

So what is the purpose of our Debteraw Tsegeye G. Medhin to have a website in his memory another person asked me? I told this him to forward this question to the Web site owner(s). As far as I am concerned, I told him that my Debteraw is a Revolutionary, an Educator, an Artist and a Democrat (READ). That is the Debteraw I know for fact and that is what I have been writing to expound. As to his fifth dimension, I think I have an access to reach him. Debteraw's color is cipher, secret writing; very pure language (B) we still can communicate. I do receive his message occasionally and that is what I tried to disseminate to the public at large. Call me by my name. I am a messenger.

And so I searched in the Internet to find out what it means in the modern Tech world. The tech word dictionary deciphers the word Debteraw as Debt Era. How true! Our world is full of debts. The real Ethiopians did not like to be debtors in the financial sense, but in the sociological sense, Ethiopians were fond of "Balewuleta" (I owe you). What a wonderful philosophical history.

What about now? What are the Ethiopians are proud of? What are the Eritreans are afraid of? Thanks to Shaebia, Eritreans are afraid to be in debt and Woyane that made them a debt nation. Frankly for me it took almost 4 decades to differentiate between Borrowers vs. Lenders, Owe vs. Own, Debt vs. Credit.

If you are like me, we need a new idea, a new conversation and a new type of leadership in financial and in business. Is there a relationship between Money, Finance and Business?

In my next issue, I will continue on the faith-love-hope along with the organizational set up for each of the Synods, the Government and the University. For today, the day of 07-07-07 let me do my numerical posting. Please, figure it out. Decipher it out for you and for your folks.

Let us decipher the following amalgams of revolutionary history TODAY!!!

MAKK ETHIOPIA		*ZAK ERITREA*	
SQUARE	**Plus**	TRIANGLE	E =7

MAKK	***Personalities***	**ZAK**
Social Revolution	***Revolutionaries***	***Struggle***
Do the right thing	AAWA	The Rebel Way
Money has its own rules	WE'ISA	The Long March
Money is a dream	SHIGEGE	The Discussion Way
Money is a nightmare	BTET	The Clandestine Way
Money is not a gift	WAZEG	The Democracia Way
Money is a present	MAKON	The Sacrificial Way
There is world without money	WOGOFA	The Path of Light

For comments and criticism: woldetewolde@yahoo.com

CALL ME BY MY NAME:

A debate with Debteraw, XIV

Wolde Tewolde alias Obo Arada Shawl

July 23, 2007

> There was neither happiest nor a saddest times in my life. It was only an open and balanced life. DEBU

Why celebrate the Millennium?
Why celebrate the Amnesty for Kinjit's leadership? Why not celebrate the Negotiation Process?

MILLENNIUM

The Americans had reason to celebrate the 2nd Millennium because of the smooth transformation of Zeros and Ones in the financial empire. The Europeans had reason to celebrate to thank for their continuing dominance with the help of Christian faith.

The Ethiopians plus the Eritreans have nothing to celebrate this particular 2nd Millennium, because neither has the Technology nor the Christian Belief to Celebrate. It would have been better to celebrate the 13th month of their calendar; at least they would have boosted their tourism industry. This Millennium Ceremony will only portray pretension and confusion. I do not know how long we can go on pretending and confusing our communities and societies, especially having participated in the Liberation Movement for four decades. Was it decades of decadence as is normally claimed by those who have never participated in the struggle for Democracy in one way or another or was it decades of fruitful sacrifice for our future? I leave the answer to the readers.

Why do we confuse current issues with Monumental Institutions of history and culture? Ethiopia is known for its rich history and Eritrea for its deep-rooted culture.

How did Debteraw explain the organizational set up of our Institutions during the past four Millenniums? Here is how: -

For four Millenniums, Ethiopia was structurally organized in three ways.

- The Monarchy was a <u>decentralized institution</u> making its residence on mountaintops to protect it from foreign invaders. When it needs to centralize or control, there will be wars to settle their disputes. The local wars can be fought in the plains face to face. What a fair game!!! The Ethiopian way of resolving disputes which was equivalent to present day negotiations.
- The Orthodox Church of Ethiopia was and is structurally a <u>centralized institution</u>. (Refer to its Synods and Dogma of the Church).
- The Nobilities were not structurally organized, but <u>loosely organized</u> on tutelage basis where there was no control and command, only Respect and Honor.

If Ethiopia was known for its institutions of <u>Centralization</u>, as in the case of the Church, for its <u>Decentralization</u>, as in the case of the Monarchy and the <u>Check & Balance</u>, as in the case of the Nobilities, why is there no continuity or better, why there has not emerged new institutions to replace them?

I know that the *<u>Ethiopian pretenders</u>* will say that they are continuing the heritage and the *<u>Eritrean confusers</u>* would say because Ethiopia had nothing in the past. Both views are wrong. It's high time to educate ourselves about Ethiopia and Ethiopian institutions.

Debteraw's Triangle of Faith-Love-Hope in the Era of AB (Anja & Bitena) has not yet seemed to pass. It is the letter **C**...that is now at stake. The Continuum of Debteraw's legacy of F-L-H is at a Crossroad. So far, I hope that we have agreed that Debteraw was/is an organizer Extraordinaire. Debteraw has no illusion that humanity was initiated in Ethiopia but he does not wish too to end of Ethiopian Millennium during the coming few months alone. Debteraw believes in Alfa Omega of Ethiopia. The current Millennium celebration is a farce especially when the entire population is lost in its history, culture and identity. The Ethiopian values are being shattered with each passing day. Debteraw says "let us identify & discovery (ID) our history & culture (HC)." Unless we examine inwardly and know what we are celebrating, it is automatically assumed that the celebration is about poverty, aids, disease, hunger and ethnic strive and above all disunity in political, social, and culture.

AMNESTY FOR KEGNAZMATCH (cud) AND GRAZMATCH (uedf)

During the 1880s and 1890s, Monarchists, Aristocrats, Clergy, and army leaders threatened the unsteady Third Republic. These groups wanted to return France to a Monarchy or to have military rule. A controversy known as the Dreyfus affair became a battleground for these opposing forces. Widespread feelings of ant-Semitism or prejudice against Jews also played a role in this scandal.

In 1894, Captain Alfred Dreyfus, one of the few Jews officers in the French army, was accused of selling military secrets to Germany. A court found him guilty, based on false evidence, and sentenced him to life in prison. In a few years, new evidence showed that other army officers had framed Dreyfus.

On January 11, 1898, Major Esterhazy, the army officer who had actually committed the crimes of which Alfred Dreyfus was accused, was judged innocent by a court martial, or military court. Two days later, Emile Zola published in a popular French Newspaper an open letter about the Dreyfus affair, titled J'accuse! (I accuse). Part of that letter appears below:

"It is only now that the affair is beginning, because only now are men assuming clear positions: on the one hand, the guilty, who do not wish justice to be done; on the other, the followers of justice, who will give their lives so that justice may triumph. I accuse the War Office of having carried on in the press an abominable campaign in order to screen their mistake and mislead the public.

I accuse the first Court Martial of having violated the law by condemning an accused on the basis of a secret document and I accuse the second court martial of having, in obedience to orders, screened that illegal act by knowingly acquitting a guilty man. As to the men I accuse,

I do not know them. I have never seen them. I have no resentment or hatred toward them. I have but on passion – that of light."

In this letter, Zola denounced the army for covering up a scandal. Zola was given a year in prison for his views, but his letter gave strength to Dreyfus's cause. Eventually, the French government officially declared his innocence. Exile and Persecution convinced the Jews to work for a separate homeland. Call me by my name. What is my name?

Public opinion was sharply divided over the scandal. Many army leaders, nationalists, leaders in the Clergy, and anti-Jewish groups refused to let the case be reopened. They feared sudden action would cast doubt on the honor of the army. **Dreyfus's defenders insisted that justice was more important and than he should be freed.**

The above may be a voice of the past, but think if it has some relevant voice in present day Ethiopia.

In Ethiopia, we had rich political history and cultural values. Debteraw knew what and where these resources were located. Unlike Debteraw, most of us pursued college education for careers only with no Ethiopian background knowledge. The struggle between the CUD leadership otherwise known as KEGNA'AZMATCH (Rightist) and the leadership of EPRDF alias known as GRA'AZMMATCHS (Leftist) has nothing to do with leadership or with justice. PhDs (doctors) and GUNS can only take sides. Both cannot be impartial. Let the Azmatchs step forward to lead or redeem us. DEBTERAW'S EPRP IS ALWAYS WITH THE AZMATCHES AND THE ZEMATCHES, if you understand what I mean. THE AZMATCHES OF EPRP's COLLECTIVE LEADERSHIP AND THE ZEMATCHES OF EPRP FOLLOWERSHIP IS STILL ALIVE AND AT LARGE. Thanks to Debteraw's leadership and fellowship. There is faith, love and hope for all Ethiopians during the coming one thousand years. Justice will prevail and Debteraw will be acquitted (faith), will be free (love) and resurrected (hope).

NEGOTIATION

All of us negotiate everyday. Resolving a problem with negotiations is very crucial. All types of negotiations, small or large, business or personal, follow a certain principle.

First of all, negotiating is a face-to-face human drama. It could be gentle or brutal. Negotiators should possess the following six attributes: -

- Authority
- Power
- Principle
- Intellectual ability
- Knowing limitations and
- Sensitivity

All these six personal characteristics define as ability as negotiators. Were the CUD leaders and TPLF power holders possessed the above qualities and requirements. I am of the opinion that because the basic parameters were missing, there was no negotiation. It was pure and simple Amnesty. This time TPLF has scored a point by going back to the 18th century style of amnesty but also have forgotten that Ethiopia is in the 21st century. Why you may, ask?

First, the principles of evaluating TPLF's own negotiating ability is doubtful

Second, the measurement of the ability and interests of CUD's leadership is underrated

Third, understanding the interests of those whom CUD and TPLF represent to say the least were suppressed and Last but not least, the awareness of how outside factor influence has been undermined. Thus, since the tools of NEGOTIATION were all missing, the name is a misnomer.

In my own opinion, there was no negotiation between CUD leaders and the power holders. There was only a third-party intervention. The Third-Party Intervention (TPI), also known as alternate dispute resolution has two basic models: that of mediation and arbitration. These models did not work in the dispute between Ethiopia and Eritrea in the case of Badme. Why do we the so-called Abyssinians keep on repeating of things that do not solve problems? Is it because the name of Abyssinia is a bad name (It is a pejorative name given to us by the Arabs)? Call me by my name. What is my name? I believe there is something deep missing. Could it be the blood of Debteraw or the process of MAN?

We will find out in due time.

Once upon a time, I sent a book to Debteraw in the field. The book was entitled "Yes to Negotiation". He wrote back to me that negotiation with TPLF could not work. He reminded me again about their modus of operand, "Zinjeron wede Bahr; Asan wede Terra." This was a quarter century ago. How true Debteraw!!! Anyhow Debteraw thanked me for sending the book but warned me that in Ethiopia the process of MAN (Mediating-Arbitrating-Negotiating) could only work in unison not in isolation. Debteraw had and still inspire us to continue in his verbatim "TEQE'RA'QE'SU". We all should promise to heed to his wisdom. Debu, do you think we as Ethiopians or Eritreans should the dictum that "*how a society buries its dead tells much about its future?* I am asking you this because you always remind us to ask the two fundamental questions of Why and How. We are waiting for your reply.

For comments and criticism: woldetewolde@yahoo.com

CALL ME BY MY NAME:

A debate with Debteraw, XV

Wolde Tewolde alias Obo Arada Shawl, August 3, 2007

A time to killA time to dieA time to reflect
Leadership 101 has arrived

Defining Moment (LEADERSHIP)

And that having been relieved from the sentences of death and from the agony of imprisonment, the fate of CUD leadership seems to be over. Last week, a new phase of struggle is made. The Team of Debteraw Website has to be commended for bringing forward into the limelight those heroes and heroine Ethiopians/Eritreans who stood for Justice and Freedom for all Ethiopians regardless of ethnicity, nationality or religion. Debteraw Team in its Web Page has launched a second step – posting-the pictures of the leaders of struggle who not only reject the TPLF's way of governance but also defy death to save Ethiopia and Ethiopians. How many of us do we know about this leadership and followership? What kind of Azmatches/zematches were they? What were their personal background, their common cause, their common bond and their political experiences? It is high time to know them closely. Hurray – Bravo – Congratulations to Debteraw's team.

Better late than never, the Ethiopian intellectuals and other experts will see for themselves who and what these heroes and heroines stood for. And to learn why and how they are living under the cruel shameless and faceless government of present day Ethiopia. The fiercest battle is no longer between the left and the right but between partisanship and bipartisanship. That is between those with ethnic names who follow the style of TPLF and those who follow EPRP's bipartisanship.

The following local title also known as the PENTAGONAL LEADERSHIP is an amalgam from past Ethiopian tradition. From the way of doing businesses, it seems that they all have forgotten the Ethiopian Revolution. I hasten to add that the DERG's way was perhaps revolutionary but it was not a Revolution in the true sense of the concept. The DERG was appropriately labeled as Fascist as it was engaged in demagogue, violence and nationalism, the hallmark of fascism. That was why it has crumbled in the end. Call me by my name. What is my name?

The KEGNATZMATCHES headed by CUD The GRAZMATCHES headed by TPLF

The FITAWRARIS headed by UEDF THE RASES headed by PFDJ

The DEJAZMATCHES headed by OLF are all advised to solve, first and foremost, their own crisis before they attempt to salvage **AETHIOPIA.**

A good thing is happening in Ethiopian politics: though On the one hand, it seems to me, that five types of leadership are emerging – fighting for partisanship albeit with dictatorial leadership style. All of them seem to fight for their own party even though all of them do not have a political party. Nevertheless, some sanity may actually be returning to Ethiopian politics. Too often, organization leaders hide their values in vague languages and programs. The leaderships of the above named organizations operate in the old system of feudalism where there was no rule of law but law of fear. The old titles seem to be replaced by Doctors and Generals! Debteraw prefers the traditional titles of GRAZMATCHes and so on, unless we can come up with better titles.

While on the other hand, The AZMATCHES & ZEMATCHES headed by EPRP also known as the EWAY Collective LEADERSHIP that demand *justice for all victims and freedom for all living individuals*. It is about leadership and follows ship in the true sense of the words. Justice and freedom are its criteria. Title is not a primary importance to EPRP. EPRP is about responsibility (disciplined) and it is about choices (Democracia)

The Eway Revolution was an initiation of all progressive forces that merged into the leadership of Ethiopian Peoples Revolutionary Party or Eritrean Peoples Revolutionary Party.

EPRP seems to be ready to tell its stories, its values and visions. How about the rest? Are they ready to do the same? The public has the right and the desire to know what really has happened in the past. It is not for revenge but for learning purposes. Call me by my name. What is my name? Faith-Love and Hope.

THE CONCEPT OF CHANGE (REVOLUTION)

ALL changes, even the most longed for, have their melancholy; For what we leave behind us is a part of ourselves We must die to one life before we can enter into another (Anatole France)

Debteraw has carried out his responsibilities for all Ethiopians as READ, namely

- **Revolutionary**
- **Educator**
- **Artist and**
- **Democrat**

Debteraw always suggest that individuals should be critical thinkers in order to be an agent for change. He worked so hard as a teacher and as an advisor to change the educational curriculum of Ethiopian schools.

He consistently advocated for making KINET (Arts) as the property domain of HAFASH, SEFIEW HZB, MASSES or however you call them.

As far as Democracy is concerned, Debteraw used to tease college freshmen students as follows "TE'TERATER YABAT NEW METERATER". This was not as some opposition group's claim that he meant for malicious intent. It was an effective guide for the new comers to be critical in their learning. I hope all of them are thanking him for his advice.

It is not about side issues such as left or right. It is about real issues of faith of the people, love from the power holders and hope from the universities Debteraw struggled to be a true revolutionary until a political system that is legitimate and acceptable to all Ethiopians be instituted.

There is an old saying that champions do not become champions in the ring – they are merely recognized there. The case of EPRP is a case in point. The three qualities that are necessary for the collective leadership of

EPRP are competence, connection and character (3Cs). For the follower ships of EPRP, trust is the fundamental issue. Trust comes in turn from Relationships. Both collective leadership and follower ship have Shared experiences, common bonds, and common causes resulting in strong glue of relationships. As a result, both groups respect, trust and reciprocate in their mutual pain or care.

THE NEW ATTEMPT (MAN)

If we keep missing the purpose of why the Ethiopian Revolution has taken place, we are again doomed to failure.

At the onset of the Ethiopian Revolution, the land question was of paramount importance to the rural population (peasants) and the question of enrollment in the university was also crucial to the urban population of Ethiopia.

Debteraw was against the nationalization of lands in Toto and he was anti quota system of enrollment to the university. Piecemeal and in isolation was not palatable for Debteraw's idea of Revolution. As we have seen in both instances, Debteraw and his party of EPRP were right then and now in regard to these issues.

What about now? What is this attempt of negotiation? It is not negotiation. It is arbitration, no it about mediation (Shimagle) and so on and so forth.

Mediation-Arbitration-Negotiation (MAN) should work in unison not in isolation.

Debteraw has told us in the past that the land issue of Ethiopia or Education cannot be done in isolation. We have to remember the issue of unity-in-diversity. It is not about size and shape when we speak about diversity. The diversity by the TPLF's of ethnic diversity and the Shaebia's language diversity is a balloon. It is designed as a marketing device for organizing people. It does not have real substance. Think of Badme and think of Kinjit!!!

The French have a marketing expression that sum up this strategy rather neatly. Cherchez le creneau. "Look for the hole." Cherchez le creneau and then fill it. Those Ethiopians who live and struggle from

European countries seem not to follow or seem to heed to EU directives and instructions.

That advice goes against the "bigger and better" philosophy ingrained into the American spirit. Americans have been taught to think in a certain way in the power of positive thinking and as a result they may sell a lot but in the process they can destroy a person's ability to find a creneau. Ethiopians/Eritreans in America do not seem to accept this bigger and better concept.

However, CUD and TPLF seem to fight for the favor of USA government. Both seem to clap with one hand. Can they do it? We shall see! A gun of the TPLF, a Vote of CUD is not compatible. What both are missing are the peoples' voice, our voices, workers, teachers, farmers and students of Ethiopia and Eritrea.

To find a creneau, EPRP has the ability to think in reverse, to go against the grain. That is if everyone else is going north it can see if it can find its creneau by going south. A strategy that worked for Christopher Columbus who discovered America should also work for Ethiopians and Eritreans.

Kindling new hope (Woman)

It is said that women have **choices** and Men have **responsibilities.**

Men from Ethiopia and Eritrea have taken responsibilities for far too long. Even Menghistu Haile Mariam has announced that he was given the responsibility to lead the Revolution. Who gave him the responsibility? Men can answer me this question. So far, I have not seen a single organization that takes care of its responsibilities seriously. Everything was for self-aggrandizement. Women have to be tested. After all this is the time for Choices. We should challenge them. I hope they will not repeat what we have done, using power for our own survival.

We must make at least one assumption; boys and girls are born differently. That is not to say that we are unequal, have different basic human rights, or that either gender is the lesser. It is to acknowledge a very basic biological reality. Maleness and femaleness are complementary, not identical.

What Debteraw and his colleagues did not focus was to build a family. Their own family was enough for sacrificial lamb. They sacrificed their own families. Should or would God revenge now? I doubt but he will give justice to all the victimized Ethiopians or Eritreans.

Conversation for women is more focused on context while for men it is on content.

Women talk to affiliate, men to pass information. Because of this, women are likely to want to speak at great length, enjoying the connectedness. By contrast men will be prone to listening for the problem and getting on with solving it. This is a perfect time for Ethiopians to be connected by women and a perfect timing for us men to listen. Let us pass information to them.

Currently we as Ethiopians and Eritreans should demand for Debteraw's release from the dungeon that he is in. Choice is the answer. By the way Debteraw's middle name is anchi **a female, Beta not Alpha. As an Alpha, Debteraw fought for the rights of Adam (Eritrean), and now he is fighting for Eve (Ethiopian).**

CONCLUDING REMARKS

It is not enough to be convinced that one's idea is different – the message must be heard, too. EPRP has terribly failed on this one.

The solution is to think in terms of opposition rather than progress. It is not a question of being better but of showing oneself to be different. EPRP has done this. What about the rest political organizations of Ethiopia and Eritrea? They will be in a better position if they do not blame EPRP. It is far better to understand it closely.

The end of the era of continuous progress as ESZ (Ezana-Solomon-Zagwe), or MTY (Minilik- Tewodros-Yohannes) should give way to an era of creativity and revelation.

EPRP is listening to new sources of inspiration. New comers are having their say as well as those people who have been struggling for over 33 years.

Finally it does not matter whether we are of that ethnic or nationality, whether we are in America or Europe, whether we have power or powerless, have killed or been killed. What counts is that we are all motivated to

IMMORTalized Debteraw. So, let us ask ourselves the question. Are we sufficiently honest to tell the truth and underline the lies, which jeopardize the future of Ethiopia? Is it about fear?

It is telling about truth. Ethiopians and Eritreans are ready for the truth. The fighting faith of Debteraw will prevail.

For comments and questions: woldetewolde@yahoo.com

CALL ME BY MY NAME:

A debate with Debteraw, XVI

Wolde Tewolde alias Obo Arada Shawl September 3, 2007

Debteraw website is a Marketplace for solution seekers Ethiopia is a country of many Writers Eritrea is a country of many Fighters The world is full of problem Creators

After the celebration of 2nd Millennium and Border Demarcation what?

The *history* of Ethiopia and the *geography* of Eritrea are perhaps the culprits for all our real and perceived problems. What about geography and what about history? Of course, there are different areas of geography and hundreds of history classification. The geography I am referring to is the Red Sea, which is irrelevant for transportation these days. The history I am alluding to is not peoples' history. It is rather about water, the source of Blue Nile. So we see, it is neither about the locational geography of Eritrea nor about the social history of Ethiopia. Or is it about color – a Red and a Blue- a red referring to sea and a blue referring to river. In actual fact the Red Sea is not red and the Blue Nile is not blue. A further confusion to our perception of natural primary color has been added to. We are just like the adage "a blind man in a dark room looking for a black cat which is not there." I hope the morning after the MC&BD (millennium celebration and border demarcation) that will take place on or after September 13, 2007, we would not be in such a blind alley for life. Will the TPLF share a *piece* of the cake they desperately want and will the PFDJ get the *peace* they desperately need? Call me by my name. What is my name?

MARKETPLACE

First of all, all intellectuals should be happy for the availability of Marketplace for their ideas, thanks to Debteraw's website. Everything that is posted on Debteraw's website is about ideas not products or services (PIS) or is that peace or piece? How do the current writers spell the spell? Every one of us is a salesman. What do we sell? The question is do we have products of our own? Do we have services to provide? The answer to the first question is that we have none but as to the second question, we have plenty of services to provide although we give our services without due consideration for cost prices. We all have ideas that nobody has in today's marketplace. Our ideas may not be current but nevertheless, they are marketable. The question is how to market them. We were not in the business of selling goods and services let alone ideas. Ethiopians were in the business of preservation of humans, animals and plants. Thanks for the regime of TPLF/EPRDF, every animal, human and plant is now for sale.

It is true that before the Eway Revolution, Ethiopian politics was limited to the Monarchy and to the Nobility occasionally blended with religion. For the majority of people, politics was alien. Ethiopians were living by socio-economic and cultural values detached of politics. However, Ethiopia has marketplaces open for seven days a week for almost an entire year. It is a wonderful place to be in any Ethiopian marketplace. I have missed those places of openness and of abundance. How come we could not emulate our open market tradition in politics and economics? That is the puzzle I could not figure out! How come our intellectuals speak and write about politics and economics if they do not know about our traditional Marketplace for goods and services and above all of ideas?

There is no question that Ethiopia under the current regime is a marketplace for products. Products from everywhere except from its own domestic product have flooded the market. An economist who used to work for the regime said once that the WTO (world trade organization) has put a double edge sword on the leaders' neck, as if the DERG was not dreaming that all Ethiopians has one big neck so as to deal with by its so-called revolutionary sword. As a result they allow everybody to sell in Ethiopia. Inasmuch as TPLF allow to be organizing in ethnic lines, it has also encouraged every Ethiopian to sell virtually in websites including our daughters and sisters whom they call it free-free market for whom? We should demand for answers. All websites are full of ads and marketing gimmicks.

ETHIOPIAN WRITERS

As I have suggested in my previous article XV, the titles that we inherited such as Grazmatches and Kegnazmatches were perhaps suitable for our current situations, as we have not come up with new alternative literature for titles to address one another. There is so much disrespect for one another within our communities.

All Kentibas, Negadras and Balambarass have come back to sell something to boost up confusion. TPLF/EPRDF also known as Grazmatches, CUD alias Kegnazmatches, UEDF alias Fitawrari, and PFDJ alias Rases OLF alias Dejazmatches have laid down their programs or practicing or non- practicing what they preach! Individual posing as Kentibas (mayors) or Negadrases (businessmen) have come in the open market place. But there is no communication tools to send the message. The bridge of trust is broken.

The battle and the battlefield have changed though our writers with PhDs do not seem to accept it. These days a lot of them have been writing on the knowledge they have acquired from their academic worlds. The artifact of the 18th and 19th centuries has crumbled. So what is that professors did not get it right? While arguing relentlessly about Ethiopia and Eritrea, we have witnessed in front of our naked eyes, the UN is composed of over 200 nations from less than hundred countries during a short period of time. In the word of Kenichi Ohmae, in his book the End of the Nation State wrote the followings: -

For many observers, this erosion of the long-familiar building blocks of the political world has been a source of discomfort atleast and, far more likely, of genuine distress. They used to be confident that they could tell with certainty where the boundarylines ran. These are our people; those are not. These are our interests; those are not. These are our industries; those are not. Itdid not matter that little economic activity remained truly domestic in any sense that an Adam Smith or a David Ricardowould understand. Nor did it matter that the people served or the interests protected represented a small and

diminishingfraction of the complex social universe within each set of established political borders."

For instance, Debteraw website has published a long article by Ato Obang Ujilu on the dialogues between two professors who are behind the current political issues of Ethiopia and Ethiopians. Their names are Al GebreMariam and Ephraim Isaac. Both names sounded Judeo-Christian. Both names of Al and Isaac do carry negative connotations. Call me by my name. What is my name? Anyway, both professors may have an interest in Ethiopia's welfare although not necessarily in Ethiopians well being. Both are viewing Ethiopia and its people from their academic fields. Specifically, Mr. Al's attempt is basically to change the justice system of Ethiopia but he is forgetting that the people in power are secretive and shrewd grown up in a feudal society. They have not liberated their minds so far. For Mr. AL changing justice system may be sound simple like changing names in a matter of seconds. Mr. AL sees from the angle of his **name** while Mr. Isaac sees it from the culture of **symbols** (I see him dressed in Habesha's qemises) But Mr. Ujilu speaks from the behaviors or values. Dozens if not hundreds both from the old and new schools of thought have begun to write about Ethiopia and Eritrea but not enough about Ethiopians and Eritreans. Debteraw would love it provided they are also reading at the same pace they are writing. Debteraw's mantra is READ, READ and READ (revolution-education-arts- democracy).

The article by Ato Obang Ujilu (I hope it is a real and an Ethiopian name) "of lies, promised joy, "shimagles", pardons and bananas" is a case in point. I am not biased in names but the meaning of names matters for me. In names, there is meaning, without meaning there is no life. NIBAB YIQETL WETRGUAME YEHAYI an Ethiopian name comes from three sources.

- Religion
- Family and
- Fashion (popularity)

The main reason why most of us do not know the meaning behind our names is that we have not attempted to decipher our desired name or live by our name. Who baptized parents or those responsible who took care of us during childhood? It was all secret and mysterious. Call me by my name. What is my name?

Another instance that I would like to point out is in relation of Dr. Fikre Tolossa of Ethiopia and Dr. Tesfatsion Medhane of Eritrea. Both academicians have achieved the academic excellence they deserve and that is why they are lecturing at Universities. We applaud for their achievement. However, both professors have not yet joined what we call the TSINHATE MUHURAN intellectual groups. What this means is that – a unitary comprehension of concept-theory-application (CTA) is lacking in their analysis of Ethiopia and Eritrea respectively. Both are theoreticians devoid of the Ethiopian and Eritrean concept of struggle and application. I wish these individuals academic knowledge could have been incorporated into the long and complex Eway Revolution. I want to point out to them that two out of three is better than one out of three.

Let me say something of somebody whose name is Ato Mandefro who was working in the Central Personnel Agency of Ethiopia. When educated people return from abroad, the first question he used to ask them was "have you written a paper on Ethiopia?" If the answer was no, he provides them blank papers and asked them to write something about their country Ethiopia. Most of them were stuck. They defend themselves that they could not have access to information and documents. Ato Mandefro was put in prison for asking "silly" questions.

Professor Tolossa's article "Alienation: a result and impact of western education on Ethiopian intellectuals dated on 8/18/07 and posted on Ethiomedia.com was mainly of complaints and concerns not solutions. If there is no recorded documentation for his analysis, why shouldn't he interview illiterate people or educated individuals who are not of his type? Or why can't he approach his own colleagues who were in elementary, high school and colleges? I am sure they know beyond his expectation. Ethiopia's case was not between modernization and civilization. It was a lack of MES (mathematics, engineering and science) to cope up with the modern world. But for intellectuals who studied social studies there was a missing link known as Freedom- the freedom of SEA (Speech, Expression and Assembly). It so happened that the masses of Ethiopia and Eritrea were and is still fighting for the actual SEA (Red). Isn't this confusion on your part? Decipher your name? What is your name? Call me by my name.

As to my best friend's book of Confederation: Professor Medhanie's complaints and concerns seem to be over, he was alienated from the masses of Eritrean people although mostly of his own making. He has proposed a confederation among many nations. How is it feasible when everyone has returned at least psychologically into his mothers' womb? Ethnicity by Woyane and languages by Shabia can be stumbling blocks. How the regime change is is possible? Is this the American way or the Eway revolution? Shouldn't we build on what we have as knowledge and assets are cumulative?

Debteraw's two main questions of why and how to every proposal and project should be considered before you write. Tsegaye Debteraw has inculcated these two questions into the minds and hearts of our generation. We should be better prepared to answer these two questions.

ERITREAN FIGHTERS

The Blue Nile River and the Red Sea are not useful for the majority of Ethiopians and Eritreans per se. currently these Blue and Red are only useful for foreign nations. For who and why will be a discussion in future articles. For now, suffice to let to rest the issue of geography and history aside and concentrate on the people's issues of politics, military, social, economy and culture.

As for me, I have geography of Ethiopia and Eritrea in my pocket, the language and the culture right in my sight. Blue Nile Basin encompasses about one third of Ethiopia's size. This land mass covers from Eritrea down to Kefa and Illubabor of 318,000 squares miles. And who will benefit from this Water Basin? EGGIKSWWT (Eritrea, Godjam, Gondar, Illuabor, Keffa, Shewa, Wellega, Wollo and Tigrai) Regions are affected by the use and abuse of this water Basin.

And who are the beneficiaries from the use of the port of Assab in the Red Sea? The Wolloyes, the Tigrians, the Godjames, the Gondares and partially the Shewans, are the potential savers of transportation cost from the smooth operation of the port of Assab. The GoGoTW (Godjam, Gondar, Tigrai and Wollo) regions are the real power brokers for the morning after. Do the other Kifle Hagers of Ethiopia need the Red Sea? No, they do not need the Red Sea for reducing transportation costs. The ports of Sudan, Massawa, Djibouti, Mogadisho and Mombassa are lined up for competition to provide services to SEEDS. But it is an established fact that competition is the lifeblood of any nation, be it in politics, social, and economics.

Eritrea has produced hundred thousands of fighters in the last forty years and still doing it. What is the purpose of these trends? It is good that people are trained for any skill- a skill that is useful. Nowadays all skills have changed be it in military, social, economics and even in politics. It is time to realize that there are four Cs that are operative in our world. These are Capital, Corporation, Communication and Consumerism. Eritrea can only be a consumer society just like any other country unless otherwise, the government has the other Cs in place. I am of the opinion that the fighters should be transformed to entrepreneurs. I would have liked the fighters to be peace keepers in the whole world. It is a noble and a payable job. The most unwise thing is to keep the youth in the trenches for indefinite period. In the name of demarcation, time, effort and energy are wasted. And above all, the demarcation is a bogus. As I have said before, the demarcation is already done in the minds and hearts of the Eritrean people right after the unprecedented mass deportation of Eritreans from Ethiopia. Technical demarcation is not the answer. Peace will not come because of the UN, AEA or AU interference. It lies within our own people who fought side by side to bring justice and democracia for all Ethiopians and Eritreans.

I find it amazing that the TPLF and the PFDJ have returned to the symbol of flag of Red, Yellow and Green. What about the Paquame, the Meskel, Timket and the Tsome rituals? You answer it. What about heroes? As far as PFDJ is concerned, there are no official heroes only the sandal and the camel. In Ethiopia, though, there are heroes here and there.

In Ethiopia, there is no value so far except the love for money that is not the same thing for the value of money. In Eritrea, there is value for being debt and corruption free. But there is no value for choices.

The best thing that I have heard so far is that PIA of Eritrea and Sebhat Nega both said that they stand or love the other people more than their own. This is a good thing. But what is the problem? Is it greed for money or power? One of them is doing right and the other is doing evil. Which one is that, please stand up!

INTERNATIONAL (global)

AEA (Americans-Europeans-Asians) have essentially begun to believe that the Red Sea Corridor and the Blue Nile Basin are intertwined. The people who live around them will have to plant seeds (Sudan- Eritrea-Ethiopia-Djibouti-Somalia) for generations to come all the way to the Third Millennium. The Physical unity of these countries of SEEDS is the real interest of AEA. Are we entitled to know what our Ethiopian Thinkers and our Eritrean Fighters plan to do after the so-called 2nd Millennium and Border Demarcation? The human brain uses only a third of its potential but in the case of Ethiopians and Eritreans, we only use an insignificant fraction of our brains. Why? Socially speaking, it is because of fear of embarrassment, wurdet in Amharic keiybluni in Tigrigna. Scientifically, speaking for fear of imperfect work and religiously speaking, for fear of interfering in God's work. Politically speaking though, I believe it is emanated from fear of persecution and imprisonment. What has happened to the struggle of liberation? What a tragedy or travesty for Eritrea and Ethiopia? Has the Revolution failed us? Yes, the Revolution by the DERG was a misnomer. The Eway Revolution of Debteraw's EPRP was real and it is still going strong.

CONCLUSION

It is worthwhile to know that the age of symbol, ritual and hero is over. The age of value has arrived and it is going to be fought within Ethiopia and among Ethiopians. Reading is not enough it should be accompanied by writing for reading and writing are complementary inasmuch as talking and listening are intertwined. We should be reminded of the wisdom of our scholars such as Debteraw who used to tell that NIBAB YIQETL WETRGUAME YEHAYI meaning that reading by itself kills while translation saves. Ethiopiannes/nist/winet can only validated through practice by faith by name and by face. Join the Tsinhate muhuran (CTA) associates.

Ethiopians and Eritreans who were born between 1941-1974 have brought political ideas into the limelight though cautiously and clandestinely. This generation for lack of name, I call it **JJJC** (33). Call me by my name. What is my name? No doubt, this generation has created the following characters.

1. Doubters represented by TPLF and CUD
2. Atheists represented by PFDJ
3. Believers represented by UEDF
4. Seekers represented by OLF
5. Everybody and Everyone represented by EPRP

And in the next Millennium, what do we expect to get? Piece-Peace-PIS or pins?

For comments and criticism: woldetewolde@yahoo.com

CALL ME BY MY NAME:

A debate with Debteraw, XVIII

Wolde Tewolde alias Obo Arada Shawl

October 13, 2007

A choice of political leadership for Ethiopia
An Engineer, an Economist or a Political Party?

Introduction: A little bit of political history

For Leadership to hold, legitimacy is the single most important element. The Monarchy legitimizes authority from God, the Almighty; The Military legitimizes its authority from the Gun and political parties claim their authorities from party mandates. In our case, the legitimacy for the Monarchy and the DERG was clear as the day light. However, the legitimacy of the TPLF is blurred. There was/is a lot of lies and deception. Some of us believe TPLF's legitimacy emanates from the State Department and some of us believe that their legitimacy comes from the people of Tigrai. Others believe that it comes from the ethnic nationalities of Ethiopia. But EPRP has gone through these assumptions and realities. EPRP has fought against all these elements of imperialism (both of American and Russian), has fought against narrow nationalism and has fought against distorted thesis of Shaebia's colonial theory. There is nothing new for EPRP to regret and to lament for today's Ethiopian situation.

The issue of legitimacy is of paramount importance to everyone and everybody. Let us have clarity on this issue before we fight on paper, on the streets, in bars, in churches and in assemblies.

The Eway Revolution was about legitimacy that emanates from individuals who will have a choice during recruitment, voting or election.

Without working from bottom up and vice versa, there will be no legitimacy for power. Based on this fundamental principle, EPRP has taken a bold and an arduous process to empower individuals. A clear case in point was about Berhane Meskel Redda. Mr. Redda was indeed a revolutionary par excellence. He has spent an insurmountable amount of time, energy and resources to organize EPLO (Ethiopian Peoples' Liberation Organization), the precursor of EPRP. Because of his talent and celebrity, many students and professionals wanted his leadership. In fact, many joined EPRP solely on his name recognition. Too many individuals have associated with EPRP because of Berhane Meskel Redda (BMR). But does this acronym of BMR resonate with this individual reality? With Berhane, there was no light, he did not believe in the Cross and he did not help individuals. So his name was a misnomer from the beginning. Call me by my name. What is my name?

The current discourse for political opposition leadership has been around two individuals, Ato Hailu Shawl and Ato Berhanu Nega. Both individuals have different experiences albeit with complementary education, that of _cost_ _and_ _benefit_. But what is at stake at the present time? Are Ethiopians looking for political leaders in the form of individuals or political parties? If so, are these two individuals apt to the leadership position? What do they stand for? Who are their constituents? Can they solve the ethnicity and the nationality question? What is their stand on War and Revolution? Globalization versus Free Trade? Demarcation versus Mass Deportation? How can they solve poverty and prosperity? And by what means? My readers should answer these questions for themselves. I for one want to express something of relevance to leadership 101 as follows.

The Engineer: It's about cost in isolation!

Ato Hailu Shawl is an accomplished engineer in his field of study. He knows the cost of Construction, the cost of Operation and Maintenance of goods and services. What about benefits? Engineer Hailu understands benefits at an individual level or more appropriately for his personal interest. What about the social benefit to our society? Ato Hailu has worked for the benefit of International organizations such as, oil industries, Highways and Sugar Corporations not to mention agriculture and consulting for

Europeans. I doubt if he had ever considered the social cost and benefit for Ethiopia and Ethiopians.

By training engineers are very much conscious of unit cost but not social cost. Let us not forget the DERG era in which five of the eleven politbureau members were engineers while the rest were military men. Both training do not dwell in rational thinking unlike other training. The rest of the population including the Ethiopian youths were forced to be involved in Dankera (dancing), which was contrary to real KINET as proposed, by Debteraw and his colleagues.

As a footnote, I had an assignment to connect Goddjam and Wellega by road via Bure-Nekemte towns. Mr. Hailu had asked me to speed up the project so that he can give it to the Russians for financing. I knew then that he was not considering the social economic benefit for the country. He was only doing his job. But I was doing my job and the public job simultaneously considering the benefit and the cost elements. As a technocrat, Engineer Hailu was excellent but as a revolutionary, he was mediocre. Another example worth mentioning was that during the dialogue (WYYT) of employees of Highway, certain groups opposed that the then manager of Highway Authority, Mr. Hailu did not qualify to join the discussion as he had 33 bedrooms in his residence. That automatically disqualify him to be a progressive worker was the complaint. To counter this silly argument, I told the group that I had 16 doors in my residence and that did not mean that access of doors disqualify me from participating in the discussion, I counter argued. Ato Hailu actually proved himself by allowing construction workers to have access to free men's (cafeteria) in the construction site. Some of his policies proved that he stood for the workers.

The point is that Ato Hailu has passed through many ups and downs including imprisonment. I remember that he gave a bold statement against the cadres of the DERG regime. I also remember that a bus ticketed for supposedly allowed an EPRP member to commit suicide humiliated him. I hope all these might help him to differentiate between EPRP, the DERG, the TPLF and the EPLF. With the exception of EPRP, all other organizations believe that might is right. For EPRP, *right is might*. It was, it is and it is going to be in the future. Ato Hailu recently said that he has learnt a lot while in prison. I hope he can now differentiate between deception and democracia, between USA, EU and E and E not as countries but as their way of life and their political system. HAILU SHAWL is a proper and legitimate name as deciphered by debteras. It is a positive name. Call me by name. What is my name?

The Economist: It is about benefit in isolation!

DR. Berhanu thinks that there is light at the end of the tunnel or rather the light is on. If I have to decipher his name, the letter B is still locked on him. I recommend Ato Berhanu to unlock his name. In his first name, there is no light but in his second name there is nature. In Ethiopia, the government is against nature. Everything is artificial. Ato Berhanu should learn at least from his father. I see that he did not learn from the first alphabet of A (ASSIMBA). Personally, I do not think he has the trade off between cost and benefit analysis. The Ethiopian economy has been an incremental development, thanks to World Bank and capitalist development of infrastructure. Dr. Berhanu and his close friends have not realized the long and hard development plan of the country. Individual projects and sector projects were materialized on their cost-benefit analysis. Now Mr. Economist thinks on political terms and even that what he call civilized and uncivilized? What does that mean? I wish he could have used a proper term of Regierungsbezirk/Bezirksregierung (urban and rural). Ato Berhanu before learning anything from Rural Ethiopia, he was appointed as a mayor for the city of Addis Ababa. Am I missing something? As an economist (I am sorry I do not know in what he has specialized), he should know something about urban planning and rural development. I hope he understands what I am saying. Ato Berhanu knows that needs are logical while wants and desires are sentimental and emotional. Our needs pushes us just so far, but when needs are satisfied, they will stop pushing us. But if our purpose wants and desires – then wants and desires will keep pushing by after our needs are satisfied and until our wants and desires are fulfilled. So what is that derives Ethiopians to push for? Is it liberty and freedom political or otherwise? Please stand up Mr. Berhanu as you have during the Imblta Groupie Era!

Ato Berhanu had joined EPRP but has been discharged voluntarily from his duty of serving EMAKKIANS (Ethiopians and Eritreans).

Nevertheless, he has worked tirelessly to demean and to undermine EPRP's leadership. I doubt whether Mr. Berhanu had grasped the working relations of EPRP leadership and follower ship, i.e. Zematzches and Azmatches. He had been falsely accusing EPRP of killing a dozen members of minorities for the purpose of empowering Amhara and Tigrian elites. When confronted that he was involved in the trial of guilty conspiracy but was released, he again lies that he was a minor. As a policy, EPRP does not send minors to fight. I suspect he went to AAssimba to save his life from the terror of the DERG and not ready to struggle for change.

Let me sketch Mr. Berhanu. He was from Markato a bustling area for workers and traders. No education only hard work. Arada a Balanced place for action and counter action. Arat Kilo or Sidist Kilo an academic center for intellectuals. I have traveled for 13 years from Mercato to Arat Kilo (3 miles) physically and mentally. But for Mr. Berhanu it took him two solid years to travel these three miles of distance. Arada by definition is the center of Addis Ababa. There seems an effort by Berhanu to be a centrist in the Ethiopian affairs. He wanted to be in Mercato and at Arat/Sidist Kilos at the same time. He should live in the Piaza. His priority should be known. He should choose as a matter of priority, education, politics or business. He cannot have them all. The economist should really try to understand the **costs** that have been paid by all Ethiopians to be free from dictators and authoritarians like that of Melese and Isayas respectively. Ask the Mercato residents and traders; ask the Arat/Sidist Kilo students and residents and above all ask the whereabouts of all the Aradas.

Party Relationship: It is about social cost and social benefit in unity

EPRP unlike, EPLF and TPLF, did not depend on personalities or on the Secretary General of the Party. A significant number of intellectuals believe that had Berhane Meskel Redda become the Secretary General of EPRP, there is no doubt in their mind that Mr. Mellese or Mr. Essyas would have been in the place where they are now. Mr. Redda would have been the Ethiopian and the Eritrean leader. But the question is would that be a solution? Probably, it would have been a solace for those who cry that EPRP is evil and weak. Too many EPRP members and associates desire victory at any cost. But that is not what the genuine EPRP aspired for Ethiopia and Ethiopians. Instead of a single man at the helm, **EPRP decided to have a weak Secretary General but a strong collective leadership.** EPRP leadership is living by example, of the people, for the people and by the people. DEMOCRACIA is the mantra of EPRP. Unless we are blind or deaf, DEMOCRACIA is the voice of EPRP. DEMOCRACIA HAS BEEN THE COLLECTIVE LEADERSHIP OF EPRP SINCE ITS INCEPTION. Not only Ethiopians but also the whole world are crying for DEMOCRACIA, thanks to EPRP leadership and membership. This means that EPRP is a winner not a loser. It became a winner though at a heavy sacrifices and losses to itself. We should not confuse that all losses of lives and material wealth were the result of EPRP's doing or undoing. All losses and victims are a result of EPRP's opponents. EPRP is a victim not a predator. According to Debteraw, EPRP was and is to educate, to empower Ethiopians and Eritreans through READ (Revolution, Education, Arts and Democracy). There is nothing wrong to read and to decipher one's name, one's culture and one's belief. Call me by my name? What is my name?

EPRP: It is about political analysis

The majority of EPRP leadership does not like manipulation, as manipulation is the enemy of Trust. Debteraw with capital D used to dig into problems, not the people. Some think that there are two kinds of workers, those volunteers and those who get paid. Not true for Debteraw. There are only volunteers, some who get paid, and some who do not.

In every high achieving organization, like EPRP, people are basically volunteers. If Ethiopian workers do not want to work but just collect a paycheck, they can do it. But the point is simple. What makes people "volunteers"? Why is it that some computer programmers produce more times than others? Why is it that some people on NASA projects work sixty or more intense hours a week without being asked or paid extra for it? And why is it that EPRP leaders work overtime and without pay?

The truth is that whether people are employees or volunteers, they do what really needs to be done only voluntarily. EPRP members and leaders "volunteer" because Ethiopia and its people expect their best to give them and to receive the best in return. And in particular during the 1070s, when Ethiopians and Eritreans were enthusiastic and behave in ways they want them to behave, the tone of voluntarism was necessary to a high performing organization of EPRP. EPRP's call was heard all over the country, and it is going to be heard again. Welcome aboard, the Eway Revolution will save you all.

Maintaining EPRP's dignity

Dignity is an internal self-respect that should never be allowed for compromise by the disrespectful actions of others. It is the result of commanding and demanding the respect of others. EPRP derives taking responsibility for its choices and actions.

It acts on principle, not expedience
EPRP faced catastrophe without collapsing
EPRP has clear boundaries and do not permit to be consistently violated
EPRP resisted slurs, attacks and meanness with like behavior and
It has high standards and lives up to them.

CONCLUSION

Our Eway revolution was to define the standard of all values as man's life; the means of our survival as the exercise of our rational minds, not our adrenal glands like that of Mellese of Ethiopia and Isaiah of Eritrea. EPRP has taught us that it is because we must be free to think and act in order to survive and flourish that we should deal with one another based on mutual consent and never through the initiation of forces. And for these reasons, the E-governments should be limited to protecting the rights of individuals, to life, liberty and land property, **and above all the right of all exiles to return to Ethiopia.**

What we here from postmodernists like the economist and his elite colleagues is that there are no standards, no right or wrong, and that is a matter of opinion and interpretation, except their own bizarre theories and hidden agendas. This line of thinking is rampant with TPLF leadership thanks to our economist and his likes.

What is needed is an unapologetic defense of the rational, responsible and principled individualism. Each Ethiopian/Eritreans should pursue the goals he love, whether nurturing a child to maturity or a business to profitability; whether writing a song, a poem or a business plan; whether laying the bricks to a building, designing the building or arranging its financing. The result would be a society in which we are each enriched, entertained, educated, enlightened and inspired by our fallen and living fellows. This is the vision of our comrades of EPRP.

CALL ME BY MY NAME:

A debate with Debteraw, XIX

Wolde Tewolde, alias Obo Arada Shawl

November 7, 2007

Up Front – Help Wanted
Qualified candidate to promote democracy within EPRP!

This is EPRP's end game, halfway to forming a true political community. As it gets under way, notwithstanding earlier battles within itself, EPRP will have to do more for its citizens to accept not only its discussions but also its agenda. The agenda is READ, READ and READ.

Call me by my name. What is my name? EPRP.

E = Ethiopia
E = ERITREA
P = PEOPLE = KINET
R = REVOLUTION = DEMOCRACIA
P = PARTY = POLITICAL

EPRP teaches its members to stand up for their beliefs and values. EPRP's shared goals are to exercise the right to practice to change the government through peaceful and democratic means. Peaceful and democratic were and are unacceptable to the people in power.

On the contrary, the opponents and the enemies of EPRP label the party as militarist/anarchist and undemocratic, YE'MYEN EKEK WEDE ABYE L'KK.

In order to test whether, EPRP was or is undemocratic, I ask readers to carefully understand the following events in the life of EPRP.

ANJA: When the majority of the CC of the party made the decision concerning the form of leadership, two individuals, by the name of Berhane Meskel Redda and Getachew Maru have attempted to abort the decision using their Celebes names to discontinue the operation of EPRP's programs. Essentially, they were against the collective leadership concept but they did not spell it. As it turns out, even their own prominent brothers who were members of the party were against them. EPRP was not and still is not based on family, friend or food (FFF) business. In short the two individuals have disgraced themselves, their party and country by creating a party (a new eprp) that ultimately brought havoc and disaster. The first test of democracy within the party was to "kill the party" as was communicated to Menghistu in writing by the new eprp.

Anja was not only an act against vote and decision but it was about "Kick it Away."

BITENA: In order to rectify the destruction that was initiated by these individuals, the representative leaders of the Party and the Army had assembled for assessment, evaluation and rectification. While these important discussions were going on, many members became impatient and abandon the struggle to go to different directions. Some have surrender locally while others surrender internationally. It was ironic that some top leaders blame the party for allowing democracy to the rank and file and left for Europe, Canada, and America. But the true leaders agreed to continue the struggle. Those who chose to continue the struggle have done so in the hope that others will join them at later stage or continue the struggle by any other means necessary but parking. And so the struggle of EPRP has been going on by any other means necessary. But what many members do not know is the fact that why and how the name of Betena label turned into reality. I believe some leaders have encouraged other members not to continue the struggle. It is a cultural thing. It was not EPRP's fault. All those who wanted to leave the struggle have left peacefully and honorably. EPRP has to be commended for this type of DEMOCRACIA – a solution for everyone and everybody. The second test of democracy within EPRP collective leadership has been solved without a fight in a civil manner. It was about "Stay Away with or without parking."

COMMITMENT: The recent congress has been a different kind of the same thing that has been done in the past, a complaint about the lack of democracy. It is only different in the sense that it happened in America where nobody is afraid of threat. Do we have to conclude that the democracy at home was better off? How come leaders walk out? What about the conviction, the persuasion and commitments? Does it mean that EPRP was more democratic under duress? What happened to the HE'S GLE HE'S method of resolving issues? That was something unique to EPRP. Actually EPRP is well known to be a breeding ground for democracy as testified by many individuals and groups. Ethiopia and Eritrea should be thankful to EPRP for teaching its children to be peaceful and democratic, civil citizens. Once again the choice according to DEMOCRACIA is among Ethinicization, Democratization or Nationalism. "Walk away" is not a democratic option. EPRP is on the verge of becoming a Democratic Institution for everybody and everyone. Has anyone heard that EPRP collective leadership has done dealing behind the back of its members, and supporters without mandate? I haven't. I have seen individuals making attempts to duplicate EPRP as an organization by even sacrificing comrades' lives in order to get some financial, economic or political reward. But in the end, they all regret to leave EPRP.

Concluding Remarks: Collective leadership is not synonymous with collective bargaining. EPRP has a long history of collective bargaining with the Labor Union as well as with political and civic organizations. Politically, EPRP's collective leadership does not mediate or arbitrate neither for the release of prisoners nor for the bargain of sovereignty of anybody. The purpose of EPRP's existence is to struggle for liberty and freedom and negotiate if feasible for justice, faith, love, and hope.

As a political Party, the organization of EPRP has been solid and true to its name. The main tree is always the same with many roots and branches.

I appeal to all debteraw website readers to take a deep look into this week's first page. Let us see if we can synchronize the three dimensional phenomenon within the same page.

On the top of the page: pictures depicting small voices from victims. On the left: see DEBTERAW himself radiating the laser guide.

In the middle: see the essence and focal point for our living in DEMOCRACIA

Let us immortalize Debteraw and his colleagues. The release of Debteraw and his colleagues is the basis for moving forward.

For comments and criticism: woldetewolde@yahoo.com

CALL ME BY MY NAME:

A debate with Debteraw, XX

Wolde Tewolde alias Obo Arada Shawl

November 17, 2007

In the beginning, EPRP's shared goal was to exercise the right to practice to change the government of the Prime Minister of Aklilu Habtewold and his brothers through **peaceful** and **democratic** means. Peaceful and democracy were unknown to the people in power.

Ethiopian security forces routinely tortured, beat, mistreated detainees under interrogation to obtain confessions or incriminating **information**. In several cases, Ethiopian authorities subjected student activists, nationalist and other critics of the regime to forced exiles and an option to go to the mountains and lowlands of

- Bale,
- Eritrea,
- Godjam,
- Ogaden and
- Tigrai.

EPRP began to undermine the regime by instilling the concept of Revolution, a political Revolution. They call this revolution as the Eway Revolution. It included the present physical geography of Eritrea and Ethiopia. Conceptually, the Eway Revolution encompassed the Blue Nile in the west, the Red Sea in the east, and the Yellow in the North and the Green in the south. This Eway Revolution has bloomed to the full in present day Ethiopia.

- The Eway Revolution walked through Mountains, Valleys and Deserts of Ethiopia. News of the Eway Revolution has spread fast locally and internationally. The Ethiopian University Service became the agent of change for the entire of Ethiopia. The University National Service became competitive with the American Peace Corps. The so-called Red State of Hamasien and the so- called Blue Amhara state just like the Red and Blue of American Democratic and Republican have became the focal point for contention. The Leftist (Grazmatches) the Rightists (Kegnatzmatches), along with the millions of Ethiopians in the middle valorize
- Justice,
- Faith,
- Compassion,
- Respect and
- Hope for everyone and everybody, yet the expense of **forgiveness.**

With this background the Monarchy of Ethiopia gave power to its citizens without fight. The beginning of the end had arrived in September 1974.

"Who is the next leader, please stand up!" was the demand and cry of all Ethiopians. By that time, two schools of thoughts have already been mushroomed between those who opted for Military Rule and those who supported the Civilian rule. The military supporters led by Mieso as was expected went head on to confront not only the Nationalist guerrilla fighters but also against the civilian Ethiopians. And so the party of EPRP became the victim of the Military regime for 17 solid years (1974-1991).

EPRP has been a school for democracy since its inception, helping its members and supporters learn to care about the world and talk about their political concerns. It was also true that EPRP also taught its members how to silence its opponents mainly through poems and writings. At times, it had to use its members of EPRA to resort to force. But EPRP's strength was in persuasion via the publication of DEMOCARCIA and through its members' discipline. Essentially EPRP was and is a breeding organization for many political leaders. It should be commended for its training for democracy.

The problem was that the majority of Ethiopians did not understand whom the "personal leader of DEMOCRACIA." The Military junta has been pursuing for the publication of DEMOCRACIA – the political organ of EPRP to catch the ringleader. The editors of the publication were few but the contents of DEMOCRACIA were the voices of all EPRP members, its supporters, its sympathizers and of the populace at large.

EPRP has believed in the history of Ethiopia that city-states, nation-states and member- states were existent long before the advent of Haile Sellassie I. All what EPRP wanted was to create a state (space) that would be peaceful, affluent and democratic, in other words, the attempt was to create a software for Ethiopia. In order to implement this shared Ethiopian dream, EPRP continued to work with the urban and the rural population of all nations and nationalities. While continuing with its vision and mission EPRP has met its first obstacle from within itself. A faction or Anja has emerged. What is this Anja thing? The procedure was simple but the consequence was devastating not only for EPRP but for the whole nation of Ethiopia. It was the first breach of Trust among Ethiopians.

What is it about?

Simply it is about **Collective Leadership.** Two individuals by the name of Berhane Meskel Redda and Getachew Maru refused to abide by the majority of the decision of party. In every Organization, particularly when it is a democratic one, one cannot ago against the decision of the majority. It is only proper to fiercely debate and discuss for ones' ideas and opinions to convince the majority, but once it is decided, it is over, it has to be carried out by the decision. Unfortunate as it was at the time, the two individuals have done their share of destruction to annihilate EPRP, the party they themselves have created. What an anomaly! "They kicked away EPRP."

Once the damage was carried out by the "new EPRP" in the cities, Menghistu further demanded the "new EPRP" to eliminate also the Army of EPRP, otherwise, Menghistu told to the Anja leaders that they could not be accepted to Menghistu's alliance. It was a big challenge for them but they informed him that they support the Peasant Revolution. Nobody knows whether they meant it or it was an impossible task. And so the DERG leader alias of Seded group went after Berhane where he was captured while to trying to escape out of the country. I have met the person who and how he captured him. It was a sad story of a failed leadership to tell.

Why was this a failed leadership? There were two main reasons, a cultural and an educational.

"Temelket Alamahn, Teketel Alekahn" was deeply ingrained in Ethiopian mentality. At the height of EPRP, there was no leader in person totally in contradiction to the Ethiopian culture and tradition. EPRP wanted to make sure that every individual could be or would be a leader. That was and is the concept of EPRP's democracy. The Party has paid a heavy price to institute this concept. It was not all for nothing though that the party has sacrificed. In terms of democratic slogan, the term has become a household word in Ethiopia. In terms of application, EPRP members have joined and became members or leaders in different organizations. This is a plus for EPRP unlike many claims and counter claims. Once the dust settles, the truth will come out. For the time being, let me give you some anecdotes from EPRP's diary.

In the Kebele where I lived, an old man advised the youth of the time not to confront the Military regime because according to him, he said "Ethiopians do not have underground places like foreign countries, please my children," he said, "do not think about underground movement." The then Youth League, the now Middle Aged said told to themselves, until the Official of the Kebele understands what an underground means, that they can work openly even by using the Kebele Office. And so they did. The entire towns, cities of Ethiopia were engulfed with underground activities. And we all know the rest of history. **The clandestine leadership of EPRP has done its work.**

The Eway Revolution also became popular in the whole countryside of Ethiopia. The DERG refused to accept reality and the youths and militias began to refuse to go to war. As Ethiopian parents became unwilling to send their children to the Revolutionary War, the DERG began to force them and so they send their children with weeping and crying.

In order to stop the invincible and invisible Eway Revolution the DERG cadres were gone wild for campaigning to stop the cry of parents. I want to share with readers a typical incident of campaign that I encountered in the town of Dejen, Godjam Administrative Region. It was during the campaign for annihilating EPRP. The officials of the DERG had gathered the police, the merchants, bank and government officials and many residents of the town. In front of the gathering, the cadre said the following, "Why are we weeping when we send our children to the War Front? What has happened to the guts (WENE) of Belay Zellek, Tewodros, Yohannes, Minilik and others? Ethiopian used to celebrate when they go to the war front. Why is this different?" he asked. As usual in those days, everybody was silent. But an old man got up and responded in the following manner. "My son, you have said the bravery of Belay Zelleke, the Minilik, the Tewodros and the Yohannes. I do not wish to repeat it." He continued to say "But my dear cadre, we are sending our children **without leaders**. You DERG leaders are here and our children are there. What can our children do without leaders? You tell me. In fact, this is a consolation for our children's death to weep and say goodbye." He finished his opinion and sat. Readers can imagine how the DERG cadre became speechless and paralyzed.

The story of these morals is meant to relate to the current situation of EPRP leadership dilemma. EPRP collective leadership teaches its followers about courage so that its members and followers learn to emulate EPRP's leadership behavior rather their words. Courage demonstrated is likely courage learned. What is courage? It is the absence of fear. The lesson members need to learn is how to face the fear of the unknown, being mindful of security considerations, choosing battles carefully. There is a difference between being foolhardy and being brave, though. The foolhardy face predictable danger that could be avoided; the brave accept danger with all necessary precautions, because it is unavoidable or because it is important to make a statement at that time.

EPRP teaches its members to stand up for its beliefs in the world at large but must demonstrate courage in its organizations. The Party of EPRP has shown both courage and fear. The EPRA did not show trustworthiness. Self-trust is evident in a person's self- esteem and confidence. Risk taking and experimentation, unavoidable, unreasonable, inconsistent or unreliable - the less likely in a stable environment without stability EPRP is hard-pressed to trust self or other.

There is a missing link in EPRA's history but there is no missing link in the history of EPRP. The struggle of EPRP will continue unabated with or without individual leadership or professorship. It is all about P (principle) and not about B (benefit) or B (blood).

Unfortunately, CIA of America and Mosad of Israel jointly decided that the Red State of Eritrea and the Blue Region of Ethiopia should be together. A Christian leader of EPLF and an all-Christian region of Tigrai was their basis for their idea of unity during the 1991 assumption of power. This false premise have created havoc in today's' Ethiopia. By the same token, they blocked EPRP not to participate in London Conference. Tacitly, I have to assume that they have given a permission to annihilate EPRP from the scene. In the same way that the DERG was looking through the wrong prism to annihilate EPRP from the source, TPLF the brain child of America is peeping through the wrong prism to kill EPRP from its source. Where is the source of EPRP, one might ask?

UP Front - Help Wanted
Qualified candidate to promote Democracy within EPRP!

IMMMORTALIZE, IMMORTALIZE AND IMMORTALIZE DEBTERAW!!!

This is the last piece for a debate with Debteraw; the next articles will be **Solutions** with Debteraw.

For comments and criticism: woldetewolde@yahoo.com

CALLL ME BY MY NAME:

A commentary on EPRP's split, XXI

Wolde Tewolde, alias Obo Arada Shawl,

December 23, 2007

Encounter

On Friday morning, a day of freedom, I came across of an old friend by the name of Kebede Essatu, a poet and a revolutionary of a kind. I always tease him whenever I see him. He had sacrificed his education for the sake of EPRP and thereby for the sake of the Ethiopian Eway Revolution. This time he somewhat teased me about the split of EPRP leadership? According to rumors he said that EPRP leaders have split and have shared the Party's asset. Or, he further asked me if there is a process of reconciliation as he came to read it on websites.

Although I do not know much of the reconciliation process, I know that there is no dividend to be shared out to anybody. However, we continued the discussion about EPRP's leadership row. I told Kebede to look for the truth. "What is the truth?" he said in his usual emotional mood. I continued to explain in the following manner:

"We all should ask," I said to Kebede, "Who holds the truth?" Did the truth about EPRP leadership in America gone with Belayneh alias known as Mersha or is it still with Assefa aka Fassika? How do you know where the truth is? Kebede asked me again? There is no truth, he seemed to utter in his inner own voice. Off hand, I told him what I have heard from the participants in the Conference as the truth. And our discussion went on for a while. Ato Kebede and I can only talk about EPRP's leadership in

America. The leadership we know about EPRP is around these two individuals in relations to the areas known as North America and Canada. That is all.

I reminded Ato Kebede that every time, there comes a fundamental change in a nation or a country or a system of government, there is bound to be a shift and a hope for finding one's niche. We have seen this during the collapse of the ancien regime of Haile Sellassie I, where a lot of people had shifted with the wind even by betraying the Monarchy - whose legitimacy comes from EGZIABHER

When the DERG whose legitimacy emanated from the military power came to end; there was a shift for which Kebede himself was a witness. By the way I have encouraged Ato Kebede to go to Addis Addis when he told me that he had three goals in mind.

- To demand the release of Debteraw and his comrades
- To open a branch office for EPRP and
- To participate in the drafting of the Constitution of Ethiopia.

Now, it is the same thing, there seems or there is a perception that the TPLF is going to collapse any time soon and therefore, there is a glimpse of hope within some groups that it is time for them to be on the bandwagon.

Kebede asked me what I think about the split in EPRP's leadership as many have asked me before, and here is what I think.

This was not narrated to him as he was with some body and that we did not want to bother the other person with our somewhat private but serious discussion.

HISTORY

31 years ago, on September 11, 1976, the military government known as the DERG officially declared EPRP as the public enemy number one. The DERG by declaring this proclamation proceeded to wipe out EPRP. A peaceful dissent by EPRP was met by savage torture and murder of its members and supporters.

After 17 years, the DERG was the one that was wiped out and not EPRP.

According to the reports made by Belayneh, Woyane, Shaebia and the Sudanese government launched a war against EPRA and presented themselves as true Ethiopian democrats. Simultaneously, EPRP was excluded from the London Conference that was meant to hand over power to the insurgents, on the pretext that they do not have a Fighting Army like that of OLF, TPLF and Shaebia.

After seven years, all of the peace loving and democrats of Woyane and Shaebia exposed themselves in bloody battles resulting in an endless war of nerves and wasted resources. Above all, the TPLF and the EPLF fighters is becoming dustbin of history. Only their leaders are reported to live comfortably and luxuriously.

After 16 years, TPLF and Shaebia are still remained unpopular governments. But the EPRP collective leadership is still remained intact with both integrity and loyalty to the Eway Revolution.

Why is this anomaly has occurred? Is it the leadership style that mattered? Or is it the democratic style that is at work?

In other words, Shaebia imprisoned 15 of their leadership comrades, Woyane dismissed five of their leadership comrades, and Kinjit fired 5 of their leadership. Ask your self whether EPRP leaders have fired their fellow leaders. Absolutely not. Only member's votes can put them down. Where is the democracy in action? I leave this for the readers to answer.

It is now a truism that is what is most important is not a country's first election, but its second and subsequent elections. And what matters is not simply that people have the right to vote, but they are offered a real Choice, under conditions that are truly free and fair. EPRP believes that this phenomenon is not happening in Ethiopia today.

Elections are one part of a democratic symphony. This should have been a reminder for Kinjit leaders and members. A full orchestra is required, including markets that reward initiative; legal structure that prevail justice, police that respect due process; and a press corpse that is free to pursue the facts and publish the truth. EPRP has learnt this not only from history books but also from bitter experience in Ethiopia.

Split Over Democracy or DEMOCRACIA?

Let me go back and speak with Kebede. Leadership and Relationship with EPRP was never about property or financial gain. It is about understanding and working together.

Two individual of EPRP collective leadership members became dictators. Assefa and Hama Tuma were labeled as dictators of EPRP. Are they really? Assefa's dictatorship is very well known in North America. Kebede knows it and Berhanu Shalleka knows it because both claims that Assefa has never oppose them let alone to dictate them.

What about Hama Tuma? Hama Tuma is a satirist. He cuts through the baloney and gets to the truth. Wit has its place in Ethiopian politics, and people always like to laugh where Mr. Hama Tuma offers them in his writings. But funny can be a distraction from the serious stuff that Hama conveys to Ethiopians. Hama Tuma writes about Ethiopian elites, the African leaders, Texan Ethiopians etc. Ethiopian culture, opposition to the war in Somalia involvement and the way Eritrea is separated from Ethiopia and so on and so forth. Mr. Tuma has always been funny in his writings for a lifetime of making people laughs and critically think. Ato Tuma tries to sound deadly earnest even, in truth, a little ponderous at times as he seeks to be a real democrat. What comrade Hama now needs is gravitas. True democracy is never achieved- it is always a pursuit

If EPRP that love liberty is weary, then those who love power will always sweep all of us away. That is indeed the fear of Hama Tuma and it is a legitimate fear. In other words, DEMOCRACIA is an Ethiopian version of democracy.

As to the question of Ato Mersha, we have gone through this before. When Kiflu Tadesse wrote a history of EPRP, we have agreed to respect each other and do the right thing until Ethiopia offers an opportunity for EPRP to be a candidate as a political party. When that time comes, Ato Mersha can campaign that he has never stopped the entire journey of EPRP's long struggle and that he has been wounded in the battle whereas Ato Kifle can claim by saying that he had written a partial history of EPRP but stopped somewhere in between. I thought we have agreed on this. Ato Kiflu has parked so to speak while Ato Mersha was actively involved in bringing back the former EPRP members back. At the beginning Ato Mersha's attempt was noble but somewhere I lost him when he was deeply involved in bringing old leaders and intellectuals back to struggle. His task was not about recruiting, it was rather about convincing individuals with new ideas or telling the future plans of EPRP. It is true that ideas can bring people but people cannot bring ideas. I am not opposing that he should not bring back old comrades to the struggle but they should be convinced first why they come back. After all EPRP is for everyone and everybody. But what every one should accept is that there is one and only one EPRP Organizational Tree and a center. In terms of space and time, there is AAssimba, there is TSelmti and Mercato, i.e. ATM.

In order to walk away from EPRP's path of struggle, one has to evaluate what the stated programs of EPRP were. For your evaluation, they are written down in the following. EPRP's declared programs

1. Replacement of the military by provisional popular government
2. Recognition of basic democratic rights
3. Political prisoners should released
4. Eritrean question must be resolved peacefully and democratically
5. Peasants must be armed
6. Economic demands must be fulfilled and
7. Ethiopia must be free from foreign domination

How many of these demands are met today? I leave the answer to the readers of this article. CONFUSED OR CONFUSING?

SECURITY, PROPSPERITY AND VALUE for all Ethiopians is at stake. Debteraw's CULTURE AND FAITH is calling us for an action. Let us free him to free Ethiopia. Here is how things should work with EPRP collective leadership

EPRP has three layers of leadership.

- Organizational leadership,
- Ideological leadership and
- Political leadership

They all work as a team and are known as **collective leadership.**

Organizational

A= V-V-V, i.e. voluntarism-vote-victory
The question of priority is very important not only for EPRP but for the whole civilized world. EPRP appeals to voluntarism by educating, persuading or agitating. No threat or cheat. In other words, the

Machiavellian type of attaining power by any means necessary is not its forte. YETM FISCHEW DQUATUN AMCHW roughly means the end justifies the means. Instead EPRP teaches, "the means justifies the ends." Once this is accomplished, then volunteers will be organized to participate or in this case VOTE. After a vote, then they considered their mission as VICTORY. But other organizations and parties do vice versa. Most of them, they prefer, victory first. Judge for yourself, which is better. EPRP members or associates whether former or current do not regret of being associated with EPRP for precisely because they were volunteers before victory. I do not want to blame all our intellectuals for not deciphering the Latin letter of "A". Our Geez letter of "LE" is reversed.

Ideological

B = 13
Decipher the letter **B,** Spin the letter **E**
Put them together and
Be whatever you want to **BE**
There are three categories of people, those who search for BENEFT = B
Those who search for BLOOD = B and
Those who search for BELIEF = PRINCIPLE
I hope when we talk about EPRP leadership, we are referring to PRINIPLE and not to blood is thicker than water or is there a benefit for me. If we are going to judge about EPRP's leadership, it is always about the belief and value for Ethiopians. Those who look for better financial benefit or for their kin's and kiths, EPRP is not for them. EPRP has been and still is a haven for Integrity, Love and Trust.

Political

C = Culture
Like any culture, the Ethiopian culture is very complex. Although many educated individuals attempted to challenge and change the Ethiopian culture, EPRP did not even try to change let alone to challenge the culture. By the way culture in the Ethiopian context culture is "a state of mind"

while in the Eritrean context it is about telling yourself about yourself. What a contrast!!

Conclusion

Only a popular and democratic government could give Ethiopians and Eritreans a chance to unite and survive. That had been the goal of the popular movement, which was betrayed by the intervention of the military. The soldiers did not relinquish power as they have initially promised (See "Confession" in Amharic by Tesfaye Lemma.)

Woyane did not hand over power to the elected Kinjit groups. And there is no guarantee that from now on, that EPRDF will hand over power if they loose in the coming elections.

Power of the people comes only when and only when the seven points of programs as proposed by EPRP comes to fruition. Although these were written and demanded a long time ago, they are still valid, after all DEMOCRACIA – the organ of EPRP warned all of us by writing the following: "ALEBABSEW BIYARSU BE'AREM YIMELESU."

For comments and criticism: woldetewolde@yahoo.com

CALL ME BY MY NAME:

Solutions with Debteraw, XXIII

By Obo Arada Shawl alias Wolde Tewolde -

February 13, 2008

The crocodiles are dead
The Animals are imprisoned
The Oak is still burning
Badme and Assab are in non-negotiating
EPDJ and TPLF live by your name
Let us give EPRP a break so as to stay in its true name!

BREACHING TRUSTS OF CULTURE AND UNDERSTANDING

A change is an essence of life. An attitude change is much needed. Practically everyday, we change our clothes, shoes, and take shower (personally I don't) food and so on and so forth. When we were young, we think differently, when we are old, we cannot think in the old way. We should grow old and be mature. In what way, one might ask?

History and Culture are our main references for survival, stability and unity. However, as elites we do not distinguish between history (by the way there are hundreds of history types) and culture (of course there are many cultures.) Our political history is full of errors. Our cultural history is not documented. Our revolutionary history is being discarded. So how can we trust one another and understand each other? It is a tough call.

As for me, the **followers** of king Minliks I & II, Tewodros, Yohannes are the real hindrance to progress and understanding. These kings have done their useful work. Their history is done. It is no use to follow their ideas of holding to and transferring of power. If reference is needed for stability, take the case of Jesus the Great who ruled Ethiopia in 1704 when the stability of the country was at its peak. It was after his death that the local lords became stronger. We should all remember that we had kings and kingdoms without *maps and demarcation*.

The point I am trying to make is that if we want change as we did in the 1960s and 1970, then we have to abide by all rules and regulations that govern human beings. For almost fifty years, I have heard the same slogans and intrigues from our elites. Don't we have the capacity to learn? Don't we read maps, least directions? When I was in high school, there were some seventy countries, now there are over two hundred countries. When I used to travel from Addis Ababa to Asmara, it used to take me three weeks, now it takes a day and a half. Can't we see this? I see in our community a lot of people (including me) carrying cell phones, for what? Is it not for communication unless we have different meanings for communication?

What is going on with our lecturers (including those who are on radio talk show) and writers? Is anybody listening to what they are lecturing or any one reading to what they are writing. I leave this for them to answer. I demand them to heed to John Adams, 1765 that wrote as "let us dare to read, think, speak and write."

Notwithstanding these elites, the general populace of E-countries have already the answers for the journalistic questions of what, who, where and when long time ago thanks to people like Debteraw. What the EE-peoples are asking now is the Socratic question of Why and How. Debteraw has fought and still struggling to do that by showering questions of why and how even to his captors.

Politics demand that some truths cannot be told. In hindsight our politics was a cheap piece of instant wisdom. We had operated on passion at the exclusion of intelligence. We should have done both then and do it now.

We need the intellectual firepower from our professors and PhDs to those of us who want to preserve it and pass it on. My partial inquiry is provided in the following paragraphs.

However, unlike the current American primary election that is based on personalities our own struggle is based on issues. Let us examine a group of individuals who were part and parcel of the progressive movements of Ethiopia.

ISSUES AND PERSONALITIES

BADME: Border demarcation as disturbing news by DR. YACOB H. MARIAM
ASSAB: Natural outlet to the Sea by NEGUSSAY AYELE, Ethiopian scholar
A lawyer and a Politician (YHM & NA)

The above two professors at the height of the Ethiopian Student Movements, were supporters of the impending Eway Revolution. In fact when the Monarchy ended its life, both individuals had joined organizations in order to promote their interests (personal or public). I believe both were seeking for political solutions between Ethiopia and Eritrea. When they could not deliver the political solution, they have resorted to the economics of transportation. What do they know about economics of transport? If they do we want them to teach us. As far as I know, Assab is not useful for transport outlet for Ethiopia. And, Badme is not a cause for disturbing demarcation.

Consider this

> Badme = Bad Me (I am no good)
> Asab = As AB (I am the father)
> A BA (bachelor of Arts) is adequate to understand the culture of Ethiopia and Eritrea least the condition of a village and an artificial port.

I am so sorry that such fine professors in their own fields of study have sensationalized the case of Badme and Assab. I can understand why UNMEE and MI (Melese and Isayas) sensationalize and internationalize the village and the outlet, but not when these enlightened and one time Revolutionaries. I would ask these professors to re-examine their assertion of "useless piece of property for Eritrea, yet a life-line for Ethiopia." Talks are cheap as they say. Your one time colleague Debteraw has a solution for your concerns. It is called AAGMELAGO (see Call me by my name: a small talk with Debteraw, part I). You wrote, "There are myriad peaceful ways of incorporating Assab with Ethiopia". Please name one.

WEBSITES OF DEBTERAW & ASSIMBA

A call for Movement: Eliminating the twin tyrants, by Mesfin Araya, PhDHelter Skelter, Topsy Truvy, by Hama Tuma, A Revolutionary writer

The self-less generation (middle aged guards) of Haile Sellassie I University, a.k.a. Tsinhate Muhuran's reasoning for the ills of Ethiopia and Eritrea are described as follows:

The student movements have created revolutionaries and nationalists. As professor Endrias Eshete wrote, "the irrationals have done their useful work, it is for the rational to carry on" I believe these so- called rational are now carrying the duty of educating the young mind of Ethiopian students, carrying out the diplomatic programs in the USA and conducting business in the name of free market in Ethiopia. It is an anomaly that those who created them are out of the country, dead or imprisoned.

Mesfin Araya, on the one hand, has written an open letter calling for the need for resolving the ensuing problems of the Horn Africa by demanding removal of the twin tyrants again without telling us why and how to do it. Definitely, there is no progress but the process has been going on since professor Mesfin played a role in Haile Sellassie I University Campus. What has happened to the Revolutionaries? Or what has happened to their idea of unity, stability and prosperity? Were there flaws in their ideology of Philosophy, Religion or Politics? Or was the methodology of struggle was wrong? Why did everyone as the professor has indicated that everyone and everybody have returned safely into his/her mother's "womb"? Can the professor distinguish between dictatorship and tyranny?

Or alternatively, do our intellectuals know that the entire system of global economy or the digital era have created havoc in our region? I wish all the professors could come together to form a Think Tank to solve the perceived problems of Ethiopia and Eritrea or what he call the "Horn of Africa." I wish they could call me by my name? What is my name?

My own way of explanation is simple and straight foreword in that there is a switch of role models. Robin Hood is replacing Che Guevara. Reverend Martin Luther is replacing Malcolm X. Makonnen Bishaw is replacing Tilahun Gizaw and son on and so forth.

Hama Tuma, on the other hand, in his article of Helter and Skelter, Topsy Turvy, vividly explored the questions of what, who, where and the when questions without the why and the how questions. Here is what he wrote: -

> "The victims always do the dying, the killers thrive. It is not a fair world. Tell me another story please."

I will tell you this. ELF (Equality, Liberty and Fraternity), the story of the French Revolution has been and is being copied in Toto by our organic and inorganic intellectuals.

Hama Tuma presented 38 statistical figures concerning the status of the whole world including USA. However, in America, unlike that of France, our struggle is for Life, Liberty and the pursuit of

Happiness (LLH). Without statistics, can we choose between these two concepts? As an example, take the case of Jerome Keviel who embezzled US$7.2 billion or Euro $4.9 billion for our discussion. Mr. Jerome is becoming movie hero for the whole world including perhaps for Melese). In France, they say he is "Mis a pied". In America, we say, "you're fired".

Is this an aberration or what? Tell me more Mr. Hama!

Mr. Hama Tuma! Who says the world is fair? Are we not struggling to bring another story? There is no fraternity and no equality in America. There is only liberty. That is our common denominator with you guys over there in Europe.

In general people don't vote based on issues. They vote based on judgment and character. I believe it is true with the May election in Ethiopia. Most of the candidates have poor judgment and character.

Mr. Hama continues to write, "People with short memories have messed it all up. Yesterday's criminal can be feted as today's hero without a pip of an apology or a mea culpa from them. The new persists and spreads. No wonder many people are confused and mediocrity has ascended to the throne." I agree completely on this one. Here is what should be done.

On one hand, while on the process of changing everyday we may make mistakes, if we do, in religious lexicon, we have to REPENT or say MEA CULPA and move on to a new direction or position. Being stubborn is ignorance; arrogance offends not only God but also humans.

While on the other hand, if we make mistakes in our political belief systems or strategies be it military or propaganda, we have to admit and REGRET and say sorry.

Both requests are acceptable by both the Almighty and the Mighty.

In Ethiopia or Eritrea, there are no role models. Before the Revolution, there were the apostles, prophets, evangelist, priests and teachers. After the Revolution, there were only comrades (a good name became sour). Among the civilian population, there were mostly titles, which we labeled feudal. On hindsight, they may be useful. Now, we have Doctors and professors. It is for this reason that I ask the "organic intellectuals" to be role models.

In Ethiopia, we have to remember that Debteras are the role model for social justice. EPRP's Debteraw is a scholar and a model for both Ethiopia and Eritrea. We are not asking to memorialize Debteraw, we are asking for immortalizing him and his works. That is the task of all the progressive elements of Ethiopia and Eritrea.

I am wondering if these educated veterans of the Haile Sellasie era as prudent and cautious politicians as Negusse Ayele and Mesfin Araya, as bold and blunt Revolutionaries as Hama Tuma and Yacob H. Mariam, have a common culture and understanding towards Eritreans and Ethiopians. If not, we have to look for other serious relationships in familial, personal, religious and historical phenomena, in lieu of political revolution.

Freud's famous case studies that seek to come up with an explanation for what happened could be a starting point.

Reading the Bush Tragedy by Jacob Weisber may help us to understand our own dilemma. It is about a plane crash with a black box that can help explain what brought the White House down in flames. A black box of ours with serious relationships is in order. Laboratory and diary can be our stepping-stone for our educators and revolutionary leaders to teach and lead us.

EPRP's DEMOCRACIA

And then there is confusion when we see DEMOCRACIA in the name of EPRP in two websites. Apparently both seems the same outwardly but inwardly, they have deep differences in unresolved issues of Eritrea. For how many years can we use the case of Eritrea and Eritreans as an issue to be resolved? Eritrea and Eritreans have not changed since Gherhi (Adam), along with Dinkinesh (Eve) the father of humanity has been created and I do not believe they will change. In fact the world is going to change into their way of life. It seems to me that some ex-EPRP leadership assumes that by using DEMOCRACIA, which was and is the mouthpiece of EPRP can become automatically the heir of EPRP. DEMOCRACIA was not and is not the mouthpiece of some individuals but the mouthpiece of all its members, associate members and supporters. It should be identified with those held incommunicado and with those who sacrificed their lives for the sake of all Ethiopians. Above all it should be under one banner and leadership.

There is something about the word "Democracies" with the letter D: D for divide, divorce, doubt, drug, and dirt. So many words with a D are on our lips as in depression, debt, debauchery, dyslexia, dementia, and dysfunction

For us Defeat and Deny are important word concepts. Let us compare and contrast the case of Ethiopia and Eritrea using the following ten criteria: -

Elimination of Corruption
Crime Reduction
Protection of private property
Reduction of Taxes
Enforcement of Contracts
Supporting the Rule of Law
Encouraging Savings and Investment
Educate their population
Become self-sufficient in food production
Stopping fight with neighbors

The above analysis may help to evaluate the current situation in Ethiopia and Eritrea. This is a choice to make for non-political individuals. Just to give them a hint, Estonia and Ireland are examples where creating it is creating not by buying but wealth.

The interest of EPRP, I believe is to challenge the governments of EPDJ of Isayas and the TPLF of Melees do not think that EPRP neither challenge the ownership of Assab nor the demarcation of Badme. It was not and should not be an issue for EPRP.

Consider these:

The Tsinhate Muhuran Akals of the Haile Sellassie I University were hoping to continue to implement the following: -

> *Representatives = Rs of EPRP*
> *(animals) Senators + Ss of EPRP known as (crocodiles)*
> Decipher the letter B and spin the letter E and be whatever you want to be.
> Bellette
> *(excellence)*
> Berhanu
> *(enlightment)*
> Beyene
> *(justice prevails)*
> Bereket
> *(blessing)*
> Bekele
> *(planting seeds)*

Call me by my name: what is my name?

CONCLUSION

The Long March of experience in the Eway Revolution and the bitter lesson of Badme war do not seem to sink in our head least in our soul. Have we learned to decipher the alphabet of English? If so we have just not progressing. It seems that we have not grasped the letter A and still we have not been able to decipher the letter **B**.

If there is no BDT (building democratic tradition), we have to BBC (building bridges for communication). Liberty is promoting virtues and excellence. Liberty is in Europe and USA and we should have it for all Ethiopians and Eritreans regardless where they live. **Let us have a common call.**

For comments and questions: woldetewolde@yahoo.com

CALL ME BY MY NAME:

Solutions with Debteraw, XXV

Obo Arada Shawl alias Wolde Tewolde

(March 23, 2008)

DEBTERA versus SENATOR

Three days ago, a girl whom I met at the Starbucks surprised me by telling me that she has never heard about ABYOT let alone to know what it meant. On the other hand, she perfectly remembers very well about the Wars of Maichew and Aduwa, Korea and Congo. She further told me that she was going to Ethiopia to get married in a traditional wedding. She prefers the marriage to be consummated in Ethiopia for cultural and religious values.

"What religious and what cultural values are talking about?" I have surprised her in the same way she puzzled me about ABYOT. I told her that I did not return home in Eritrea since 1972 and to Ethiopia since 1986 for lack of traditional, religious and cultural values.

I believe that the Ethiopian Revolution aka known as the Eway Revolution was to be remembered. It was not destructive, as some writers wanted us to believe. The Eway Revolution should be understood in its proper context of change, i.e. Revolution via Democratization.

I was about to explain to this young and vibrant lady what ABYOT or the Eway Revolution was/is meant, when suddenly her ride came to take her home, i.e. Ethiopia. We will discuss about ABYOT, Tradition and Marriage when she returns in about three months. But in the mean time, let me switch to a different and explosive topic for America and Ethiopia.

The Eway Revolution is not about nationality, ethnicity, language or ideology as was subscribed in Ethiopia and Eritrea as indicated below.

Leaders	Tenets	Symbolic Tools
Haile Sellassie I	Christianity	The Lion of Judah Menghestu Haile M.
	Socialism	The Black Lion Mellese Zenawi
	Ethnicity	Star of David in pentagram Essayas
	Language	Camel, olive tree and colors

For Debteraw and his political Party, EPRP it is none of the above. For Debteraw and EPRP, it is about the Ethiopian Security and the Eritrean politics by means of Revolution via Democratization.

For Ethiopia, the E-Way Engine (EWE) has brought a new way of thinking, thanks to Deteraw and his political party, EPRP.

For America, the Search Engine (SE) has brought a new way of thinking, thanks to Obama and technology.

However, the politics and experience of Debteraw and Obama are markedly different in many ways but similar in some ways. The origins of race, color and religion (RCR) are traced in Ethiopia, but they are nowhere a threat to Ethiopia as they are to America.

SENATOR BARACK OBAMA (FLF)

This week Obama spoke loudly and vividly something that was simmering on underground. The talk of race, color and religion were everywhere and but nowhere as an issue for - America is believed to be a melting point for everything. RCR was not discussed in public as a political issue. Now Senator Obama talked about it in such a way that it will help America because of his mixture of races. What races? Obama did not say it enough. He should have said that he is from a black and a white skin color. It is all about the color of the skin. This is what we call in Ethiopia K'L'S. He should have confirmed that his skin is a mixture. Instead Senator Obama says time and again that he is a unifier and not a divider. His reasoning is that has adapted various cultures by living in different places with different people. That is the trouble. It is not the mixed culture that will assist him to be a president. It is the single value that will unite the country. After all, Americans are known by their Flag (13 stripes and 50 stars), by their Latin alphabet and by their Freedom (FLF) and not by their culture, as Obama campaign wants us to believe.

Obama's value is embedded in his name rewritten in Latin alphabet. Did he live by his name? Or alternatively, does his name signify something? That I do not know.

DEBTERAW TSEGEYE GEBRE MEDHIN (FFF)

In Ethiopia a person's skin did not matter. The same womb can deliver black or white regardless. In Debteraw's country a human being is a human being. He is an Ethiopian, a child of God regardless. But in recent years, especially after the so-called modern education, things have changed. Some individuals began to hide their identity, especially after the Italian colonization. Some intellectuals began to hate their identity. They were captured by false pride of being educated without the "Alphabet" of GE'EZ. Here comes the scholar Debteraw Tsegeye into the picture.

Without the development of GE'EZ Ethiopia/Eritrea would not have been civilized. Civilization by definition is of mental exercise and record keeping. In the absence of GE'EZ, or any other alphabets enormous things would not have been possible. Philosophical thoughts, Biblical religion and Organization of societies would not have been possible without the written word. GE'EZ had and will continue to have great impact on social, economic, political, cultural and educational investment sectors.

What is GE'EZ? Fidel or Abugida?

I want to leave the answer to be discussed by my readers.

U-T (HePe) ever since we know how to read and write, we have never thought of where it came from or how it was evolved. The answers to these questions were only told by foreign researchers mostly enamored themselves to be known as Ethiopinists. Inasmuch as they themselves were foreigners, they had to say that GE'EZ came to Ethiopia from outside the country via South Yemen.

Scholars of Ethiopia like Debteraw insisted that GE'EZ is an indigenous script and language. In order to dispel or reveal the truth of the value of GE'EZ language and in order to communicate with the alphabet of it, Debteraw became a debtera instead of a priest and had deciphered the content of the language of Ge'ez in terms of Qine-qidase-wazema-trgum-sewasw (QQWTS) and this has scarred not only the high priests but also the high government officials. While on the other hand, Debteraw went to college in order to understand the values of the western world written in Latin.

Those who became literate and educated in Latin alphabet are basically against Ethiopia and Ethiopians– essentially against themselves. Their own identity is at stake. What a tragedy?

First year students who attended Geography 101 class used to tell us that PMWM starts by teaching about Ethiopia in the following manner. He starts from the North, Eritrea is stone, Tigrai another stone and before saying more some students withdrew from Geography class thereby becoming ignorant of their own country. What do you call this? Hatred or ignorance?

Another example as narrated to me by a friend was as follows. While Emperor Haile Sellassie I was visiting the library of Alemaya College, the emperor asked the Dean of the college whether the library houses GE'EZ books. The dean bowed without saying any thing. Haile Sellassie again asked him the same question, the dean again bowed. The Emperor said, "Is that the answer", the dean bowed for confirmation. So we can see why the responsible officials like the dean of Alemaya, the lecturer of Geography in Addis Ababa never like to promote the true educational system for Ethiopia. The history of Axum, Meroe and Egypt (AME) do not seem to sink in the minds of our educated professors. Call me by my name. What is my name?

As if that was not enough, Mesfin Wolde Mariam is making sure that Debteraw will never see sunlight while he (PMWM) is alive. What a travesty? The reason is simply because Debteraw is literate in GE'EZ and English and he knows the difference between knowledge and wisdom unlike the professor who only negotiates his way via information.

Mesfin writes about Obama and not about Debteraw! Can anyone ask the professor why he is not writing about Debteraw? This question should be added to the 20 questions posed to the professsor by www.EthioLion.com) to become the 21st question. What a tragedy? Is he an Ethiopian or is he a mixture of cultures as Obama himself. I am wondering!!!

Semitic, Hamitic or Cushitic as a language was not an issue for Debteraw. The choice of FIDEL (GE'EZ) as in ATT (Amharic-Tigrigna-Tigre) and the Latin alphabet together are of fundamental importance for our peoples' communication. The Afaan Oromo, with a modified Latin alphabet called Qub'ee as presented as Oromo Script is another alphabet to compete with GE'EZ. What a wonderful world of choices!!!

For comments and criticism: <u>woldetewolde@yahoo.com</u>

CALL ME BY MY NAME:

Solutions with Debteraw, XXVI

Obo Arada Shawl alias Wolde Tewolde,

April 1, 2008

This is not for April the Fool!
Exclusively for EPRP members and associates

The History of EPRP

Despite many confusions and claims, EPRP's political history was and is simple and straightforward. The **Issue was clear:**

DOMESTIC Affaire

In the South of Ethiopia, it was about Land to the tiller (Me're't L'arashu)
    In the North of Ethiopia, it was against Reactionary Bureaucracy ((Ishi Nege) *FOREIGN Affaire, it was against Anti-Imperialism both capitalist and socialist Imperialism*
    The **Vision** was obvious
    One Flag, One Alphabet and many Freedoms (FFF) The **Method** was defined
    Peace in the North and Democracy in the Center for DEMOCRACIA to prevail everywhere and anywhere. (More on this issue is forthcoming).

The Current Status of EPRP

Some individual people tell me that EPRP's thrill is gone. I tell them that there was/is no thrills with EPRP. EPRP is about responsibilities with oneself and society. That is the first indication of a responsible party.

EPRP is about responsibility, helpfulness and confidence. When I speak in such a manner, some opponents tell me bluntly that I do not sound as either a member or a supporter of EPRP. In fact, they point out that I sounded like a Republican.

I wish the EPRP (d) understands what Republican means. I wish they could present themselves as Republican or democrat within the party of EPRP.

Inasmuch as EPRP has led as a vanguard party to show all organizations and groups why and how they should struggle, EPRP is still in the forefront of struggle for DEMOCRACIA. The party of EPRP still leads and teaches by example.

.EPRP's opponents whether from domestic or foreign countries have painted the Party for what it is not. The shocking part though is that some veteran leaders accuse of themselves as members of an anti-democratic political organization in Silence for quite a long period of time. This is unheard of in the history of EPRP (there is should not be conspiracy theory within EPRP). Even the Guerrilla fighters of EPLF and TPLF label EPRP as a democratic organization. In their language, the EPRP (Ethiopian People's Revolutionary Party) gives guidance to EPRA (Ethiopian People's Revolutionary Army) and not vice versa as practiced in their own organizations. (See more articles on the relationship between EPRA and EPRP).

CONFLICT RESOLUTION IN EPRP'S TRADITION

Externally, so far, there was no confusion in EPRP's vision and mission towards the people of Ethiopia as a whole.
Internally though, EPRP has faced with two major conflicts of A, B, and numerous minor conflicts in the letter of C embedded in the letter of S.

> A= Anja
> B= Bitena
> C= this is the third stage. It is about cooperation or Separation. After all C is part of S, which is Secrecy and Conspiracy.

ANJA: This was a faction of a serious nature regarding leadership style and operation. Two decision makers of the party dissented against the majority's decision of the party and acted wild in decimating the party they have helped to create. In other words, they were found guilty of undemocratic action and by the will of the majority, they were ousted from responsibility (mind you not from power) and by fate they were banished. The case was closed democratically and honorably. This should be **Number One Lesson** to be emulated by all organizations and parties. It is the legacy of EPRP collective leadership, pure and simple. After all, it was about responsibilities and commitment and not about power. So far, nobody is complaining. I hope it does not crop up in the future.

B'TENA: This was a concept of re-evaluation of EPRP along its lines of struggle after the so-called "Red Terror". The leaders have assembled for almost three months for re-evaluation of its past and to assess of its members willingness whether to continue the struggle. In the mean time, many of its freedom fighters disbanded not into abyss but into societies. I have witnessed this phenomenon in Dessie, Wollo, in Gonder, Gonder (Begemder) in Addis Ababa, in Kenya and in Washington. This should be Number Two Lesson to be emulated by all organizations and parties. After all, the meeting was long and democratic to consume such a long time. It was obvious that many members and supporters became, for lack of a better word, disfranchised from EPRP. EPRP has always welcomed them despite some disgruntled individuals.

The **C** groups for lack of name a.k.a Walk away, Teletafi, splinter or any other name attached to them as many of their ideas were contrary to EPRP's method of struggle, DEMOCRACIA. EPRP was known for its long-term plan and revolutionary struggle and not coup d'etat (Gultcha bi'le'wa'wet Wet'Ayataftim). Every time individuals or groups feel weak, hopeless or even when betrayed, they have been resorting to condemnation of EPRP leadership and against some prominent members. Instead of joining gracefully and honorably or alternatively abandoning EPRP (my friend calls this phenomenon-Parking), some of them became enemies of the party. I believe it may be in the Ethiopian/Eritrean culture of blame, a culture of blame inculcated only in winning. They should be reminded that EPRP accepts the culture of losing. EPRP has liberated the minds of its members to be whatever they want to be but not as an enemy of the party.

All of the splinter groups have the obligation to tell the Party and its _**collective leadership**_ so as to resolve the issue or the vision peacefully, amicably and democratically. PAD is acrimony for Peace- amicable-democracy.

Sometime back, ASSIMBA Team reminded us of a looming danger of crossing the Rubicon (in their language the Redline).

Now the moves of EPRP (d) seems tantamount to crossing the Redline, setting the stage for deeper involvement in Ethiopia's ethnic and Eritrea's language political confusion and crisis.

Leaders of this splinter group do not seem to have long-term strategy for taking their members on more assertive role for change of regime or for the release of DEBTERAW and his comrades.

COLLATERAL DAMAGE

These days, there is a lot, it seems of collateral damage, between Issayas and Melese (I&M), between Obama and Clinton (O&C) and Hailu and Mesfin (H&M). What is to be said of EPRP? What has happened to the concept of collective leadership? I thought the leadership issue was resolved by the Anja a.k.a the Ha and Le faction, two individuals were responsible and they received their penalty either from the party or from the enemy. It is done and closed.

How about the Bitena? These too have come to pass. From 3-5 individuals have taken the responsibility for encouraging to be disbanded. This has taken place over twenty years ago. I do not understand why people dwell on revenge instead of resolution. Some of us slumbered for a long time and suddenly came to realize that EPRP is still alive. That is a healthy position to be in. But there is a cost to pay, a simple cost called RECOGNITION. Those who continued the struggle in the name of EPRP should be commended and never negated. And in return, those who had continued along the lines of Debteraw have to understand why those who did not continue for various reasons. After all EPRP is about doing the Right Thing and not much about the Wrong Thing. And so I would like to ask why is this current of Duplication or Copy is necessary?

For the sake of clarity let me ask my readers the difference between the following two dual words: Duplicate vs. Copy

Rabbit vs. Hare

Duplicate:

- Identically copied from an original
- Existing or growing in two corresponding parts, double
- Denoting a manner of play in cards in which partnerships or teams play the same deals and compare scores at the end, i.e. Duplicate bridge

Copy:

- A reproduction
- To follow a model or pattern,
- Imitation

What is the difference between a rabbit and a hare? There are of the same kind with a little physical and social difference that only experts can tell.

What has happened now is unprecedented in the history of EPRP. The only political party that has passed the test of time is EPRP both internally as well as externally. This Party, at no time has seen such an unholy alliance in its name and character. Many have stolen its name, slogan and emblem but never its vision, mission and value. I wish the EPRP (d) could come up with courage, principle and vision instead of story telling and copying materials. (More on this coming)

What is needed now, is about an image or a strategy. Leaders of EPRP should not pay any cost. Dr. Tesfaye Debessai and his followers have paid the cost. Tsegeye Debteraw and his colleagues are still paying. What kind of price should the current leaders pay?

What is needed of them is the following:

- They should be **Fearless leaders** i.e. speak the truth (like Hama Tuma)
- They should follow a **timeless principle leaders** and (Fassika Bellette)
- They should be **visionary leaders and followers** (As Azmatchs & Zematches together)

Sustain:

- **To keep in existence or continue**

Preservation, Rehabilitation and Protection of Ethiopia is the name of the game and not revision of EPRP. Call me by my name. What is my name? It is EPRP and not EPRP (d). Let us not confuse our community and societies. One Flag, one Fidel and many Freedoms.

For comments and criticism: woldetewolde@yahoo.com

CALL ME BY MY NAME:

A Commentary, XVIII

Wolde Tewolde alias Obo Arada Shawl

November 1, 2007

As Ethiopians we had dignity. We used to embolden ourselves with pride and self- respect. But these days, no matter how dignified an Ethiopian may look, whether he is an ethnos, a nationalist or an internationalist, whether he is rich, or homeless, he/she needs to restore a sense of dignity and pride. Actually dignity and pride are the qualities that each member of our society must recognize, in himself/herself and in others. If we do not recognize our own dignity and that of others, then respect is lost.

In fact, dignity is the reverse side of the quality of respect. Dignity is something we have and that which we do not want to be damaged. Respect is something we give to others. Even children have dignity. When we don't show children any respect, it threatens their dignity.

Our current political crises have also brought our true dignity to the surface.

- Soldiers and guerrilla fighters who fought to the end for their respective goals
- The Revolutionaries who refused to be put down by an unfair leaders
- A small nation that refuses to be disregarded
- Priests who want to delve into serious theological matters and
- The Exiles who refuse to give up their motherland or fatherland's rights

All these reflect in our human dignity brought to the surface by these crises? A geographer, an economist, an engineer, a journalist and an artist have betrayed our causes. I am a glad politician – political scientists and revolutionary politicians have not betrayed us.

The leader who forgets his own dignity and behaves in ways that cause others to lose regard for him compromises his ability to lead. Such is the case of many current Ethiopian leaders from the government, congress or some political party leaders.

Dignity however is not to be confused with pomposity, a puffed-up self-importance. It is not an illusion, delusion or grandeur. It is a quality that shines through at all times, but especially in trying times. EPRP collective leadership has been a shining example in this regard. In order to be qualified as collective leadership, the PAC (Party-Army- Community) must be provided (packed). EPRP has a long history of making this a reality. What and how is the component parts of this organization should be indicated in the following manners?

EPRP's PARTY (Integrity)

In a sense, integrity means that intellectual, spiritual, psychological, ethical and social parts are congruent parts with one another. Despite EPRP's clandestine activities, its integrated operations must let the right hand know what the left is doing. An integrated leadership doesn't speak out of both sides of its mouth. EPRP doesn't espouse always being honest and aboveboard, and then suggest that in order to do business with others, it has to be dishonest. If being dishonesty is ok by EPRP, then being honest and aboveboard is not. Lying or asking one's members to lie, undermines the belief that others live in integrity.

Beating the other fellow by any means sends the message that EPRP has neither core nor center values. Integrity doesn't mean rigidity, but it does mean holding dear in every way the various parts of its personality and its life must be a reflection of its entire societies. With due respect to other religions, inasmuch as for the Catholics has a center in Vatican city, for the Jews, Jerusalem and for Muslims Mecca, Ethiopian and Eritrean Orthodox Christians have Axum as their center. How many of us know this? Most of us think that Axum was center for politics or trade. How about the Protestants? Where is their center? Can anyone tell me, please?

EPRP's ARMY (Trust)

When we put trust in an organization, we generally have confidence in that organization's honesty, dependability, and integrity. EPRP has exhibited stellar qualities that help Ethiopians and Eritreans decide to trust it, but so far, the Party did not earn peoples trust.

It is not enough to be convinced that one's idea is creative; the message must be heard, too. Trust can only be given as a gift. Once given, trust must be constantly nurtured, for it is a fragile quality and can only be undermined through one misstep. All it takes for trust to be broken is one big lie, one wrong affair. That is why, first, the Haile Sellasie regime, later on, the DERG, last, the EPLF, and now the TPLF has constantly been attempting to sow mistrust among Ethiopians and Eritreans. The army of EPRA had a secondary role to play while in Tigrai, Gondar and Godjam. The party of EPRP has been guiding the army unlike all other liberation movements in the country. This is the right and proper way to lead. Many people including EPRA members think that the EPRP army is a fighting army. It is and was a revolutionary army. What this means that unless and otherwise, the Peasants knew their enemy, they are not supposed to bear arms. First and foremost, they have to be liberated themselves before they liberated others. In other words, the recruitment was very crucial. Threats and cheating was not allowed in recruiting peasants. (More on this on later issues.)

EPRP's COMMUNITY (dignity)

Dignity is an internal self-respect that members do not allow to be compromised by the disrespectful actions of others. It is the result of commanding and demanding the respect of others. EPRP derives its dignity from taking responsibilities for its _choices_ and _actions_. Our task or vocation in life has little to do with dignity. Whether they clean toilets, heal plants or people, manage the mailroom or the ministries, EPRP members have dignity, for dignity is embedded in the personality of EPRP, not in the job or profession. Too many members and associates of EPRP had career professions and government positions, and still thousands are serving national and international organizations. It is also true that some are abandoned the ultimate objective of EPRP programs and policies. Nevertheless, EPRP was and is the single political voluntary organization that had/is sacrificed its own lives and resources for the simple reason that Ethiopia and its people should deserve social and individual justice, albeit with dignity.

Trust can never be taken for granted. It must be constantly renewed. If trust is broken, it is possible to reconcile and restore, depending, of course, on the severity of the break. There are some elements that perpetually try to destroy or undermine any positive happenings. That is one way of explaining Third world mentality. If one is not a third world mentality, she/he should understand that knowledge and wealth should always be cumulative phenomenon. In our case, the Haile Sellasie government had undermined the struggle of the Ethiopian/Eritrean Patriots' struggle against Fascist Italy. The DERG has destroyed the hardware and software of Haile Sellasie's cumulative of knowledge and wealth. The TPLF is destroying what the entire generation of Ethiopian cultural icons and natural resources. EPRP on the other hand, has preserved all cultural, religious, historical and social values. The main contention for EPRP was the political governance of the country. It demanded that the entire Ethiopian political system should be changed for good. The demand of EPRP was correct then and is correct now. It is positive step. The right to vote is central to DEMOCRACIA. It is a matter of time before everyone is on the same page with EPRP.

CONCLUSION

All we can do is to study closely, EPRP's history in terms of Arts, Education, Revolution and Democracy (READ).

Lessons have to be learned from EPRP's political experience, organizational and voluntary sacrifice. The hallmark of EPRP has been in the areas of principle, trust and dignity and to a lesser extent of respect for others. The class struggle has somewhat definitely blurred its members and associates to disrespect others. EPRP leaders and members will respect their opponents, inasmuch as they expect respect from others, given an atmosphere conducive to debate and discussion.

For comments and questions: woldetewolde@yahoo.com

CALL ME BY MY NAME:

After the symposium

Obo Arada Shawl alias Wolde Tewolde -

July 13, 2008

TPLF seeks Light where there is none
EPLF seeks Victory where there was once
OLF seeks Democracy on the ground
EPRP seeks Knowledge above ground

Ten days ago, on July 3, 2008, a symposium was held in Washington, DC. The main purpose of the symposium according to Assimba Forum was to reach a consensus on how to fight for the release of TSEGEYE GEBRE MEDHIN alias popularly known as DEBTERAW.

On the agenda of Assimba forum, it was stated that DEBTERAW was to be seen from three dimensions, that of human, professional and public. In other words, DEBTERAW is a prisoner of conscience, an educator and a political figure.

Debteraw as a prisoner

Although the organizers of the event did invited many representative organizations and institutions that are related to the Human Rights aspects of DEBTERAW, few have come to participate in the one-day event. As at now, it is not definitely determined why many of the invited speakers did not show up. But among those who showed up include the following: -

- Mesfin Mekonnen representing, Human Rights Council (HR2003)
- Captain engineer Fantahun Kahsay representing Solidarity committee for Ethiopian political prisoners (SOCEPP) and
- Dr. Mankelklot representing one of the Ethiopian Mass Media

The representative of Human Rights appealed to all the attendees of the symposium that as Ethiopians, we should be aware of at least, the fate of our human aspects if not for the animals and plants of Ethiopia. He said that there are tons of human right abuses in Ethiopia among them the abuse on DEBTERAW who has been imprisoned in incommunicado by the TPLF regime since 1991. It is time that we campaign for the implementation of the HR2003 so that our problems could be resolved peacefully. Ato Mesfin spoke on the current progress of H.R. 2003. He promised that if the Senate passes the legislation on H.R. 2003, it would have enormous impact on the Ethiopian societies as a whole.

Engineer Fantahun has spoken at length about what it means to be imprisoned for so many years as he was a victim himself. He was forced to abandon his profession to dwell on the rights of prisoners of Ethiopia.

Dr. Mankelklot has advocated for a change in his own words "to carry out a revolution".

However, he neither elaborates on what kind of revolution nor the methods of revolution. He elaborated on a lot of issues of concern to all Ethiopians.

Debteraw As An Educator

Many individuals, young and old, have presented DEBTERAW's works of non-visual arts. He was presented as one of the best of Ethiopian artists, educators in democracy and revolution. DEBTERAW's acumen of struggle and change for all peoples of Ethiopia was par excellence. He was depicted as the alpha omega of One Flag, One Fidel and many Freedoms. In order to testify this, a well-known person from Sweden was scheduled to be a guest speaker for the occasion.

Unfortunately, this person by the name of Hailu G. Yohannes alias known as GOMERAW could not make it. It is sad that Ato Hailu is in what is known as in G"ZOT.

DEBTERAW & GOMERAW. What do they have in common? Both are revolutionaries, educators, artists and democrats. The only difference is that one is imprisoned INSIDE the country while the other is held ABROAD. **Let us free them to free ourselves.**

Debteraw and Gomeraw are twins in terms of Ethiopian, Arts and Literature with the background of Orthodox religion. Both did not believe in an organized religion. In the Orthodox Church, religion is relatively connected to DEMOCRACIA. The true knowledge and wisdom emanates from the monasteries of Ethiopia and Eritrea and not from the Board Rooms of Corporation or from the Vatican of Rome. Whatever the case since both are held in prison, we cannot discuss the issue of Ethiopian Orthodox Christianity. I had planned to discuss the issue of religion vis-à-vis politics during the symposium, but for technical and for lack of speakers on the subject of religion, we were forced to abandon the topic altogether.

Debteraw As A Public Figure

What makes Debteraw's case as special is that DEBTERAW is an icon of a well-known political party organization popularly known as EPRP that became a target for harassment and banishment since its inception. DEBTERAW was number one target of the DERG era and still remain number one enemy of the TPLF regime.

On the one hand, EPRP was and is represented by the concept of one Flag, one Fidel and many freedoms. Because of many disinformation and propaganda towards the Ethiopian rainbow and the Geez script, even its own supporters wrongly condemned EPRP.

On the other hand, as freedom is precious, it is also costly. Many Ethiopians and Eritreans either afraid of its cost or its practicality, they do not stand with EPRP at least in the open forum. Because of these fears and tribulations, people from ERHCO and the Mass Media of Ethiopians did not show up in the one-day event for DEBTERAW. What a travesty!

The symposium was both a success and a sad story. This day and date was a day of special importance to hundreds of Ethiopians, Eritreans and to thousands of EPRP members, supporters and sympathizers. This day was meant to be the beginning of the end. The beginning of what and the end of what, one might ask?

We are living in a time akin to the Roman Empire when people stopped believing in what might call the main organizing principle of their society and instead pioneered new forms of community in which to live out of the realm of moral life. EPRP should be judged by posterity, as all of us should be ultimately. The DERG, EPLF and the TPLF are dictated and justified in the first instance not by political principles but by an extra-ideological perception (correct or incorrect) of imminent benefit or threat. EPRP's stand was correct.

Even today, unlike EPRP's mainstream political party, in Ethiopia and Eritrea, expediency rule and principles are expendable. It is time that a new beginning should be on the horizon. People had enough of „blood is thicker than water" as espoused by EPLF and OLF and „what is in it for me" as espoused by TPLF.

Concluding Remarks

Debteraw Tsegeye's revolutionary struggle is about courage and faith. It was not about dethroning the king, deposing the DERG or eliminating EPRDF per se. It is about ***fighting for*** not fighting back. EPRP owns a piece of Ethiopian and Eritrean political history. These days" arguments abound. There are 10 sides to every story and very little agreement from one version to the next.

However, EPRP only negotiate with those who have something to gain by giving EPRP what it wants. EPRP see a clear way to take revenge on someone who wronged it. Of course, the best revenge is always to be so fabulously over the whole thing that EPRP couldn't careless. EPRP's internal coping mechanism is getting a workout healing and then forgiveness. If members of EPRP are feeling sore, at least they can take solace in the knowledge that is good for EPRP.

The one-day event symposium as expected had audience who listened to the divergent point of view, found common ground and willing to embrace new visionary ideas. Thanks to Assimba forum, especially to the balanced conduct of Ato Sewyew and Ato Elias. It was a wonderful event for a change based on a human cause.

For comments and criticisms: woldetewolde@yahoo.com

CALL ME BY MY NAME:

A commentary on a death of a fallen hero

Obo Arada Shawl alias Wolde Tewolde -

April 9, 2008

What is his name?

Retta Adane was his given name. I used to call him as Rettaw just to upgrade him from his two syllabuses name. However, he has refused to do so. My idea of a third letter is to avoid Black vs. White type of conversation, in other words, avoiding them and us. We always have a third arm or leg in the Ethiopian context. Retta used to tell me that there was only two-way struggle. He was saying there is still two Ethiopia, one for the privileged class and the other for the underclass. He chose to side with the underclass. Retta recognized that he came from a privileged class but he abandoned it for the sake of the majority of Ethiopians. Nonetheless he lived in both worlds fighting tooth and nail.

What are his accomplishments?

Academically, Rettaw has an associate degree. He was an accomplished photographer, career wise. Professionally, he was a real REVOLUTIONARY. He fought in the cities, in the metropolitan areas, in the mountains, and across deserts and ghettos of Ethiopia and America. He had sacrificed his comfortable life to combat grievances for a better tomorrow in political, social and economic matters for all Ethiopians.

How did he live?

Unknown to his family and many of his friends, he had lived a comfortable life. A life of freedom and liberty. He freely moved between the Badme (Zone of Washington), namely Axum and Zula restaurants. He had been sending messages of free spirit and life. Retta traveled physically from America (A) to Ethiopia (E) and from Addis Ababa (AA) to AAssimba (AA). He showed us the way of alphabetical travel from A-E. Having left the party, Rettaw has been traveling mentally and spiritually from Axum (A) to Zula (Z). Retta has traveled from A-Z, a complete study of the Latin alphabet. What a noble journey! Call me by my name. What is my name?

His Weakness

The hallmark of EPRP and EPLF was discipline. One is internal and the other external. Retta did not like both of them. As a result he abused himself albeit without abusing his own organization, EPRP.

His Sense of Humor

Retta's sense of humor was impeccable.

One day, I met Retta while traveling in a city bus and he asked me whence I was coming from. I told him that I was coming from a public meeting where Negede Gobeze, Aregawi Berhe and Eyassu Alemayehu were attending. He was taken aback. He labeled them in the following manner:

Mr. A as ki'lo (innocent)

Mr. E as selay (spy) Mr. N as feri (coward)

How can you put these three together, he asked me, mockingly? I said to myself as (sic) spy-innocent-coward. I did not tell him to decipher any of my alphabetic letters. I know he was trying to be funny.

At another time, I met him again in a city bus. This time I have asked him from where he was coming. He said, "I have been to my doctor, a doctor who told me that I would only live for three months but when I returned to see the doctor for my final appointment, I found out that he was dead. I must have misunderstood my doctor. He was prescribing death for himself." I teased Retta that he must have suffered from the deadline.

He smiled because he knows that I know that he was not afraid of death. I laughed, laughed and laughed as usual for his sense of humor.

Another sense of humor of Retta as was narrated to me by one of his comrades was as follows. As his friend was addressing a gathering, by saying "ladies and gentlemen" Retta added a third category by addressing a "those in between". This has happened in Italy some twenty years ago. Retta was ahead of his time and he was teaching by example. Of course, this was contrary to his "them and us".

During his career, I think Retta was employed temporarily by Tamrat Lyne a one time prime minister of Ethiopia. Retta has lost his job, as did the prime minister. Retta had a photograph taken from Makalle field of donkey's mating season. Whenever he wants to scare or test people's mentality or culture, he shows them the picture as they gasp, "he is crazy." He was teaching his countrymen to face reality lest culture shock breaks them.

The lesson Retta is leaving behind

It is said that Mark Twain aptly described about mysteries, the mystery of God, Death and of Life. For most Ethiopians God and death are certain but not life.

Retta's death was not sudden and unanticipated. He is divorced, unattached, have 3 children and his whole life revolved around the concept of EPRP as the head of a family, community and society. He no longer felt safe when EPRP and a whole lot of his comrades died, exiled and imprisoned. Nevertheless, he deeply believed in the ultimate success story of EPRP.

How do the Retta comrades at this age and stage of life grieve? How do they overcome the complete emptiness and fear? Well, he has lived enough time to teach and to struggle albeit with harmony, peace and freedom with himself and his surroundings. Retta is to be emulated in his personal courage.

Grief is natural and normal. It hits us in different ways. For some of us, it is as if a stone is sitting on our chests until we can barely breathe. For others, it is a fact that can't be faced, so much so that they keep busy from dawn to midnight drinking or working. Grief is like a blanket, smothering us with sadness and fear, but in the case of Retta, there is no grief for he has carried out what he wanted to accomplish

And so it is with all of us. Good books and politics will ease his comrades' pain though these are not the only options. Prayer will encourage contemplation. We all have lost a truly special person. We all will carry a bundle of sorrow on our back if we miss his point of view and life style.

Those who have attended the burial ceremony informed me that many have regretted of not knowing him enough to appreciate his life. I know most of them were frustrated and angry at his behavior. We should look for the best in everybody. If we had the patience to listen and see long enough and keep on waiting, their good side will come out. I wish I had asked him what wisdom he would impart to the world if he knew it was his last chance. I suspect he would say "Retta lived for 30 years after a terminal diagnosis for freedom."

Tell him how much we miss him and ask him for advice on how he coped up during rough times.

He won't answer; imagine what he would have said, "vive EPRP and continue the struggle"

For comments and criticisms: woldetewolde@yahoo.com

CALL ME BY MY NAME ADDRESS:

A Commentary

Obo Arada Shawl alias Wolde Tewolde

October 13, 2008

This is a response to some queries emailed to me by (Ato) Berhanu Tesfaye. My response may be politically incorrect. The questions are placed at the bottom of the article for reference.

1. 36-years of struggle by EPRP
2. The need for Research
3. Reasons for the fallout
4. Cursed generation
5. Six main parties

36 years of struggle

EPRP's struggle was not only about 3 decades of struggle. Politically it was and is a struggle of a century. It was also about five centuries of struggle for social, environmental and cultural change/revolution.

Politically, EPRP in principle recognizes the efforts and attempts of Miniliks" *modernization*, Tewodros's *concept of Unity*, Yohannes's *religious faith* and Haile Sellassie's *efforts for education*. All these four kings lived in the last hundred years and they are the source of the perceived problems of the nationalists. DEBTERAW and his Revolutionary political party, EPRP foresaw the will and the sacrifice to further Modernization program through Unity and the value Belief through Education. But this unity and education goes further into centuries when Ethiopia lived without printing privileges.

According to DEBTERAW, however, modernization did not meant the importation of manufactured goods but through creativity and innovation by AEthiopians unlike that of Minilik who strived to access to the products of by scientists. DEBTERAW believed that Arts – littérateurs, art and culture collectively known as KINET could play important role in the development of Ethiopia.

The RE i.e. Yohannes's belief could only be furthered by education alone. I guess that was why perhaps DEBTERAW became an educator/teacher. So you see Ato Berhanu, 36 years is nothing compared to the centuries of cultural and political change? In today's terminology, EPRP was software as opposed to Shaebia or Woyane's hardware organizations. In other words, unless and otherwise we collectively understand the history and culture (HC) of AEthiopia, there are plenty of years ahead of us before we reach our goal. The contribution of EPRP to the consciousness of AEthiopians to politics as well as to Arts and

Literateaure should be recognized.

I am not denying the fact that EPRP's struggle for collective leadership, trust among its members, justice for everyone and everybody by way of DEMOCRACIA was perfect. It was full of missteps and errors.

Research

Who is going to do the research? Are there researchers who are interested in what EPRP has done or what has not done? I see and hear only people who only condemn EPRP. How much does the research cost? Professors and PhD. holders or others should address such questions… Most of the organizations you mentioned were doing something of value. I cannot emphasis to you the fact that some are good at actions while others are good in theories. EPRP has the traditions of having designers-planners-theoreticians and practicing individuals and groups. It is known as Sin"huate M"huran (እንሕተ ምሁራን).

Reasons for the fallout

You seem to be puzzled by addition, subtraction, multiplication and division. It is the nature of mathematics —which is necessary in all walks of life. We cannot do without arithmetic let alone mathematics. There is no way to avoid this phenomenon. I think you ought to read about philosophy, psychology, sociology and economics. It will help to grasp the nature of human beings.

Cursed generation

Why do you use this word "curse"? It is not a proper word to use in politics. It is very unfortunate that Ato Kiflu Tadesse used "that generation while writing his book, „the generation". That was a misnomer. He should have used an appropriate term instead of that generation. It is an abstract word – compare this to "that one" used by Senator McCain against Obama, which is interpreted in different ways. AEthiopians especially the youth are interpreting "that generation" as vague and foolish. It should be explained time and again with cyclical nature of life.

The generation that BT is referring was the generation that was <u>selfless</u>. The generation of AEthiopians who were searching for victory based on vote on the basis of voluntarism not on adventurism. And it is improper to call „that generation" a cursed generation. What do you call this generation of today?

Six main parties

I cannot tell you that neither the life struggle between *EPLF and ELF, OLF and TPLF, MEISON and EMALEDHI* nor between *EDU and EPRP*. You have to do your own studies and research, though I can give you some guidance as to where to find data.

What I can elaborate to you is on the real fallout of EPRP from the others.

To make it easy for you and a lot of others, I have to use the following written documents in Amharic about EPRP's strategy and methodology.

አለባብሰው ቢያርሱ በአረም ይመለሱ
ፍሬ ነገሩ፡ የአክሊሉ ካቢኔ በእንዳልካቸው ካቢኔ መተካቱን የሚቃውምና መሠረታዊ ለውጥ የሚጠይቅ
ጽሑፍ (This was the first warning for AEthiopians by EPRP)

የኢትዮጵያ ሰፊው ሰርቶ አዶር ሕዝብ ይቅደም
ፍሬ ነገሩ: የመሳፍንት ስርዓትንና የውጭ አገር ከበርቴዎችን የሚቃውምና ከሣራተኛ፤ ከገበሬ ከወታዶርና
ከምሁራን የተውጣጣ ጊዜያዊ መንግሥት እንዲቋቋም የሚጠይቅ። (This was a response to DERG's

slogan "ETHIOPIA TIKDEM".

ለውጥ ለሕዝብ – በሕዝብ
ፍሬ ነገሩ፤ ዴሞክራሲያዊ ስርዓትን ለማምጣት ሕብረተሰቡ መታገል እንዮሚገባው የሚያትት።

(This was a reply to those in doubt about the Revolution)

ትክክለኛው ጎዳና
ፍሬ ነገሩ፡ መሳፍንት፤ አሳራሽ፤ አቀባባይና የቢሮ ከበርቴዎች የለውጥ ተቃዋሚዎችና የስፊው ሕዝብ ጠላቶች
መሆናቸውን የሚያትት። (This was a reminder to all opposition groups at the time)

አልሾሹም ዞር አሉ
ፍሬ ነገሩ፡ ሕገ መንግሥቱ የሕዝብን መሠረታዊ ነፃነቶችንና ስብዓዊ መብቶችን የሚያረጋግጥ፤ ኤኮኖሚው ለስፊው ሕዝብ ጥቅም እንዲውል የሚያቶርግ፤ በኢትዮጵያ ሕዝቦች መሐከል በእኩልነትና በፊቃዶኛነት የተመሰረተ አንድነት እንዲገነባ መሠረት የሚጥል መሆን እንዳለበት የሚያትት። (this was written in response to MEISON's derailment of the Revolution by giving the DERG green light as a Revolutionary group and this has become the beginning of the end for all our ill defined history of the Eway Revolution.)

Dear Woldetewolde

It is a nice piece of idea to give us some highlights about the nature and some core inception of the ELF, TPLF and EPRP but i differ in your ideas in such a way that all the three have the same zero sum game in bringing democratic rule and the rule of law because all of them have different visions from inception, ELF as you stated it focus on geographical liberation which is the same as EPLF but what astonish me that of EPRP, at inception being the core party to bring democratic rule in Ethiopia in conjunction with unity did not moved a millimeter during the last 36 years, why? Is it a curse or a blessing to the ruling party as well the Ethiopian people? Why always we prefer division and subtraction than addition and multiplication? What is the core reasons that after a while we disintegrate in all sectors of our struggle?

The above issues need detail research in terms of physical, mental and circumstantial evidences in the past years but to me the major fall out are simple and straight forward the reasons being: -

- €€€€€€€ Egoism
- €€€€€€€ Cultism
- €€€€€€€ Nobody knows better than me
- €€€€€€€ Refuting discussion on issues but focus discussion on individuals
- €€€€€€€ (Maybe not sure), parties use some source of income to fill their bellies

Since I also call myself the product of this cursed generation which believe in division and grabbing new names whenever and whenever the branch start to grow, I did not belong to one or another party which were established in the beginning of the struggle whether we like it or not belong to four. Six main parties EPLF (ELF), OLF, EPRP, MEISON, EDU, EMALEDIH?

Would you please elaborate me some of the real fallout if they are different from the above.

With regards,
Berhanu Tesfaye

RECONCILIATION

Reconciliation for EPRP is all about having justice for ME and We. If really we want to be reconciled with EPLF, OLF, MEISON, EDU and EMALEDIH and other recent comers, here are two thoughts for consideration.

Advice for anti-EPRP:

The zebra of ነጭ ሳር in Gemu Gofa belongs together for one zebra is weak, many are powerful. That is their strength. It is our strength too. No person can live alone; it is not possible. We need each other. When we come together we are powerful. This wisdom is as old as humanity. Aesop, the Greek storyteller who lived many centuries ago, put this wisdom to words when he wrote in "The Four Oxen and the Lion," "united we stand, divided we fall." It is as simple as that; community is in our bones. AEthiopians are not particularly strong or fast, but their ability to cooperate with others to think, to communicate and work together makes them powerful. Mr. BT and others should think how to decipher his/their name in terms of GEEZ, Latin and Numbers, then try to communicate from the lowlands (ቆላ) to the highlands (ሞጋ) and vice versa. It is not about language, it is about temperament and understanding.

Advice for EPRP members

> *Gratitude unlocks the fullness of life. It turns what we have into enough, and more. It turns denial into acceptance, chaos to order, and confusion to clarity. It can turn a meal into a feast, a house into a home, a stranger into a friend. Gratitude makes sense of our past, brings peace for today, and creates a vision for tomorrow.*
>
> *-MELODY BEATTIE*

EMPATHY IS REACHING OUT WITH COMPASSION

Empathy is crucial for living for oneself and others. It is empathy that helps us to connect our own desire for happiness to that held by others and to understand how similar we all are despite our differences. Empathy also unites.

DEBTERAW's EPRP was no short of empathy and happiness.

EPRP should be grateful for all its opponents for fighting a political Revolution and in return the Nationalists, the Monarchists, the Renegades and the Fascists will accept their wrong doings in the name of truth, justice and freedom.

Education was of paramount concern for DEBTERAW as such we should strive to achieve it.

The search to find DEBTERAW and his comrades should be given priority not for their sakes and their families but also for JUSTICE and DEMOCRACIA to prevail

For comments and criticism: woldetewolde@yahoo.com

CALL ME BY MY NAME:

A tribute to DEBU

Wolde Tewolde, alias Obo Arada Shawl

December 5, 2007

TSEGEYE DEBTERAW has challenged many of the basic assumptions and beliefs of why and how Ethiopians have approached the natural world as opposed to the artificial world. Debu's provocative thoughts and actions have inspired some and infuriated others, but no one can dispute his premise: that it is time for all Ethiopians to develop a new and more sustainable relationship with Ethiopia's ECOLOGY.

Debteraw reminds us that the task of solving ecological, cultural, intellectual and spiritual (ECIS) problems is not just only a matter of Revolution but of law and morality. Connecting abstract legal notions of property to land holding in Oromo land and communal aspects in Eritrea is not enough. Debteraw's enlarged sense of responsibility and community in our dealings with the land issue, which is not solved even at the present moment, was his essence for his long struggle.

In short, for DEBU justice and the Land Question of (DEGA-WEINA-KOLA) are interchangeable and they are the main issues and should be our obligations to pass to the future generations.

Debteraw predicted that others will govern the daily lives of Ethiopians and that the emerging power holders the DERG and his cronies will aggravate their helplessness. He enlightened me by arguing that

- The products/services we should buy
- The transport system we use and
- The homes in which we live

All are to be controlled by others. "We will be offered choices, but they will be limited choices", Debteraw used to argue with us. Is this not a true prediction? Do we need a scientific proof? As for me, I have seen what products I could or couldn't buy during the DERG era, I have seen how my residential place was controlled and I know how the transport system have and still working against the interest of Ethiopians.

As at today, everything what DEBTERAW TSEGEYE GEBRE MEDHIN has predicted forty years ago, the time I met him has happened and is happening. We should stop this madness of land misuse, family break and community disintegration.

The point to be made about this understandable sense of confusion and helplessness is that our problems are societal in scope, which means that our solutions must be equally broad. Organizations, political or otherwise can adopt some resolutions and sanctions, but their range of action is limited - absent of a decision to drop of society and return to the "fields or guerrilla" mode of warfare.

EPRP of DEBTERAW can rise up to confront this complexity only by joining together as a community and a people to demand justice for HIM, YOU and US.

What we can do? We can set out what to do as part of the solutions- what we value and what we want and demand to the current local, regional and global power holders of our houses, products/services and our means of transport. It is time to challenge and confront TPLF, EPDJ, EU Parliament, the UN, China and the State Department.

As for me, DEBTERAW in his first interview transmitted his ideas of solution in the transport system as **AGGMELAGO.** This is a ROAD MAP for all Ethiopians starting from the RED SEA (from sea level) to RAS DASHEN (highest mountain). I hope we will deal with this concept in great length in due course.

For comments and criticism: woldetewolde@yahoo.com

CALL ME BY MY NAME ADDRESS:

A Commentary

Obo Arada Shawl alias Wolde Tewolde

October 13, 2008

This is a response to some queries emailed to me by (Ato) Berhanu Tesfaye. My response may be politically incorrect. The questions are placed at the bottom of the article for reference.

1. 36-years of struggle by EPRP
2. The need for Research
3. Reasons for the fallout
4. Cursed generation
5. Six main parties

36 years of struggle

EPRP's struggle was not only about 3 decades of struggle. Politically it was and is a struggle of a century. It was also about five centuries of struggle for social, environmental and cultural change/revolution.

Politically, EPRP in principle recognizes the efforts and attempts of Miniliks" *modernization*, Tewodros's *concept of Unity*, Yohannes's *religious faith* and Haile Sellassie's *efforts for education*. All these four kings lived in the last hundred years and they are the source of the perceived problems of the nationalists. DEBTERAW and his Revolutionary political party, EPRP foresaw the will and the sacrifice to further Modernization program through Unity and the value Belief through Education. But this unity and education goes further into centuries when Ethiopia lived without printing privileges.

According to DEBTERAW, however, modernization did not meant the importation of manufactured goods but through creativity and innovation by AEthiopians unlike that of Minilik who strived to access to the products of by scientists. DEBTERAW believed that Arts – littérateurs, art and culture collectively known as KINET could play important role in the development of Ethiopia.

The RE i.e. Yohannes's belief could only be furthered by education alone. I guess that was why perhaps DEBTERAW became an educator/teacher. So you see Ato Berhanu, 36 years is nothing compared to the centuries of cultural and political change? In today's terminology, EPRP was software as opposed to Shaebia or Woyane's hardware organizations. In other words, unless and otherwise we collectively understand the history and culture (HC) of AEthiopia, there are plenty of years ahead of us before we reach our goal. The contribution of EPRP to the consciousness of AEthiopians to politics as well as to Arts and Literateaure should be recognized.

I am not denying the fact that EPRP's struggle for collective leadership, trust among its members, justice for everyone and everybody by way of DEMOCRACIA was perfect. It was full of missteps and errors.

Research

Who is going to do the research? Are there researchers who are interested in what EPRP has done or what has not done? I see and hear only people who only condemn EPRP. How much does the research cost? Professors and PhD. holders or others should address such questions… Most of the organizations you mentioned were doing something of value. I cannot emphasis to you the fact that some are good at actions while others are good in theories. EPRP has the traditions of having designers-planners-theoreticians and practicing individuals and groups. It is known as Sin"huate M"huran (ጽንሐተ ምሁራን).

Reasons for the fallout

You seem to be puzzled by addition, subtraction, multiplication and division. It is the nature of mathematics —which is necessary in all walks of life. We cannot do without arithmetic let alone mathematics. There is no way to avoid this phenomenon. I think you ought to read about philosophy, psychology, sociology and economics. It will help to grasp the nature of human beings.

Cursed generation

Why do you use this word "curse"? It is not a proper word to use in politics. It is very unfortunate that Ato Kiflu Tadesse used "that generation while writing his book, „the generation". That was a misnomer. He should have used an appropriate term instead of that generation. It is an abstract word – compare this to "that one" used by Senator McCain against Obama, which is interpreted in different ways. AEthiopians especially the youth are interpreting "that generation" as vague and foolish. It should be explained time and again with cyclical nature of life.

    The generation that BT is referring was the generation that was <u>selfless.</u> The generation of AEthiopians who were searching for victory based on vote on the basis of voluntarism not on adventurism. And it is improper to call „that generation" a cursed generation. What do you call this generation of today?

Six main parties

I cannot tell you that neither the life struggle between *EPLF and ELF*, *OLF and TPLF*, *MEISON and EMALEDHI* nor between *EDU and EPRP*. You have to do your own studies and research, though I can give you some guidance as to where to find data.

    What I can elaborate to you is on the real fallout of EPRP from the others.

    To make it easy for you and a lot of others, I have to use the following written documents in Amharic about EPRP's strategy and methodology.

አለባብሰው ቢያርሱ በአረም ይመለሱ
ፍሬ ነገሩ፡ የአክሊሉ ካቢኔ በእንዳላካቸው ካቢኔ መተካቱን የሚቃውምና መሠረታዊ ለውጥን የሚጠይቅ
ጽሑፍ (This was the first warning for AEthiopians by EPRP)

የኢትዮጵያ ሰፊው ሰርቶ አዶር ሕዝብ ይቅጦም
ፍሬ ነገሩ፡ የመሳፍንት ስርዓትንና የውጭ አገር ከበርቴዎችን የሚቃወምና ከሠራተኛ፤ ከገበሬ፤ ከወታጦርና ከምሁራን የተውጣጣ ጊዜያዊ መንግሥት እንዲቋቋም የሚጠይቅ። (This was a response to DERG's

slogan "ETHIOPIA TIKDEM".

ለውጥ ለሕዝብ – በሕዝብ
ፍሬ ነገሩ፤ ዴሞክራሲያዊ ስርዓትን ለማምጣት ሕብረተሰቡ መታገል እንዮሚገባው የሚያትት።
(This was a reply to those in doubt about the Revolution)

ትክክለኛው ጎዳና
ፍሬ ነገሩ፡ መሳፍንት፤ አሳራሽ፤ አቀባባይና የቢሮ ከበርቴዎች የለውጥ ተቃዋሚዎችና የስፊው ሕዝብ ጠላቶች
መሆናቸውን የሚያትት። (This was a reminder to all opposition groups at the time)

አልሸሁም ዘር አለ
ፍሬ ነገሩ፤ ሕገ መንግሥቱ የሕዝብን መሠረታዊ ነፃነቶችንና ስብዓዊ መብቶችን የሚያረጋግጥ፤ ኤኮኖሚው ለስፊው ሕዝብ ጥቅም እንዲውል የሚያቶርግ፤ በኢትዮጵያ ሕዝቦች መሐከል በእኩልነትና በፈቃዶኝነት የተመሰረተ አንድነት እንዲገነባ መሠረት የሚጥል መሆን እንዳለበት የሚያትት። (this was written in response to MEISON's derailment of the Revolution by giving the DERG green light as a Revolutionary group and this has become the beginning of the end for all our ill defined history of the Eway Revolution.)

Dear Woldetewolde

It is a nice piece of idea to give us some highlights about the nature and some core inception of the ELF, TPLF and EPRP but i differ in your ideas in such a way that all the three have the same zero sum game in bringing democratic rule and the rule of law because all of them have different visions from inception, ELF as you stated it focus on geographical liberation which is the same as EPLF but what astonish me that of EPRP, at inception being the core party to bring democratic rule in Ethiopia in conjunction with unity did not moved a millimeter during the last 36 years, why? Is it a curse or a blessing to the ruling party as well the Ethiopian people? Why always we prefer division and subtraction than addition and multiplication? What is the core reasons that after a while we disintegrate in all sectors of our struggle?

The above issues need detail research in terms of physical, mental and circumstantial evidences in the past years but to me the major fall out are simple and straight forward the reasons being: -

- €€€€€€€ Egoism
- €€€€€€€ Cultism
- €€€€€€€ Nobody knows better than me
- €€€€€€€ Refuting discussion on issues but focus discussion on individuals
- €€€€€€€ (Maybe not sure), parties use some source of income to fill their bellies

Since I also call myself the product of this cursed generation which believe in division and grabbing new names whenever and whenever the branch start to grow, I did not belong to one or another party which were established in the beginning of the struggle whether we like it or not belong to four. Six main parties EPLF (ELF), OLF, EPRP, MEISON, EDU, EMALEDIH?

Would you please elaborate me some of the real fallout if they are different from the above.

With regards
Berhanu Tesfaye

RECONCILIATION

Reconciliation for EPRP is all about having justice for ME and We. If really we want to be reconciled with EPLF, OLF, MEISON, EDU and EMALEDIH and other recent comers, here are two thoughts for consideration.

Advice for anti-EPRP:

The zebra of ነጭ ባር in Gemu Gofa belongs together for one zebra is weak, many are powerful. That is their strength. It is our strength too. No person can live alone; it is not possible. We need each other. When we come together we are powerful. This wisdom is as old as humanity. Aesop, the Greek storyteller who lived many centuries ago, put this wisdom to words when he wrote in "The Four Oxen and the Lion," "united we stand, divided we fall." It is as simple as that; community is in our bones. AEthiopians are not particularly strong or fast, but their ability to cooperate with others to think, to communicate and work together makes them powerful. Mr. BT and others should think how to decipher his/their name in terms of GEEZ, Latin and Numbers, then try to communicate from the lowlands (ቆላ) to the highlands (ደጋ) and vice versa. It is not about language, it is about temperament and understanding.

Advice for EPRP members

> *Gratitude unlocks the fullness of life. It turns what we have into enough, and more. It turns denial into acceptance, chaos to order, and confusion to clarity. It can turn a meal into a feast, a house into a home, a stranger into a friend. Gratitude makes sense of our past, brings peace for today, and creates a vision for tomorrow.*
>
> *~MELODY BEATTIE*

EMPATHY IS REACHING OUT WITH COMPASSION

Empathy is crucial for living for oneself and others. It is empathy that helps us to connect our own desire for happiness to that held by others and to understand how similar we all are despite our differences. Empathy also unites.

DEBTERAW's EPRP was no short of empathy and happiness.

EPRP should be grateful for all its opponents for fighting a political Revolution and in return the Nationalists, the Monarchists, the Renegades and the Fascists will accept their wrong doings in the name of truth, justice and freedom.

Education was of paramount concern for DEBTERAW as such we should strive to achieve it.

The search to find DEBTERAW and his comrades should be given priority not for their sakes and their families but also for JUSTICE and DEMOCRACIA to prevail

For comments and criticism: woldetewolde@yahoo.com

CALL ME BY MY NAME ADDRESS:

A Commentary

Obo Arada Shawl alias Wolde Tewolde

October 13, 2008

This is a response to some queries emailed to me by (Ato) Berhanu Tesfaye. My response may be politically incorrect. The questions are placed at the bottom of the article for reference.

1. 36-years of struggle by EPRP
2. The need for Research
3. Reasons for the fallout
4. Cursed generation
5. Six main parties

36 years of struggle

EPRP's struggle was not only about 3 decades of struggle. Politically it was and is a struggle of a century. It was also about five centuries of struggle for social, environmental and cultural change/revolution.

Politically, EPRP in principle recognizes the efforts and attempts of Miniliks" *modernization*, Tewodros's *concept of Unity*, Yohannes's *religious faith* and Haile Sellassie's *efforts for education*. All these four kings lived in the last hundred years and they are the source of the perceived problems of the nationalists. DEBTERAW and his Revolutionary political party, EPRP foresaw the will and the sacrifice to further Modernization program through Unity and the value Belief through Education. But this unity and education goes further into centuries when Ethiopia lived without printing privileges.

According to DEBTERAW, however, modernization did not meant the importation of manufactured goods but through creativity and innovation by AEthiopians unlike that of Minilik who strived to access to the products of by scientists. DEBTERAW believed that Arts – littérateurs, art and culture collectively known as KINET could play important role in the development of Ethiopia.

The RE i.e. Yohannes's belief could only be furthered by education alone. I guess that was why perhaps DEBTERAW became an educator/teacher. So you see Ato Berhanu, 36 years is nothing compared to the centuries of cultural and political change? In today's terminology, EPRP was software as opposed to Shaebia or Woyane's hardware organizations. In other words, unless and otherwise we collectively understand the history and culture (HC) of AEthiopia, there are plenty of years ahead of us before we reach our goal. The contribution of EPRP to the consciousness of AEthiopians to politics as well as to Arts and

Literateaure should be recognized.

I am not denying the fact that EPRP's struggle for collective leadership, trust among its members, justice for everyone and everybody by way of DEMOCRACIA was perfect. It was full of missteps and errors.

Research

Who is going to do the research? Are there researchers who are interested in what EPRP has done or what has not done? I see and hear only people who only condemn EPRP. How much does the research cost? Professors and PhD. holders or others should address such questions… Most of the organizations you mentioned were doing something of value. I cannot emphasis to you the fact that some are good at actions while others are good in theories. EPRP has the traditions of having designers-planners-theoreticians and practicing individuals and groups. It is known as Sin"huate M"huran (ጸንሐተ ምሁራን).

Reasons for the fallout

You seem to be puzzled by addition, subtraction, multiplication and division. It is the nature of mathematics —which is necessary in all walks of life. We cannot do without arithmetic let alone mathematics. There is no way to avoid this phenomenon. I think you ought to read about philosophy, psychology, sociology and economics. It will help to grasp the nature of human beings.

Cursed generation

Why do you use this word "curse"? It is not a proper word to use in politics. It is very unfortunate that Ato Kiflu Tadesse used "that generation while writing his book, „the generation". That was a misnomer. He should have used an appropriate term instead of that generation. It is an abstract word – compare this to "that one" used by Senator McCain against Obama, which is interpreted in different ways. AEthiopians especially the youth are interpreting "that generation" as vague and foolish. It should be explained time and again with cyclical nature of life.

The generation that BT is referring was the generation that was <u>selfless</u>. The generation of AEthiopians who were searching for victory based on vote on the basis of voluntarism not on adventurism. And it is improper to call „that generation" a cursed generation. What do you call this generation of today?

Six main parties

I cannot tell you that neither the life struggle between *EPLF and ELF, OLF and TPLF, MEISON and EMALEDHI* nor between *EDU and EPRP*. You have to do your own studies and research, though I can give you some guidance as to where to find data.

What I can elaborate to you is on the real fallout of EPRP from the others.

To make it easy for you and a lot of others, I have to use the following written documents in Amharic about EPRP's strategy and methodology.

አለባብሰው ቢያርሱ በአረም ይመለሱ
ፍሬ ነገሩ፡ የአክሊሉ ካቢኔ በእንዳልካቸው ካቢኔ መተካቱን የሚቃውምና መሠረታዊ ለውጥን የሚጠይቅ

ጽሑፍ (This was the first warning for AEthiopians by EPRP)

የኢትዮጵያ ሰፊው ሰርቶ አዶር ሕዝብ ይቅቶም
ፍሬ ነገሩ፡ የመሳፍንት ስርዓትንና የውጭ አገር ከበርቴዎችን የሚቃወምና ከሦራተኛ፤ ከገበሬ፤ ከወታቶርና
ከምሁራን የተውጣጣ ጊዜያዊ መንግሥት እንዲቋቋም የሚጠይቅ፡፡ (This was a response to DERG's

በኢትዮጵያ ሕዝቦች መሐከል በእኩልነትና በፈቃዶኝነት የተመሠረተ አንድነት እንዲገነባ መሠረት የሚጥል መሆን እንዳለበት የሚያትች፡፡ (this was written in response to MEISON's derailment of the Revolution by giving the DERG green light as a Revolutionary group and this has become the beginning of the end for all our ill defined history of the Eway Revolution.)

ትክክለኛው ጎዳና
ፍሬ ነገሩ፡ መሳፍንት፤ አሳራሽ፤ አቀባባይና የቢሮ ከበርቴዎች የለውጥ ተቃዋሚዎችና የስፊው ሕዝብ ጠላቶች
መሆናቸውን የሚያትች፡፡ (This was a reminder to all opposition groups at the time)

አልሻሹም ዘር አሉ
ፍሬ ነገሩ፡ ሕገ መንግሥቱ የሕዝቡን መሠረታዊ ነፃነቶችንና ስብዓዊ መብቶችን የሚያረጋግጥ፤ ኤኮኖሚው ለስፊው ሕዝብ ጥቅም እንዲውል የሚያቶርግ፤

በኢትዮጵያ ሕዝቦች መሐከል በእኩልነትና በፈቃዶኝነት የተመሠረተ አንድነት እንዲገነባ መሠረት የሚጥል መሆን እንዳለበት የሚያትች፡፡ (this was written in response to MEISON's derailment of the Revolution by giving the DERG green light as a Revolutionary group and this has become the beginning of the end for all our ill defined history of the Eway Revolution.)

Dear Woldetewolde

It is a nice piece of idea to give us some highlights about the nature and some core inception of the ELF, TPLF and EPRP but i differ in your ideas in such a way that all the three have the same zero sum game in bringing democratic rule and the rule of law because all of them have different visions from inception, ELF as you stated it focus on geographical liberation which is the same as EPLF but what astonish me that of EPRP, at inception being the core party to bring democratic rule in Ethiopia in conjunction with unity did not moved a millimeter during the last 36 years, why? Is it a curse or a blessing to the ruling party as well the Ethiopian people? Why always we prefer division and subtraction than addition and multiplication? What is the core reasons that after a while we disintegrate in all sectors of our struggle?

The above issues need detail research in terms of physical, mental and circumstantial evidences in the past years but to me the major fall out are simple and straight forward the reasons being: -

- €€€€€€€ Egoism
- €€€€€€€ Cultism
- €€€€€€€ Nobody knows better than me
- €€€€€€€ Refuting discussion on issues but focus discussion on individuals
- €€€€€€€ (Maybe not sure), parties use some source of income to fill their bellies

Since I also call myself the product of this cursed generation which believe in division and grabbing new names whenever and whenever the branch start to grow, I did not belong to one or another party which were established in the beginning of the struggle whether we like it or not belong to four. Six main parties EPLF (ELF), OLF, EPRP, MEISON, EDU, EMALEDIH?

Would you please elaborate me some of the real fallout if they are different from the above.

With regards
Berhanu Tesfaye

RECONCILIATION

Reconciliation for EPRP is all about having justice for ME and We. If really we want to be reconciled with EPLF, OLF, MEISON, EDU and EMALEDIH and other recent comers, here are two thoughts for consideration.

Advice for anti-EPRP:

The zebra of ነጭ ባር in Gemu Gofa belongs together for one zebra is weak, many are powerful. That is their strength. It is our strength too. No person can live alone; it is not possible. We need each other. When we come together we are powerful. This wisdom is as old as humanity. Aesop, the Greek storyteller who lived many centuries ago, put this wisdom to words when he wrote in "The Four Oxen and the Lion," "united we stand, divided we fall." It is as simple as that; community is in our bones. AEthiopians are not particularly strong or fast, but their ability to cooperate with others to think, to communicate and work together makes them powerful. Mr. BT and others should think how to decipher his/their name in terms of GEEZ, Latin and Numbers, then try to communicate from the lowlands (ቅላ) to the highlands (ሞጋ) and vice versa. It is not about language, it is about temperament and understanding.

Advice for EPRP members

> *Gratitude unlocks the fullness of life. It turns what we have into enough, and more. It turns denial into acceptance, chaos to order, and confusion to clarity. It can turn a meal into a feast, a house into a home, a stranger into a friend. Gratitude makes sense of our past, brings peace for today, and creates a vision for tomorrow.*
>
> *-MELODY BEATTIE*

EMPATHY IS REACHING OUT WITH COMPASSION

Empathy is crucial for living for oneself and others. It is empathy that helps us to connect our own desire for happiness to that held by others and to understand how similar we all are despite our differences. Empathy also unites.

DEBTERAW's EPRP was no short of empathy and happiness.

EPRP should be grateful for all its opponents for fighting a political Revolution and in return the Nationalists, the Monarchists, the Renegades and the Fascists will accept their wrong doings in the name of truth, justice and freedom.

Education was of paramount concern for DEBTERAW as such we should strive to achieve it.

The search to find DEBTERAW and his comrades should be given priority not for their sakes and their families but also for JUSTICE and DEMOCRACIA to prevail

For comments and criticism: woldetewolde@yahoo.com

CALL ME BY MY NAME:

A commentary

Wolde Tewolde alias Obo Arada Shawl,

August 13, 2007

In 1986, a group of Ethiopian graduate students were enrolled at the University of Virginia Tech. On the first week of college day, we attended a conference on "Futuristic" seminars. The futurists explained at length on countries that would progress and regress. In the end they enumerated those countries without future. Ethiopia was listed as a futureless country. At that moment all my Ethiopian colleagues left the conference, as they were upset. I stayed not only until the question and answer session but also even after the conference has formally closed. I had to get a real explanation for their prediction.

Having talked to some of them, I found out it was based on shallow reasoning and scientifically or statistically untenable.

On the 2nd week of our stay, someone in the cafeteria asked us from where we came. When we told him that we are from Ethiopia, he said that at least, here in America we have something to eat. Then I asked him and his friends how they came to know about Ethiopia. I explained to them that there were only five ways of knowing Ethiopia during those days. Because of

- Haile Sellasie I
- Abebe Bikila
- History Books
- The Bible and
- Famine

None of them seem to know the other four except the last one, which was the famine of 1984, the issue of the time upon which they based their conclusion.

On home coming day, all international flags were hoisted on the campus of VA TECH. The only flag that was not hoisted was the Ethiopian Flag. Mrs. Sally came to where we were sitting and asked us why one of us did not hoist the Ethiopian flag. Mrs. Sally is the lady who welcomes and looks after the international students. In her welcome address, she told the attendees that she wished that America had a history like that of Ethiopia. We had no explanation to tell Mrs. Sally that none of us take the initiative to hoist the flag. The Ethiopian flag was so sacred that no one touches unless he is some sort of an official of a government or a church was our last resort to tell the tale.

Where were our geography or history teachers? Who are our geographers? What were the sources of our history? Did we learn any sociology class? And who are our sociologists? Do we know the history of the flag? What is its significance? A lot of questions should be answered.

You be the judge. As for me, I have done my homework. Thanks to Debteraw's training manuals. Call me by my name. What is my name? READ, READ and READ.

Question: What is your name?
Answer: I have a nickname; I have a pen name; I use my father's name; my name is Hayes, AL, Jason, and Jolly etc. etc.

Question: Who are you?
Answer: Abyssinian, no I am an Eritrean, no I am an Oromo, oh no, I am an Amhara or I am a Tigre etc. etc. No, No and No, I am an AETHIOPIAN. What a Mess!!! Call Me By My Name.

What is my name? What about now, at the dawn of the 2nd Millennium? Do we know?

- Those who died since the beginning of the Revolution
- Those who are still in prison
- Those who are missed in action

According to our culture, the Birth, the Marriage and the Death (BMD) should be celebrated. The first two need no explanation. But the Death part needs elaboration. Do we celebrate like the Shanklas with pomp and joy or do we grief for life or do we honorable bury our dead? I do not know why, someone has to tell me.

In Debteraw's case, it is reported that an individual from Maichew reported that he has shot him in person. To misinform about the death of Debu was a deliberate attempt by TPLF officials to make us believe that he is dead so that there would be no political prisoner under their custody. But no one will believe them that Debteraw is not a political prisoner. And we all know that Debteraw refused to cooperate with TPLF officials. As it is clear to the outside world Debteraw is still alive and well. I personally meet him once in a while by an Econcept.

But as Debteraw's editorial rightly asked for the timely release of Debteraw. It is better for everybody if he is released without bond or signature. DEBTERAW abhors both of these. That is, to true to his nature, Debteraw is a true Ethiopian, no baggage, only Trust and Courage.

Finally, the message is clear, if TPLF have killed Debteraw, their teacher, our teacher, let us all bury him properly because as it is said, "the burial of the dead tells much about the future of any society." Ethiopia is no exception. **WILL ETHIOPIA WILL BE FUTURELESSS** as the futurists in VA TECH had predicted? Absolutely not provided WE IMMORTALIZED DEBTERAW.

For comments and criticism: woldetewolde@yahoo.com

CALL ME BY MY NAME:

A commentary

Wolde Tewolde alias Obo Arada Shawl

June 1, 2007

Politics: It is an open ended Relationship. We can build or we can destroy the bridge of Relationship.

It is a matter of choice. I for one have chosen to build the bridge. Actually it was my profession to build a bridge. In the field of Ethiopian politics, the ELF, OLF, EPLF, TPLF, and the rest liberation fronts have chosen to destroy the bridge. I believe because their leaders were mainly men and men usually think in terms of space – a physical space while women conceptualize in terms of Time. The era of women has finally arrived in the Ethiopian societies. Hopefully the story of MAKON within EPRP will be a guiding light for all of us - men and women.

EPRP has never attempted to destroy a bridge. EPRP considered itself as a human bridge and I want to testify that it is not dead and cannot be dead provided people are open to understand its political history, its members, supporters and its leaders. I for one have made an effort to answer the following questions for my personal judgment. By the way, I am not an EPRP apologist. I am against sky-is- falling rhetoric.

Do we know the political history of EPRP?
Do we know its members?
Do we know its supporters?
Do we know its leaders?

Until we know or make an effort to answer these basic questions, I think we should withhold our judgments.

Let us examine the following two judgmental comments, one of which almost self-assuredly gave rationale for the death of EPRP, the other self-consciously labeled names but in the end genuinely accepted the right information. I hope the anonymous commentator will make a sound judgment after reading these commentaries and the articles of call me by my name. Democratic solutions will emerge with real names. Call me by my name!

Comments (1)

Anonymous names usually emanate from three sources.

1. *Fear of retaliation.*
2. *Because of a hidden agenda and*
3. *Out of respect of one's own culture.*

Although the previous commentator is anonymous, the questions are not uncommon and must be answered. That I will gladly attempt to answer some of his/her queries, and in the process to reiterate on Ato Tedla's comment. Here are the following ten cardinal questions that I have picked up from his/her comments.

1. *"EPRP is dead…" Was that not the reason why the Ethiopians Elected Qeeneejit and fight for democracy?*
2. *Which EPRP are you talking about?*
3. *EPRP was made without by itself without the Ethiopian people Election.*
4. *If EPRP is thinking for the Ethiopians, is it the time to talk about itself?*
5. *Was it not better to co-operate with others in order to get rid of Woyane!*
6. *If EPRP knows Woyane very well and Woyane is afraid of EPRP; when is it going to show its power?*
7. *Do not repeat some more mistakes*
8. *The Worlds Politics has been changed a lot*
9. *Do not be stubborn like mule*
10. *Have a nice day!!*

And here are the relevant replies for your concerns. I hope these frequently asked questions should at least give you a glimpse of understanding of why EPRP still exists and how it operates.

The reason why Ethiopians elected Qeeneejit and fought for democracy was not upon the death of EPRP as such. On the contrary, the opposite was true. It was a test for the government whether it will abide by the rule of Election Law. And the government has failed miserably. EPRP is alive unless we have different meaning for death and life. For your information EPRP's slogan and Party Organ is DEMOCRACIA. Check for the publication. It is the only mouthpiece of EPRP. I doubt those who have negative comments about EPRP have never seen let alone read the Publication. And it is also true that many members and supporters did not receive DEMOCRACIA. Many have perished because of this Publication. It was and is the Essence for the Life of EPRP. It is said that whenever an editor of DEMOCRACIA is killed or imprisoned, it is a sure sign that EPRP is dead. But can we kill ideas? I leave the answer for you. I believe this question is twisted. The soft revolution by Qeenjit to topple the regime did not work for the simple reason that there was no common cause, bond or experience (CCBE). As the name suggest it is just coordination and the coordination was out of tune! Call me by my name.

Since its inception EPRP is one and only one. The Party is made of rocks and not with sands. Starting with its name, EPRP stand for E = E, People = public; Revolution >< Reform; Party = Politics. It is like the A'Abay River and the B'ahri Erythrism that never change while the people, the plants and the animals that live around these places die and transform. Both geopolitical of River and Sea just named after colors of BLUE & RED, which they are not. Call me by my name not by my color. True some members of EPRP have betrayed the Party; some have switched sides not because of cause but because of lack of communication, propaganda machine, lack of confidence resulting in confusion. And currently some attempt to cheat that they still belong to the true original Party of EPRP but only pay lip services. I believe that the most dangerous confusers are not those who betrayed or abandoned the struggle but those who still pretend that they are or belong to the one and only one EPRP.

If you need further information, we should attempt to understand the history of Anja and Bitena. In a nutshell, ANJA was a phenomenon of a faction or split from EPRP leadership. It was based on a choice of a Secretary General whether who would be a powerful and dictatorial or a weak Secretary General with Strong Collective Leadership behind him. I hope by now every Ethiopian or Eritrean has understood the right choice of EPRP's stand on **collective leadership**. The whole concept of EPRP lies in Collective Leadership. The merits and demerits will be debated with Debteraw SSEEGGYY!!!

The second wave of EPRP's internal problem was what was known as B'TENA. This is a cultural phenomenon. It is still current in our societies. What it means is that "if I am dead, EPRP is dead, if EPRP is alive, I am alive." It is a tautological argument. But EPRP is a voluntary organization; no one forces to join unless one wants to. EPRP is not about nationalism, religion, or ethnic background. It is about ETHIOPIANISM (not to be confused of course with Ehiopiawinet, Ethiopianess etc.). It is about freedom and democracy. It is about the free people since time immemorial. It is not about slavery and freedom. It is about God given freedom to keep it alive. Enslave yourself and then liberate yourself is not the EPRP's way. I believe those who were involved in the concept of B'Tena have regretted in hindsight and the majority have rejoined the Party. Cutthroat competition is not for Ethiopians. It is not meant for them. EPRP understood its peoples' inner culture for Ethiopian societies are based on community of equals.

The AB story, that is, of ANJA & B'TENA was internal and twenty years have passed since EPRP has moved to ABC…Cooperation with all its ex-members as well as with its trustworthy opponents.

Finally, let me say that the Oak Tree of EPRP is one but with many branches. Call me by my name. What is my name?

EPRP of course was and is organized without the election. It is the whole purpose of why it is still struggling. EPRP believes deeply in Election process and not in Appointment Process. If we miss this concept, we are missing the whole survival of Ethiopia. EPRP says "NONE" to the question 'what is in there for me?' or 'blood is thicker than water'. It only stands for Principle of Justice for ALL ETHIOPIANS. If we see argument or complaints, it is only a way of doing business wit EPRP Community.

EPRP does care for all Ethiopians as individuals, as families and as communities. At this time, EPRP is not talking about itself or its members. It is voicing daily about the fate of all Ethiopians and Eritreans as human being as they deserve a better respect and dignity. When EPRP members were young and bold, they did not know what they were doing, now they have matured and believe me they know what they are doing. They are doing, at least the right thing for Ethiopia and Eritrea.

EPRP has cooperated with all organizations, groups, parties or movements. The history of EPRP is a history of cooperation. Practically, every individual or organization has taken advantages from EPRP's cooperation. EPRP did not consider cooperation as weakness but strength. But cooperation does not mean to surrender one's core value beliefs. EPRP did not and will not cooperate with any thing that it considers it anti-DEMOCRACIA. EPRP's, motto has been always "you can use us without abusing us"!!!!!

EPRP does not consider Woyane as its own personal enemy per se. EPRP considers Woyane's deeds and mission as contrary to the wishes of all Ethiopians. If you are asking that Woyane fears EPRP, it is because EPRP holds the moral Truth, and the truth hurts as they say. Maybe the question of fear comes to mind. Otherwise the street talk of Woyane is fearful of EPRP does not hold water. Nevertheless, it is a common knowledge that Woyane has /is been against the interests of all Ethiopians whether out of fear for EPRP or out of ignorance or something else, no one can tell. The Woyane has a history of revenge first against the Amharas, then against EPRP, then against OLF and then against the Eritreans, and then against Qeeneejit and now against Somalis and tomorrow who knows against who they are after. Only Mariam Tsion of Axum knows!!! EPRP and Woyane do not see eye to eye for Woyane moves with Fear whereas EPRP in Faith or courage.

What mistakes are you talking about? If you do not make mistakes, you cannot progress. By the way, mistakes, errors, wrongs and damages are synonymous in Amharic. No one is perfect. Only Jesus Christ was perfect, and for that he was crucified. Sometimes, I wonder maybe EPRP leaders like those of Debu, Debesai, Walle, Tselote etc., etc. were perfect to be sacrificed. Memories and pictures do matter. Are we are talking about simple mistakes? What about the bad memories imposed on them? What about the lost pictures of their families? Whose mistake is it to be raped, disposed, and imprisoned and to be refugee and asylee? Please put the blame where it belongs. EPRP is the victim in the so-called Ethiopian Revolution. Please, tell me the specific mistakes committed by EPRP apart from the common street talk of "they are responsible to cause the revolution". Oppression and exploitation were rampant in Ethiopia, the O representing Oromia and the E representing Eritrea. All what EPRP did was to guide through the right path and you are the witness now what was at stake and still at stake. What: Freedom and Justice. How: Via DEMOCRACIA. For these slogans EPRP suffered and is still suffering.

What is my name calling me by my name? Don't forget though that there were and still are some destructive EPRP members!

Yes, the World has changed. Changed into what? First, there were Humans (ARTS) in Africa, and then it was transformed into Science while in Europe and later Science yielded to Technology in America, becoming as AST. So now where are we going? Back to Human ARTS or to the STARS. The only solid change we see is that communication has changed. Instead of our verbal or written word, we have switched to the E word. That is about it. In our case, the verbal and visual are still alive and well. But thanks to Woyane, we have abused the word of TRUST in God, in Human and in Societal Harmony. It is good to remember that EPRP is not the one, which has brought havoc through revolution!

(Remember the Eway Revolution has been stolen or distorted first by the DERG and now by the TPLF.) The damage is long overdue. The more you change, the more you don't change.

Principles do not change. The flow of Abay River does not change, the sun rising in the East does not change even the Ethiopian skin will not change!! Politics of EPRP should change. But currently, EPRP is not in the business of politicking. If politics is a Relationship, then the current Relationship of EPRP is sour. It is a human survival. Politics of government for Election has not started in Ethiopia. Politics of Appointment is still in operative. The lineage of Minilik and Yohannes still lingers on. But EPRP has gone a long step away from these two lineages towards that of Tewodros of Gondar, Haile Sellassie of Harar and Iyasu of Wello. Changes come with understanding of the other party. Let us try to understand EPRP. Give it a try to forgive EPRP. May be it is holding a panacea for all Ethiopians.

Have a nice day. What a wonderful wish. Thank you very much. We need more of it. Thank you Ethiopian Mothers, Daughters and Sisters (MDS) of EPRP Community and Eritrean Fathers, Sons and Brothers (FSB). Ride on EPRP.

Comment (2)

Tewolde: Hi

Thank you very much for commenting on my article of May 13, 2007. I have already told you my name, which is Wolde Tewolde. It may sound funny especially for African American. But hey my parents gave it and I have to live by it. My other pen name is Obo Arada Shawl. I created this name simply to tell people that I am also from the urban areas of Addis, Asmara and Dire Dawa or rural Oromia. That is as far as my personal name. So you have two choices to address me.

But the title of the article is related to Tsegeye, Ssegeye, or using any Latin letter. The first reason was that foreigners couldn't say the Geez SSSSSS. Try this with your children, if you have any. It won't work. The second reason is that there are prominent names similar to this Tsegeye. People get confused. In conformity to your wish, I want to clear with names first. The third reason is that there is a saying in Tigrigna, which says "Shim Yimrh, Tuwaf Yebrh", roughly name guides, candle lights. Also in Amharic, "Melke T'fu B'Melk Y'degfu". But the most important part of these series of articles is to know about Tsegeye Gebre Medhin also known as DEBTERAW. He is living incommunicado somewhere in Tigrai. He is one of the best leaders of EPRP. By the way, I like your name, if it is a true name. Do you live by your name? Can I call you by your name?

Postscript

"All men are created equal" and that government should be "of the people by the people and for the people" that there should be "liberty and justice for all", said Abraham Lincoln. "All" mean all the inhabitants of our planet. EPRP's planet was beyond Eritrea and Somalia.

Ex-EPRP members should speak of character built, friendships made and comrades lost. But instead they are speaking of background ethnicity, money made, titles earned.

A nation reveals itself not only by the men it produces, but also by the men it honors, the women it remembers. The Millennium to be soon celebrated is not meant for celebration, it is supposed to be REMEMBERED. Remembering the thousands of men and women who lost their lives for freedom of political history, cultural art, and life. This is a thought not a sermon!EOE.

For comments and criticism: woldetewolde@yahoo.com

Call me by my Name, Address or Title ...

NAT

By Obo Arada Shawl

June 7, 2009

On Ferenji

I am ignorant
I am ignorant, please educate me
Answer me why the C.I.A. aspire to **yoke** the Blue & Red of Aethiopia
Answer me, if you know
Why the European Parliament wish to **untie** the yoke
Tell me, if you know
Why the Asians penetrate unto us

On Nationality

I am ignorant,
Educate me why Mr. Afeworki wants me to be an Eritrean
Tell me also why Mr. Zenawi, his ally don't want me to be an Eritrean
Answer me why the Oromos want me to be an Oromian, If and when they become Independent
Not from Eathiopia but from Abyssinia
Educate me why I cannot be a Somalian
Do I have the right to be a citizen of any country?
Please tell me if I can't be

On Religion

I am ignorant,
Educate me why the Pentecostal Christian wants me to join them
Tell me if you know, why the Catholics want my misery Tell me again why the Protestants dearly love me Answer me, why the Muslims find interest in me
Educate me, why the Jewish Community admire my company
How ignorant can I be?

On Language

I am ignorant,
Answer me, if I am qualified to be an Amharic speaker
Please, tell me if I am an Amhara Answer me, what an Amhara is For I know many languages Based on languages
Where does one belong?
In America, Asia or Europe
Tell me if you know

On Politics

Strange as it may sound,
I love the sound of BR (ብቀ)
Than the BR itself (Blue and Red states)
I love EE countries, in fact everything about E Strange as it may sound, I don't like the Asian mix For I am Yoga
Connected to by land and Rainfall Connected to History and Culture (ሃቀ) I am an Eathiopian

CALL ME BY MY NAME:

Solutions with Debteraw, XIV

Obo Arada Shawl alias Wolde Tewolde

March 13, 2008

Confused or Confuser

Am I confused or a confuser (no such word is found in the English Dictionary, though)? My pen name is Obo Arada Shawl, which signifies that I stand for Rural Ethiopia, inner cities of Addis Ababa and Asmara respectively but my real name is Wolde Tewolde. Am I creating some confusion for my readers? If there is, please let me know as our given Names signify something of value.

In my previous article, actually it was a commentary on professor Mesfin Wolde Mariam who might intentionally or unintentionally lived in a confused environment or smart enough to confuse others during our lifetime. In the past, I had attempted to save Ethiopians from confusion made by a prominent Poet, deceitful geography professor and by an emotional journalist in Diaspora. I have always believed since years back that three professions (personalities) namely of Arts, Geography and Journalism can create distortion on any Ethiopian realities.

MWM (Geographer)

I do not want to go on answering the twenty questions posed to professor MWM by EthioLion.com. Besides, no one asked me to do so despite my plea. However, since the professor cannot stop meddling in the affairs of innocent Ethiopian/Eritrean lives, we have to continue to reveal and disgrace his personality a la mode of CC (combat & challenge) and TT

(Tagel & Tateq) style of struggle. CC was the name of the publication of EPRP whereas TT belonged to MEISON's. Both style of struggle were anemic to MWM. He likes Yaz & Leqeq despite his pretension as a leftist professor. When the EthioLion editor pleaded with the professor as to when to get off from the Ethiopian peoples" back, I responded that he would never do that until he finds out his DNA. When I wrote that comment I did not mean his DNA in order to find out his paternity or his criminality record. I was trying merely to locate his space in life, namely his political geography.

Now, true to my prediction, he wrote an article on Obama (see Abbaymedia.com). He labeled Obama's presidential race as a spirit. What kind of a spirit, one may ask? This kind of jumping into conclusion is what harmed our people and country. I am sure this is another blunder by the professor to be seen in the near future.

Every time there is a wind of change or a hope for change professor MWM jumps and make some serious mistakes including some irreparable damages. For instance, the professor had joined a panel of eleven PhD holders that was formed to demarcate the Ethiopian polity under the DERG. He also joined the group of so-called independent Ethiopians who went to London to witness the surrender of the Ethiopian government to EPLF/TPLF/OLF. This time, the professor had joined with three PhD holders and three Masters. One can go on listing his calculated or erratic activities. What I do not understand is why many Ethiopian intellectuals follow his example instead following the right people regardless of their titles. Call me by my name. What is my name? (Girzmatch, Kegnazmatch, etc. etc.)

I do not know whether it is true or not, but one simple explanation of the professor's attitude of character and personality is given like this.

- In his professional field, at a certain time during a proposed meeting of some local Amhara officials to be held somewhere in rural Shewa village, they did not know the location of the village and so MWM was summoned by the Emperor Haile Sellasie I in order to locate the meeting place and so the professor true to his geography knowledge pinpointed the village. From there on, the

Emperor reported to have said that „there is nothing that Mesfin does not know". Could this be a reason for his arrogance?
- In his family life, when asked why he wanted a divorce from his wife, it was circulated that he said, "Two husbands couldn't live in the same house". Let us hope that Mideksa has liberated him this time around.

Our Issue, Then

How do we handle our aspirations for Unity, Peace and Democracy? At the time when I met Debteraw, our communication was three dimensional, in religious terms (father-son-holy spirit), familial (husband-children-wife), governmental affairs (monarchy-church nobility), political (party-army-masses) and so on and so forth.

Specifically, Debteraw used to insist that the practical solution for bringing Unity-Democracy- Peace was through READ (Revolution-Education-Art-Democracia). For Debu and me the letters of A&E are one and the same (usage in pronunciation as first & fifth). However, their contents were fundamentally different from mine as AE = Arts and Education (he was excellent in Kinet and Education). For me, the letters of K& W were/are relevant as KW = Knowledge and Wisdom. Our common agreement for working together was based on Revolution and Democracia (RD). By the way every nation has progressed via Research and Development while ours was set on Revolution and Democratization.

Our Issue, Now

I do not want to go into detail as why each leader/professional, country/countries or global organizations aspire to indulge in Ethiopia or Eritrea. Suffice to indicate to my readers in a nutshell what is behind agendas of our time.

So what is our stand on these issues? What do we need to do? Let us discuss them.

On Domestic affairs

- Engineer Hailu for Costs
- Economist Berhanu for Benefits
- EPRDF/TPLF for confusion

On Foreign affairs

- USA for Strategic purpose of fighting Terrorism
- UNMEE for Employment
- AU/EU/China for Trade and Aid

Our Issue then and now

Domestic and foreign: Although all organizations, groups and individuals attempt to resolve the Ethiopian issues, they all do it in around about way. That is by switching places for the letters of U (unity), D (democracy) and P (peace). Changing names will not help to solve the problems of Ethiopia and Ethiopians. Prioritizing, yes.

EPRP for Unity, Democracia and Peace

For EPRP, it is not about prioritizing. It is about putting the three letters together. They have done this for four decades now. EPRP's main tasks as at yesterday, today and tomorrow were, are and will be as follows: -

- Visionary Solutions
- Fearless leadership and
- Timeless principles in
- Domestic and
- Foreign sectors.

What I wanted to bring to the attention to all my readers is that there is no Unity in Diversity as Debteraw has been fighting for a long time. We cannot go on using the same phrase or mission of Vive La Difference! I believe now that we have to bring <u>*Unity in Clarity*</u>. That is why I am asking intellectuals and other literate Ethiopians to expose their true nature in terms of Names, Symbol, Ritual and Values. Call me by my name? What is your name?

True to the nature of Debteraw Tsegeye's proposal for Ethiopia, I still insist to continue to dwell on the political solution based on Ethiopian History, Culture and DEMOCRACIA. He used to call this HCD. It is purely based on Ethiopian political History, Cultural and social/religious path (AAgmelago). To put it simply, let us see what has been said and presented to Ethiopians both at home and abroad.

EPRP is a unity of a political party, peace at the top of Red Mountain (<u>ASSIMBA.com & Assimba.Org</u>). Democracia in Eritrea and Ethiopia.

- *Let us share our experiences*
- *Let us write our shared experiences or perish as they say and*
- *Let us finish the Marathon of struggle with ADE*

When the war broke out between EPLF and TPLF and later agreed to settle their dispute through an arbitration but never materialized the agreement, but continue in disrupting the peoples" daily lives, I proposed in such a way that Europeans should settle in Zala Anbesa to administer them, to let America to settle in Assab so as to develop the Red Sea and to let the Chinese to let them to settle in Badme to develop agriculture. At the time, nobody heeded my call. What about now? I have now different types of proposal. Here it is.

For EPRP, Ethiopia is a **<u>Center</u>** for the Universe and Eritrea is a **<u>Key</u>** for the World.

It is about **CK. It is that simple.**

Proposal

The senator from Wisconsin, Russ Feingold described Ethiopia as demarcated/bounded by a failed state of Somalia, by an ethnic cleansing Kenya, by a genocidal Sudan and by an inaccessible authoritarian Eritrea. Of course, the senator forgot to add the country of Djoubiti. <u>*It is inconceivable without D for our project of SEEDS country.*</u>

For comments and criticism: woldetewolde@yahoo.com

CALL ME BY MY NAME:

Leadership style unfolds in Eathiopia

By Obo Arada Shawl

January 13, 2012

- EPRP leadership aimed for Ideology - Politics - Economics in the order given
- TPLF leaders aimed for Idea- Communication- wealth in that order
- EPLF leaders aimed for Faith - Love - Hope in that order
- OLF leaders aimed at DEMOCRACY – LOVE –LIBERTY in that order

Thesis

Leadership and management are two concepts sometimes interchangeable just like freedom and liberty. It has been very unfortunate that most Eathiopians have failed to recognize or deliberately avoided to differentiate these concepts.

The headlines above indicate the true path followed by each organization to liberate or democratize the country known as Eathiopia. To the naked eye or to the uninitiated, it seems that Ideology of EPRP equals to the Idea of TPLF and that the Faith of EPLF is equal to Democracy of OLF and so on and so forth, but deep inside they are far apart in consciousness than awareness. If the reader wishes to play with the equations, let him/her do so. I am just posing these equations for food of thought. The readers can challenge among themselves. For me the answer lies somewhere else.

In my previous symbol of BBB where the right hand B represents benefit: what is in there for me as being practiced by the TPLF Leadership,

B on the left represents Blood: blood is thicker than water as practiced by EPLF leadership and the middle B represents belief for freedom and democracy as practiced respectively by the leadership of EPRP and OLF.

Despite four decades of struggle for whatever term we give it (liberation, people, revolution, and front etc.etc.) we still are unable to pin down our differences. Why? We are cowards. We all confuse our folks by not telling what is in our minds. For instance, those who want benefit, why don't they say it loud and clear and those who want to help their ethnic why don't they say so. Why hit around the bush. The majority of Eathiopians are tired of hearing denials by Shaebia's supporters; lies by supporters of Woyanes and regrets by EPRP's adherents and tampering of the true nature of DEMOCRACIA by OLF followers.

Freedom in its simplest form is the opposite of FEAR. We should not camouflage it with other names and concepts. Why are the leaders of EPLF, TPLF, EPRP and OLF afraid to admit their mistakes or ignorance if there is any? After all, we all learn from our failures and not successes. *This is the thesis.*

Anti-thesis

As far as I am concerned, the EPLF leaders are afraid to admit that their colonial theory was dead wrong especially in the wake of the Ethiopian Revolution.

The TPLF leaders were totally wrong to follow and adopt the politics of EPLF and the Ideology of EPRP. TPLF leaders should not have been caught in between Revolution and Counter revolution for Peasant revolution does not last long as it did in Woyane I.

The EPRP leadership was short of explaining the role of democracy and its objective stand on peace to the Eathiopian public at large rather than its circle of influence. OLF leaders have failed to vocalize their stand to their own people as opposed to their so- called enemy.

The following authors have clearly been lost in the "jungle" of Eathiopian secrecy and conspiracy for achieving leadership style. *This is the anti-thesis.*

Synthesis

2011 is a year for the perception of EPRP's collective leadership.

Makonnen Araya (MA), an author of a book titled "Negotiating a lion's share of freedom" elucidates how the leadership of EPRP operates in their daily lives, in cooperating, leading and deciding. Ato Makonnen has vividly described the living conditions of Northern Eathiopia. It was not a living condition not to subscribe to a Revolution. The Eway Revolution was justified.

What was more significant for Ato Makonnen is the peaceful condition of leaving the on going Revolution. Mr. Makonnen has resigned from the organization of EPRP and now lives in the West Coast of the United States of America

Another book authored by Ato Ayalew Yimam narrated that he spent many years trying to find the inner core leadership of EPRP and in the end he thought he found it but it was "empty shell and does nothing except protecting its inner circle". Ato Ayalew in his book titled "Yankee, Go Home" ultimately has escaped from EPRP and currently resides in the East Coast of the United States of America.

Menghistu Haile Mariam in his book titled "Tiglachin" wrote on page 461-462 "that as usual those who decide and those who prepare the trap were EPRP's high members of leadership. Berhane Meskel Redda (BMR) and Getachew Maru did not agree to assassinate me. Menghistu believes "that EPRP members did not agree all the time including killings. This and other information were possible to get from those who rectify their decisions willingly gave their words once they returned from their party thrown and bitten by the population." Rhetoric's of Menghistu Haile Mariam, dictator vs. democracia is exposed. *This is synthesis.*

Menghistu is in Zimbabwe, Africa badly beaten and shamed of his actions. We hope we will hear more of him.

EPRP is still well and alive in its democratic struggle. It has endorsed its successor of Youth Generation known as WeKind.

On November 19, 2011 while celebrating its 39th year of anniversary of EPRP, some of its leadership members have reiterated their decision of their successors which is the main thing in the Eathiopian politics for succession.

The question is who is right in knowing the nature and style of leadership of EPRP. The answer is no one. It goes with the territory. EPRP is for DEMOCRACIA and Freedom. Freedom and democracy belongs to the Eathiopian people. As it was not for Haile Sellasie or Menghistu, it will be for neither Issaiyas nor Melese. The people will decide. *This is the conclusion.*

The Eathiopian struggle for Eway Ethiopian Revolution will continue with its unique style of leadership and membership.

TRUTH WILL PREVAIL

For comments and questions woldetewolde@yahoo.com

CALL ME BY MY NAME & ADDRESS;

A Commentary Solutions with DEBTERAW-The Burning Issue or the Entertaining issue!

November 23, 2008

- One was born in Eritrea's village dominated by Catholics and the other was born in Gonder town dominated by Orthodox Christian
- Both were Revolutionaries one in political science the other in artistic songs
- One is a professor by profession and the other a singer by trade
- Both individuals are Arada and from Arada – if you know what I mean!
- One lives in NY, where anything goes and the other lives in Addis, where everything fails.

The professor is Mesfin Araya (PhD) and the singer is Tamrat Molla (Ato). Why are you comparing these two individuals, one may ask. One of them is my friend and the other is from my Kebele. Although I have personal knowledge about them, I do not wish to write something of a personal nature. My interest in writing this article is about issues that concern all of us, old, adult or young, male or female, literate or illiterate. I believe there is a missing link between what singers grasp and what theoreticians or Revolutionaries were supposed to understand and apply.

A week ago, two events have happened, one Online Web and the other on Radio Wave. My comments might help to educate _readers_ and _listeners_. Please, read the speech and listen to the interview.

A commentary on the Professor's speech

Professor Mesfin gave a speech on the occasion of EPRP's 36th anniversary. It was true that EPRP was a vanguard for the Ethiopian Revolution, because revolution by definition was anti establishment. Notice, It was not about *change*!!! For that reason too many progressive student leaders, workers, trade leaders, teachers and progressive bureaucrats had joined the EPRP and of course, thousands if not millions had followed what EPRP was doing, saying and writing in the publication of DEMOCRACIA.

What about now? How do literate people like the professor show or lead EPRP members or supporters to get going, especially at a time when there is a rift or confusion in issues of names and addresses? A slogan to call that EPRP is the sole political leader for Ethiopia is not tenable. We do not have to be an EPRP apologist to feel a twinge of pity for the insult condemnation of the party. The Revolutionary Party had and has to tolerate all names and abuses. EPRP was and is not about leadership per se. It was about the burning issues of peace in Eritrea and dismantling the land tenure system in the rest of the country. Since all our bets were on democracy, EPRP since its inception to the current DEBTERAW's dungeon prison and beyond has not yet to be fulfilled.

What is democracy? Call me by my name and address.

"There is no river that you did not cross, no mountain that you did not climb and there is no blood that you did not split."

The above may be a figurative statement but it does not beat to the tune. The statement sounds very militaristic. It has no democratic tone.

But EPRP was and is about democracy. It is about capital D not M. In fact, the infamous slogan coined against the works of EPRP was. Those who became enemies of EPRP were not only the DERG, the EPLF or the TPLF but it was and is WE – the civil society that had difficulty in understanding FREEDOM OF CHOICE. Is this not the same thing what the current opposition groups are portraying? Democracy is not embedded in our culture. It is a cultural thing – political at that. What is democracy and what is leadership?

Suffice to say at this time that Tesfaye Debessay (PhD), a Catholic, Tsegeye G.M. aka DEBTERAW, (an Aethiopian scholar) and Osman

Ahmed (Engineer), a Muslim have worked together hand in glove with the understanding of common bond, balance and boundary (CBBB).

I do not want to go on commenting on professor Mesfin's message at this time. There are too many flaws open for argument."

EPRP had plenty of educators and Revolutionaries but not plenty of business leaders – least political leaders. AEthiopia needs high-profile politicians, intellectuals and business leaders collectively what I call.

Professionals do not wear masks, however, history and politics is their witness.

Is the professor seeing miracle or mirage? All post discussions about EPRP centered on diversity of thought and vigorous debate on issues and being able to surround oneself with people with whom you disagree without being disagreeable, because we feel that it is going to lead to a better answer. What is the better answer? That is the burning question of the time. One possible answer is how to organize. If I were the professor, I would train and organize many EPRP members and supporters in his University, which would not be difficult for him.

A commentary on the singer's speech

Although the purpose of the interview was meant to get financial and moral support for Tamrat's deteriorating health conditions, Abebe Belaw, the radio monitor, raised issues of political nature. The singer was hailed as a hero for fighting against feudal titles or feudalism.

What is Feudalism anyway?

Feudalism is a term used in the early modern 12th Century long before Gondar was founded. It has legal as well as military obligation where lords tenants (and kings live not in the political system we know today. In feudal system, on the one hand, the status of a person depended in everyway on his position on *the land*, while on the other hand, land-tenure (determined political rights and duties.

For almost 400 years, several Neighborhoods or Quarters have traditionally divided Gondarians. Those who claim power from the dynasty of king Solomon such as the Hamasiens and the Shewans usually had no fixed capital. By 1635 FASSILIDES had founded his rule at Gondar.

Gondar became an old imperial capital of the historic BEGEMDIR (the land of the Beja tribe). For a singer as Tamrat feudalism may be difficult to define precisely as a working definition. I have no doubt though that Tamrat knew the social aspect of feudalism.

EPRP has defined feudalism by analogy as Semi-Feudal where there were (███████ aristocrats erfs in practically in all northern Ethiopia and landlords and tenants in the rest of the country. In short, oppression (███) and exploitation (has become the norm in Tamrat's days. He has seen it in Gondar and he has seen it in Addis Ababa being practiced.

In order to alleviate the political oppression and the economic exploitation, EPRP with its committed and dedicated members and supporters had gone into a territory where no man has gone before so to speak. The liberated and the conscious Gondarians fought Melaku Teffera to the bitter end.

Singer Tamrat – though technically rebelled against his father, he did not rebel against *the root causes of the problem*. His song was just a reflection of the popular demand of the time, after all art is the reflection of the populace.

I have attended the ratification of the DERG's Constitution in our Kebele. The meeting was scheduled to last for four hours. The Kebele cadres spoke for half of the time only on and Tamrat was the top speaker on the issue of DIKALa. No wonder the DERG has to collapse on its own merit. Later on, we have learnt why the issue had become important as Menghistu Haile Mariam begotten a child out of wedlock. One wonders where this child is today.

The point I am trying to make is that the singer did not or could not have played a role model for eliminating feudalism. He was only an instrument who did not understand the feelings of his father let alone the source of feudalism. By the way EPRP has never fought a cultural war. It was very careful not to indulge on people's culture. On the contrary, many individuals assumed names of minorities to diffuse oppression. I believe the famous name Hama Tuma must have come to be something to do with it.

Concluding Remarks: One-Seven-Eleven

I have always believed in the process of democratization, which incorporates, conceptualizing- designing-planning-programming and budgeting (5 tasks).

In EPRP's lexicon, (5).

Alternatively,

- Information officer
- Organizer
- Strategist
- Manager and
- Leader

And by slow accretion of small changes over long periods, EPRP's vision, mission and value has taken place as Professor Mesfin has pointed out in his speech. But it should be remembered that the contribution of EPRP was undoubtedly via DEMOCRACIA – the rule of the people, by the people for the people. Democracy is not about division; it is about Unity in a unique way.

Neither the type of call by the professor nor the claim of the singer is warranted.

DEBTERAW has shown us all those Revolutionary steps progressively for almost 40 years and we should continue to uphold if we so desire to unite the whole country known as AETHIOPIA. DEMOCRACIA is the way and let us choose to pick one or two tasks as specified above but not grapping all of them at the same time.

For comments and questions: woldetewolde@yahoo.com

CHALLENGING EATHIOPIANS ON THE FOURTH OF JULY!!!

SOLUTIONS WITH DEBTERAW, XI Call me by my name, address and title -

July 4, 2009

In the recent past months, there is a simmering movement towards settling scores of politicking between Eritreans and Ethiopians. Such instances are

- Federation vs. Confederation
- A repeat of the slogan for struggle via "Bale or Bole" (EDIAL)
- Formation of a youth league for EPRP
- Crying wolf by the leaders of Shaebia and Woyane for Unity and Power Abdication
- A promise to reveal the existence of the Ark of Covenant by the an Ethiopian Cleric and so on and so forth…

All the above could be taken as a sign for positive thinking for final arrest to the Eway Revolution.

However, on close analysis, there are very important elements "missing" from these movements.

Scenario one: In the designs of God and in the eyes of men, "all men not women were created equal" Who created Eathiopians? Or alternatively, what is the day or the date for the INDEPENDENCE of Eathiopia? Miazia 27, Meskerem 2, May 24 or July 4? Do we really understand the meaning of Independence, Freedom or Liberty in the context of Eathiopia? Is this enough to be a challenging question? If there was no beginning date for Colonialism, we should not look for one as Independence.

Let us start with July 4, 1776. Was this date and year the Independence Day for America? Was this calendar an adoption or Declaration of Independence? If we know the answer to this question, I hope Eathiopians will come to their senses to talk about arnet or nezanet. አርነት: ነፃነት common terminology. Who struggled for what and for whom?

The Eritreans might have mismatched the Italian Colonialism to Ethiopian Colonialism that did not exist. I believe their long struggle was for freedom and liberty and not for Independence. If it was for Independence, it must be an independence from Italy. This should be the topic for reconciliation. Ethiopians should accept the independence of Eritrea and Eritreans in return would accept that their Independence Day was a culmination of European colonialism. This should be the challenging question before moving on to the next movement.

Scenario two: Sports and Entertainment do not seem to be part of these movements. The fact that the soccer players from Eritrea and Ethiopia crisscross in order to avoid each other instead of coming together. This year for instance, Ethiopians are in Chicago, Eritreans are in California and the Oromos will held their own on Atlanta, Georgia.

On the one hand, The Eritrean soccer federation does seem to grasp neither the adoption nor the declaration of Eritrean/American Independence. The Federation was hiding or rather sandwiched between the day of the Martyrs and the day of Family/Religious Festival known as ንግደት. I do not believe that their agenda was and is about sportsmanship. If it is, we have not seen it yet.

While on the other hand, The Ethiopian Sports Federation was/is not participating in the agrarian societies where food is plenty with missing "sportsmanship and comradeship". The Ethiopian Sports Federation was in a unique position in the sense that political groups, business people and civic communities gather in one place. Unfortunately, a quarter of a century has passed without making significant contributions to either development or cooperation among people of all walks of life from Ethiopia.

Can any one explain this anomaly of our struggle for change and revolution? Art, Entertainment and Sports industry should take center stage for reconciliation and development. Without these three sectors of Industry, little will be accomplished in the case of Eritrea and Ethiopia let alone in the Horn of Africa.

A reminder to all Revolutionaries of Eway Ethiopia

- You were involved in the struggle to bring *peace and democracy*
- You had the courage to fight for your *Rights*
- You were imprisoned for your *thoughts*
- You died for your *beliefs* and
- You are going to die for your Blue and Red Nation (**BRN**) but not for your currency (BR) A message to all anti-Eway Revolution
- Forgive and move on
- Stand for Eathiopia
- Ask questions of why and how
- Differentiate between Tabot and Constitution

Then

- Tell the truth for it will set you free
- Confess to not only to your God but to your fellowmen
- Speak to Power without fear
- Dare to be open to disclose your ID
- Search for the whereabouts of DEBTERAW

Why DEBTERAW?
For DEBTERAW is the one who taught us that

R is for REVOLUTION Not for RACE
E is for Eritrea and Ethiopia
Not for ETHNICITY

·

That is why we should re-examine the *RE as a subject not as a predicate.*
In short let us all TAKE THE HEAT FOR OUR INALIENABLE RIGHTS LET US TAKE A STAND FOR OUR DEMANDS not dreams
TAKE THE HEAT FOR OUR INALIENABLE RIGHTS LET US TAKE A STAND FOR OUR DEMANDS
Happy Four to all!!!

ማን ያቸንፋሌ፧ Colts versus Saints?
ሽጉጦች ወይስ ቅደሶች? እምነ ት ወይስ ሀይማኖት?

ከአብ አራዲ ሻውሌ 3-3-10

መግቢያ

በአንዶ በኩሌ፣ በስሜ ሌጡራ፣ መፍትሔ ከቶብተራው ጋራ በሚሌ ርእስ ስጽፍ ሰነ ባብቻሁሁ፣ ሆኖም አመርቂ የሆነ ነ ቀፌታም ሆነ ምስጋና አሊገኘሁበትም አግኛች ከሆነ ም አሊውቀውም።

ጽሐፌ ያተኩር የነ በረው በምሁራኖች በተሆይም ,በአካዲሚያ' ማዕረጋቸው ብቻ ሆመጠራት የሚሽቀዲዮሙእንዮነ ድ/ር፣ አንጀነ ር፣ ኤኮኖሚስት ወዐተ ነ ኝ እየተባባሳ ምያውነና ጥበቡ ሳይኖራቸው በንደፈ ሒሳብ (ቴዎሪ) ብቻ እየተነ ደከመፍትሔ ይሌቅ ሙግትነ የሚያስቀደሙግኡዜ ምሁራንን ከጽንሒተ ምሁራን (ረሰርችርስ) አጋር በመሆን በኤትዮጵያ ምዴር ሆሚዮረገው የ_ሥርዓት(Eway Revolution) ሆውጥ ይረዲሌ ከሚሌ በጎ አስተሳሰብ የመነ ጨነ በር። ነ ውም።

በላሊ በኩሌ ዮግሞ በመኑ እየተቀያየረ ስሆነ መረጃ ,አንጽርመሽን' ብቻውን ብቁ ስሊሌሆነ ማሆት ጌዛው ያሆፈበት ስሆነ በእውቀትና በጥበቡ መራመዴ ስሆአስፌሆግ ሆዙሁም የሚረዲ የእንግሉዜኛ ቁነቁ ስሆነ በእንግሉዜኛው

ቁንቁ ቢጻፍ ሆአሁኑና ሆመጫው ትውሌዴ ጠቀሜታ ይኖረዋለ በሚሌ ግንዚቤ ነ በር።በተጨማሪም መዜገብ ቃሌቶቻችን ሆማሳዮግ።

በሽጉጦች ወይስ በቅደሶች?
በዙህ ጽሐፌ የዚሬ ሶስት ሳምንት እሁዴ ቀን ማሆትም እንዮ ኮኔ አቆጣጠ 02-07-10
ስሆተዮረገው 44ኛው (XLIV) የሱፐር ባውሌ ፉትቦሌ አስመሌክቶ ነ ው። በአሜሪካ ታሪክ ውስጥ ወዮ 107 ሚሉዮን ገዮማ የቲቪ ፕሮግራም ተመሌካች የሳበ ጨዋታ ነ በር።

በዙሁ ጨዋታ ሳቢያ ምክንያት አባቶች ያስተሊሆፉሌን አስተሳሰብ (የሚታረሙውን አርመን?) ሆመጫው ትውሌዴ ትምህርት ይሆናሌ ብዬ ስሆ አሰብኩ እነ ሆ መሌእክቱ እንዮሚከተሆው ቀርበዋለ።

የዚሬ አርባ ዓመት ገዮማ ሆሱራ ጉዳይ አሥመራ ሄጀ ስሆ ነ በር አባቴ በጦርነ ቱ ምክንያት ከዓደ (አገሩ) ተፈናቅሌ አሥመራ ከተማ አገኘሁት። በዚዛው የጠዮቀኝ ጥያቄ እንዱህ ነ በር። ,ራዱዮን ሲያወራ አንዴ ሰው በቶረቱ ዴንጋይ ያስፈሌጣሌ፣ ምሊጭ ይበሊሌ፣ አሜሪካኖች ጨርቃ ሊይ አረፉ፡ የሚሌ ነ በር። ምንም መሌስ ሳሌሰጥ ,ይህ ሁሉ ውሸት ነ ው፡ ብሌ ሲጨርስ ,እነ ሆ አሁን ቶግሞ የውንዴሜ ሌጅ 'ጀሆሽው' ሆነ ዋለ
መሰሆኝ መስቀለን አይሳሆምም ያሁው አነትስ፡ ብሌ መስቀለን ሲያወጣው ቾሌ ብዬ, መስቀለ በእንቲአነ ።መስቀለ ቤዚነ ' እያሌኩ ስሳሆም ያሆ ቃሆ- አጋኖ ጠፍተው የነ ብሩ ዓይኖቼ በሩ። የመጨረሻ የተሰናበትኩት በዙሁ ሁኔታ ነ በር።

ነ ገሩ እንዱህ ነ ው። ዴንጋይ የሚስፈሌጠው ሰውዬ በዮሴ ከተማ በአንዴ ሆቴሌ ውስጥ ተከራይተነ ነ በር። ካራንቡሉችንን ከተጨውትን በኋሊ ዴንጋዮን በቶረቱ አስፈሌጡናሌ።
የጨርቃ ጉዳይም በኪሴ መጽሐፍት ይዝሆሁ ፣ ,የሰው ሌጅ ጨርቃ ሊይ አረፈ፡ የሚሌ ሽፋን ነ በረበት።

ይህ ሁኔታ በእምነ ት ወይም በሃይማኖት፣ በሰሊም ወይም በግጭት ወይም ቶግሞ በሊሊ የቅራኔ አፈታት ተመሌክታችሁ መሌሱ ሆእናነ ተ አንባቢያን እተውቫሆሁ።

ይህንን ታሪክ ሀሌጀ ስነ ግሩው በፍጹም ትርጉም የሆሽ ይሆንበት ነ በር እስከ አሁፈው የ44ኛው (XLIV) የሱፐር ቦሌ ጨዋታ ዴረስ።

የፉትቦሌ ሙሉውን ጨዋታ ሃመጀመሪያ ጊዜ ከሌጀ ጋር ሆኜ አየሁት። ሌጀ ጨዋታው ሳይጀመር ማን ያቸንፋሌ ብሎ ጠየቀኝ።

ሌጀ፡ ማን ያቸንፋሌ?

አባት፡ ማንና ማን ናቸው?

ሌጀ፡ Colts against Saints (ኮሌትsና ሳይንትስ) አባት፡ ይኸማ ምን ይጠየቃሌ፤ ቾል ብዬ ሳይንትስ አሌኩት ሌጀ፡ ሆምን?
አባት፡ ከሽጉጥና ከመስቀሌ ማን ያቸንፋሌ ትሆኛሀህ? ሆነ ገሩ አንተ 'ጄንጤ' መሰሌከኝ፤ ነ ሀ እንዳ?

ሌጀ፡ ብሆንስ?

አባት፡ በመስቀሌ አታምንማ!

ሌጀ፡ መሊእክት መስቀሌ ይሸከማሌ እንዳ?

አባት፡ ታዬያ ሽጉጥ የሚታጠቁ ይመስሀሌ?

ሌጀ፡ በፈገግታ , በቾልታ ከሆነ ፤ ባሀሽጉቶች ነ ው የሚያሸንፉት አንተ በምትሆው ግና ቅደሳን ናቸው የሚቀናቸው ሆነ ገሩማ እኔም የሳይንትስ ቶጋፈ ነ ኝ ብልኝ አረፈ።

በመጨረሻው ውጤቱ እንዮተጠበቀው ሆኖ፤ በእረፍት ጊዜ 10-3 በሆነ ውጤት አሆቀ። በ13 የተሆከፍኩ መሆኔን ሌጀ አውቆ ኖሪዋሌ መሰሌ በውጤቱ ሳይገረም የቀረ አይመስሆኝም።
J=10 : C=3 JC=13= Jesus Christ ብሆህ አይዮሌ የምትቦረዜርው ብል አስቶነ ገጠኝ። ሌጀ እኔ የምጽፈው ሆነ የምሰራው የሚያውቅ አይመስሆኝም ነ በር ምክንያቱም የአሁኑ በመን ሌጀቻችን እኛ እናውቃሆን፤ እናንተ ሸማግሆዎች ምን እንቶምትሌና እንዳት እንቶምታስቡ ግራ ስሆሚያጋባ ነ ው እያሌ ከወሌጀቻቸው ስሆሚርቁ አውቅ ስሆ ነ በር ነ ው።

ሆማን ኛውም መቶበኛ ጨዋታው ካሆቀ በኋላ ሰፋ ባሆ መንገዴ ስሆ የአሜሪካ ፉትቦሌ ጨቃታ አስረዳኝ። ከዜርዘሩ ባጨሩ እነ ሆ

'ዴሪው ብሪስ የሚባሆው አቀባበይ ተጨዋች (Quarterback) ቀቶም ብል ሆሳንዱያን ቻርጀር ሲጨወት የሚወረውርበት እጁ ተጎዲ።በዙሁ ምክንያት የፉትቦሌ ሙያው ተብሊሽ ተብል ተገመተ። የሚቀጥረውም ጠፋ። ነ ገር ግን አሊባማ ስቴትስ ሄድ የእጅ ጥገና አዮረገ።

የእግዚአብሔር ጉዲይ ሆኖ በሊሊ በኩሌ ቶግሞ አሠሌጣኙ ሺያን ፓይተን (Coach) ሆመጀመሪያ ገዘ የአሠሌጣኝት ቦታ ተሰጥቶት የቅደሳት (saints) ቡዴን አሠሌጣኝ (coach) ሆኖ ተቀጠረ።

አሠሌጣች ብሪስን ,እኔና አንተ ሆነ ን ይህ የወቶቀ ቡዴንና በካቴሪና ምክንያት የወቶቀ እስቴት ከወቶቀበት እናንሳው፡ ተባብሆው እነ ሆ ከአራት ዓመት በኋላ ሆዙሁ ታሊቅ ዴሌ በቁ። ብል አስረዳኝ።በ2009 ውዴዴር ሲጆምሩ 13 ጨዋታ በማቸን ፍ ሆጥል ማሆፍ
አንቶኛ ሠፍራ ይበው ነ ው ያሆፉት።

እንግዱሁ ብዘዋቻችሁ እንዲያችሁት በመተማመን ብሪስ የተናገረው እንዱሁ የሚሊ ነ በር።
,ይህ የእግዚአብሔር ጥሪ ነ ው።' የሕጸን ሌጁ ዓመት በዚው ዕሆት ስሆዋሆ ብሪስ ሌጁን በማቀፍና በመሳም አከበረ። የኒው ኦርሉንስ ከተማም ፈነ ቶቀች።
ካተሪና
ተቸን ፈች፤ ዓሆምም ትምህርት አገኛች።በሰይንትስ ቡዴንና በገሌፍ ባሕር ሰሊጤ እና
በኒው ኦርሉንስ ከተማ ውሆቶት ተፈጠሩ። ተስፋ፤ ሀሌም እና ትግሌ ተቀናጁ። ኢትዮጵያም ከምትከተሆው ብሌሹ ሥርዓት የሚያዴናት ይሆን? ማን ያውቃሌ?

በእምነ ት ወይስ በሀይማኖት?
መስቀለ ምንን ያሙሆክታሌ? ሆምንስ በኢትዮጵያ ወሌ ክፍሆ ሀገር ውስጥ ሆምን ቀራጨ አሆ? የጉራጌ ብሔረ ሰብስ ሆምን መስቀለን በከፍተኛ ቶረጃ ሉያከብሩው ተነ ሳ? መስቀለ የሚጠሊ ወይ የሚፈራ ነ ገር ሆኖ ነ ው? ወይንስ ጌታ ሲሰቃይ ሊሆማየት በሚሊ ሰበብ
ነ ው? እኔ አሊውቅም።

ጄሆሻዎቹ መስቀልን እንሆ ሹጉጥ ነ ው የሚያዩት ማሆትም የግዲያ መሳሪያ ብሆው ስሆሚቆጥሩት አያምኑበትም፡፡ ጸንጤዎቹ ቶግሞ መስቀሌ የሃይማኖት ጉዲይ ስሊሌሆን በቀጥታ

እየሱስን ማግኛት ስሆሚቻሌ መስቀል የመገናኛ መሳሪያ አይሆም ይሊሌ፡፡በሊሊ አነ ጋገር እየሱስ ሲነ ሳ እንጂ ሲሞት ማዩት ይሳናቸዋሌ፡፡ የአሁን ወጣት ኤትዮጵያዊ ፖሆቲከኛ ዓይነ ት፣ ስሆ አሳሆፋችሁት ስቃይ አትንገሩን ባዮች፡፡

እንዮን አባቴ እምነ ት ከሆነ ግና መስቀሌ እግዘአብሔር ሆሰው ሌጅ ሆማስተማርና ሆማዲነ አንደ ሌጃን ሌኮ በእኩያን ሰዎች ሲሰቃይ በባይናችን አይተነ ሁሊም አምሊክን እንዴስታዉሰው እና እንዲንረሳው ይመስሆኛሌ፡፡

በተጨማሪም ሆእንዮን አባቴ ቀይ፣ብጫ፣ እና አረንጓዳ ሰንቶቅ የቤተ ክርስቲያን አርማ እንዮመሆኑ ሌክ እንጉ መስቀል ከእግዘአብሔር ጋር ቃሌ ኪዲነ ሆመግባት የሚጠቀምበት

የመገናኛ መሳሪያቸው ነ በር እንጂ እንዮአሁኑ ፖሆቲከኞች ባንዲራ የኔ ነ ው ያንት አይቶሆም እያ ሕዘብ ከሕዘብ የሚያፋጅ መሆነ አሌነ በረበትም፡፡

በእኛ አብዮት እምነ ት ከሆነ ቶግሞ እንቶሚከተሆው ይሆናሌ፡፡
የኤትዮጵያ አብዮት የመሩት ጉዶች የኢየሱስን ትምህርታዊ አካሄዴ ሲያስተምሩ ሁሰቃይ እንቶሚቼሊ እያወቁ ትግሊን ሆኤትዮጵያ ሕዘብ ሲሊ ተሰውተዋሌ፡፡
ነ ገር ግና በአሁኑ
ጊዘ እንቶ ሞኞች እየተቆጡሩ ይነኛሊ እንዴያውም አሌፍ ተርጄ መቀጣት አሆባቸው የሚሊም አሌ፡፡ የዙሁ አቀንቃኝ የሆነ አንዲንዴ ያጄንጤ ተከታዎች እኛ ብቻ ነ ን
ያትግሊቹሁነ ፍሬ መብሊት ያሆብነ እያ ይነኛሌ፡፡ የክርስቶስ መስቀሌና መነ ሳት
የአንዴ ሳንቲም ሁሆት ገጽታ መሆናቸውነ ይረሳሌ፡፡ በዓሆማዊ አነ ጋገር
ያሞተሌሽ ቀርቶ የገቶሆሽ በሊ አባባሌ ነ ው፡፡

አስተሳሰብ/ውይይት
ቶብተራው ሆይማነቶኛ ነ በር? ብሆው የሚጠይቁኝ አሊ፡፡ መሌሴ የሆም አማኝ ነ በር ስሊቸው
ክሬዙ ብሆው ይተዉኛሌ፡፡

ብዞ ጊዜ ሰዎች ኢትዮጵያውያን ሀይማኖት ተቆች ናቸው ብሆዉ ሲገልጹልኝ እሰማሀሁ። በእኔ አስተያየት ግና አይዮሆንም ነ ውᎅ ብዞ ኢትዮጵያውያን መጽሐፍ ቅደስ ሊሆማንበብ ዋና ጉዳያቸው አዴርገውት ነ በርᎅ ክርስቶስ ባስተማረው ትምህርት ሊይ ብቻ እያተኮርን በባሕሊዊና በኦርቶድክሳዊ ቤተክርስቲያን አስተምሮ እንዴናተኩር ሆነ ናሌᎅ ይህ መጥፎ
ነገር ነ ው ወይስ ሸጋ ጉዳይᎅ እንወያይበትᎅ

ሃመሆኑ በሀይማኖትና በእምነ ት ያሀው ሌየነ ት ምንዴን ነ ው?
በእንግሉቦኛ መዝገበ ቃላት ብዞ ዘርዘር መግሀጨአሀ። የተፈጥሮ ሀይማኖት፣
የተዋሕድ ሀይማኖት፣ የራዕይ ሀይማኖት፣ የአይሁዴ ሀይማኖት፣ የጣዖት
ሀይማኖት፣ የኤትክስ ሀይማኖት የመሳሰለት ሁለ ይገኛለᎅ

እነ ዙህ ሀይማነ ቶች ከእምነ ት ጽንሰ ሐሳብ ጋር ተቃራኒ ናቸውᎅ
እምነ ት እምነ ት ነ ውᎅ ፌዜ=ብሎፍ (Faith-Belief) የግሌ ነ ውᎅአንዴን
ግሆ-ሰብ
ጥንካሬው የሚቴካው በዙሁ ነ ውᎅ ሀይማኖት ግና ብዞዙን ተሰባሰበው
በአንዴ ሊይ ማመንን ይሆዋሌᎅ

ሀይማኖት የሚያስፈሌገው እምነ ትን ሆመቆጣጠር ነ ውᎅ እምነ ት ቶግሞ
በበኩለ ሀይማኖትን ሆመግታታ ነ ውᎅ በላሊ አነ ጋገር ሀይማኖት የሰው ሌጅ
እግዙአብሔርን ሆማግኘት (Reach Out) የሚያመሊክት ትርጓሜ ሲኖረው
እምነ ት ግና እግዙአብሔር መቀበሌን ያሙሆክታሌᎅ

አሁንም በላሊ አነ ጋገር እምነ ት የመጨረሻ ግብ አይዮሆምᎅ በቀለለ አማርኛ
እውነ ት
፣የአእምሮ ቅበሊ፣ ጉዳይ ነ ውᎅ

ሀይማኖት ግዲማዊ (ውጨዊ) ነ ገር ነ ውᎅ እምነ ት ቶግሞ እኛኑ ምንነ
ታችን የሚገለጽ ይሆናሌᎅ ሀይማኖት እምነ ታችን የምንገሌጸበት ባሕሊዊ
ሌምድችን ይጨምራሌᎅ

እምነ ት የእውነ ትን መሰረታዊ ግንዚቤያችን ነ ውᎅ ዓሀምን በምን መነ ጸር
እንዮምንረዲት፣ ሆያትቆቹ እሴቶች ቅዴሚያ እንዮምንሰጣቸው፣ የትቆቹ
ቅደሳት፣ የትቆቹስ ሀቅ ወይ

ውሸት፣ ምንስ ሆማግኛት ብሆን ነ ው የምንኖረው ሆሚሆው ሁሊ መፍትሔ ሰጪነ ው።

እንዞ እኔ ከሆነ የኢትዮጵያ ተዋሕዶ ክርስቲያን ሃይማኖት አይኦሆም ምክንያቱም የሰው ሌጅ ሙከራው ዎ እግዚአብሔር ሆመዴረስ የሚያፍርገው ጥረት ሳይሆን እግዚአብሔር ራሱ ሆሰው ሌጅ እንዶሚኦርስ እምነ ተ-ኢትዮጵያውነ ት ስሆሆነ ነ ው።

የኦርቶድክስ እምነ ት በግሌ የተመሰረተ በፈጣሪው (እግዚአብሔር) እና በተፈጠረው የሰው ሌጅ የሚያተኩር ስሆመሆነ ይመስሆኛሌ።

የኢየሱስ ክርስቶስ ጉዳይም በሕይወት-በሞትና በመነ ሳት ያሆ ክስተት ስሆሆነ ኢትዮጵያውያን ወዴቀው እንዮሚነ ሱ እሙን ነ ው።

በአሁኑ ጊዜ ምን መኦረግ አሆበት?
መስቀሌ ምንዴን ነ ው? ሆክርስቲያን ሕዜብ ምንን ያመሆክታሌ? ባሆፈው ሳምንት ሆምሳሌ የአሜሪካን ም/ፕረሲዮንት ሚስተር ጀ ባይኦን በግንቦራቸው አመዬ ተቀብተው በጋዛጦ ታይተዋሌ። አመዴ የመስቀሌ ሳይሆን አይቀርም፣ አቶ ባይኦን የካቶሉክ ተከታይ ናቸውና።

አባቴ መስቀሌን ያሳሆመኝ ዋናው ምክንያት መስቀሌ ‚ቃሌ በቃሌ‛ ሁያዴነ ን ሳይሆን በምግባራችን እንኦ ‚ምሌክት/ኦርማ‛ ማሆት እንኦ ባንዴራ በዕሆቱ የሰው ሌጅ ቸግርን መቁቁም እንኦሚያስሌገው ክርስቶስም በመስቀሌ ምክንያት መሸከምም ሆነ በመስቀሌ እንኦ ሰው እንዴናውቀው ተብሌ ነ ው። አሁን በፈሌምና በቴሊቪጅን እንኦሚያሳዩን ዋይነ ት።

በኢትዮጵያ ኮሚኒቲ አካባቢ የአቶ ሀይሆ ገሪማንና የአቶ ዓሉ ሁሴን የስቃይ ፈሌም እያየነ ነ ው። ከፈሌሙእየተማርን ነ ው ወይስ እያመን? መሌሱ ሆአንባቢያን።

እኔ ቶግም ከአባቴ በሳይንስ ሂሳብ አስቤ ሉሆመጣሉት ሆመግባባት ስሌ ዜም ብዬ ስሆ ዮንጋይ አስፈሉጨና ጨርቃ ሉይ ማረፍ ሌከራክረው አሌፈሌገሁም፣ በጊዛው አያስፈሌግም ነ በር።

ያሁኑ ሌጆ ,ጄንጤ' ነ ህ ስሆው ብሆንስ ማሆቱ መብቱ ነ ው። ሌታስተምረኝ አትችልም ሌትመርጥልኝ አትችልም የሚሌ ስሆሆነ ሆማብራራት አሌፈሆግኩም። አያስፌሌግም።
,ሀይማኖት የግሌ ነ ው አገር ግና የጋራ ነ ው' ተብል የሆ።

መጥምጥሚያ
ኤትዮጵያውያን በምን ምክንያት ነ ው ሏስማሙያሌቻለት ሆሚሆው ጥያቄ እንዶሚከተሆው ሆምግሆጽ ተሞክሯሌ።ጽንሰ ሄሳቡ የተወሰዮው ከሪክ ዋረን (በፐረሲዮንት አባማ ምረቃ ጊዘ ቃሌ-ቡራኬ የሰጡቄስ ናቸው) መጽሏፍ ነ ው።

አንዶኛ፤ በጥፋታችውና በፀታችው ምክንያት ከጥፋታችው እየሽሹ ወይም ከአፍረታቸው እተቀበቁ ይገኛል ይሌ። በአሁን ጊዘ በርከት ያለ ኤትዮጵያውያን ቶግሞ በፀፀትም በአፍረትም ምክንያት ነ ገሮችን እያባባሱ ናቸው ።

ሁሆተኛ፤ በይቅርታ ጥሊቻችውንና ንዳታችውን እንዲያበርዶ እየጦጋሙባቸሆው ጊዛያቸው ሁኔታችውንና ዶርጊታችው በቸንቅሊታችው ተሽክመው በውስጣቸው እያሩ ወይም እኖ በንብ እየፈነ ዶ ናቸው ይሌ።በጥሊቻና በንዳት ስሆሚነ ዶ ኤትዮጵያውያንም በብዚት አለ።

ሶስተኛ፤ በፍርሀት እየተነ ዶ አስከፊ ሙከራ፤ ያሌጠበቁት ሁኔታ፤በእምነ ት ና በፍቅር ወዮሪት መራመዶ ስሆአቃታቸው ነ ው ይሌ ቄስ ዋረን።

ኢሕአፓ ፍትህ ሆማስገኝት ብል ብዘ አባልቹና ቶጋፊቹ ስቃይ ስሆዮረስባቸው ፤ ኤርትራዊያን አርነ ታቸውን ሆማኘት ሲባሌ ብዘ መስዋእትነ ት ከፈለ፤ ነ ጻነ ታችው ካገኙ በኋሊ ቶግሞ ያሌተጠበቀ በባዶሚ ጦርነ ት ሳቢያ ብዘ ⬜መዶ አዘማዶ ስሆተሰዋባቸው። ብዘ ኤትዮጵያውያን ቀይ ባሕር ,ያኛ ባሕር ነ ው' ብሆው እምነ ት ስሆነ በረባቸው ቀይ ባሕርን ሆማስጠበቅ ሲሊ ብዘ ብዘ መስዋእት ከፍሆዋሌ። በዙሁ ሳቢያ ፍቅርና እምነ ት ስሆጠፉ ብዘ ኤትዮጵያውያንን ቸግር ሊይ ናቸው።

አራተኛ፤ በፍቅር ንዋይ ሆተጠመዶ እዶሜያቸውን ሙለ ሆመበሌጸግ ብዘ ቶስታ ሆማግኝት፤ ብዘ ሀብት የበሆጠ ቶሀንነ ት ስሆሚሰጣቸው ስሆፈሆጉ። ,ስግብግብነ ት' ብቻውን ጊዛዊ ቶስታ መሆኑን ስሆማይገነ

በቡ ፤ ሀራስህ ዋጋ መስጠትና ሆንብረትህ ዋጋ መስጠት ሌየነ ት እንዲሆው ስሆማያውቁ ብዘ ችግር ውስጥ ይወፈቃላ ይሊለ ቄስ ዋረን፡፡ በእኛ አገር ቶግሞ፣ ሆምሳለ የወያኔ መሪዎችን አርአያ ት ይመሆከተዋሌ፡፡

አምስትኛ፤ መፍትሔው ከእግዘአብሔ ጋር ግንኙነት ሆኖ ሳሆ ፍሊገቻቸው የተመሰረተው ሁላም በላልች አሆኝታ ስሆሚሆን ክፍተኛ ችግር ይገጥማቸዋሌ፡፡ቄስ ሪክ ዋረን .በአለማ ሊይ ያተኮረ ሕይወት' በሚሌ መጽሀፋቸው እንዮ መፍትሔ ገሌጸውታሌ፡፡

እንዮዙሁም በእኛ ኮሚኒቲ ብዘ ሕዜብ ,ወገንተኛነ ትን' ሲያጠቃው ይታያሌ፡፡ምናሌባትም ከእምነ ት ወይ ከሀይማኖት ጉዴሆት ሳይሆን አይቀርም በሚሌ ተስፋ ይህንን ሆውይይት አቀረብኩ፡፡ ከዕውቀት ማነ ስ ከሆነ ቶግሞ ይቅርታ እጠይቃሆሁ፡፡

ጥያቄ ወይም አስተያየት ካላችሁ

For comments and questions: woldetewolde@yahoo.com

DEBTERAW

–Missing Link or PersonFootprints of Assimba–

Debteraw and Wallelign, I

By Obo Arada Shawl January 13, 2010

TPLF's chaotic style versus EPRP's party substance

On the eve of the departure of the Monarch, Emperor Haile Selasie, everybody and everyone was excited for a big change of leadership including the King of Kings, himself.

The educated class of M'huran and the Tsinhate M'huran collided head on ideological as well as on the political agendas for Ethiopia. But for the average man or woman, there was no difference between the two concepts of – ideology & politics. Instead of battling on the concepts for change, both sides of MEISON and EPRP mainly fought over the question of legitimacy for political power and over the merits and demerits of Military rule.

MEISON (All-Ethiopia Socialist Movement), EPRP (Ethiopian People's Revolutionary Party) were the two contenders to teach and disseminate the power of ideology and politics to Eathiopians. On that account both have succeeded to a certain degree.

Notwithstanding their accomplishment, today both organizations have failed to rescue their leadership. I am referring to the leadership defined by Abera Yemaneab of MEISON who has been kept in EPRDF's prison indefinitely and DEBTERAW's hostage drama kept incommunicado in Woyane's base camp.

As a movement, MEISON is finished. It has no mass base as the "educated class", the class that was associated as an instrument for the DERG's inhumanity, headed it.

And the DERG is finished on its own merit. Technically both MEISON and the DERG were counter-revolutionaries disguised in revolution.

The Nationalists of TPLF and EPLF were not revolutionaries either. Every single action associated either with the TPLF or EPLF has grown more unpopular over the years.

When we look back since the TPLF's coming to power, the Ethiopians, initially the Eritreans, then most of the ethnic societies were motivated by TPLF's campaign for electoral politics. There was no substance but style.

All along, EPRP was informing and acting against the chaotic role of relationship and governance of the TPLF. Nevertheless, its enthusiasts adopted TPLF's methodology of fabrication and maneuvering.

In contrast, opposition parties, many of them as fractious and outspoken have become interested in substantive political issues. They decry the dangers of selling/leasing lands, about Article 39, arresting opponents and censoring/shutting mass media.

Their concerns are valid. These are public issues of fundamental importance.

The Unfinished Revolution

EPRP stands for the entire Eathiopian population for the peasants as well as for the urban dwellers. It does this by promoting peace and harmony among peoples and nations through the process of democratization.

The Eathiopians have turned decisively against the class of M'hur Akal and against all its theoretical/ideological works. At the same time, the Eathiopian public has moved against Melles and the Issais regimes that began their popularity soared but now sunk to low level of approval.

Both Melles and Issais epitomizes as products purchased by consumers and has come to regret it and that the consumer want their money back.

In a sense, both leaders have never been more than their education although for some people was more than enough. Both leaders have neither experience nor accomplishments for their positions they are in.

Their accomplishments should be reexamined against their stand on global trade, global culture, global climate or religion.

On domestic issue, for Eritreans, there is no room for fake elections, no free market and no free lunch.

Our M'hur Akal is educated beyond its intelligence. Their resolution, moral clarity and an ability to understand and to connect with great many people are unknown. Only the Tsi'nhate M'hur Akal has not been fooled itself for which their country and its people will not forget.

TPLF and EPLF have misjudged the times and the country of Eathiopia. Thanks for the seeds of Assimba; the long struggle of DEBTERAW and the spirit of Wallelign live on.

The Eway Ethiopian Revolution

The Eway Revolution is a search engine and it is the path that DEBTERAW and his Revolutionary Party followed. The base is Assimba mountain, it is being negotiated by DEBTERAW's life and death situations and finally reaching the goal of Wallelign to become one strong, stable, democratic and open society in the name of Eathiopia.

DEBTERAW is more than an individual person. He is the missing link in the Eway

Ethiopian Revolution – a revolution that has changed Ethiopia forever and for better.

TRUTH WILL PREVAIL
For comments and questions: woldetewolde@yahoo.com

CALL ME BY MY NAME:

A discussion with Debteraw

Wolde Tewolde alias Obo Arada Shawl

June 13, 2007

Little Knowledge is dangerous (Anglican church) Silence is golden (Coptic church)
Too much information is lethal (Vatican)
Wisdom is everything (EPRP collective leadership) Balancing is an Ethiopian ACT

So far, the collective leadership and the Party of EPRP have survived many ups and downs. The AB (ANJA & b'TENA) story within EPRP is relegated to history. The concept of B'tena has been realized by almost everybody for its social and cultural havoc. ANJA belongs solely to the leadership style whereas B'TENA refers to the members or followers of the Party. Both leadership and follower ships should equally share accountability and responsibility Anja and Bitena respectively. However, before relegating them into archives, we need to put them in their proper perspectives.

Collective Leadership

The first test of the leadership style has happened as a result of the defection of the eight members from the small nucleus of the armed forces in Aassimba, immediately following the land reform proclamation. Among many of the main topics discussed by the central committee in preparation for the conference was the issue of democracy within the Party of EPRP. At the time, many Ethiopian student leaders were conscious of the role of a Secretary General in many Communist movements as an evil ground against its members. Kiflu Tadesse in his book "The Generation" put it in the following manner: -

In many of the communist parties, the post of the Secretary General had produced very powerful and autocratic leaders. In some cases, the Secretary General replaced the party and became its embodiment. In the days of the student movement, those who seemed ambitious for office were regarded with suspicion. The nature of democracy was deemed important, especially for a clandestine organization where the membership had difficulty in controlling its leadership. The experience of the organization, coupled with that of the international communist movement, had enabled many of the central committee members to look for a remedy to the problem. Kiflu continued to write, Some EPLO CC members had discovered that the role of the General Secretary could be quite detrimental to the internal democracy of the organization. Some of the leading central committee members had misgivings about Berhane Meskel's attitude and handling of issues as Secretary General. Working in Berhane's absence in Addis Ababa for almost a year, the other central committee members had developed a working relationship they felt was harmonious and effective, and saw no need for supervisory function performed by the Secretary General. The harm that the post caused to the internal democracy of an organization seemed to outweigh it benefits. After some discussion, it was decided to propose an amendment to the constitution abolishing this post as being incompatible with party democracy and to replace it with a central committee secretary with purely technical functions. (Kiflu P: 237)

Berhane Meskel Redda, the then Secretary General was furious about the power change. That was the basis of ANJA or Split within the EPRP leadership. The Party of EPRP along with its members and supporters has suffered in particular and the Ethiopian populace in general as a result of this split. As every body knows it, it was bloody and devastating experience to all Ethiopians. As it happened concurrently with the Red Terror, it did not only created confusion but also became an anomaly though professor Gebru Tareke unwittingly called it an aberration.

Have we learned from it? I hope so! I am sure had Berhane Meskel got his way, the Party of EPRP would have been in power a long, long time ago. I know thousands have joined EPRP for the simple reason because Berhane Meskel or others like him with impressive personalities were involved in EPRP. But hey, deep at heart all Ethiopians do not want powerful individuals. That is our culture. A collective culture, and I am proud to be one of it. Until we build a system of government like that of USA or some European countries, we cannot afford to have powerful individuals who will eventually be dictators in due course. It is human nature to abuse power unless one is governed by the Rule of

Law or controlled by a Check and Balance System of government. For such a struggle, EPRP would be an asset for Ethiopia and a model for all Africa. Is my name compatible with my deeds? I am Debteraw of EPRP. Call me by my name. No individual dictatorship in Ethiopia!

Along this line of collective leadership, EPRP also designed a slogan "People's Provisional Government". Why because Ethiopians have to participate not to be led blindly. We are still at that demand after 33 years! What price for Democracia! Signing documents like that of Kinjit leaders in Diaspora is hardly a consolation. EPRP's leadership and followers are not bonded by signatures but by faith and noble cause. If the collective leadership and the followers at large were working hand in glove, why then B'tena took place? The following paragraphs will elucidate.

B'TENA (Disorganization)

After being informed or as was during those days, when one becomes conscious, the next step was to get organized. According to the study conducted by EUS (Ethiopian University Service), the northern part of highland Ethiopia was mostly organized on a village or AaDI basis. The rest of Ethiopian regions were largely sparsely inhabited and scattered.

The balance between freedom and control came into power play. The supporters of the DERG mainly MIESO have delimited the urban areas into Kebeles and the rural Ethiopia into Gebere (Peasants) Association. EPRP leadership was concerned with this type of delimitations as an infringement on the freedom of peoples' rights. EPRP followers also have sensed that MIESO's intension was not genuine. I, for instance knew Wondimu Desta, the French educated architectural engineer who was genuine enough to delimit Addis Ababa into economic zones. But it was abused by the DERG and it is still abused by the current government. This type of KiLiL zoning heavily paralyzes CUD. What a travesty- Zoning for development transformed into chaos and imprisonment!

To counter that attack or rather to overcome this obstacle of freedom of movements, EPRP formed a Zonal sector in the urban centers and a Regional sector in the rural areas. The rest is history. Members of EPRP have been underground and aboveground for a long period of time with the difficulty of distinguishing the real enemy from the true comrade.

EPRP community was from the beginning a genuine community of individuals who really believe in "unity-in-diversity". The Party believed then and now, that the greater mental diversity of the members, it is better so long as each can recognize that others however, alien are sincerely loyal to the common enterprise of Eritrea and Ethiopia. As Olaf Stapledon, in his book of Philosophy and Living wrote:

Genuine community entails that the members of the community shall be bound together in mutual enrichment and mutual obligation either by direct personal contact or by the established will for community. It is impossible to have genuine community without a resolute will that all members of the community shall be treated with respect and kindliness which every individual desires to receive from his neighbors. Personal intercourse and the abstract will for community may be regarded as the two kind of cement which consolidate communities." (Olaf P: 292)

As it was explained in previous articles in "civilized society", there is very little to deserve the name. Civilization is after all, is not a modern convenience or a mechanical power. It is only a process of advancing to more civil mode of behavior from a less mode of behavior. In other words, civilly is treating people as persons in services of immediate _social contact_ and in _social organizations_. The fabric of Ethiopian culture is congruent with these social relationships and organizations.

Back to the B'tena phenomenon, given the background of EPRP formation after a long movement of students, workers and teachers consolidation, it was natural, that the workplace, the home and the office (WHO) to be in consonance to move foreword to push Ethiopians for a better nation.

But many organizations, governments, Fronts and in particular TPLF was undermining EPRP. The main reason behind EPRP's failure was not as popularly propagated because of B'tena by its own members and followers or by the RED TERROR or by the work of ANJA. It was simply as a result of Woyane's evil doings. Here is why.

Firstly, TPLF denied EPRP to operate in Tigrai province.

Secondly, TPLF tipped the DERG in Makale to stop EPRP recruits from joining EPRA. It was both an act of sabotage and an act of selfishness'.

Thirdly, TPLF hoodwinked or duplicated EPRP in various forms disguised as EPRP similar to the Geek legend of the "Trojan Horse".

Fourthly, TPLF prevented EPRP's from participating in any forum in the country and outlawed EPRP since it came to power in Ethiopia.

Finally, the most devastating evil of all-evils was the assault on EPRP's base area of Go jam and Gonder and still holding EPRP's leadership like Debteraw incommunicado for over 16 years.

So B'tena is a misnomer. It is neither the fault of members of EPRP leaving the Party nor the fault of the collective leadership for failing to regroup its members; it is the sophisticated work of the TPLF taking advantage of Ethiopian gullibility. It is that simple and obvious.

Conclusion

The enemy as in 9/11 did not come from outside, rather there was no enemy. We have been told that the Eritreans wanted to sell their country to foreign powers or nations. Sixteen years have passed, yet they have not cut the deal and they do not seem to do that in the near future or ever. The TPLF is an enemy within. It is controlling all aspects of economy and freedom. The concept of KiLiL and Free Market is anti-freedom of movement and anti-socioeconomic freedom respectively.

On the one hand, the leadership of ELF had the tendency of following the Baath Party, TPLF had the ideology of Enver Hoxha, EPLF's leadership were followers of Mao's ideology, Mieso story was about following Marxism-Leninism. While on the other hand, although many EPRP supporters like those of ESUNA, were contemplating to follow varied ideologies, Debteraw's EPRP was against pursuing foreign ideology of any sort. The collective leadership of EPRP aspired to find their own ideologies based on their history and culture- the issue of originality and practicality. It was true that some individual leaders were emulating Che Guevara, Ho Chi Mi and Kafka or from religious history some individuals were in the footprint of Jesus' or Mohammed's or Buddha's goodwill practice thus fulfilling the good will of their fellow men and to all human beings for that matter.

As a policy, EPRP collective leadership has always been inward looking. The previous regime had a policy of hospitality towards foreigners. None of the alumni of Haile Sellasie I University has the desire to work in the ministry of interior. Most of them wanted to be a minister for foreign affairs. What about now? I leave judgment to readers.

Q&A with READ

In all the past conversations with Debteraw, it was intended to spell out Who Debteraw is and What he stood for; I hope we have achieved something in return. We have come to the conclusion that Debteraw is equivalent to READ, i.e. a Revolutionary, an Educator, an Artist and a Democrat. Our core problem is the inability to READ. Those who read are in a single digit! Do you believe that? We better believe it! In addition, those illiterates have stopped to listening; instead they have resorted to talking. Our slogan or program should be "READ TO ME" DEBU!

For the time being, I have conducted an interview with Debteraw and here are his current thoughts and ideas.

Question: Can you tell us in simple words what distinguishes Haile Sellassie, Menghistu and Zenawi or between the Monarchy, the DERG or EPRDF/TPLF?

Debu: Haile enjoys mystery; Mengistu prides in false promise and Zenawi is insidious. Haile believes he is one of the chosen people even if he is not. Menghistu believes that he can control everybody including nature. Zenawi believes that he can be a copycat of Melese Tecle who was dedicated to the cause of Democratic Ethiopia. Zenawi wanted to be accepted both as an Eritrean and as an Ethiopian based on blood. But the question is not about biological; it is about an idea of history, culture and political value. It is a fact that he took what he though was his hero, Melese Tecle without understanding what he stood for. Call me by my name! That is the fallacy of the TPLF leadership who at the same time cannot operate in harmony with themselves. I am sorry to say that many who were born from both sides of parentage are still suffering. EPRP has solved this dilemma long before it started its revolutionary struggle. Unlike Kiflu who wrongly portrayed the ethnic background of EPRP leaders as from this ethnic or that ethnic background, EPRP has waged its struggle on the basis of common cause, common bond and common experience. Individuals like Obo Arada Shawl, for instance, have become both Eritrean and Ethiopian simultaneously based on their beliefs of Democracy and Justice.

Question: What does present EPRP stands for?
Debu: The letter E stands for both the country and its people. There is no one without the other. That is EP= Peoples of Ethiopia. R=Revolution and P= political party which replaces the line of Haile Selassie who was the 225th king of Ethiopia. That is how EPRP got its name. It was a difficult task but it will get there. If there is any letter to be left out, it is the letter R that may be replaced by Respect, Relationship and Rehabilitation.

Question: What is the solution for Ethiopia?
Debu: AAGMELAGO is an Ethiopian ideology of futuristic concept embodied in cultural, religious and politics of governance bundled up together. It is a roadmap for progress and stability for the whole of Ethiopia.

Question: It was easy for you to share what you believe in, because of your intuitive, but it is harder for us to back up everything with facts and figures?
Debu: Let my work speak for itself. Science and Technology has not touched Ethiopia. By this I do not mean about the science of Earth, Life and Space. I mean of cells, atoms and electromagnetism.

Question: Your sense of humor or organizational skill was exemplary. You were able to transform something from simple to fabulous in less than five minutes, for instance in organizing EPRP, how did you do it?
Debu: By becoming down-to-earth humble, open and honest!!!

Question: Who are the men and women behind the idea of EPRP leadership?
Debu: The mouthpiece for EPRP was and is the Weekly Publication of Democracia. At the beginning, Tesfaye Debessay, Yohannes Berhane and myself became the editors. All three of us showed what commitment means and what a showdown with oppressors of life, happiness or health. DEMOCRACIA is my name. Every man or woman whose thoughts and feeling is expressed or written in this Publication is already a leader. Decipher my name – it will also reveal my deeds.

Question: What is Earth-Life_Space means to you?
Debu: I have studied these mysteries in my father's monastery. All three are one and the same. The right question is what is politics and what is religion. EPRP's mission was to ask the questions of WHY and HOW. The question of Why belongs to politics or religion and the question of How is the realm of science.

Question: Some people say that EPRP is dead; it should be left in peace. What do you say?
Debu: Is this Truth, opinion of fact? It is a TOF (tough) question? Let everybody answer it?

Question: Do you have energy leaks caused by judging others?
Debu: I spend my energy on creativity and on restoration. Judgment halts progress. When we as leaders judge others, we inhibit our own forward motion. Also, when we judge others, we are not doing our job because we are not in sync with the energy that moves us forward. Jesus said to Peter, "What business is it of yours what I say to John? Keep your eyes on your own forward motion". John. 21:21-22. *I say to you one day at a time while focusing on the future.* This should be the motto of EPRP.

Question: What advise do you give to leaders?
Debu: Leaders must have not only vision and communication skills but also tremendous personal resolve. While leaders attract followers, at any moment they must be able to walk away from them, lest they become followers themselves.

For comments and criticism: woldetewolde@yahoo.com

EYONA: Fusion of cultural communities

By Oash Tewolde

December 3, 2012

A quarter of a century ago, an Ethiopian scientist asked me "to sum up" the Eathiopian Student Movement. He asked me this question because at the time, I had written an article on how the Ethiopian college student movement was initiated. My writing was based on college presidential campaign speech entitled "Right is Might versus Might is Right?" As we now know, Asmara's call for struggle has emanated from the premise of "might is right" while in Addis Ababa, the Word was "right is might."

Readers can take their own conclusions. As to my friend, the scientist, he moved to Ethiopia for good, right after the joint forces of EPLF and TPLF entered Asmara and Addis Ababa respectively. However, currently, I am told that he is back to the United States for resettlement. I intend to meet him and find his "sum up" on the ground.

Another quarter century is passing by without any conclusion of movement. The EPLF has changed its name to Eritrean Front for Democracy and Justice (EPDJ) and the TPLF incorporated itself as Ethiopian People Democratic Front (EPRDF). The EPLF prides itself that it is serving the Truth. What 'truth' is in today's world? The leadership of EPDJ needs to tell how and when truth will be served as opposed to claiming that they are serving truth. After all, truth hardly dwells in vacuum. The correct way is to tell and show for whom the bell tolls.

The TPLF also laurels itself on transforming poverty. What is poverty? Does poverty depend on food, consumer or durable goods? The concept of poverty envisaged by the TPLF leaders is incompatible with the Ethiopian peasants. It is a common knowledge that Ethiopians live historically on Dega, Weina or Kola regions. Of course, the majority of them inhabit the Weina Dega climatic zone. By Ethiopian standard, these are not considered poverty stricken. Those who live on the Dega are naturally healthy and happy until the pursuers of Truth and Poverty came to their habitation.

Those who inhabit the lowlands of Eathiopia traditionally were nomadic. It is also true that these people suffer from malaria and their cattle from tse tse fly which is deadly. But nowadays, their land has become desirable thanks for the innovation of technology.

So the question of Truth and Poverty are not the real obstacles to the Eathiopian populace. It lies somewhere else. In this and in subsequent articles especially during the 2013, I want to deal with the issues and ideas that became hindrance to our moving forward.

The Student Movement be it in Eritrea or Ethiopia has played a major role in the political, social and cultural matters. The "might versus right"debate that was initiated in the 1960's would have been a clear solution had it not been hijacked by the TPLF and EPLF adherents.

The simple and immediate issue that comes to one's mind and heart is the fact that the Ethiopian Revolution and the Eritrean War was obscure. War is not the same thing with that of Revolution.

The Eritrean Liberation Front (ELF) had a clear agenda for war. It was based on a colonial theory of liberation. According to ELF leaders, Eritrea should be independent from colonial masters of Italy or Imperialism however, we define it and were to achieve Independence (mind you not Harnet & Nazanet); the Front was destined to carry war on colonialism before the issues of freedom and liberty. It was a question of prioritizing for them.

Revolution for the ELF leaders was secondary issue despite many denials by some writers on the subject. The EPLF on the other hand, had no clarity on its objectives. The EPLF leaders did not separate the colonial theory of liberation from the true nature of the Ethiopian Revolution which I call the Eway Revolution. It took some forty years for someone like Tesfai Temnewo to come out and to testify the path of EPLF Revolution. Mr. Temnewo forcefully narrates the innuendoes, lies and rumors that abound among EPLF members and fighters.

According to Tesfai, only less than a dozen people died for their beliefs and convictions of Ideology. The rest were either succumb to fear or slaughtered like mute sheep as a result of lies and conspiracy. For what? It was purported for Independence and not for freedom and liberty as the truth seekers wanted us to believe. Thanks for Tesfai Temnewo for having to disclose to us that Essais was elected one time and as such he has continued to exercise his elected power. And we all have read Essais's declared objective in "WE and Our Objective" although frankly it was very hard to understand even for an educated let alone for the uninitiated labeled as Hafash. I think the author knows what he wrote. If it is Essais's dogma as was claimed by many that he wrote it, and then I believe he is carrying his mission in order to accomplish his vision in accordance to his own strategy and understanding and we should not blame him for that. The opposition did not get it and we did not get it. Period. It is like my scientist friend who did not understand the Eway Revolution. The Ethiopian Revolution cannot be arrested and sum it up. It is a continuum process.

What we get from Tesfai is the fact that Essais is still an elected leader since day one. I believe Eritreans especially his comrades in arms are incapable to impeach him for he is faring in terms of corruption better than his colleagues. My own understanding is that opposition groups can bring alternative to his dogma of power based on Chinese PLA. Can we learn from the current 18th Congress of Peoples' China? I believe we can at least to sum up their way of doing business and politics.

What about the TPLF's war on poverty? Do we believe it? The people of Tigrai were told that they will be liberated from the Amhara domination. What domination? The Amhara populace was poverty stricken themselves. The people of Tigrai did not struggle only for liberation but also for honor, value and purity. The leadership not only lied to their own people but also to all Ethiopians and Eritreans alike. They said they believed in Eritrean Colonialism but they participated in the elimination of ELF, the true holder of Colonial Theory. The TPLF claimed to believe in the true Ethiopian Revolution and yet, they have killed the Ethiopian Revolution. They lied and lied to the bitter end until grabbing power as in the Melese case. And now they will continue to lie and cheat until the name Ethiopia is erased from the map of the Earth and that the majority of Eathiopians will become a minority in their land if not in their country.

So what is the solution? My own opinion is that the Student Movement has to finish or 'sum up' what was started by its predecessor. The student members of the time have now matured and have become professionals, diplomats and politicians. The next generation of student movement should focus on education, training and voting (ETV).

It is imperative to ask what the objective of the Eritrean/Ethiopian youth organization in North America also known as EYONA. This student youth organization will continue to pursue the true nature of Ethiopian Revolution a.k.a. Eway Revolution.

This Youth will understand the difference among all three successful Revolutions. The Russian Revolution led by the Bolsheviks, the Chinese Revolution led by PLA and the American Revolution that was led by the 13 colonial states of America. In my own opinion, these three Revolutions are the only ones to be emulated by the Eathiopian youths worth in the annals of history. Of course, the fourth one which I am very much interested to impart to Eritrean and Ethiopian youth is the Eway Revolution which started in the 1960 and still continues to the present day Ethiopia and Eritrea.

What is this Eway Revolution? Is it one way ticket? Is it backward, downward, upward or forward as in President Obama's slogan? Time will show in which direction the Eway Revolution will head. A preliminary sense of direction will be revealed in year 2013. There is an early indication that it will take the format of the American Revolution. Let the old generation of Student Movement pass the baton to the new ones for the new ones have access to all information and knowledge. We can only give them wisdom without strings attached. The history of Eway Revolution although fifty years old has an added advantage of a prominent wars – the war of Aduwa. Revolution and War should be separated. We should not be confused by the elites and Ph.D. of Eritrea and Ethiopia as we are being confused by the patrons of the current Orthodox churches. We had enough of confusion. The tools of communication should be carefully chosen. One of our instruments of communication is to comprehend culture – not the Eword, the Written, the Mword or 3rd word but the real way of life of the alliterate and the illiterate of Latin alphabet and the literate of Geez.

TRUTH WILL PREVAIL.
For questions and answers oboaradashawl@gmail.com

SOLUTIONS WITH DEBTERAW, I:

Call me by my name & address

By Obo Arada Shawl

November 13, 2008

Introduction

13 days ago an ordinary name Obama became not only an historical event but as well as a household word. It is the only name that ends with a vowel "A" in the American Presidential names. Arusi or Arsi, the smallest state of AEthiopia begins with the letter "A". What's is in a name? Call me by my name.

In AEthiopia ኤትዮጵያ as opposed to ኢትዮጵያ there are thousands of people with the name of Obama. They live in the borderline of Sidamo, Gemu Gofa, Wollega and elsewhere. The point is what does Obama stand for? For me, it is deciphered in the following: -

O = 10
B = 13
A = VVV M = 13
A = 111

Deciphering OBM will result in 36 years of Struggle by EPRP. Is it a coincidence or Divine? What about the letter "A"? According to the teaching of DEBTERAW the letter "A" as in Latin is deciphered and stands in upside form for **Volunteerism-Vote-Victory.**

Who is the Oboma of Ethiopia?

This kind of question has been asked by million of AEthiopians in million times especially at the beginning of the onset of the Eway Revolution.

What is interesting and a dumb question at the same time, people like Getachew Garedaw from Germany asks the same question (see www.ethiolion.com). Artist Tesfaye Lemma in his book entitled "Confessions of the DERG (የዯርግ ኑዛዜ) has displayed as a cover book of Haile Sellasie's picture that was taken just six weeks before his downfall and Mengistu's clenched left lined up for history. On the cover of the book, there is also a big question mark invoking the unknown next leader for Ethiopia. Many educated AEthiopians were predicting the blood bath after Haile Sellassie's departure. On the contrary though, nothing has happened. The killings and imprisonment that ensued following the downfall of the Emperor was not for the lack of new leaders but for an idea far greater than free speech, free self-expression and free assembly as put foreword as DEMOCRACIA.

Many people misunderstood the Eway Revolution, a revolution for a political system dubbed as የፖለቲካ ስርዓት

On the one hand, after Menghistu, people were worried as to what will happen to Ethiopia as a country as opposed to leadership? The question if and when Menghistu leaves was not about who will replace him, for Menghistu has gone from the minds and hearts of all Ethiopians long time before he was gone. AEthiopians were worried what kind of system of government they will get. For the ordinary people the question of DEMOCRACIA was paramount. All throughout their lives, AEthiopians have been fighting for their liberties and social justice.

On the other hand, foreign experts who proposed the London Conference for the transferee of power were sure that nothing bloody will happen if the guerrilla fighters were to take power and if Menghistu leaves peacefully, but on the contrary, two years of bloody war as opposed to revolutionary war were ensued and too many killings and imprisonment is taking place even to this day both in Ethiopia and Eritrea. Why one may ask? The answer lies not in leaders but in leadership, i.e. political party leadership.

What is Political leadership?

Campaign for election or legislation has more than two sides while a politician's analysis is the same. And it does not matter whether the issues are local, state or national, they all work the same way. Elected officials are likely to behave given the same vote or money.

When the Woyane's came to power, they pretended as if they were operating in a la DEMOCRACIA by pretending as if people were free. We have seen this with Ginbot election result. The Woyane are still in the mentality of appointment not election. Most opposition groups are doing the same. Such is why EPRP has diagnosed as feudal system of political mentality. Most of our educated and non- educated seem to desire for appointment and not election. I can see why EPRP has failed in promoting the leadership style that is desired. I know many people from EPRP members will complain about this failure. But everyone and everybody should fail once in a while, as not failing will only show that we have not been trying. But EPRP has been in the struggle for many decades.

What EPRP wants to differentiate is the part between a politician and a stateman in as much as it has spent 3 decades of differentiating between a Revolutionary and a Nationalist.

What is a statesman, anyway? According to Harry Truman a statesman is "A politician that has been dead 10 or 15 years." How true! AEthiopia had hundreds of statesmen.

A statesman is someone who acts to do what is right regardless of the political risk. It's someone who puts the public good ahead of partisan politics. A statesman is one who makes decisions based on what is right, not on what is popular.

DEBTERAW's contribution to election

First of all politics involve money and votes. In AEthiopia, we do have neither of these two factors. Secondly, we do not know whether we were politicking locally (at woreda level), statewide (at awraja level) or nationally (Kifle Hager). Let us remember that Ethiopia was divided into ጠቅላይ ግዛቶች፣ አስተዳዮች፣ እና ክፍለ ሀገሮች

This was a step forward in thinking of changes – colonizing- administering- regionalizing had to mean something for aspirant people.

But the TPLF came with a different mode of thinking, backward thinking. Without understanding the nature/use of money and the tools for democracy, the EPRDF embarked on the road of capitalism. There are many mysteries of Capital none of them easy to grasp for the EPRDF parliamentarians. The hour of capitalism's greatest triumph is in its hour of crisis. The fall of the Berlin Wall and the present financial crisis are good examples for the triumph of Capitalism. The fall of the DERG was an opportune time for the triumph of political system in Ethiopia. The TPLF and the EPLF blew it. In actual fact, the TPLF has doubled their crime by attempting to destroy DEBTERAW and his EPRP. That was not an opportunity for triumph but a crisis for their downfall. Ethiopia cannot be a Capitalist nation without the tools of Capitalism.

EPRP, on the other hand, unlike TPLF and EPLF, has followed the right path from **voluntarism – vote – victory.** DEBTERAW is leading us to voting system and then declare victory. The victory of EPLF, TPLF and the Kinjit is short-lived because victory is only meant for them. It is the reverse in the case of EPRP.

In my earlier article, (See www.debteraw.com call me by my address, III) I have indicated that the federal state of Sidamo will be a state for diplomatic mission whereby the crisis around the Horn of Africa will be resolved diplomatically. The Boranas, who are the true source of democratic culture and Oromifa language with no bias for any type of religion and class, will be a source of diplomatic relations for what the so-called Abyssinians are lacking for. Let EPRP search and appoint capable and honest Sidamonians to join the Mission, Vision and value of EPRP. By definition, the Sidamas, the Wolaytas, the Gurages, the Gurjis, the Derassas the Oromos, the Amharas the S"me T"ru Hamasien and even the Ras Tefferians are settlers in the state of Sidamo.

Obama vs. Debteraw: lessons to be learned

History is made in two ways. By dramatic occurrences often surprising such as the fall of Berlin Wall in 1989 and by slow accretion of small changes over long periods. These are harder to notice while they are happening but often more significant than the isolated, surprising events such as the coming to power by the DERG, the assumption of power by EPRDF and the election of Ginbot.

These two are usually are interrelated only in geographically and politically stable societies such as the USA.

Obama made history in the way DEBTERAW has embarked to make history. Power concedes without a fight or demand. In the case of DEBTERAW, it is a fight but in the case of Obama it is a case of demand. We all have collective memories but one moment is the American experience. Notice the crying of Jackson and of Oprah. Both cried for different reasons. EPRP members and supporters are crying for Debteraw as why is still … ተሰወረ

Notwithstanding the above memories, comparing DEBTERAW and OBAMA Both men are educated Both men are humble Both men are articulate Both men are likeable and Both individuals have a lot of heart and are very passionate about issues facing their respective countries. They both saw the problems and the possibilities and did not bother for confrontation and a list of grievances.

Above all both men campaign for change except DEBTERAW call his አብዮት (አቧ) Revolution. And the commonality is change via education. It is to be recalled that DEBTERAW became more radicalized after the „Educational Sector Review for Ethiopia". In fact, education (not of East or West) but have AEthiopian became the core value for EPRP's struggle.

For Obama it is change + transformation = Hope

For DEBTERAW it is revolution + hope = social justice

Why did the change of Obama worked and not for DEBTERAW's EPRP? Is it because of the word *change instead of revolution? Would it make a difference had AEthiopians use change instead of revolution?*

Absolutely not. A revolution should have to take place in Ethiopia just like in America or elsewhere before election to take place. The Ethiopian Revolution was correct to have taken place. The only problem that people cannot see up to the present time is that the true Revolution that was envisaged by DEBTERAW's EPRP has been hijacked by the DERG, sabotaged by the EPLF and aborted by the TPLF.

Veteran EPRP members and associate members recount battles both past and ongoing. Thanks to DEBTERAW's existence, EPRP continues to survive and thrive. As many opponents seem to charge DEBTERAW and his EPRP as "concealed communist", it was not true as his party affiliation and political position was clear and untainted.

If you want to understand the Eway Revolution, Obama is for pop culture and DEBTERAW was not. (See call me by my address: A commentary on Marathon and Sprint that was posted at www.debteraw.com *on August 23, 2008.*

Concluding remarks

DEBTERAW lived and operated in a society of WE whereas Obama lived and operated in a society of ME. Given the present time, what lessons do we have to learn about the shift from ME to WE?

DEBTERAW is still with us, not alone. He fought for social justice and for his personal freedom and yet he is denied his personal freedom let alone social justice.

Le us fight to free him as he is considered as the "father of AEthiopia" or at least, let us witness his death in the manner the "mother of Africa", Miriam Makeba who died this week while doing her passion on stage. She was the voice for liberation when she staged at the Haile Sellassie I university in 1963. DEBTERAW is our voice.

To be an obstructionist or confrontational to EPRP's vision, mission and values is futile and unnecessary once we have found the truth about DEBTERAW who is sacrificing his life to the betterment of all AEthiopians. Let us build on the accomplishments of DEBTERAW'S **voluntarism, vote and victory. That is how Obama did it.**

Thanks for Barack Obama for showing to all AEthiopians who could not see the ideal and the method of struggle by DEBTERAW and his EPRP. Literate AEthiopians in Latin Alphabet have to start with the letter of „A" as in ARUSI which includes „5".

Literate AEthiopians in GE"EZ have to start with the letter of U = U which is equivalent to UNITY, ETHIOPIAN UNITY through STRUGGLE OR CAMPAIGN.

TRUTH WILL PREVAIL

For questions and comments: woldetewolde@yahoo.com

SOLUTIONS WITH DEBTERAW, II

Call me by my name, address and task ⊒

By Obo Arada Shawl

December 13, 2008

Background Information

Aethiopia is a beautiful country. That is the only reason why the Aethiopians have kept their Independence intact. How, why and what kind of beauty? I leave the real answer to my readers.

But for me and for others who think like me, Aethiopia's beauty lies in its natural-ecological beauty expressed in 13th months of sunshine as in Ethiopia and 3 seasons in just 2 hours of vehicular travel as in Eritrea. In other words, Aethiopia is endowed with mountains for cooling purpose and it is located near the Earth's Equator for warming purposes. Isn't that something of value to be thankful to God or to our ancestors? Adam and Eve (A&E) ገርሃ እና ድንቅነሽ

According to legend, the people who have inhabited this Land are righteous, humble and God fearing people. With my own experience, these Aethiopians didn't differentiate between names, boundaries and careers. They all lived as nomads, herders, tillers, traders, warriors, bandits or teachers (debteras included).

Philosophically, these Aethiopians had lived on the principle of "live and let live" regardless of name, address or career differentiation. All of them are governed by Market Place በአገር ገበያ and not by Wall Street. I have been visiting markets – from Monday to Sunday as was part of my job and they all were located and based on open market. The amazing part, most of them speak their own dialects or languages with no sense of fear or indignation for not knowing the language of neither of the merchants nor of the government in power. To classify them on language basis is pure racism. There is neither market place for ideas nor for products that govern Aethiopians as at to date.

Technically, though, the Aethiopians were living in 17th or 18th centuries, as 90% of the land mass is without communication and transport services.

Those who conceived this situation had embarked upon developing freedom of social movement and the open economic market fabrics of the Great Society into the 20th century. Not in technical terms but in **philosophical, ideological and political** contexts.

Kiflu Tadesse who authored the book on "The Generation" has this to say

> This is a book about a generation of Ethiopians who embarked on an arduous struggle to transform its country. The first members of this generation were born in the early 1940's and the youngest in the early and mid 1950's. *It was a generation of activists who came together because of altruistic aims and goals.* It was a generation that was visionary, idealist and perceptive and consisted of the most enlightened and brightest citizens. Many of the members of these groups were among the privileged few who had access to modern education. Most of them were successful academically and many were honor students."

* Emphasis is mine

However, a widespread ignorance of a crucial nature in politics, philosophy and economics is apparent in today's Aethtiopia. What has happened to the Ethiopian Eway Revolution? Was there something wrong with the stars or the Revolutionaries? What has intervened or what has happened in between the following years? The answer should come from my readers. Decipher the letter B. You will find the answer.

1961 - 1974	= 13 years
1974 – 1987	= 13 years
1987 – 2000	= 13 years
2000 – 2013	= 13 years

- Hint: Menghistu brothers; international conspiracy against Aethiopia; peace deal and the dawn of DEMOCRACIA

If we cannot figure out the years of the software indicators for reflection, conspiracy, peace and downfalls for 52 years, then surely all our docile educated class have reason to believe that WMD (Wallelligne Makonnen – DEBTERAW) have brought to Aethiopia real WMD (weapons of mass destruction).

If this is the case, we have to revisit the software path of the Eway Revolution. Again, Ato Kiflu continues writing in his preface as follows

"An effort is made to portray events, incidents, decisions and activities realistically. Detailed analysis and interpretations of the activities are not provided, only the account of the history itself. This was done for the sake of fairness and with the intention to express the actual feeling of the fallen comrades. *It is the intention of the author to tell their story the way it was made and the way they want it to be told and retold.* The correctness or wrongness of events or decision is not the main focus, but an explanation of why things happened the way they did and the attenuating circumstances that influenced decision making."

** Emphasis is mine

This week, I have visited the office of EPRP in Washington, DC. Although I have made several visits in the past, this is my first time to observe a special item of interest. Was it the set up of the office? No. Was it the variety of books? No. Was it the rack on which computers was place? No. Was it the radio room? It was none of the above.

It was a painting, hanging on a wall that attracted my attention. I have seen it a dozen of times but never figured it out the way I did it now. ልብ እንጂ ዓይን አያይም የሚሉት ትክክል ነው። The painting has been in the office for almost 2 decades, but to my amazement, I did not give the attention they (the personalities) or it (the painting) deserves.

Now that I have, what does this painting represent in EPRP's office? Who were or who are these personalities? These three individuals were true comrades who honestly believed to be the pioneers in idealizing Aethiopia but only if they would be involved in the Eway Revolution. All three portray different family and education background but above all their true passion in each of the following areas of

- Politics
- Revolution and
- Philosophy

Matters to all of the Great Society of past Ethiopia and the future of Aethiopia, for understanding these three departments of knowledge is a priority. I believe that without these precondition, nothing will go forward and albeit backward. For EPRP, these tasks have been carried out by many of its members and supporters and so the task of the party of EPRP will be focused on organization and leadership.

On Organization

Anyhow, let me go back to what I can decipher from the painting where I can contribute to the truth.

They are from left to right

1. Wallelligne Makonnen ዋለልኝ መኮነን
2. DEBTERAW and ፀጋዬ ገብረ መድህን
3. Tilahun Gizaw ጥላሁን ግዛው

As widely believed to be, nameless and faceless members of EPRP and supporters are considered to be followers of Marx-Engels-Lenin. But that was and still is not true. Aethiopian Revolutionaries were not reading or following what Marx, Engles or Lenin have written or said, or as the paintings of MEL as displayed on Revolution or Meskal Square. The majority of EPRP supporters and associates were following their own national heroes of Wallelligne-Debteraw- Tilahun (WDT ወዲት). Let us briefly examine what these personalities have represented and are still representing.

Wallelligne Mekonnen: on collectivism

Wallelligne was a person who deeply believed in independent thinking. He was an individualist who believed that collectivism in any form was wrong especially the type of Russian or the Chinese style. I am actually referring to our way of organizing principles -on the basis of nationalities - is very wrong. Organization should not be based on languages alone. Even by the standard of Stalin's definition, language is one among many. True to Wallelligne's nature, language be it any language including Amharic by itself is not a criterion for an identity. Wallelligne believed that language is only a tool for communication and a tool for thought processing. Nothing else. That was actually the main reason why he wrote the article on nation and nationalities in order to dispel oppression, as many believed that the culprit is the language of Amharic.

Since Wallelligne was a political science student as such, he was writing, thinking and acting on political level. He knew that the Amhara was a symbol of political affiliation not an economic or a cultural affirmation. He did not only address the problem of the national question but he had also attempted to redress it. It is up to us to follow his solution in the right context and in the correct way and not a' la Woyane's way. Wallelligne Mokonnen Kassa did not recommend the future of Eritrea as a state of nine nationalities or as many as eighty-one something in the Ethiopian case and worst at that solely based on geography or ethnic languages.

As to his organizational affiliation to EPRP, he was recruited or has recruited others on an individual basis not on a group or national as it was the case with the Woyane and Shaebia's way of recruitment. Any EPRP member was convinced to join the organization on a personal level and not by threat or cheat. Wasn't this a wonderful way of organizing a revolutionary political party. There is no regrets whatsoever for those who has joined on this principles of organization.

I have no doubt that Walleligne would abhor the concept of ethnic rule. Ethnic rule with all its dogmas and rules, traditions and dialects would surely be a mental disaster. Tribes will subsist on the edge of starvation and at the mercy of natural disaster. A man of self-esteem like Walleligne would not accept the notion that the content of his mind should be determined by muscles, namely by the means of unspecified string of ancestors.

Determinism by Marxism is far superior to ethnicity. Collectivism based on language should be abolished. That was not the idea of WMK. Due Consideration might be given to the article of October 23, 2008 (call me by my address: Solutions with DEBTERAW, III). The proposal was not mainly based on the three individual's wish, but of thousands especially with mixed parentage.

Tsegey Gebre Medhin – DEBTERAW: on myth

The mystic's doctrine that men must give credit to God for all their virtues and vices was unacceptable to DEBTERAW. Religion encompasses ancestral or cultural traditions, writings, history and mythology as well as personal faith and religious experience. Ritual myths of performance practices or patterns associated with temples or centers of worship, preliterate oral traditions that may vanish as the written word becomes the story and the literate class becomes the authority. Aethiopians must blame for all their sins upon themselves, is the mystic's doctrine. The principle of men's right to their own life, their liberty, to the pursuit of happiness would be the ultimate goal of all Aethiopians after the Eway Revolution as declared by DEBTERAW and his party.

However, social myths reinforce or defend social values or practices. On the one hand, in our cases, we have seen nationalist modern scholars such as Tecola Hagos (a Tigrian nationalist), Jordan Gebre Medhin (an Eritrean nationalist) whose works of studies was/is as exposed by Girma Bekele in his writings on *ethnocentrism* is distortion of the highest form.

DEBTERAW, on the other hand, expounded the traditional story, typically involving supernatural beings or forces of creature, which embodies and provides explanation. Justification (etiology) a religious belief or ritual or a natural phenomenon was clarified by DEBTERAW, Tsegeye G Medhin to anybody who needed at the time of the revolution.

Not all traditional stories are myths. For instance, a person or thing held in awe or generally referred to with near reverential admiration on the basis of popularly repeated stories be it real or fiction is not a harmful myth. Those who knew DEBTERAW personally can testify.

So what is wrong with being debtera? DEBTERAW has enlightened the Aethiopian population through traveling – physically, philosophically, socially, spiritually and above all via the Eway Revolution from Assimba via Tselemt, via the Abay river back to the Market Places of Aethiopia.

For those of us who do not know the difference between a debtera and a priest, the former is mostly responsible for education (spiritual life of community) whereas the latter has a representative function. Unlike that of the Jewish debtera, the Aethiopian debteras were part and parcel of the church hierarchy for they are poets, writers, musicians, dancers and healers. DEBTERAW has opposed the interference of the state into the affairs of the church and vice versa. By the way, the Independence of Aethiopia has been kept by the work of the debteras. The distinction between the task of the debtera and the priests is the same between personal and business matters.

Tilanhun Gizaw: on altruism

Tilahun Gizaw was the elected student president of USUAA. Tilahun was from the nobility of Tigrai state. His sister was married to Emperor Haile Sellasie's son.

Tilahun has been taking courses in Sociology, which was not popular at that time in Haile Sellassie's University.

However, from our class discussions and personal conversation, Tilahun had the following core beliefs

- The right to own property over random search and seizure
- Liberty over oppression
- Natural right to life over the constant fear of death

After his failure to become a student president, he studied the true nature of Aethiopian societies condition and desire first hand. Unlike the unholy claim that he was against the fortune's of his sister, Tilahun finally took the idea that when Aethiopians have the opportunity to choose, they will choose to be ruled by the consent of the governed not by the coercion of the Ethiopian State. This is what we globally call nowadays as the rule of law, not by the whim of the rulers. How true Tilahun was.

As to his altruism, I do not think, Tilahun had believed in this concept. I also think that the author Kiflu Tadesse's statement of altruism did sink or match with the beliefs of most Revolutionaries let alone with all Aethiopians. Why? It is an appropriate question. Here is why.

Altruism is a condition, which refers to people who keep sacrificing themselves and their values. We have seen this state of conditions during the DERG era, the Anja era, the TPLF and the EPLF era. That is to say that altruists sacrifice their friends to enemies, their allies to their antagonists, their convictions to anyone's wishes, the truth to lie, their strength to anyone's weakness and the good to any evil.

There is a misconception about altruism in the Eway society. Altruism is confused with kindness or due consideration to others. In fact, altruism is a moral theory that preaches that man must sacrifice himself to others. In our revolutionary struggle, many people thought that the comrades should place the interest of others above their own and that they actually are required to live for the sake of others. Was this not our Aethiopian core of confusion? If it is not let us discuss and solve our problems.

The reason why Tilahun Gizaw participated in the Eway Revolution was simply to ameliorate the economic and the social conditions of all Aethiopians via the politics of democracy – allowing the will of the majority to prevail while protecting the rights of the minority, including the Royal Family.

Concluding remarks

Unless the term „generation" has different meanings to Ato Kiflu, a generation is defined as the average time between a mother's first offspring and her daughter's first offspring. This makes a generation around 30 years in length. Compare this with 33 years of Jesus Christ as one generation. Sociologists mostly accept the classification of generation of Silent (1925-45); the Boom (1946-61); the Thirteen (1962-81); the Millennial (1982-2000) and the New Silent (2001-?). Ato Kiflu should rename his title of his book; otherwise, the generation he is referring to is dying out. It is time for detailed analysis and conceptual understanding of a generation. The struggle is still continuing with or without DEBTERAW. But Ato Kiflu seems to forget WDT. Let us all visit the EPRP office for a reminder of the living and the fallen comrades as Ato Kiflu has displayed a poem on the page of his book.

Ethnicity has a history of endless and bloody warfare. We should not wait for that to happen. Our only hope would be to be organized on a common cause and common ground. DEBTERAW has shown us the way to dispel mythology, Wallelligne has written and struggled until death to bring the solution to the problem of nations and nationalities and Tilahun has shown the courage for what was right and honorable in defiance to his social class. The painting that is hanging on the walls of EPRP office is a true reminder of Aethiopian role models for political leadership.

In other words, these three giant personalities have shown us

- How to know ourselves
- How to love our country and
- How to differentiate one's ally from the enemy

TRUTH WILL PREVAIL

For comments and questions: woldetewolde@yahoo.com

CALL ME BY MY ADDRESS:

Solutions with DEBTERAW, III

Obo Arada Shawl alias Wolde Tewolde -

October 23, 2008

ETHIOPIA is a center of the whole wide world www
ERITREA is a key to Africa

EPRP is a model for political party in the 21st century
We're defined by what we pass on to the next generation

I am from: Say it Loud and Clear
ARUSSI, where the letter A will be comprised of voluntarism, vote and victory after the final path of the Eway Revolution.
BALE where the letter B is still being deciphered so as to become a lasting solution to ▮▮▮ a name that will include Eritreans and Oromians. (Budget/Bicycle/Bomb)
ERITREA where the head of ▮▮▮ as opposed to
GEMU GOFA equivalent to GG where GG =14 states confirming government of the future
GODJAM the home of three quarter of AEthiopians for their lifeblood
GONDER where history and the future of governments is located
HARARGHE where unity, love and diversity resides
ILLUBABOR where the beautiful and young animal and rainfall rejuvenates *KEFA* where the home of the number one drink of coffee Arabica originated *SHEWA* where Amharic, the future lingua franca for Africa perpetuates
SIDAMO where all international conflicts could be solved following Obama's election

TIGRAI where T = the last alphabet in Latin, Alpha and Omega coincide/ converges
WELLEGA where Biblical Wisdom prevails
WOLLO where Quran Wisdom prevails

If I am unable to call you by your name, then I will call you, at least by your address. Where is your address? ABE GGH IKS STW W? With the exception of HTW (███████) which are compatible with Latin letters, the rest 10 states of AEthiopia are subject to be deciphered by its respective nationals and nationalities.

Repeatedly, I have come to a conclusion where our history and culture (HC) alias known as are the real culprits for all our perceived ills and poverty.

In the last few weeks numerous articles have been posted in defense of nationalism, religious freedom and political leadership. Articles written by Dr. Aleme Eshete along with Dr. Fikre Tolossa as posted in www.mahder.com; Dr. Abeba Fekade's posted at www.assimba.com Metho Obang as posted at www.ethiox.com Petros Tesfaghaber as posted in www.awate.com and Zewge Fanta as posted in www.Ethiomedia.com have indicated on these issues.

Basically these articles are all written to either defame the past Revolutionary struggle of AEthiopia or to belittle the Eway Revolution. The articles that were posted in the five websites will lead us to the basic question of unity with Capital U. The methodology for uniting the country, according to Wallelegne is DEMOCRACIA whereas that of Tewodros's was by the sword. Which one is right, Walle's method or the Teddy method? In order to answer these questions, we need to go back to the basics of our Revolution.

In doing so, readers may not be derailed from the true path of progress in making that

- Amharic to be the lingua franca language for Africa
- EPRP to be the true model of political party in Ethiopia
- Ge'ez aka Fidel to be the media of communication throughout the continent of Africa
- Recognition of Agaw's role in its true Ethiopian perspective and
- Accepting the primary color of the Ethiopian flag as an identity as in many African nations has done so.

At the expense of going into details in commenting each article, I chose to comment on only two individuals who were involved in the Eway Revolution. One is from Wollo and the other from Eritrea. Call me by my address. Where is my address?

Abeba (PhD)

The ills as Dr. Abeba attempts to explain come from hallucination not real. If we look it through the prism of history what is history? I recommend many of my readers including Dr. Abeba to read a book entitled **"What is History?" (Reference will be provided upon request).** Otherwise, let Dr. abeba write about religious history, that is, if she is a Catholic or a Muslim. Otherwise, the history of Gragne Mohammed and Yodit Gudit is over with. They were incidents of history. I wish Dr. Abeba's concentration were on mothers' issues as women's' issues are different than mothers' issues.

If I am not mistaken, Dr. Abeba seems to dwell on social, religious and political issues wrapped up in sexism, which in the final analysis lead us in mental health regression. I wish Dr. Abeba had chosen the politics of government, i.e. people's government as proposed by EPRP three decades ago. The issue of sexism and religion has been dealt with if not in the past three Millenniums but also during the era of Eway Revolution.

Dr. Abeba! Don't you think that having friends is a touchstone for people's lives? For friends according to Elaine Zelley, PhD a professor of communication at La Salle University in Philadelphia who studied female friendship sums it up like this:

"Friends provide a social network, companionship and emotional support."

I shall have to ask each and every one of my readers to ask the following rhetorical questions and tell me whose profession is needed to solve our problems in Diaspora.

- The friendship pool that seemed so deep in our teens and 20s have gotten shockingly shallow.
- Our oldest friends are scattered all over the globe with some wonderful exceptions
- Finding and cultivating new friendships is just hard
- On top of all that, who has the time!

As AEthiopians, we are not different than being social animals. We do not need to be reconnected but to share experiences. What experiences? Political, social, cultural, religious or sexism? Name it, we have it all.

The DERG, due to its credit has somewhat eliminated the fever of religious zealots.

MAKON, the female comrades of EPRP had resolved the sexism issue in Ethiopia and Eritrea a long time ago. For now, I hope Dr. Abeba will first research about her Wollo man's dream and method of struggle, as others have not yet discovered his mission and vision. By doing so, I know that Dr. Abeba will help millions from mental retardation and alienation.

Petros T. Conspiracy Theory of Nov 27, 2007

Petros wrote a long article of the 1970s student movement while he was in the Haile Sellasie I university. It was a well-established fact that the majority of Asmarino students were disengaged in the then Ethiopian student movement despite Petros's claim. He may be exceptional to be involved in the Ethiopian politics or he may be either an Ethiopian with an Eritrean background or who was born in one of the 13 provinces of Ethiopia or attended/educated in Ethiopia. I do not know his education or his birthrights to negate his claims. The analogy of Wallellegne vs. Tewodros is an appropriate test for further discussion in order to arrive at the truth of our struggle.

Zawge Fanta wrote, "Walleligne misunderstood his country and its people as much as the people misunderstood him." I know for sure that Walleligne did not misunderstand his country and its people; on the contrary, he knew his country and its people very well that he had to sacrifice his life for their cause. It is also true that many Ethiopians misunderstood Walleligne. It is more so because the TPLF leaders deceived to nominate him for their cheap propaganda machination by organizing

Although Eritreans were given the choice to participate in either with the Eritrean Liberation Fronts or with EPRP, Mr. Petros seems to confuse the issue of Nazanet with Harnet. Freedom was advocated by the elites of EPRP whereas the Eritrean elites were advocating for Independence.

Having achieved Independence for Eritrea, now the EPLF government is searching for democracy and justice as it has renamed its military organization by Peoples' Front for Democracy and Justice (PFDJ).

For EPRP, the cart does not come before the horse. EPRP has been advocating DEMOCRACIA and justice even before its formal formation. May be Mr. Petros could not see the student movement as democratic body. Let us not forget the history of election in the university. Nobody can deny that there was an academic freedom at least on campus level. Dr. Tesfatsion Medhine can elucidate to Petros the academic freedom that existed then.

The most amazing story (distortion) is when Mr. Petros claimed that the tools for hijacking namely the bomb and the gun were imported from Asmara. What a ridiculous idea as if one could not buy them from the "Somalia Tera". As to the other distortion about professors Mesfin Araya and Tesfatsion Medhine, I will let them respond.

Concluding notes

Almost for 40 years, since Walleligne Mekone's article was written, a silent debate was going on inside the elites mind. This silent debate seems to come to the public debate once more hopefully in the open forum. I hope this debate will dwell on Walleligne's deepest political beliefs such as whether WM was a liberal, a conservative at heart or a closet radical? Or was he a more subtle and moderate political figure who embraced Tewodros's, then discarded Monarchism (Teddyism) in pursuit of a restless ambition? Is there evidence to entertain both views? Was WM an analyst or an ideologue?

Was WM liberal to be ironic and self-questioning rather than messianic for all Ethiopians? Sometimes events call for courage and clarity not a sense of irony. And courage may be required to confront a genuinely radical and passionate Revolution. Even a closet radical would resist hijacking. Any conflicted woman or man (WM) with ambitions of reconciliation of the nations and nationalities might attempt to reconcile. But it is only the passionate, committed, courageous moderate like Walleligne Makonnen could succeed. Isn't this ironic with Walle, the hero? If it is not, let us see what the EPRP's 36 years of unabated and continuous political struggle would prove to the world.

The editor of Ethiomedia wrote "we hope Zewge's first-hand account would clear the fog that had shrouded the life of the student activist who rose to national prominence during the turbulent final years of the reign of Emperor Haile-Selassie." What a wishful thinking! Ato Fanta was perhaps his close friend but he was not his comrade friend. The struggle is not about personal friends; it is and was about ideas of change. Ato Fanta and his likes speak about girl friends and monetary things, but WM and his likes speak about progress and civility. I do believe that there is no "last hours for Walelgn Mekonnen." It will be perpetual.

It is essential that the debate between Monarchism vs. Democracy should be clarified. The people's government as proposed by EPRP is once again is being challenged by a so-called "government in exile". Walleligne's article and hijacking could not be understood out of the context of EPRP's struggle for change. No doubt WM was an agent of change and he was not alone. Millions have died for his ideas and are still dying and disappearing at an alarming rate. There are three main reasons why we keep harping at the wrong side of political history.

- Eritrea was not separated because of Walleligne's article. It was rather that Eritrea was a cause for his untimely death.
- That the TPLF leaders have disguised themselves in the hood of Wallelign – the sort of the Trojan horse.
- That the current leadership of EPRP lacked the gut and the will to defend Walleligne from being labeled as an agent of the Eritrean Fronts.

EPRP's support group around Washington DC are going to celebrate this week their 36 years of struggle for DEMOCRACIA. What does this mean? Go back to the blue line in the caption. How do we do it? That will be the question this week for EPRP. Will the name and picture of WM would come up for discussion and display or will he be forgotten as his comrade in arms DEBTERAW?

For comments and questions: woldetewolde@yahoo.com

SOLUTIONS WITH DEBTERAW, IV

Call me by my name, address and task

By Obo Arada Shawl

January 20, 2009

If you are a Christian, repent
If you are an atheist, contact
If you are a cheat, stop your cheating habit
If you are a liar, walk to leave
If you are an Aethiopian, live and let live
"Dreams of our forefathers"

The unfinished journey of DEBTERAW
Versus
The Finished journey of B. Obama

On March 23, 2008, an article on Debteraw vs. Senator, was posted on debteraw.com call *me by my name: solutions with Debteraw, XXV* and http://mahder.com. That article was based on the differences between DEBTERAW and the Senator. It was about race, color and religion.

Today's article is based on the similarities between DEBTERAW and President Obama's education and experiences.

In as much as DEBTERAW has graduated from a prestigious university, like that of Obama, DEBTERAW started to work as a teacher though the school officials would not allow him to teach beyond 2nd grade. When the new government came to power, the then current government officials wanted DEBTERAW to serve under their directions. DEBTERAW refused knowing that those officials were not genuine but "opportunists". When the DERG appointees for education began to pressure DEBTERAW not only to work but also to cooperate with them, lest he will be classified as anti-revolution. As usual, DEBTERAW came with his new harmless creative device. That is, he told to the Board members of Education that his father is aging and that he was soon to take over the Zuquala Monastery as his primary job. The Board members were astounded at his request for resignation from teaching profession. Of course, clandestinely, DEBTERAW was educating and organizing a political party. The rest is history, as they say.

Let us have a look at these similarities

1. Obama worked as a community organizer for 3 years and
2. DEBTERAW worked as political organizer for three years.
3. Obama served as practicing attorney for 3 years and
4. DEBTERAW worked as editor-in-chief for a political publication known as DEMOCRACIA.
5. Obama served as a Senator for 10 years (both for US and State legislator).
6. DEBTERAW is serving full time Revolutionary for political reforms.
7. Obama used to lecture on part time basis and
8. DEBTERAW used to serve churches on part time basis.
9. Obama authored two books, one on dreams of our fathers and the other on the audacity of hope for future generations.
10. DEBTERAW authored numerous publications, books and poems.

As a result, Barack Obama has become the President (E) of a powerful nation on the whole world while DEBTERAW ended up as a prisoner of conscience of an ancient but civilized nation.

Obama has started his journey from Philadelphia – the source of the American Constitution but DEBTERAW has yet to travel from the red mountain - ASSIMBA – where the *seeds - (Sudan-Eritrea-Ethiopia-Djibouti-Somalia)'s CONSTITUTION will be drafted.*

Obama has traveled through B&D (Baltimore and Delaware) to reach Washington DC

ወደ- WDC

DEBTERAW has yet to travel via ADAA ዓ(ዶAssimba-Dessie-Addis Ababa) to reach the new flower, Addis Ababa. (See Tedla Asfaw's regret as his knowledge of ASSIMBA revealed not by his fellowmen but by outsiders)

Concluding remarks

Obama is considered a product of Martin Luther King as well as Malcolm-X. His rebellious character is not by "any means necessary" as that of Malcolm X. Instead of working in places where Harvard graduates prefer to… Obama chose to negotiate his way through the downtrodden population of Chicago West Side.

DEBTERAW chose to work with Lab Adder ላቧእዶaሯnd Gebar ገባ-ሯthose who worked by their sweat and taxpayer Aethiopians.

Obama is lucky to live in a political system with all its checks and balances intact. He is also lucky that he lives in a country - physically surrounded by two Oceans, sea and land whereas DEBTERAW's Aethiopia's physical geography is surrounded by dry land, sea and rivers and with no political system familiar to all its citizens.

Obama was born around the time when President Kennedy pronounced as "Ask not what you can do for your country, ask for what you can do for your country" whereas DEBTERAW was a high school student when President Kennedy's speech reverberated all over the world. Besides, DEBTERAW WAS BORN IN SOCIETIES THAT HONOR SACRIFICE IN ONE'S COUNTRY not a dream.

Obama is 47 years old and he is the 44th president of USA. Let us hope that on Obama's 50th birthday, DEBTERAW's provisional political government will be put in place with the help of the 44 churches in DEBTERAW's Tabots of Gondar and so God help all.

The Lab Adder and the Arso Adder have now become politically conscious thanks to DEBTERAW and his EPRP. What is now required is an immediate release of the true son of Aethiopia and Aethiopianism from TPLF's dungeon.

TRUTH WILL PREVAIL
For comments and questions: woldetewolde@yahoo.com

Postscript

The Aethiopian Student Movement has taken almost the entire life span of President B. Obama. We do not know whether this is the beginning or the end of political and civil liberties for the Black Movement in America. Besides, President (E) Obama did not say. We have to wait and see.

But as to the Aethiopian Student Movement, it is high time to bear fruit. Despite this Movement and in spite of DEBTERAW'S down payments, Aethiopians have not been able to choose their government democratically. The institutions of the church should be left alone, the bureaucracy should be democratic and the freedom of speech, self- expression and assembly (SEA) should be respected.

The difference between the developed and underdeveloped is not based on material wealth alone but on the cumulative culture of knowledge and experience. EPRP has developed such a knowledge base and experience by keeping its name, address and task.

Americans are united around BO. (ቦW) hy is it not possible to UNITE, if not for all Aethiopians, at least for those who at one time or another has been associated with DEBTERAW's path of struggle? ሁ ሉ ዪE…ሃሆዪ. Iyf ou believe DEBTERAW's path was and is wrong, let us discuss and iron it out. I truly believe that the way of DEBTERAW is similar to that of President of Barack Obama.

A prominent political commentator was asked why all Americans want President B. Obama to lead them. His response was "we need him more than he needs us." Maybe this is true for all Aethiopians that they need DEBTERAW more than he needs them.

SOLUTIONS WITH DEBTERAW, V

Call me by my name, address and task

By Obo Arada Shawl

Febreuary 13, 2009

I have plenty of questions but I do not have the answers

The persistent past of political economy

For the last 150 years, the ideologies of Marxism, Nationalism and Liberalism have divided not only the Adam & Eve Society in particular but also had divided the whole humanity. Ideology refers to systems of thought and beliefs by which Aethiopians as a group or individuals had attempted to explain how the social system functions and the principles applied. The Marxists led by EPRP, the Nationalists led by EPLF and the Liberals led by EDU were at the center of economic analysis before and on the eve of the Revolution. The Eathiopian Student Movement has attempted to explain the Eway Revolution in such a manner.

On the one hand, the conflict among those Eathiopian intellectual groups was based on three moral and intellectual positions that have revolved around the role and significance of the market in the **organization of society and economic affairs.** The three ideologies were -

- Economic liberalism ጥቅም
- Marxism ለእድገት እንስራ VISION OF EPRP
- Economic nationalism ጥቅም ለጁ ብቻ VISION OF EPLF

The Liberals of EDU and the traditional Marxist of EPRP consider the integration of a society into world economy to be a positive factor in economic development and domestic welfare. Both agree on this position.

EDU like most liberals were for economic development via trade. But their domestic sources of growth were to depend on foreign flows of trade, capital and technology.

Marxists, on the contrary believed that the external forces could promote economic development only by breaking the bonds of Aethiopian conservative social structures. And that was not desirable though necessary condition.

The Nationalists believe that the world economy only operates to the disadvantage of their domestic economy and domestic welfare. Trade in their view was an engine of exploitation and for underdevelopment only.

These three controversy of EDU, EPRP and EPLF over the role of world market economy in the global distribution of wealth, power and welfare constituted the underlined problems of Aethiopia, as a result of these positions, EDU had collapsed quickly during the Revolution, EPRP still persists and EPLF is still fearful of global economy. Today, we can still speak of ideologies not of "theories" as applied to trade, investment and development. Once more, the current governments of Aethiopia are confusing issues of TID (trade-investment-development). What a tragedy!

While on the other hand, many copycat organizations such as the DERG, TPLF, and many others have differed on broad range of questions such as:

- What is the significance of the market for economic growth and distribution of wealth among groups and societies?
- What ought to be the role of markets in the organizations of domestic and international society?
- What is the effect of the market system on issues of war and peace?

Each of these three perspectives has strengths and weaknesses. It is clear now for the entire whole wide world that no perspective provides a complete and satisfactory understanding of the nature and dynamism of these ideologies. Together all three can provide useful insights for our future.

These were the main issues for our Eway Revolution. I believe that the Aethiopian Student Movement had embarked on a political Revolution to be followed with economic revolution and it is in this light that the struggle of EPRP should be evaluated and judged. Not the other way round. I heard a group who were discussing on why EPRP did not build roads and bridges. What an argument!

Having said this let me go to the current irregular conditions to be concluded by suggestions for posterity.

ANOMALIES that may persist in the future

Paguemen 13 is equivalent to Friday the 13th

Paguemen is the 13th month in Aethiopian Calendar, which consists of only 5 days (September 6-11). The slogan of "Ethiopia a country of 13 months of sunshine" has been a welcoming gesture of tourists. But most important is the fact that Aethiopians do not pay bill as they work for free during this month. What a wonderful concept!

Friday 13th is a superstition about a day of good or bad luck. The fear of Friday the 13th is called Paraskavedkatriaphobia = 23 letters which is derived from the Greek words of Paraskevi = Friday Dekatreis = Thirteen and Phobia = Fear

The history, rate of accidents, occurrence and its social impact of phobia of thirteen are too much to tell. Suffice to say that the number 13 was considered as irregular transgressing completeness. The number 13 is incomplete as reflected by the 12 months of the year, 12 signs of the Zodiac, 12 hrs of the clock, 12 Apostles of Jesus, 12 tribes of Israel, twelve gods of Olympus and so on and so forth.

From Jesus to Christ

This week "Frontline" on PBS (public broadcasting service) is broadcasting this journey to the public. It is important to see this program. No judgment here.

DEBTERAW vs. OBAMA

When I compared these two individuals in terms of education, experience and ability, individuals scolded me for my views and some websites refused to post the article of comparison. My message was simply to expose the fact why and how Americans put their man on top of the job while we Aethiopians put our man with the same caliber in dungeon.

What about now? This week we are witnessing that President Obama is celebrating Honest Abe who kept the American Union pursuing Civil War and Emancipation. By the way Abraham Lincoln used to worship in 1313 N.Y. Ave. NW. Washington, DC.

This week we are approaching the third wave of Eway Revolution that will herald the end of TPLF and EPLF tyranny and dictatorship respectively. No doubt DEBTERAW's long struggle in keeping EPRP alive and intact for the purpose of Unity and Revolution of Ethiopia will be celebrated. It is a matter of when and where.

Unification Churches vs. All Souls Church

What is the difference? Both Churches are located along the 16th street, to be specific; Unification Church's address is at Columbia Rd., NW Washington, DC 20009. The address of the All Souls Church is located at 2935 16th street, NW Washington DC 20009

The are located on 16th street along the Golden Gate to the White House facing each other though their entrance is located from different location. The thing I don't understand is why all the meetings organized by Ethiopians are held in the Unification church. I might add that the Symposium that was organized for DEBTERAW was held in the same church. The organizers for DEBTERAW, I believe chose this place for its low budget. But there are rich organizations that have and still conducted their meeting in this unification church.

May be Ethiopians love unity than diversity!

On Adam & Eve

Who comes first E or A? Eve was tossed from the Garden of Eden for a minor offense but now she is dealing with her mate, children and disappointed father as described in Elissa Elliott's Eve. Elliott asks was Eve the first lady? Who knows may be it was Lucy of Aethiopia!

Innocent and Lucy ገርሂ እና ድንቅነሽ

The archeological bones that were discovered in the highland of Eritrea and in the lowlands of Ethiopia are named to reflect the wishes and desires of people. Of what people! People of the gods or of GOD, I wish I knew the answer.

What is preferred to be an innocent or a beautiful? Innocence is a hallmark of old generation while beauty is a hallmark of this generation. Can't Aethiopians have both attributes? Cash flow has destroyed our innocence. The current rulers do not seem to grasp the concept of finance let alone cash money. Should we not be aware of the history of money since king Ezana's time? Let us first learn the use of money before we try to run for money.

Also, a piece of advice to our women folk, where do you stand in the following ranks of history. When a woman is between 15-20, she is supposed to be wild like Africa, When she is between 20-25, she is beautiful like America When she is between 25-30, she coarse like Germany When she is between 30-35, she is mature like France When she is between 35-40, she is rough like Russia and When she is between 40-45, she is old like England <u>On Issayas (E) vs. Meles (Z)</u>

How does Issayas apply his name in relation to the Bible? Does he sign his name with an E or an I? Why is he not forthcoming to his identity? Why did he keep people guessing who he is and his philosophy? I bet nobody asked him directly for he does not believe in questions, as he does not delve in democracy of any sort except in jokes.

What about Melese? Why does he not use his given name? Is he still in a disguise format? Who is he and what is his personal philosophy and what does he want out of the Ethiopian and Eritrean people? Why does he behave in a tyrannical way? I bet deep in his heart, he is GUILTY about his friends who died for real DEMOCRACIA. Fear is killing him just like his predecessor Menghistu Haile Mariam.

On Iyassou (E) vs. EPRP

What about Iyassou? Why does he not use the letter E? He is one of the founding members of EPRP. He is also one of the leading collective leaders of EPRP. Since he is still in the business of struggle of empowering the people of Ethiopia and Eritrea via DEMOCRACIA, I understand his position to use pen name also known as nom d'guerre የትጥቅ ሹራ and so on in various languages. What is in a name, call me by my name?

Why do current/ex members and supporters blame Iyassou for nothing? If he is not a democrat with a capital D, he is a democrat with a small d. has he not fought all his life and is he not still fighting to establish a system of democratic government in Aethiopia. Or is fighting with ideas and thoughts are irrelevant in the struggle for Aethiopia? Is it not true that the pen is still mightier than the sword? In actual fact, our fighters have not used swords but guns and bombs, which they have not manufactured themselves.

What is better for Aethiopia or Eathiopia or Ethiopia? What is in a name? What is the solution? A choice among, Dictatorship as in Eritrea, Tyranny as in Ethiopia or Democratic Republic with EPRP will have to be made soon. We need to choose!

On Afric a's Ghad afi

President Ghadafi openly admitted that no democracy is needed for Africa. He is now the head of the **African Authority.** What a shame!!!

What is the relationship between Libya, Eritrea and Somalia? I wish I knew the answer.

On Al Gore vs. Earth

Al Gore, the Nobel Peace winner told the Senate Committee, … "would bring a screeching halt to human civilization and threaten the fabric of life everywhere on the Earth – and this is within this century, if we don't change."

When John Kerry, presidential candidate asked Al Gore to tell the Senate Committee about the energy solution, he quickly answered that it is Geothermal

"Geothermal energy. This has great potential; it is not very far off."

I bet Al Gore know the territory of the Afar from where Lucy came. The Afar land was and still is hell – a burned face of the Earth. Geothermal is plenty in the Afar land. I hope he was not speaking about this land – an inconvenient truth!

Trillion is 1,000,000,000,000 = 13

The year of many trillions is in place for stimulus and bailout. Could the year 2013 be for solutions for our perceived solutions?

CONCLUSION

Currently in Aethiopia, Will power is in short supply, but good intentions abound. How about a kick in the rear by external forces if good intentions can't cut it? A kick from Issayas or Melese in our case, a kick from Ghadafi in the case of Africa or a kick from President Obama in the case of America. Definitely a kick from President Obama and DEBTERAW would be desirable as both are qualified for a kick! But not from the others.

For us, there was a call from DEBTERAW. While he was corresponding with me about his whereabouts I asked him what the solutions would be for all Eathiopians. He said the solutions lies in AAGMELAGO (see this in call me by my name...). Since DEBTERAW had suggested this term some years back, I have been trying to figure it out as what he meant by that concept. By the way Geothermal is plenty in Eathiopia. I wish Mr. Gore have seen the place where the human civilization is discovered and where the Geothermal energy is located. Currently, Mrs. Lucy is in Washington Seattle while the geothermal energy is along Awash River.

What a coincidence of history and culture HC = HC A clash of Geez and Latin letters.

Or a convergence of alphabets!

TRUTH WILL PREVAIL

For comments and questions: woldetewolde@yahoo.com

SOLUTIONS WITH DEBTERAW, VI

Call me by my name, address and task

By Obo Arada Shawl -

February 23, 2009

*For whom the bell tolls Ethiopiawinet is abstract Ethiopianism is concrete
Since there seems no agreement
What about the alternative medicine of Aagmelago as inspired by DEBu!*

The unfinished journey of DEBTERAW
Versus
EPLF, TPLF and OLF

The why and the how's: Today is the beginning of Fasting...

COLONIALSM?

Colonialism is as old as society itself. However, the term colonialism took a more sharp and specific meaning during the 19th century when colonialists saw it as an extension of "civilization" from Europe to "backward societies".? Was Aethiopia a backward society with no so-called "civilization"? What is the stand of EPLF, TPLF and OLF as at to date? Perhaps regret! Call me by my name, what is my name, colonizer or colonized? Explanation is required!

In addition colonialism was seen as a search for

- Raw materials,
- New markets and
- New fields of investment.

What about MMI (material-market-investment)? Was Aethiopia fit for colonization to take place based on these criteria? EPLF, TPLF and OLF, please tell us more on these issues.

At other times, colonialism was colonization that desire to physically settle people from the imperial country. Who was imperial in the Aethiopian case? More explanations, please! Resettlement or migration tells us different stories.

Typical aspect of colonialism include Racial and Cultural between the ruling and the subjects such as the followings

- Political
- Legal domination   = Your action speaks louder than words
- Exploitation of the subject
people

Colonialism was seen as a key cause of uneven development. What is the stand of EPLF, TPLF and OLF concept of uneven development? Is ignorance bliss in this case?

Finally, contrary to the EPLF, TPLF and OLF claims of being colonized, the term colonialism may also be used to refer to an ideology or a set of beliefs used to legitimize or promote the system. As such the colonizers of Aethiopia seem to be the EPLF and the TPLF in concrete terms and the OLF in abstract terms.

Colonialism was often based on the ethnocentric belief that the morals and values of the colonizer were superior to those of the colonized – otherwise known as Racism or pseudo- scientific. What is the purpose of ethnicity? It is either racism or something else. All Aethiopians demand explanation.

AETHIOPIANS?

- Those who were born in geographical Ethiopia alias MAKK
- Those who have and still are struggling in the Eway Revolution
- Those who are married to Aethiopians and
- Those who were adopted to be Aethiopians and
- Others who qualify for any other reason not mentioned above

DEMOCRACIA?

It is in our culture to judge and be judged. In Aethiopia it is of judges, by judges and for judges?

The culture of WE is deep in our culture as a result we have been judging others by our standard. Aethiopian strive to behave in virtuous morality not by edicts and votes.

Interestingly enough, President Kennedy's speech at the time "ask not what your country can do for you but ask what you can do for your country" reverberated in the Student Movement which really touched the CIA Opportunists. The radical student movement, not only were aware of their culture of voluntarism but also they were ready to sacrifice for their country. They did not need President Kennedy's appeal.

DEMOCRACIA – the political organ of EPRP has been published its 34ᵗʰ and 35ᵗʰ year this month. The first call is for the youth to take charge of their beloved country Aethiopia (USAE) while the second issues is about Yekatit የካቲት ግም ሲል.

DEBTERAW's call for action

- Know what the Americans and Israel's want out of Aethiopia
- Know the interests of the Chinese and Russians
- Know where the interests of Europeans lie
- Know why the Arabs and Muslims want to be involved in the game of chess
- Strategize how the leaders of EPLF and TPLF abdicate their power.

A hint for removing the leaders of EPLF and TPLF.

1. The EPLF leader is a dictator for he does not believe in the concept of democracy let alone DEMOCRACIA
2. The leader of TPLF is a Tyrant who cheats in the name of democracy but exercises his power in a tyrannical way
3. Ask for justice in the name of DEBTERAW for Shaebia claims that their main objective is searching for justice while Woyane knows very well that they are keeping the rare Revolutionary/

Patriot incommunicado for fear of flourishing open and free DEMOCRACIA in ኢትዮጵያ.

NB: This month of Yekatit has seen many adventures, many sharp changes of fortune. Since 1974, all Aethiopians have seen war, revolution, execution, madness, sexual scandal, power corruption, religious conversion and attempted assassination but not POWER ABDICATION. Why, why and why? Can one find it by fasting?

TRUTH WILL PREVAIL

For comments and questions: woldetewolde@yahoo.com

SOLUTIONS WITH DEBTERAW, VII -

Call me by my name, address and title

By Obo Arada Shawl -

April 1, 2009

It was a comedy of the King to be an investor in education
It is a tragedy for Dictator Essayas to invest in education
It is a double tragedy for Tyrant Meles to be an investor in education

ምሁራን M'huran refers to the Professional servants
Versus
ጽንሐተ ምሁራን Ts'nhate M'huran refers to
the Public servants (politicians)

BACKGROUND DATA

- 49 years ago, during the coup d'etat by the Neway Brothers, there were less than 100 students in the University
- Over 90% of the Eathiopian population were illiterate in Latin alphabets
- Less than 15% of the population used to go to school
- Only 5% had completed grade 12
- Some 60% were made to fail the Ethiopian School Leaving Certificate (ESLC)
- Only a half-million students were enrolled in elementary school
- There were about 170,000 students in High School.

POLITICS

Source: The Generation by Kiflu Tadesse

Everybody knows that people are the most important assets in any organization more so for EPRP. The struggle for Labor versus Capital was well known for EPRP member organizations and allied supporters. Contrary to many elitist elements that oppose the EPRP, the active members of EPRP have always attempt to merge politics, science and technology in their endeavor to revolutionize Eathiopia. The Eway Revolution was meant to change the Monarchy, to separate the Clergy from the state and to encourage those so-called "Nobility" class to join the working class. A political decision!

There is nothing more unpredictable than politics. Some Eathiopians see politics as hopeful and as essential to achieving humanity's dreams and potentials. For other Eathiopians, politics is a necessary evil, or a conspiracy of the elite. Don't we all know that both views are correct?

But what is politics? It is about people and it is about power. No one can be safe with either one. EPRP is in the business of peoples' power, which is embedded in DEMOCRACIA and not in the power of the gun. This can only be done via investment in education a la M'huran and Tsinhate M'huran style.

EPRP leaders and members recognize both Chairman Mao's dictum that "politics is a war without bloodshed" and in Winston Churchill's words "that in war you could be killed only once, but in politics you can be killed many times".

What is education after all?

Education normally is an act that refers to any experience that has a formative effect on the minds, character or physical ability of an individual. Technically, education is a process by which society, via schools, colleges and universities and other institutions transforms cultural heritage, accumulated knowledge, values and skills from generation to generation. That was the aim of the Student Movement.

The right to education is a basic human right. Civil and political rights, life, liberty, freedom of expression, equality for social and economic rights, rights to participate in culture, to work and so on, are all Human Rights Issues.

Modern education was introduced into Ethiopia with the full support of Haile Sellasie I. No doubt modern education was due to him. In fact, he became a patron of the University. He had eleven colleges named after him.

Was he wrong to be a patron? Was it symbolic or substantive should be the right question? What about now? Can we say the same of the prime minister of Ethiopia and president of Eritrea?

To be a patron of Education, one has to be aware in the relationship of *concept-theory-and practice* in Educational Investment. Haile Sellasie was appointing ministers who were armed only with theories and at that - merely acquired from college's books. In other words, there were almost no ጸንሐተ ምሁራን አካል involved in Haile Sellasie government.

ONE MANDEFRO

As I recall Ato Mandefro was an officer in the Central Personnel Agency (CPA). As part of his task he used to ask the graduates who came to apply for a job whether they have done some research/study about their country - Eathiopia. If the applicants did not possess thesis or dissertation papers written on Eathiopia, Ato Mandefro will hand them plain papers and ask them to write what they know about their country-Eathiopia. It was a good device for the recruiter man to distinguish the educated class namely ምሁር እና ጸንሃተ ምሁር አካል.

However, during the DERG era, most graduate applicants were from the Socialist countries and as they were caught off guard, they had no clue what he was demanding of them and as retribution the disgruntled candidates labeled Ato Mandefro as anti-revolution and as a result he was sent into prison. What a tragedy it was for Eathiopia!

MILLION MANDEFROS

In today's Eathiopia, we are all Mandefros. We want to know about Eathiopia. Thousands are attacking the educated or disrespecting them.

Why? Because many of them are unable to write about Eathiopia's core problems, though most of them can discuss, analyze and suggest solutions for other countries.

Most of the educated class gives two main reasons for not writing about their country:

- No data on Eathiopia
- No access or freedom to write

As to the first reason, unless they initiate to write, how could there be any data. The population is the data. The Eathiopian population is the primary source of data. Those who have written about Eathiopia and for Eathiopians are called ጽንሃተ ምሁራን አካሎች....

As to the second reason, it is good enough to fight for their political rights and focus on their respective change of government. Nobody will do it for them; they have to take the lead. They ought to lead and not to follow the illiterate body.

MAIN REASON FOR NOT LEADING

Governance is a craft (secret power), not merely a talent (genius). It involves careful sorting of ideas and priorities. The Eway Revolution entailed knowing the foundations upon which the Monarchy, the Clergy and the Nobility (MCN) were based. EPRP's first priority was to install a Political Institution i.e. a system of governance of the Eathiopians, by the Eathiopians and for the Eathiopians firmly stamping an idea and a trademark known as DEMOCRACIA. From the start, it was very clear for EPRP to believe in that

- The Monarchy was outdated and was destined to be replaced
- The Clergy had become subservient to the Monarchy and that the Church should distance itself from the Patriarch
- The Nobility would be transformed into working class or Bureaucrats i.e. progressive ones.

For this EPRP was and is being isolated politically and sanctioned economically by the so-called "Nobility" who are still confusing the working class and the peasantry.

CONCLUSION

Long before EPRP was formally formed, there were many graduates who had undermined the crucial role of alumni associations. A would have been a vibrant function of alumni association was curtailed due to elites like Samuel Alemayehu who was the president of the Alumni Association during the reign of Haile Sellasie. The other culprits were the president of the university, the academia and some professors. The Tsinhate M'huran Akal were barred subtly from running institutions and research centers that could have contributed to the over all development of Eathiopia

The Tsinhate M'huran Akal including Debteraw had faced multi-faced obstacles. Though in general, the college student body were opposing the administration of the University along with the lecturers mode of operand, the would be EPRP leaders and members were mainly agitating against the subject matter that was being taught in the university college of Haile Sellasie. The struggle was not targeted against the administration or the professors per se; it was rather to bring a new understanding of the Eathiopian reality show.

Today, The main reason why DEBTERAW is in prison is simply because he is the leader in Tsinhate Muhur Akal. His usual rhetorical question is to ask questions of WHY and HOW? If any individual asks such questions, he/she would have to succeed not only personally but also professionally. That was DEBTERAW's belief.

It's time to believe in it (Education/information) It's time to absorb it
It's time to translate it
And it's time to abandon titles
But to embrace Tsinhate Muhur titles
Let us heed
President B. Obama's call
"The future belongs to the nation that best educates its citizens."
In order to save our children and our people

TRUTH WILL PREVAIL

For comments and questions: woldetewolde@yahoo.com

SOLUTIONS WITH DEBTERAW, VIII

Call me by my name, address or title

By Wolde R. Tewolde

April 9, 2009

> It is not about reaching out
> It is about holding on to values
> It is not about winning or losing battles It is about achieving
> objectives That EPRP should be judged Anonymous

This article is the first in a three part series depicting Assegid Wolde Amanuel, the _student_, the _professional_ and the _public servant_. AWA died on USA soil but was buried in Addis Ababa on March 29, 2009. This is a tribute and a testimony of a patriot who was misunderstood not only by his friends, colleagues and foes alike but also by his own sisters. Besides, many living murhuran would hopefully understand how the Eway Revolution – the very tenet that Assegid stood for - was and is functioning. By doing so, I hope that AWA and many others like him would be exonerated from the wrong perception perpetuated by all living Eathiopian souls. In addition, this may open up a dialogue with ሙሁራን Muhuran versus ጽንተ ሙሁራን Tsinhate Muhuran. AWA's funeral service was held at St Michael's church two weeks from today. Assegid was still popular even in his death. There is no better testimony than his wife and the church clergy who eulogized him to the best of their knowledge about AWA.

Background

Assegid W. Amanuel and I have nicknames for each other. He used to address me as a Wollamo and I used to address him as a Dorze. Why did we address each other in that manner? My own experience with Assegid was during a football match when I have observed Assegid playing football on barefoot while it was raining. Gayo Haleke, the Godson of Germame Neway and Assigid were my favorite soccer players. Although both were playing barefoot and my eyes fell on Assigid's. That was when and then that I related AWA to the Dorze ethnic whom I saw mixing mud with sand with their bare feet. I bluntly asked whether Assegid belonged to this ethnic group and he bluntly responded as if I was a "Wollamo." Since that day, we had very close and warm relationships.

In other words, I have read his *feet* and he had read my *face* – physical readings. It was because of Assegid that I have maintained to tell to everyone and everybody that my mother had deliberately created scars on my face that would be equivalent to a car tag so that nobody will have difficulty in identifying me. I am glad that I have a definite identity since Assegid's reminder. Assegid was not angry when I had addressed the way I did and I think he told me that he was one of them – a hard working people. For some period of time, I did believe him. This image reading was so destructive that thousands died or lived in anger. As we went to college our scopes had widen and literature readings have helped us all to change our attitude towards one another.

The Ethiopian Student Movement liberated us to be open and address the way we feel, of course with no qualms or malice towards none. But later on, from physiological to behavioral reading came to our senses and we had developed this name calling to a higher-level while in colleges and professional fields. For us and for thousands like us, to say Dorze, Wollamo, Agame, Galla, Amara, Gurage, Kimante, Tigri, Shankla or any other name-calling did not mean a thing. We were liberated from our ignorance not so because of available curriculum study or books written about sociology on Ethiopia but because of our engagement in the Ethiopian Student Movements, in sports and of course later on as a result of our working with the Eathiopian rural population.

But when I met Assigid in Washington, DC, I addressed him the way I did in Ethiopia. Assigid told me that things back home have become serious and advised me not to use such languages. What has happened? I asked him. Assegid told me only "ነገሩ የምር ሆነዋል" That was the end of that. We parted – he went to Ethiopia and I remained in America. One can compare this name-calling based on phonology with that of today's addressing one another based on ethnicity and language. What a tragedy!!!

General Wingate High School

For those readers, who do not know about Wingate – he was the major leading a small British – led regular force known as "the Gideon Force". Orde Wingate joined with the irregular Ethiopian patriots fighting the Italian occupation in Ethiopia. After the defeat of the Italians during the 2nd World War, Haile Sellasie I allowed to be named this prestigious high school after the British General.

What did this school produce? What kind of school was it? Who are the alumni? Where are they now? Have they contributed to the development of Eathiopia yet? Or to the destruction of Ethiopia? Although, the school is my alma mater, I have not appreciated the contribution of its alumni to Eathiopia's development, especially when the school at the time was supposed to be on par with that of Harvard in USA, Oxford in Britain or Sorbonne in France.

Orde Wingate left Ethiopia without bidding goodbye to Emperor Haile Sellasie I. Writing on Wingate, Wikipedia put the following" Wingate was most concerned about British attempts to stifle Ethiopian Freedom, writing that attempts to raise future rebellions amongst populations must be honest ones and should appeal to justice."

The British government - the sponsor of the school, had a good system of running the school. We were highly trained to be disciplined, respectful and responsible citizens of what country I do not know. After graduation, some left for England, some to France and others to the USA. I cannot account all those who went abroad for further studies. But Assigid was one of those who went back to serve his country and people and he did in his profession until his sickness took his life.

Assegid W. Amanuel as a bureaucrat in road transport

The first progressive graduate students were employed in the Ethiopian Road Transport Administration. It was the first test of their progressiveness. The sector of road transport was the ideal place for becoming rich albeit through corruption. But none of the graduate bureaucrats became corrupt officials. On the contrary all of them became careful not to indulge in any corruption. And what was interesting everyone and everybody were working in harmony and served the public in honesty and efficient manner. In my view, these graduates were the first group who honestly and diligently embraced to enter the old bureaucracy and change it upside down for good. **In other words, Road Transport was a place for the continuation of the Eathiopian Student Movement by other means.**

But who were these people besides Assegid? It was better for me to name them in accordance to my visits when I usually enter their respective offices. Amazingly, they were paired in their ethnic backgrounds. Assegid was housed with Lulseged both from Harrar affiliation; Ibsa Gutema and Bekele Geleta both from Wollega region sitting in one room; Gebru Mersha sitting with Yirga Tessema from Gurage region and Wallellign Makonnen and Sine sitting together. These five pairs I used to visit and have coffee or tea in their respective offices addressing them in their ethnic nicknames and we were all enjoying it. Deep inside, we were coming to together for a long haul to help the Eathiopian people for a fundamental change. And we did and still we are continuing the long struggle. I believe most of my readers know the whereabouts of these individuals and what they have done to the betterment of Eathiopia.

While working at the Commercial bank, I had come with many businessmen and bankers, but it was no match for my desire to quench the modern young bureaucrats that I have observed in the transport sector. The working relationship of these graduate students had given me a great hope for any kind of development that would have taken place in Ethiopia. I learnt right there that there was hope and desire for progress provided that certain dedicated individuals were allowed to exercise their power in government to bring a positive change. The type of bureaucracy that was in them was almost perfect. It was a model for me and probably for thousands of Eathiopians. Of course, one major part of their success story was because of their boss by the name Ato Shimellis Adugna. He gave them the power and the choice to conduct their daily business. That model of coming out fresh from a university, serving businessmen, the government and above all the public should have been emulated. I believe also that many have somehow followed their bureaucratic path.

It was undeniable that if not all, most of these young bureaucrats have continued to change the political landscape of Ethiopia simultaneously on a professional as well as on political levels.

It was in this setting that Assegid should be viewed as an expert in transportation and later on communications sectors. He was one of the best whom I call Tsinhate Muhur Akal. Why do I say this? Because, Assigid lived the live of the poor, he knew the living conditions of the land lords, and he understood the need of transport and communications in the country. He acquired the knowledge to qualify him to be a transport expert and all that was required of him was to put it in practice. For this, he was blamed for not helping his friends and relatives to become rich.

Assegid was there to help when help was needed, I would think that he had helped his classmates to have jobs but that does not make him a corrupt person. It was a noble thing if he had assisted the Wingaters provided that they were qualified for the task demanded but not at the expense of the public trust. What I do not understand is that why some people complain that has worked with the DERG. Why cannot we understand that people work for their profession? Let us compare AWA's public service with that of the banker's (governor) profession of Tadesse G.K.

In reality, Assegid has helped the movement of people and goods from one region to another. We are were we are because, we have seen one another, fought against each other, exchanged goods and services and we even have communicated with one another. Isn't this phenomenal? I think it is. One can argue that he facilitated the logistics of military and forced resettlement of people from the highlands to the low lands. But that was another matter. Neither the war policy nor the resettlement policy would have involved Assegid WA. He might have been a communist cardholder by default. AWA's name should be deciphered as a person who volunteered to be a public servant and who had hoped to vote for a final victory (VVV). He died without seeing his wisdom (VV) being implemented. I hope his children will witness his vision and mission being accomplished. God Bless his soul.

TRUTH WILL PREVAIL

For comments and questions: woldetewolde@yahoo.com

SOLUTIONS WITH DEBTERAW, IX

Call me by my name, address or title

By Obo Arada Shawl

April 23, 2009

> There was/is China for EPLF to emulate
> There was Albania for TPLF - a black hole - where no
> information would escape There was false-revolution by the
> DERG that nationalizing would become panacea. Then,
> there was/is EPRP that tries to score Political Capital.

At elementary school, he joined the underclass, at high school level, he became an outstanding soccer player, on college level he became a political activist, after his return from abroad he became professionally a decisive liberated man. That was Assegid Wolde Amanuel (AWA).

The PROFESSION

As I have repeatedly attempted to explain, the Eway Revolution should not be confused with that of the Socialist Revolution by the DERG. The Ethiopian polity and policy should be separated when we discuss issues of a national character. The Ethiopian polity of the DERG era was based on the Russian model whereas the economic policy was based on the American system, mainly guided by the IMF and the World Bank.

In other words, the Eathiopian bureaucrats were sandwiched between a _political_ and an _economic_ Revolution. For simplicity, I would like to compare two bureaucrats of a separate ministries, that of a ministry of Transport and Communication and Financial Institution. Of course, the minister of transport & communication was AWA whereas the Governor of Ethiopia's bank was Tadesse G. Kidan.

Both professional individuals were educated in social sciences that are not exact sciences. Both professionals were not directly involved in the in the Eway Revolution though in politics it is usually about people in large groups and comprises one of the followings

- Ideology – Parties
- Social order – Societies
- Nation – nations

Minister Assegid was leaning towards ideological politics though he was committed neither to MIESO nor to EPRP political structure but he was a keen onlooker about EPRP's movement for he knew that only political solutions via political parties would bring peace and stability to the nation. Tadesse G. Kidan was more or less was very much looking for the social order of the nation. In other words, both professionals were experts in their fields of study but their fields of study would not make them political leaders but tools or means for transporting goods and services as in the case of Assegid or financial instruments in the case of Tadesse.

It is high time that all ordinary citizens of Eathiopia (HAG) should realize that communications and money are solely tools. At the same time, it more relevant to all politicians to understand that DEMOCRACIA, is a means or tools that guides one to attain its aspiration or goal.

We should not forget that Eathiopia during the DERG era was operating under the concept of militarism and engineering design. Out of the eleven-politburo committee, seven were military men and five of them were engineers. By their training the two categories of militarism and engineering do not possess cool thinking. The Eathiopian masses in (urban areas) under the DERG and the Woyane masses in (rural areas) were involved in dancing that was also an emotional phenomenon. In that aspect, both AWA and TGK were not different than the rest of us in being led by mass emotions.

It is imperative to self analyze what the role of the ሙሁር during the eras of emotional distress that was rampant in the DERG's revolution. I would point out how the Muhur ሙሁር አካል was confused and cowed so much so that each blames the other profession without understanding the root cause of their dilemma.

In Marketing as in Architecture (MA- not to confuse with the degree), both professions do support other professions contrary to most Eathiopian professionals. We have witnessed and still are witnessing that one Muhur Akal attempting to demean if not to destroy the other Muhur Akal of a different profession. Why is that, can any one dares to tell us, please?

I can understand though, that since communication and financial operations are difficult to grasp by the common people, the two positions of the two ministers was hard to evaluate.

Take for instance that Professor Getachew Haile, my teacher, and Ayalnesh, my soul mate both praised Governor Tadesse G. Kidan. Why? I believe because both of them have attempted to evaluate TGK from his social order and not from his political ambitions. Because of these evaluation and appreciation, there seems a kind of mistrust among victims of the DERG regime. It's to be recalled that professor Getachew Haile and Ayalnesh, the Eway Revolutionary, were both victims of the DERG and the TPLF regimes respectively.

Unfortunately, AWA did not write his side of story but TGK did in his book "ስጠ ዐያሁ" albeit he told us half of the story of his service to the DERG.

CONCLUSION

In my first article on AWA, I have quoted from anonymous source the following

> It is not about reaching out
> It is about holding on to values
> It is not about winning or losing battles
> It is about achieving objectives
> That EPRP should be judged

Assegid Wolde Amanuel and Tadesse Gebre Kidan should be judged by their personal achievement, by their professional accomplishment and by their public services and not via the prism of working within the DERG regime.

For those readers who doubt about the interconnection between the Ethiopian Student Movement, the Eway Revolutionary professionals and the true Public civil Servants, you are encouraged to read "call me by my name: a debate with DEBTERAW, XX that was written and posted on November 17, 2007.

For those first time readers about DEBTERAW, the above article was the last debate with DEBTERAW. We are currently communicating with DEBTERAW in finding lasting solutions for our people and country Eathiopia.

With that background, let me close by quoting the following paragraph from the same article "There is a missing link in EPRA's history but there is no missing link in the history of EPRP. The struggle of EPRP will continue unabated with or without individual leadership or professorship. It is all about **P** (principle) and not about **B** (benefit) or **B** (blood)."

TRUTH WILL PREVAIL
For comments and questions: woldetewolde@yahoo.com

Postscript

While writing on Assegid's student political activity, I was told verbally and in written form that I was biased because he was my friend and that I should never praised AWA's wife for she had violated the customary law of not testifying about one's husband especially when one is dead. And that she should never raise the issue of his sisters' dispute. What is your stand on this controversy? Let us discuss.

SOLUTIONS WITH DEBTERAW, X:

Are Eathiopians defined by Arts or Religion?

Call me by my name, address and title -

Obo Arada Shawl

May 23, 2009

History of Arts

Any real history starts at the grassroots. Any one of the following seven disciplines is a type of visual art. This may be a simplified version of what we know about visual arts means. Eathiopians do not seem to have problems in distinguishing these types of arts.

Visual Arts

1. Drawing
2. Painting
3. Sculpture
4. Architecture
5. Printmaking
6. Film
7. Photography

It is true that the first five disciplines of drawing, painting, sculpture, architecture and printmaking were mainly found in the Orthodox Eathiopian Churches - though missing from the views of the general populace.

The phrase **"the Arts"** as a term was discussed scholarly and it was quite often limited to the following:

1. Music
2. Rhetoric
3. Dialectic logic
4. Grammar
5. Astronomy
6. Geometry
7. Arithmetic

Just like the visual arts it was again categorized into seven disciplines. With the exception of geometry and arithmetic, the rest five disciplines were quite known in the Orthodox Eathiopian Churches. Although this category started during the 16th century, in our case, mostly the debteras were the critics to be heard, the rest of us had to comply with the Orthodox Christian form of Arts.

It seems that I am crediting too much to the Orthodox Churches ledger in terms of ኪነት Ki"net. As time passes bye and as if these categorization were not enough to make us confuse, the above seven Arts came to be known as the **"Fine Arts"** so as to distinguish them from the "useful arts". Useful Arts - people were too busy or lazy to have need for education. Here comes the conflict of visions for the Arts.

As the difference between science and art become sharpened, the phrase "Fine Arts" came to mean anything that has been associated/created to please the senses.

After losing the sciences, the list now includes the following four elements as well as what we normally think of as "Art".

- Music
- Dance
- Opera and
- Literature

With the single exception of the Opera, Eathiopians are good in Music, dance and Literature. This is the art that DEBTERAW used to promote with specially emphasis on Literature- the domain of DEBTERAW. And the so-called scientific analysis by the educated classes of Eathiopia have added more confusion to the Eway Revolution that was underway to rectify Minilik's concept of modernization, Tewodros's act of unity, Yohannes's handling of religion and Haile Sellasie's type of education.

My first reaction about Arts was in relation to the death of Tilahun Gessesse. A commentary was written entitled "what is Art? What is Artist?" And it can be read at <u>SOLUTIONS WITH DEBTERAW, a comm en tar y on th e "a rts of de ath."</u> In the commentary, I concluded by stating that Tilahun Gessese has dwelt very well on the triangle of Love-Family-Friendship whereas DEBTERAW Tsegaye and Yemane Baria were aiming at the trio for Liberty-Unity-Justice – the Eway to 23rd century of ETHIOPIA ኢኢትዮጵያ

It is important to remember that during the 20th century, "fine arts" came to be categorized as

- Visual Arts
- Auditory Arts (music, drama, spoken literature)
- Performance Arts (visual/auditory or combination)

The place and role of the Arts in the Eway Revolution

During the era of Haile Sellassie, Art was performed or housed only in two places, in the Hager Fikr ሀገር ፍቅር theatre and at the Haile Sellassie I National Theatre ብሔራዊ ቲያትር these two places were meant to display and encourage the elites of Eathiopians to be patriotic and nationalistic respectively. Those who frequent Hager Fiker Theatre were destined to be patriotic whereas those who go to the Haile Sellasie Theatre were lured to be nationalistic. Unfortunately, those attendees at the Haile Sellasie became hyphenated Eathiopians. The main reason was that creativity was discouraged but carbon copy of foreign materials encouraged. That was a place and a time when the two Tsegayes G. Medhins collide – one for domestic creativity and the other for foreign adaptation. Of course, the National Theatre became a place for confusion and alienation.

Fortunately, there were „what I call the third tier of Eathiopian Artists" such as Tesfaye Lema, Telela Kebede, Awlachew Degene and many other heroic artists who lived under duress or had to leave these two places involuntarily.

During the DERG era "the Arts" was carried on a similar manner with tightly controlled in the name of their "fake revolution". In fact, as the top men in the power of the DERG were only military and engineers, there was no way to engage the broad masses ሐፋሽ Hafash in the Arts. But thanks to DEBTERAW and his Political Party, EPRP that ኪነት Kinet has flourished albeit under clandestine በሕቡዐ circumstances. Access to the unsung heroes and heroines to make Arts live and well to the broad masses of Eathiopia was encouraged by EPRP albeit at a high cost.

While the DERGists and the Nationalists were busy propagating the Youth with arming with hate and violence, EPRP with the help of its leadership prominent among them DEBTERAW were teaching by example how to love one's country, respect for one self and to empower others by means of poems, literature and discipline. The result is what we see today. Have a look closely at each individual person.

In other words, politicians, activists and citizens of Eathiopia should re-evaluate their stand on what ኪነት means and how it is applicable to their daily lives. In order to do that, let us examine and relate the case of the following three Artists.

- Wogayo Nigatu a case of ***Performing Art***
- Tesfaye Lemma a case of ***Living art***
- DEBTERAW Tsegeye a case of ***Enduring Art***

Let us start by asking how, where or why. Of course, the **how** question is relevant to Wogayehu Nigatu, the **where** question is for Tesfaye Lemma and the **why** question relates to DEBTERAW.

In other words, how did Wogeyehu Nigatu die at such a young age? Where is Tesfaye Lemma currently located despite his efforts to develop and promote Eathiopian Arts? And why is DEBTERAW IS STILL HELD INCOMMUNICANDO? I believe the answer lies deep in each of us who are interested in the Eathiopian Arts?

Now that we have established that we all cannot live without some sort of Arts, let us understand the basic forms of Art.

Art has two parts, a **Form** and **Content.**

Form includes elements of art, principles of design and physical materials that artists use.

Content is based on idea that portrays what an artist means, what an artist actually portrayed and above all how people react to the artist's actual or intended messages.

Let us take for instance, the following incidents

- What Mellese Zenawi has said in relation to the Eathiopian flag,
- What Issayas said in relation to the Ethiopian state
- What Wallellign has written in his essay in relation to an Amhara mask and
- On DEBTERAW's pun of words concerning Haile Sellasie's betting on the throne. All four had opinions - after all that was why the main reason they received education – to express opinions. But to say what they said and to write what they wrote

ጨርቅ ባንዴራ (መለስ) through the prism of arrogance
ኢትዮጵያ ሃያላን ባይኖሩ ኖሮ ... lack of understanding of social history
አስከ መገንጠል(ዋለልኝ) through the prism of family dispute
ዴሞክራሲ ያለ ጎዮብ (ፀጋዬ) through the prism of Arts

Should be judged and evaluated based on

- Place
- Time and
- Circumstances, otherwise it is an historical for all of us not to discern the differences.

DEBTERAW's works is full of content – the form of Arts – that has influenced religion, politics and society in general.

Our years of war and revolution in terms of politics and social influences as perpetuated by Artists and citizens of Eathiopia who were summarily executed in a historical context brought us mixed feelings of revulsion, anger and sorrow.

Though no fault of DEBTERAW and his political party, he is in prison for what power holders have pronounced and for what many cone artists have composed and sung.

What about Religion

There is a huge difference between an organized religion and a non-organized religion, the former not only it is relatively recent but also it is based on some rational or scientific phenomena, while the latter depends on faith alone.

So what is the main religion of Eathiopians? I bet there is no clear answer for my question. Obviously, there are all kinds of Christians such as Orthodox, Catholic, Protestant, Pentecostal, Jehovah, etc. etc, but they are all Christians – or are they? Please, someone explain to me in lay terms. Eathiopians are Muslims with Sunni or Shiite affiliates, but they are all Muslims – or are they? There are Eathiopians who practice Judaism, and there are people who are anti-Christ or no religion at all. So why is that religion suddenly became an issue in Eathiopia or is it going to be?

Is that because of the return of King Yohannes" children posed as atheists? Maybe the absence of followers of Teddy's unity, or lack of education despite Haile Sellassie's effort for economic development and nationalism or the lag of scientific modernization as frequently blamed King Minilik of Shoa? Does the future have to catch up with the past?

I do not understand.

As far as religion is concerned, the elites of Eathiopia were not educated, as Christian Evangelists no as Madras's though have had attended Christian and Moslem universities. The Christian elites were educated in Addis Ababa University while the Muslim elites were educated in Cairo universities. This condition relates before the Eway Revolution.

The Eway Revolution had encouraged for religion to travel from Arat Kilo and reached Mercato via Arada (AKAM).

Arat Kilo was/is a place where churches, palaces and universities conglomerate.

Arada also known as Piazza harbor businesses, entertainment and government (BEG).

Mercato was/is a place where a mosque and a church stand side by side harmonizing people to people and business transactions of all goods and services.

So where does DEBTERAW and his political party stand on religion? I believe DEBTERAW and his political party, EPRP stands independent of all organized religions. I believe DEBTERAW had tackled the issues of

- Personal and family
- Social and cultural
- Politics and economic
- Church and ministry and
- Theological and Spiritual issues,

As separate entities.

If this is not the correct idea and method by DEBTERAW, what then was/is the alternative one? For this DEBTERAW IS STILL HELD INCOMMUNICADO. Do we live for Arts or Arts serve us all? It is high time to stop acting and become real people. It should start from the top down - DEBTERAW SHOULD BE FREE.

TRUTH WILL PREVAIL

For comments and questions: woldetewolde@yahoo.com

CHALLENGING EATHIOPIANS ON THE FOURTH OF JULY!!!

SOLUTIONS WITH DEBTERAW, XI

Call me by my name, address and title -

July 4, 2009

In the recent past months, there is a simmering movement towards settling scores of politicking between Eritreans and Ethiopians. Such instances are

- Federation vs. Confederation
- A repeat of the slogan for struggle via "Bale or Bole" (EDIAL)
- Formation of a youth league for EPRP
- Crying wolf by the leaders of Shaebia and Woyane for Unity and Power Abdication
- A promise to reveal the existence of the Ark of Covenant by the an Ethiopian Cleric and so on and so forth…

All the above could be taken as a sign for positive thinking for final arrest to the Eway Revolution.

However, on close analysis, there are very important elements "missing" from these movements.

Scenario one: In the designs of God and in the eyes of men, "all men not women were created equal" Who created Eathiopians? Or alternatively, what is the day or the date for the INDEPENDENCE of Eathiopia? Miazia 27, Meskerem 2, May 24 or July 4? Do we really understand the meaning of Independence, Freedom or Liberty in the context of Eathiopia? Is this enough to be a challenging question? If there was no beginning date for Colonialism, we should not look for one as Independence.

Let us start with July 4, 1776. Was this date and year the Independence Day for America? Was this calendar an adoption or Declaration of Independence? If we know the answer to this question, I hope Eathiopians will come to their senses to talk about arnet or nezanet.አርነት፡ ነፃነት common terminology. Who struggled for what and for whom?

The Eritreans might have mismatched the Italian Colonialism to Ethiopian Colonialism that did not exist. I believe their long struggle was for freedom and liberty and not for Independence. If it was for Independence, it must be an independence from Italy. This should be the topic for reconciliation. Ethiopians should accept the independence of Eritrea and Eritreans in return would accept that their Independence Day was a culmination of European colonialism. This should be the challenging question before moving on to the next movement.

Scenario two: Sports and Entertainment do not seem to be part of these movements. The fact that the soccer players from Eritrea and Ethiopia crisscross in order to avoid each other instead of coming together. This year for instance, Ethiopians are in Chicago, Eritreans are in California and the Oromos will held their own on Atlanta, Georgia.

On the one hand, The Eritrean soccer federation does seem to grasp neither the adoption nor the declaration of Eritrean/American Independence. The Federation was hiding or rather sandwiched between the day of the Martyrs and the day of Family/Religious Festival known as ንግደት. I do not believe that their agenda was and is about sportsmanship. If it is, we have not seen it yet.

While on the other hand, The Ethiopian Sports Federation was/is not participating in the agrarian societies where food is plenty with missing "sportsmanship and comradeship". The Ethiopian Sports Federation was in a unique position in the sense that political groups, business people and civic communities gather in one place. Unfortunately, a quarter of a century has passed without making significant contributions to either development or cooperation among people of all walks of life from Ethiopia.

Can any one explain this anomaly of our struggle for change and revolution? Art, Entertainment and Sports industry should take center stage for reconciliation and development. Without these three sectors of Industry, little will be accomplished in the case of Eritrea and Ethiopia let alone in the Horn of Africa.

A reminder to all Revolutionaries of Eway Ethiopia

- You were involved in the struggle to bring *peace and democracy*
- You had the courage to fight for your *Rights*
- You were imprisoned for your *thoughts*
- You died for your *beliefs* and
- You are going to die for your Blue and Red Nation (**BRN**) but not for your currency (BR) A message to all anti-Eway Revolution
- Forgive and move on
- Stand for Eathiopia
- Ask questions of why and how
- Differentiate between Tabot and Constitution

Then

- Tell the truth for it will set you free
- Confess to not only to your God but to your fellowmen
- Speak to Power without fear
- Dare to be open to disclose your ID
- Search for the whereabouts of DEBTERAW Why DEBTERAW?

For DEBTERAW is the one who taught us that

R is for REVOLUTION Not for RACE
E is for Eritrea and Ethiopia

Not for ETHNICITY

·

That is why we should re-examine the *RE as a subject not as a predicate. In short let us all*

TAKE THE HEAT FOR OUR INALIENABLE RIGHTS
LET US TAKE A STAND FOR OUR DEMANDS not dreams
TAKE THE HEAT FOR OUR INALIENABLE RIGHTS LET US TAKE A STAND FOR OUR DEMANDS
Happy Four to all!!!

AWA: student activist, professional and public servant SOLUTIONS WITH DEBTERAW, XII

Call me by my name, address or title
By Obo Arada Shawl - July 23, 2009

This is the final piece of article written in memory of a student **activist**, a **planner** in transport & communications and a public **servant**. His name was Assegid Wolde Amanuel (AWA). His professional address extended from Moyale in the south, Assab in the east, Karora in the north and Kurmurk in the west labeled as MAKK ኢትዮጵያ. His job title was an economist and later a minister of Transport & Communications. His civil title was **Ato** Assegid as opposed to ግራዝማች ፤ ቀኛዝማች ወይም ኃድ

Introduction

In the past two articles, I have indicated AWA's participation in the Ethiopian Student Movement as well as in his professional expertise in transport & communication sectors of the Ethiopian economy where it is believed that Transport and Communication are the nerve centers for any meaningful development.

Aethiopia is considered to be a backward nation not because of its lack of social, religious or cultural factors but of its undeveloped modes of transport and communications. In Aethiopia almost 80%-90% of its passenger and freight are moved by traditional mode of transport such as walking and horses for traveling, pack animals such as donkeys and mules for transporting goods and services.

As a public servant, AWA has facilitated the movement of Aethiopians *to and from*. Doing so, the interaction of peoples of Aethiopia whether in going to war or running away from war was accomplished by AWA's responsibility via his professional understanding of public service not military service. In other words the interactions of T&C have brought the Eathiopian people to a better understanding of cooperation though not necessarily of coordination (CC).

Public Service

I know that there are individuals who think that working under the Monarchy or the DERG would automatically qualify them to be servants of Haile Sellassie and Menghistu but not of the Public. Such ideas emanate from people who were neither ever landed in professional jobs nor do have a clue about a clandestine political struggle – where freedom of any kind is banned. I bet the contribution of those professionals who had worked under the Monarchy or the DERG could weigh more than those who were in the battlefields. Let the benefit and cost analysis begin to roll– sabotaging the aims and objectives of militarism as well as of feudalism.

Public sector is about "budgeting" whereas in the private sector it is about "cost". Transport and communications sector in Eathiopia was and is public, private and autonomous. From this we can understand how difficult it was to evaluate and pinpoint AWA's role in this sector of economy especially when it was dominated by a public policy dubbed as the "revolutionary Ethiopia".

By the way, what is public policy? Public policy is an attempt by a government to address a public issue. In public policy, there are three parts (PPP),

- Problems
- Players and
- Policy

The *problem* in AWA's case was the issue that needed to be addressed namely the transport of people, goods and services.

The *player* is the individual or group of individuals that is influential in forming a plan to address the problem in question. Again in AWA's case the Central Planners of the DERG dubbed as the agents of the so-called revolution had their models from GDR and Moscow whereas the model of T&C for Assegid was from the West, resulting in a conflict of visions.

Policy is the finalized course of action decided upon by the government in this case Menghistu and his military cronies. AWA has nothing to do with top level of decision-making body. In most cases, policies were widely open to interpretation by non-governmental players, including those in the private sector. In this case, the role and influence of AWA was limited due to his non- membership holder of workers of Ethiopian party alias COPWE.

How was Public policy defined? It is defined as the course of action or inaction taken by government entities in regard to particular issue or issues. Normally, public policy was to be embodied in constitutions, legislative acts, and judicial decisions. The era of AWA's public service was the era of revolution and counter-revolution.

Ministry of Transport & Communications

Politically if not psychologically, anything that flies in the sky, crawls on land, swims in sea or water, was under the "Ministry of the DERG". Technically and in practice though it was a different matter. Everyone and everybody had his/her own game plan. A country of conspiracy and secrecy, the end result is what and where we are now.

However, for the ministry of transport and communications where AWA had spent his entire professional and public life, the following procedures were relevant

The rational model for the public policy-making process can be divided into the following three parts:

- Agenda setting
- Option-formulation and
- Implementation.

Within the agenda-setting stage, the agencies such as the Highway Authorities and government officials from the Central Planning used to meet to discuss the problem at hand. In the second stage, option-formulation, alternative solutions are considered and final decisions are made regarding the best policy. Consequently, the decided policy is implemented in the final stage. Implied within this model is the fact that the needs of the Aethiopian societies are a priority for the players involved in the policy-making process. Also, it is believed that the government will follow through on all decisions made by the final policy.

Unfortunately, those who frame the issue to be addressed by policy used to exert an enormous amount of influence over the entire T&C process through their political affiliations, personalities, and personal interests. The final outcome of the process, as well as its implementation, was therefore not as effective as that which could result from a purely rational process. The Public policy though it continued to be vital in addressing economic and social concerns of societies, the DERG, notwithstanding along with its loyal friends had collapsed on its own weight.

AWA had the skills and knowledge to understand not only the complexities of transport and communications but also the feudal mentality of many of his colleagues' vis-à-vis his revolutionary contemporaries' vision and mission. The following facts and figures could indicate the nature of AWA's industry in which he was involved.

On the one hand, the costs of infrastructure is astronomical as shown in the examples below

- Roads cost $410,000 per km
- Railways cost $900,000 per km
- Ports cost $40-60 million per berth
- Airports cost $300 per 1 passenger capacity

The above figures are in us dollars and are obtained from World Statistical Data

On the other hand, demand for freight and passenger was very high. Transport is essential not only in developed nations but also in developing countries that we tend to take for granted.

Transport and communications not only are expensive but also they are complex in the sense that we have also what is known as the "hardware" and the "software" infrastructures. AWA was mainly involved in the "software" infrastructure and as such it was/is more than we think we know enough about people to be involved in this type of infrastructure investment. AWA was a classical example to be misunderstood.

AWA has definitely assisted in the development of transport and communications such as roads, ports, airlines, railways, river and sea development as well as in the "software" infrastructure investment that were/are mostly financed by the World Bank and international finance capital. A case in point was that AWA has sent his employees for further studies for over two years while other ministers and authorities send their trainees for short duration in order to buy consumer goods from abroad notwithstanding the long term benefits of our country Eathiopia.

Democracy

AWA's support for DEMOCRACIA did not seem to be born out of a naïve sense that democracy means or will necessarily brings rapid economic progress. Unlike many of his colleagues AWA did not define democracy in terms of procedural terms to the protection of civil liberties, participation in decision-making, voting election and governance reforms. AWA knew when such democracy fails, people will have to resort to another form of government. The MIESO group as well as GINBOT 7 had confirmed HIS POINTS of view.

AWA's Democracy was a substantive outcome like economic development or social justice.

Demand for Democracies emanates from

- Understanding democracy
- Political awareness
- Political knowledge
- Formal education and
- Membership in the student movement

The above criteria had solidified AWA's belief in a public service that was based not only on a fundamental change of economics but also on a political system of government.

In contrast to AWA's work colleagues the right to rule is ascribed to an office rather to a person. AWA was loyal to laws and to the "Eway Revolution". AWA did not pay loyalty to the big bosses either to Emperor Haile Sellassie or the Dictator, Menhgistu and in return AWA's subordinates were expected not to pay loyalty to him but to the laws and institutions of Aethiopia.

For AWA, no challenge was more profound than controlling corruption as he had believed then that when public resources bleed and as public officials serve their own ends rather than the public good. AWA's dilemma was not to be deciphered so easily.

On the hand as economists love to say, AWA understood

1. As Development and governance suffer by the policy of the DERG
2. As the conflict intensifies by the nationalists Aethiopians would turn to alternative regimes. While on the other hand, AWA has realized that

No country in Africa was suffering between democracy and pseudo democracy than Aethiopia as

1. Civil liberties were constrained
2. Opposition rights were tenuous

Because of the above dilemma, AWA's aspiration was geared to the following two principles

- To achieve sustainable development, democracy would not stand still; freedom alone will not be enough
- Democratic institutions to control corruption and constraint would have to be installed.

The exercise of power by the DERG may have seemed to AWA as the delivery of public goods, not private ones. He might have believed sometimes that the revolution was in the right course. This was his dilemma. He was detached from the true clandestine revolution that was going on by DEBTERAW'S EPRP.

AWA was in conflict with the current president of Ethiopia, Girma W. Giorgis as well as with the chairman of All Amhara party, Hailu Shawl, not because of their political positions but because of their personal ambitions and greed while dealing with investment in transport and communications. That was AWA that I know serving the public good.

Conclusion

The shaping of public policy in Aethiopia is not only a multifaceted process but that it was very complex. AWA could be considered as an advocacy group who had attempted to influence public policy through knowledge and participation without political pressures.

Because of AWA participation in the student movement to define the problems faced by the lack of progress and his commitment to be at the service to Aethiopian public, he was a typical an Eway Revolutionary who would have confirmed his struggle for a subtle transform of change in toppling the ethnic government, the international attempt to deplete the potential resources of Aethiopia that have been preserved for centuries by the Orthodox churches and the Monarchies. We salute his effort in the "Eway Revolution" to initiate DEMOCRACIA.

AWA was not in a position to educate the general public but in a position to the public policy makers to explain about the nature of problems in transport and communications and how to solve them not by decree by POSDCORB, an acronym coined by Luther Gullick for (Planning-Organizing-Staffing-Directing-Coordinating-Reporting-Budgeting). In my terminology, I call AWA as ጸንሐተ ምሁር akal not only because he had participated in the Aethiopian student movements but also he was a professional who could evaluate and limit funding from the World Bank and other international organizations. That was a public service in its own right.

Time and history will tell whether AWA belonged to the SAD or MAD generations of Ethiopia.

TRUTH WILL PREVAIL

For questions and comments: woldetewolde@yahoo.com

Eritreans versus Ethiopians: choosing sides?

SOLUTIONS WITH DEBTERAW, XXIII(13)

Call me by my name, address or title

By Obo Arada Shawl alias Wolde Tewolde

August 13, 2009

> "You have a Republic if you can handle it"
> *(Thomas Jefferson, President)*

> "You can't handle the truth"
> *(Jack Nickelson, comedian)*

The above quotations should be born in mind when we discuss issues of Eritreans with Ethiopians. The first quotation was in response to a question "what do we get?" posed by a woman who was waiting for Thomas Jefferson to announce the type of government American should have. The second was quoted from a film titled "A few good men", an answer for Tom Cruise's question.

In the Eritrean case, PIA (President Issayas Afeworki) has delivered to the Eritreans what they wanted – Haar"net or Nazanet - whichever it is, I cannot figure it out.

In the Ethiopian case, the so-called politicians, remnants of the DERG regime and the apolitical individuals who seem disinterested not only in finding solutions to our people's problem but also in distorting the true past history of the Ethiopian Revolution. Or alternatively they are against the Eway Revolution for fear of the unknown. In other words, these are the groups who cannot handle the truth that was set by DEBTERAW and his Revolutionary Party (EPRP).

It will be in the context of Independence versus Truth that I am putting myself into the current debate and discussion among the following contenders.

But before commenting on the pro and cons among and between these groups of individual's opinions and value judgment, I have to re-post (I might add at the time that a couple of webmasters declined to post it) the following article that I have written almost ten years ago. I am forwarding it to be posted again hoping that will educate my readers to catch up with the current discussion and debate about Eritrea and Ethiopia.

AS IS, here is the article
DEMOCRATIZATION NOT RECONCILIATION
By Wolde Tewolde
13 January 2001

A little bit of history

My knowledge of ancient and medieval history on Eritrea, written or oral, has been very limited, but I have witnessed an era of history between the end of Italian colonialism and the beginning of the Millennium. Here is the summary.

For 1 month (2001-?), Eritreans are pleading for reconciliation/ democratization
For 2 years (1998-00), Eritreans were fighting for Territorial Demarcation
For 7 years (1991-98), Eritreans were muddling for Economic Reconstruction
For 17 years (1974-91), Eritreans were seeking for self-determination, Democracy and Socialism
For 12 years (1962-74), Eritreans were combating Ethiopian annexation
For 10 years (1952-62) Eritreans were opposing UN Federal arrangement
For 11 years (1941-52), Eritreans were fighting against British Administration
For 51 years (1890-1941), Eritreans were fighting against Italian colonialism

All in all Eritreans have waged battles and wars for 110 years. But the most prominent armed guerrilla war went unabated for 30 years (1961-1991) thanks to Awate's single bullet. It was an era of mission and vision but not of value.

B-13 group has motivated me to write. Although their analysis of the Eritrean condition was fairly accurate, B-13's characterization of the situation as „*national crisis"* was incorrect and hence their call for national unity and reconciliation were inappropriately alarming and perhaps deceptive. Nevertheless, one has to give them credit for speaking out loud.

If we accept that Eritreans struggled against Italian Colonialism, British Administration, self- rule, Ethiopian oppression and Tigrean mass deportation for over a century, when was the real national crisis? Was it at the beginning, the middle or the end? I leave this to the reader. We cannot discount the fact that TPLF or EPRDF however you want to call them have endorsed the Referendum for Eritrean Independence. The only thing that we are unable to ascertain is whether the battle at Badme were meant to be as a jumpstart for TPLF's hidden agenda or simply a test of the waters by the PFDJ for asserting their power on the ground. This will definitely take time to find out. However we take it Eritreans, under no circumstance, were in a national crisis at the end of 1st Millennium. B-13's characterization as „national crisis" was totally wrong and misleading. B-13 demanded for national debate, and it is a common sense that there should be no national debate during such crisis. May be this is a la Eritrean academicians and medical doctors, I do not know. I am hoping now that B-13 will continue to demand a National debate and not back off from their previous demand.

I have promised my readers to air my thoughts and opinions on each of the three issues.

Out of the eight topical issues and concerns raised by the B-13, only three deserve proper attention for public debate. These are the followings:

1. *National Unity and Reconciliation*
2. *Collective Leadership and*
3. *The Constitution*

For this month, I am dealing with the first issue of unity and reconciliation.

NUR (National Unity and Reconciliation)

In my article of 13 December 2000, I have indicated that National Unity for Eritreans was achieved with the culmination of a National War that was fought not only at Badme but also in all Fronts. The war was perceived as a reversal from the incorrect stand by the TPLF organizational theory of Ethiopian colonialism. The TPLF has also blurred the correct stand of self-determination as proposed by the Revolutionary party of Ethiopians and Eritreans with that of their colonial theory. An additional factor, which blurred the rationale for war between the EPLF and TPLF, was that both organizations proclaimed as Marxists determined to fight Imperialism both that of the United States and the Soviet Union. The real war between Eritrea and Ethiopia under these „Liberators" liberation was fought for confusion (hidden agenda). At best the TPLF with the Ad whites at the helm desperately desired to gain access to the Red Sea and make Ethiopia a "prosperous country" or at worst to bring down the Ham knights who want to keep Eritreans at a "poverty level". Who knows may be the Ad whites thought that the Ham knights were Italians to be given lessons after 115 years? I do not know. Just the same, for the majority of Ethiopians the War was fought for their National flag (rainbow) and for their ethnic identity (ED). Access to the Red Sea was not an issue for the majority of Ethiopians.

EPLF's wars against Yemen, Djibouti, Sudan and Ethiopia were fought not for acquisition of lands but perhaps for an assertion of national colonial independence. These small wars were the real tests for Independence of Eritrea from invaders (socialists), intruders (proponents of democracies) or from colonizers (imperialists) all mixed up in a bug. Just the same, for the majority of Eritreans, the Red Sea and the city of Asmara symbolized not only their survival but also as their national identity. As a result the identical issue of <u>*pride and security*</u> was finally sealed with the accommodation of thousands of mass deported of Eritrean origin from all over Ethiopia. <u>*National unity of a different kind unparalleled in their history was achieved.*</u>

If the unity of purpose was achieved, why then B-13 and others are asking for a unity and reconciliation? Really where is the confusion coming from? As indicated in the brief history of struggle, most Eritreans had a straightforward kind of methodology of combat with the single exception of the future that is understandable. The answer lies, I believe, between the years of 1974-1991. This was the time when Eritreans and Ethiopians were floundering for NDS (Nationalism, Democracy and Socialism). If this is so we need a re-examination of the class struggle, democracy and capitalism.

It is obvious that people can be confused with so many fundamental issues for so many years and it is also understandable for many people to blame one another and demand for an immediate Reconciliation because in their minds and hearts, reconciliation is synonymous with peace. Once the fuzzy questions of NDS (Nationalism, Democracies and Socialism) are finally cleared to the majority of Eritreans and Ethiopians, prescription will be simple. Why do we need reconciliation, will reconciliation bring peace? The answer probably is no.

What is reconciliation anyway?

The world is a better place without confrontation but whenever confrontation arises reconciliation is the solution. Most nations and individuals believe it is better to gain from stability rather than from chaos. What is reconciliation then? Reconciliation follows confrontation. As pointed earlier, Eritrean organizations were involved in recruiting their members by a) by educating b) by tricking and c) by threatening. I do not have facts and figures as to how many Eritreans were educated for what they were fighting for, how many were cheated and how many were threatened to join. Whatever has happened, the nationalists got what they wanted. That means that they are automatically reconciled with the nation of Eritrea (The authorities prefer to call it a State, do not ask me why). On the other hand, some so-called old enemies were allowed to enter Asmara freely without any reprimand. At least, I have not heard of no one who was not welcomed or put into prison because he/she visited his/her native land. But on the other, I have heard tons of stories about others who refused to follow EPLF's line of ideology, market and religious practice, to say the least, who were harassed.

<u>Is it the wrong say to oppose petitioning, reconciliation, fighting or democratization? What is the right way?</u>

Awate opted for an armed struggle and it was clearly to redress the annexation by Ethiopia. This took a little over 40 years. The irony is that fortunately or unfortunately, EPLF has carried out ELF's mission of Independence from colonization and annexation (Haa"rnet). Simultaneously, the group of C-13 of Cairo had initiated a professed dream of struggle for Eritrean peace, democracy, and Independence. Fighting and Independence go hand in hand as we saw in C-13's vision and Awate's mission.

What about Democracy and Justice?

PFDJ has the correct name for pursuing the issues of democracy and justice. So far, the Party or the Organization has not lived up to its true name, as it is neither involved in democratizing nor in creating social justice. The PFDJ is reportedly involved in a sort of business venture neither entrenched in private nor in social nature but in a mixed sort of economy (I do not understand what it means for today's world). Anyhow Democracy and Justice should go hand in hand. EPLF has gun in one hand and democracy and/or justice in the other.

What about Reconciliation and Democratization?

These two concepts are interchangeable. The lack of understanding democratization process will leave us for reconciliation option only. Followings are some samples why reconciliation is essential and urgent.

1. Awate.com's mission statement calls for "the reconciliation between the past and present".
2. Gebre Fesshazion: the Reconciliation theory and the Eritrean culture of debate of December 01, 2000 write, as "The Eritreans are the most unified people in the continent". Gebre continued to argue, "Nowadays the issue of democracy is the hot spot among Eritreans in the Diaspora. No one disagree about it; but everyone can be different about the time of its implementation. Eritrea does not need reconciliation". Again Gebre clearly confuses politics with policy issues.
3. Men hot Woldemariam in his articles of Reconciliation and National unity, calls reconciliation a vital term in Eritrean politics.

What about petitioning and crisis management?

When the so-called national crisis emerged, B-13 presented rather E-mailed their petition and demanded for a crisis management. These two concepts let alone to be interchangeable; they do not go hand in hand. By the way, how many of those 13 in Cairo or in Berlin were Democrats, Independents or Socialists? Some on should figure it out. But after 1991, there was no discussion of about Democracy, Socialism not even about the nature of capitalism. Everyone was for grubbing material wealth at any cost.

A little bit of advice for all Eritreans

On the one hand, compassionate and informed people whether Ethiopians or foreigners of any country admire the tenancy and endurance of the Eritrean people. While on the other, mean and uninformed Ethiopians and foreigners will loathe your perseverance and desire for liberty and equality. But above all, there are real people who wonder when the EERA (Eritrean Educated, Refugee and Asylee) will come to an end. An acquaintance of mine from the Jewish Community told me to be imperfect. He said that Christ was perfect and that was why he was crucified. Human beings can only be in excellence. God may be "slow to anger and yet quick to forgive." Thing about this wisdom.

What do we need for final solution? I can present three areas of concern for discussion

1. FAMATA
2. MAN
3. WRT

The above acronyms will be discussed in future articles.

Menhot named our situation as "collective insanity" I prefer to call it "collective ignorance". I know many readers rather "hearer" will be offended, but take it easy, the world is much simpler than the previous full century.

According to the writer, quoting from a document „Nehanan Alamenan" – translated as "our objectives and we" might have put us in the wrong direction. Obviously, if it says we, then it doe not represent the Eritrean people (unless he is an emperor), it implies a section of the population.

I have not read the said document and I am not interested to read it. It sounds as a Machiavellian type of governance. Mr. Woldemariam pleads for reconciliation a la Mandela type. Both are not feasible. Machiavellian is buried for good by the Information Age. Mandela's case is a case of race and discrimination. Eritren liberation is liberation from fear of retribution and a desire to share power. What are needed are „a la Democracia", „a la Democracia", and „a la Democracia". What is Democracy? Every one of us should study and understand its history, concept and application. It is not enough to repeat the word.

As an opposition Party, ELF has a daunting task ahead for its members. First and foremost, they should regroup or reorganize and be formidable political party. I believe there are there main reasons for the ELF to become an opposition not a loyalist party.

1. ELF was the victims of aggression
2. It can redress what has been done by EPLF and
3. ELF members can feel elevated that they were part of the long struggle for national independence and now they can be part of the reconstruction effort.

But before anything else, ELF should democratize itself internally. For without justice and democratization, ther is **Eritrea without Eritreans.**

Conclusion

We have to *equate democracy building with reconciliation*. If Eritreans don't want democracy, then they do not need reconciliation. But I know many want reconciliation. So stop that nonsense that democracy is not for Eritrea.

Democratization and democracies is the solution for Eritreans and its neighbor. Young people can learn from mistakes. Old people like myself do not seem to be learning from past failures. Eritreans and Ethiopians should do the following: -

1. Avoid the culture of blaming
2. Stop giving excuses for everything
3. Avoid negative attitudes

To be continued …with Commentary

"TOO LATE, TOO SUPERFICIAL (A Brief Comment on the ICG Report on Ethiopia) | LAUGHTER IS THE BEST MEDICINE"

A Commentary and a Proposal on Eritreans versus Ethiopians: Choosing Sides? -

SOLUTIONS WITH DEBTERAW: XIV

Call me by my name, address, or title (NAT)

By Obo Arada Shawl

September 13, 2009

> *Our Revolution is based on nurturing the SEEDS, whereas the revolution of MIESON groups and all other subsequent groups and fronts was bent onto the destruction of the seeds*
>
> ~W. Kassa M.

By way of Introduction

Many individuals representing websites, magazines, and political organizations have presented their pros and cons whether to ally with the leader of Eritrea, Isaisas Afeworki. In my previous article of <u>Eritreans versus Ethiopians: choosing sides?</u>, I have promised my readers that I would comment on the views and opinions of the pundits and advocates for Ecountries (Ethiopia and Eritrea). It is to be recalled though that most of them have dwelt on the relationship solely based on President Isaisas's open statement without the wishes and value of liberty for the Eritrean and the Ethiopian people in general.

Neamin Zeleke has produced a piece of article entitled <u>"The im perati ve fo r Ethi opians deali ng with Eritrea"</u> that became a precedent that ensued with a snowball argument and counter- argument among rivals and enemies without dealing with the issues and problems that put us all simultaneously into these messes and progresses – contrary to many activists and protesters claim, I believe that the Revolution in Ethiopia and the war in Eritrea were not a zero-sum game.

My view is based on these individuals' opinions and views; it is not targeted against their personalities. It is rather focused on the issue of struggle of **INDEPENDENCE** for Eritrea, on the one hand, and on finding the "uncomfortable" **TRUTH** that was historically and politically based on the Eway Revolution. Eway is my way of explaining what actually took place and is taking place in both Eritrea and Ethiopia to people who once were and still are "outside the realm of change aka Revolution".

In the early 1960's, Ethiopian elites were fed up with the status quo. Berhane Meskel Redda (BMR), a prominent founder of EPRP who later turned against his own party used this phrase "the revolution will not be televised" as frequently as he can. It was a song written by Gil Scott- Heron in relation to the then „eroding democracy" in America. That "silent revolution" spearheaded by the "Crocodile group" of the Addis Ababa College has continued to the present day albeit moving at a faster rate via the engine known as the "Animal Group" of DEBTERAW. Both groups were basically known for their covert and overt operations respectively. And their followers include ዝንብር ነዲኡ ነይነግር

(A doer does not tell even to his own mother) ሞያ በልብ ነው (action lies within the realm of the heart).

In conformity with an Orthodox method of operation, ግራ እጁህ ያዯረገውን ቀኝ እጁህ አይወቀው - the Eway Revolution went underground በሕቡዕ Be"H"buEE in the initial stage but later on, many revolutionaries came out in the open defying any regime that does not stand for Eathiopian *Security*, *liberty* and *Justice*. (Notice that EPRP's official slogan was unity, democracy and peace). In other words, in EPRP's parlance Security = Unity Liberty = Democracy Justice = Peace

Not dealing with these three pillars of value in the order given will tear Aethiopians apart to the core. It is time to deal with these **Truths if we desire to move forward and not backward,** as many activists and protesters in Eritrea and Ethiopia seem to suggest.

The Eway Revolution is a change in thinking, changing of hearts and minds of Aethiopians. EPRP did not televise the Ethiopian Revolution for it is a concept about *national security, communal liberty* and *individual justice* not readily recognizable by millions of Eritreans and Ethiopians.

In a nutshell, the confusion among the majority of Eethiopian readers arose simply because of the lack of information that took place between the years (1974-1991). This particular period was not only blurred for a lot of Ethiopians but also, to a large segment of the Eritrean elites. Currently, these "lost" Eritreans are either searching for the "Hafash's" ሐፋሽ political power base or seeking revenge for being misdirected by "EPRP" now turned into PFDJ. For this reason, their struggle is deemed to continue by any other means necessary for democracy and justice.

As far as the sequence of Eritrean Independence is concerned, I have presented my case scenario in http://www.debteraw.com/, although it was written a decade ago, which I still believe is valid.

The majority of Eritreans got what they wanted (Republic?) though the elites do not seem to embrace it for lack of DEMOCRACIA.

As to the "uncomfortable" **Truth** in relation to the Ethiopian Revolution, here is what I have to say.

Journalists or advocates for a cause

We all know by now why and how the "stalemate situation" between Eritrea and Ethiopia that was primarily caused by the two autocratic leaders is nearing ten years. We also know that both leaders were allies for a little over a quarter of a century. This may seem a long period of time for those individuals who did not participate in the political affairs of either Erithrea or Ethiopia. But they should be consoled by the dedication of those individuals and political groups who had waited for almost half a century in order to bring *justice* and *respect* for all Aethiopians irrespective of their nationalities.

As at today, there is neither individual justice for Eritreans nor collective respect for Ethiopians —the basis of our social history.

It is in the context of socio-**political history** that we should be able to delve into partnership with either leader of Eritrea or Ethiopia.

As per the current discussion and debate, two assumptions seem to prevail:

1. If the government of Isaisas fails, Eritreans will automatically rejoin with Ethiopia
2. And if Meles's government collapses, Ethiopia will be able to restore Eritrea as its province.

The above arguments are not only untenable but naïve at the core.

However, I have no reason to doubt the sincerity of those who want to ally with the president of Eritrea or distance themselves from prime minister of Ethiopia. But the rationale for dialogue should not be construed as a negotiation that would be based to be a pawn in the game of the instability of the REGIONS of SEEDS (Somalia-Ethiopia-Eritrea-Djibouti-Sudan). EPRP's motive force was and still is to nurture seeds as opposed to the destruction of SEEDS. (It is to be recalled that some circles had perpetually accused EPRP for sabotaging the wars against Somalia and Eritrea.)

Don't we remember when the Ogadenis became victims of an experiment for T- 60 (driverless tanks) supplied by the Soviet Union and a dogfight between an American jet F-5E and a Russian MiG-21MF? Don't we know now that the Ethiopian regime is sending troops to Somalia and that the Eritrean government in turn is shipping guns and ammunitions in retaliation? What is the purpose? I do not think it is about planting the seeds for harmony and cooperation but rather of destruction of the SEEDS.

Now, the former Italian Somali-land is again a victim of the proxy war of the "mini powers" of Eritrean and Ethiopian leaders. What a tragedy for all to see? Don't we learn from experience?

As a footnote, we should be able to have learnt from our experiences - only the bad side of things- so as not to repeat them. But it seems to me that the so-called Abyssinians strive to learn positive things from their bad experiences – there is no need to learn the "good"- there are role models and mentors to emulate. In Aethiopia, elders, academicians - አንሕተ ምሁራን, civilians (the honorable ones), religious (the faithful one), military (the professionals) and revolutionaries (public servants) are our role models and mentors. We *follow* their footprints and we *learn* from their mistakes. These should be our new guidelines.

We had enough of conspiracy and secrecy from the so-called "Abyssinian" community. That methodology is one good reason why the opposition groups are not succeeding to achieve their goals whatever it is.

The lack of professional journalists and the lack of trusted and credible educators is hurting Aethiopians more than ever before.

Let us examine the pros and cons for cooperation or confrontation as proposed by the journalists and advocates. For convenience let me categorize the groups of discussant into the followings:

GROUP A: Includes Dawit W. Giorgis (Agent) Neamin Zelleke (publisher) Elias Kifle and Hassan Umer Abdella (journalists) and the others who support the idea of becoming an ally of President Isaisas of Eritrea. Their proposal seems to emanate from Neamin's article as well as from Elias's interview with president Isaisas.

In the article authored by Ato Neamin Zeleke "The imperative for Ethiopians dealing with Eritrea" was written on June 12, 2009 and entailed these main points which is quoted as follows:

"Ethiopia's national salvation could only be a reality if Ethiopian patriotic and democratic forces have a base, and outside support to wage their multi-pronged struggle. The requisite is for a sovereign country to become a trusted ally of Ethiopian opposition forces and provide them all around support."

Ato Zeleke seems to argue that just because the opposition needed a base, they should sell their freedom if not their soul. His statement is ridiculous. Only cowards or foreign troops need a base. The mountains of Nakfa, Aasimba, Tulu or Dedebit bereha, Chercher, Simien mountains or the valleys of Awash, or the deserts of Afar have been used as bases for those he calls „patriots and democrats". The people are the bases. Mercato was the base for EPRP. The palace of Minilik was the base for MIESON and that of Asmara was a base for ELF. First, Ato Neamin should believe in what he wants and then act upon it in order to find a long lasting solution (Ze"LLeKE!!! Call me by my name). It is high time for all of us to find other plausible excuses for our dealership and trust-ship.

While endorsing Neamin's proposal Shaleka Dawit has said a lot of things in his article of June 29, 2009 _"the way forward for Ethiopia and Eritrea._ Here are some of the highlights:

- "Not relating with the Eritrean government is a misguided position"
- "Despite the fact the process of uniting Eritrea with Ethiopia was flawed with technical and strategic errors, the people of Eritrea believed sincerely and sometimes manifested in extreme ways that I have not seen anywhere else in Ethiopia"
- "I am the only one survivor from the pioneer group"
- "The flag and unity of Ethiopia" is paramount
- "I was an active part of the revolution"
- "There is some evidence to the claim that the student movement unwittingly allowed itself to be used by forces that had inimical agenda to Ethiopia's interest."

Shaleka Dawit is a narcissus. His own writing style says a lot about him. He writes I and my colleagues; I and I, instead he/she, they and I. All the above quotations made by Shaleka were either shallow or dishonest statements. I don't need to go into details.

According to his personal stories, Shaleka Dawit was not involved in the interests of Aethiopians. In fact he testified that he was

1. A soldier of fortune
2. A foreign minister and
3. A governor for a province that was claimed as "colonized". Dawit has never considered or imagined himself as an administrator or as a public servant but only a governor (colonizer)!!!

Sheleka's positions had nothing to do with the welfare of Aethiopians. The only time he was appointed to serve the Ethiopian refugees was the time when he runs away from the action of relief on the pretext that colonel Goshu Wolde became his immediate boss in lieu of Menghistu.

Shaleka Dawit's claim that he had been on college campuses at home and abroad that might have qualified him to be a knowledgeable and an authoritative person. But that alone wouldn't guarantee him to be an expert and give advice especially when he is not asked by the victims let alone by the victors. I think it is time for him and me to give way for the Eway generation of Eritrea and Ethiopia.

An article by Hassan Umer Abdalla entitled: <u>Ethiopia and Eritrea: the imperative to be clearheaded in order to find our way forward.</u> Here are the highlights of what Mr. Abdalla has written.

> "As I used to point out repeatedly in my Tobiyya articles it is a reflection of the anomalous eccentricity of *yal teTenTaqeqe Fichi Yal Tesaka Gurbtinna l"a sort of "unconsumed divorce and impossible neighborliness" between Ethiopia and Eritrea,"*

Mr. Abdalla may have written hundreds of articles on Tobiyya about እስጦጽያ but he seems to have been in the fringes of the nature of Revolution that liberated us from our social, educational and religious feudal mentality. Ours i.e. modern politics is about relationship in whatever form to bring peace, harmony and prosperity. (Concepts for politics are available within this article).

Mr. Abdella by quoting the journalist Tesfaye Gebreab "an anecdote of an Asmara lady with a *koboroo* dancing dazzlingly the traditional *Guaylaa* on occasion of Eritrea's Independence Day in the streets of Asmara" As I used to point out repeatedly in my Tobiyya articles it is a reflection of the anomalous eccentricity of *yal teTenTaqeqe Fichi Yal Tesaka Gurbtinna l"a* sort of "unconsumed divorce and impossible neighborliness" will not in any way move us in the right direction between Ethiopia and Eritrea.

The story goes by a journalist who asks her "Adiye; why are you dancing so passionately?" Oh, my son, we are celebrating the glorious day of our freedom from the Ethiopian occupation" She replies. The reporter asks her further, "by the way, can I have your name" and the good old lady retorts back with apparent and unfeigned innocence "my name is Ityobiya".

Was this anomaly in the minds of the lady or in the journalists" vocabulary? She was perhaps liberated from her own name, I would not know. What is in a name? Call me by my name are two different things. Harnet and Nazanet though interrelated are two separate concepts.

Mixing up her name with that of a country Ethiopia does not make sense. Her given name was ኢትዮጵያ and she got what she wanted. I don't see the reason why journalists like Tesfaye and Abdalla cajole the lady's name with her feelings. Come on Mr. Abdalla, (call me by my name, what is my name?). The Eway Revolution was meant to decrease if not erase such petty things of belittling the common people. I don't believe you are taking revenge on Umer or Omar. Do you?

The above journalistic approach is killing the nation of Aethiopia in as much as the DERG cadres had diminished it to nothing with revolutionary phrases. Mr. Abdella continues to write

> "There is no doubt that the Ethiopians have to deal with and engage Eritrea as state and the Eritrean people both as individuals as well as organized entities whenever the opportunity offers itself. It is inevitable that the Eritreans and Ethiopians, by simple logic of geography, if not history will live, side by side as neighbors of two states or as citizens of one state as they used to do just less than two decades ago. One need not be a futurologist to understand that. In politics both geography and history are constant variables. But the most constant and permanent seems to be geography."

Mr. Umer Abdella again writes on

"Again, if my memory comes to my aid, the United Nations General Assembly in its 1950 deliberation on the disposal of Eritrea enumerated the following three main justifications for the resolution it adopted on the establishment of the federation between Eritrea with Ethiopia:

1. The historical ties between the two peoples
2. Ethiopia's need for a sea outlet
3. The peace and stability in the region

I am not so sure the whether non viability of Eritrea as an entity was also taken into consideration as a factor for affiliating Eritrea with Ethiopia in an unequal federal arrangement that ever body today, concedes was doomed to fail from the beginning"

The third choice seems to discuss and debate about Regions. That concept has had its days too. We are on a higher level of politics of cooperation or confrontation. We all have choices which way to go.

What is geography and history for Mr. Umer Abdalla? Is he referring to physical geography or political geography? What is history for Mr. Abdella? There are hundred types of history. Which history is he referring to?

Mr. Abdella's main contention seems to rest on UN Resolutions. Even then, he is not referring to economics, social, cultural, religious or political nature. We have come a long way to where we are.

Ethiopians and Eritreans are demanding the nature of our leaders, whether they should be FEARED or LOVED. In other words or in modern terms all EE people are after the rule of law, democracy and freedom. It is not even about peace and stability in the region. It is rather a question of LEGITIMACY. Is it the power of the gun or the power of people? That is the question. Let us wait and see who will win. As a professional journalist, Mr. Abdella should have lead the other journalists in reporting what has been said or seen and not to give judgments with whom to ally or not to ally. Inasmuch as the cadres of the DERG have withered away for lack of **clarity,** it is also inevitable that the journalists of the current regimes will wither away for lack of **integrity.**

GROUP B: includes Saleh Gadi (webmaster) Mintesnot (political observer) and Ayalsew Dessie (Ex-member of EPRA), Mersha Yosef (ex-member of EPRP collective leadership)

> "But, the real debate has to start in earnest. It has to also be realistic. Although the focus of the discussion is the way forward we must be forced to frequent the recent past again and again. It not only geography that we must deal with but also we must come to terms with our recent past history as well."

The above quotation is from Hassan Umer Abdalla" article. This quotation would have elevated Mr. Abdalla to the Group B or C if he had been sincere about the Eway Revolution. The recent past may not be well understood by Mr. Abdalla.

"More of Red Tears" written on July 2, 2009 by Saleh (Gadi) Johar and posted on Awate.com Mr. Johar responds critically to Shaleka Dawit's proposal on relationship with Eritrea. According to Johar, Shaleka Dawit is a career soldier, a politician, a leader and an intellectual, which scares him to death. According to me Shaleka Dawit is none of the above (see my comments on Shaleka).

It is an axiom that people are afraid of the things they don't know. Mr. Johar would like to be a history teller whereas Shaleka Dawit is a history writer. Both desires are at a loggerhead especially these eras of deception and lies. No one will win the argument. What I can say about these two individuals is that both have nothing in common as their point of reference is only religion, which is in turn a private matter. I hope in the future both individuals participate in the discussions and debates about politics of Erithrea and Ethiopia together or solo. As of now, Woyane has opened the Pandora box of ethnicity and Shaebia has closed the freedom of religious practice. Both actions are dangerous.

At this juncture, I want to point out from Saleh's article for my readers.

"I was once talking to an elderly and respectable Amhara neighbor. In the course of our conversation, I mentioned a friend and tried to describe him to my neighbor. I told him that my friend grew up in Addis Ababa and that he is Amhara, and that his name is Omer. My neighbor wrinkled his forehead and snapped his head up in surprise: someone with a name like Omer cannot be an Amhara; he is a Muslim!"

Saleh continued to write

I don't want to bore you with that surprise
lesson I learned from my neighbor.

It was easy to remember Haile Sellassie (and his predecessor's) policy of building a nation state: an Ethiopia centered on the Amhara nationality and the Orthodox religion. The rest, if they were not willing to assimilate and shed off their identities, would practically be relegated to second-class citizens, if not worse."

As far as names are concerned, I have been writing why and how we got our names and further challenged my readers whether they are tuned to their names. I leave the answer to my readers and to Dawit himself whether he is living the life of king David. As far as I am concerned, he is not. There may be a change in his final part of his life, I cannot predict but I hope he does.

As to Haile Sellassie's desire of a Christian state, I do not see any problem with that wish. Many nations were Christians let alone Ethiopia that have embraced Christianity long before Christ was born. Am I to oppose if a nation wants to be a Muslim nation? The answer is no.

The saddest part of our groups, such as Mersha and Ayalsew, is the unexpected and unwarranted reaction to the suggestion of Zelleke, Shaleka or Elias to be an ally of Eritrea. These ex-members of EPRP should have known better than the rest of the ordinary members about the relationship of EPRP with EPLF and ELF in the same way that EPRP had relationships with MIESON, at least in the initial stage. It was only when fundamental issues of value changes that EPRP had parted company. The first question that should have come to Mersha and Ayalsew was to ask what fundamental change has cropped up for EPRP to be an ally with the leaders of Shaebia or TPLF. The famous reminder of Mersha to EPRP members was በራ ከአራጁ ይውላል ወይ? Is there any change of heart or mind that comes from president Isaias or Prime Minister Mellese towards the value and struggle of EPRP? I did not see it coming either from Ayalsew or Mersha about personal relationships and vendettas. (NB. Ayalsew versus Dawit; Mersha versus Iyassou– check their writings and listen to them on radio interviews)

GROUP C: Iyassou Alemayehu (member of EPRP collective leadership), **Tsegaye Kassa "collaboration with Eritrea is betrayal of the Ethiopian nation"** *Fanta Zewge and many others dwell on the issues to be addressed as opposed to be simply an ally.*

It is within this group that I want to elaborate, and perhaps convince that the correct position lies within this group for certainly the solution lies in here provided that we soberly and critically use our voices of reason and our common sense.

The most important piece of writing from this group is that of Fanta Zewge and so I chose to dwell on writing in the hope that it is inclusive for the other members of the group. Here is the quotation from Zewge's article entitled „the liberators going north coming south" Certain Political Figures from the wide field of Political Parties of Ethiopia are considering some sort of armed struggle. Their main objective is to remove the dictator who is reportedly preparing to step down. The armed struggle is a noble mission so long it is to free the people from an oppressive regime. However, the implications of the armed struggle are complex to be left to the actors and Engineers of the armed struggle. First, it must be realized that the armed struggle powered by EPLF that helped TPLF to grab power in 1991 is a sticky issue by it. Objections to the plan are mounting. Second, the armed struggle is seen as a back door to power, and so, a mission to replace a dictator by another. Third, the idea that a dictator of a tiny state, a province of Ethiopia for decades and centuries being consider as a liberator to the proud Ethiopians has become a shameful and humiliating experience. The author explores these issues. With or without armed struggle, the Ethiopian people will free themselves and the dictatorial regime with its "Ethnic Federal System" shall come to pass. Anticipating new era, the author has presented conceptual models by which to establish Economic and Political Administrative regions based on the natural and cultural features of the country. Ethiopians have to undo the damages and restore the nation to its original conditions. And to modernize the country, modern systems must be adopted. For that purpose, the author has presented conceptual models of Economic Regions and Political Administrative entities. These shall give an idea of the framework for establishing a new Federal System of Government.

Armed struggle: Ato Zewge on armed struggle, writes "the armed struggle is a noble mission so long it is to free the people from an oppressive régime. However, the implications of the armed struggle are complex to be left to the actors and engineers of the armed struggle." This is well said. (Compare and contrast between nationalists and revolutionaries.)

And I plead with Mr. Zewge to find out by the historical differences among the armed guerrilla fighters how they had been conduction their field operations. i.e. the relationships between educating-organizing-arming.

Original conditions "Anticipating new era ... Ethiopians have to undo the damages and restore the nation to its original conditions". What is the basis of origin? Physical or mental origin, there will no be original condition for a new era. That is against change or revolution.

"Modern systems must be adopted to modernize the country," Is this not a contradiction, Ato or Mr.? How do I know with which title you would like to be addressed, the original title of Ato or the modern of MR or no title at all?

Political entities The leaders of Eritrea and Ethiopia do not distinguish physical geography from political geography, since professor MWM did not teach them. Instead Enver Hoja or Mao's theory of isolation guided both leaders. Besides, Ato Fanta seems to have the belief system of hatred towards these leaders since he wrote, "For Ethiopians there shall be no worst insult than being ruled by hordes of High School drop-outs"

Honestly, both leaders are articulate and knowledgeable. The problem with the leaders is that they are using their talents and skills for the wrong cause. They have played hide and seek in Sahel, they have played hide and seek in Badme war and they are playing cat and mouse in Somalia. Don't tell us they are dropouts. They are cunning and clever at the same time. Besides, there are thousands of dropouts from high school who are ready to lead the country. Graduates from High school would have been enough for a population with over 80% illiteracy.

An economic region Mr. Zewge whether out of conviction or anger believes that, and I quote, "Eritrea is not an important land by itself. What makes Eritrea important is Ethiopia. Eritrea is not a factor to Ethiopia's progress" If that is the case, why do subsequent leaders of Ethiopia always link with Eritrea? Was it for gaining benefits or for scapegoat? Mr. Zewge not only is stuck with the old economic models based of sea transport and raw materials. Mr. Zewge and others are advised to grasp the triple resources of „SSS" as economic model for the 21st century and beyond.

If Ato Fanta's concept of importance is out of conviction, it will be a milestone for many Ethiopians not to squander their time, energy and resources on bringing Eritreans to the table. I will be one of them, as I will watch you on how you will implement your Federal States based on your conceptual model of diving the thirteen provinces roughly into two.

Let me tell you an event with how Menghistu H. Mariam decided to divide his Ethiopia for the purpose of planning. The experts came up with two alternatives for discussion in planning commission. Before the discussion commenced, the three experts showed to Menghistu alternative proposal to be presented to the Council of Ministers and their experts. Instantly, Menghistu decided on the spot that the Planning Regions should be formed into seven regions (the two alternative proposals were to divide

Ethiopia into 5 or 7). And so the Dictator's decision was done. Many of the attendees were puzzled why the Dictator decided the way he did. A joker and a thinker by the name of Osman clarified Menghistu's calculation that dividing the fourteen provinces by two instead five was much simpler.

I wish good luck to Ato Fanta since nobody is coming a liberator either from the north or south.

Ato Fanta's ideas of economic regions and political entities may work but only in Godjam region– as model for the rest of the country.

In order to be clear with the past and move on to the future, it is proper to remind once again the long and arduous struggle of EPRP for it will not only liberate the minds of its members and supporters but also it will help others to liberate their minds and hearts so as to be free in life and in death.

I find it necessary even at the expense of repeating of my past articles. The following part should be used as a reference guide in conjunction with my commentary. It will be useful for any person who wants to know and understand the history of political revolution in both Ethiopia and Eritrea as depicted in the following pages

A little bit of Revolutionary History in Ethiopia Independence for Eritreans

On the onset of the Ethiopian Revolution, intellectuals representing various academic domains came up with their version of what the people need and want. Apart from their wishful thinking of progress and hope, most of them were not qualified to analyze the urban problem with which they were associated let alone to assess the needs and desires of the rural population.

However, two schools of thought emerged, dominant among them were EPRP and MIESON. To recap the history of the Ethiopian Revolution, there were three major enemies to be tackled by all progressive revolutionaries. These were

1. **Feudalism**
2. **Bureaucracy and**
3. **Imperialism**

In order to combat these enemies of progress; the following slogans were devised,

1. Land to the tiller (in relation to Feudalism) meret la"Arashu መሬት ለአራሹ ተዋጉላት አትሸሹ
2. Combat the pretenders (in relation to Bureaucracy) አስመሳይ ምሁራን ይጋለጡ
3. Imperialism: Paper tiger የወረቀት ነብር ነው (EPRP's slogan) (Man-eater system) ሰው በላው ሥርዐት ነው (DERG's slogan)

Although both EPRP and MIESON organizations had similar ideological background on the above issues, MIESON had a better understanding of political theory in terms of philosophy. EPRP was not only equipped with revolutionary history but it had the added advantage of spelling out clearly and simply the demands and wishes of all peoples of Ethiopia.

It is to be noted though that the nationalists of ELF/EPLF and TPLF use slogans against Feudalism and Bureaucracy in the following manner - "Amhara" in relation to Feudalism and "opportunists" for the Bureaucracy. It was and is ironic for these nationalists to claim to have fought against Imperialism of the West and East. The end result for these groups concerning capitalism and socialism (both types labeled as Imperialism) is nothing but confusion. The current governments of both counties are either scared of globalization or enamored with it. As in the past, there is neither clarity nor basis for their actions of policy in both countries.

What were the Issues that drive MIESON and EPRP apart?

The basic questions that divided the intellectuals of MIESON and EPRP were the following:

1. **Who** will replace the Throne of Haile Sellassie I, the crown prince or a political party?
2. **What** is the nature of the military vis-à-vis the objective condition of the nation of Ethiopia?
3. **When** and **where** is the question of nation and nationalities resolved?
4. **Why?**

5. **And How** is the question of DEMOCRACIA i.e. SEA (freedoms of speech, expression, assembly) is applied?

Legitimacy: MIESON's choice as an answer to the question of *who* was the Military Junta. EPRP rejected the idea of supporting the Military known as the DERG to take over the responsibility of leading the Revolution. EPRP's argument was based on the assumption that the DERG could not be a Revolutionary but only a Fascistic group. The DERG has ruled Ethiopia for seventeen years and MIESON, the advisor of the DERG collapsed on its own merit. As a result of the first mistake to the first question of who, the second follow-up of the nature of DERG became irrelevant. These fatal mistakes caused by the MIESON group has taken place simply because the group had no clear understanding of the conditions and facts of Ethiopia on the ground.

As to the third question of nations and nationalities, MIESON's stand was correct in the sense that there was only one nation, politically speaking. EPRP's stand on nations and nationalities were based on Revolutionary concept of using family as a model of explaining conflicts. EPRP used to argue that the unity of a family is not only essential to any conflict resolution but it is also necessary. EPRP continued to argue further that if either of the parents has unruly and unholy behavior towards the marriage or the family, divorce is recommended, for the sake of the children, but education (consciousness) always should precedes, argued DEMOCRACIA, the mouthpiece of EPRP.

Truth for Ethiopians

If we really want to distinguish between the struggle for *independence and the truth* of how we reach to where we are today, one has to examine and understand the following methods of struggle. For here lies why and how neither all the liberators for Ethiopia, Eritrea, Oromia or Somalia or any nationality could neither Cooperate nor Coordinate (CC) their struggle for a common cause.

STEP ONE: Know Your Enemy ንቃ፤ ወዳጅ ከጠላት ለመለየት
STEP TWO: Get organized ተዮራጅ፡ ውጤት ለማስገኘት
STEP THREE: Take Arms ፍላጎትህን ለማርካት Tatek alamahn lemasakat

The only organization that has followed these three steps was EPRP. The rest started with arming the people without identifying their true class enemies. In other words, their struggles were carried out in the reverse order i.e. mastatek-maderjet-mankat. Due to its credit, MIESON did not reverse the order of struggle but isolated and categorized them, which was equally fatal to the real way of struggle for change.

In other words, for MIESON everybody and everyone should be in the same level of education, same level to be organized and the same level for being armed.

EPRP rejected this idea of first, second and third. For EPRit the people will be organized as they get conscious (educated) and they will bear arms, as they are organized እየነቁን እንዋራጀለን እየተዋራጀን እንታጠቃለን. This process was the last straw that killed the back of the camel so to speak that separated EPRP from all organizations. It was the correct way and it is still the right method alias known as the Eway Revolution.

Who would show us or convince us if those armed without being educated can be re-organized for a civic duty other than banditry. That is the dilemma we are in. Civic and civil societies that lasted for thousand of years have now become militarized. Aethiopia was not and should not be societies of "Uniforms." We seem to forget the CONCEPT of ZEMETCHA!!! Mobilization for collective security for Country, God and Family as told by oral history.

Anyhow, in as much as the false statements about the reconciliation between MIESON and EPRP have bombarded us, seemingly the same argument is circulating about the reconciliation between EPLF and TPLF. As far as I can understand, the reconciliation between MIESON and EPRP was totally wrong. In politics, it is not about personal vendetta, it is rather about public issues and values. EPRP and MIESON have agreed to work together simply for the following main reasons.

1. That the DERG failed to be a true Revolutionary contrary to MIESO's conviction
2. That national question of Eritrea and nationalities of Ethiopia went astray due to fault of either MIESON or EPRP
3. That MIESON's stand on limited Democracy (የተገቶበ ዲሞክራሲ) has been abandoned.

4. That the slogan for PEOPLE's PROVISIONAL GOVERNMENT as proposed by EPRP is still desired by many political organizations including, of course, MIESON. Is this not the burning and current issue for both sides of the aisles so to speak!!! Both organizations cooperate together on matters of issues not for reconciliation per se. And I believe the same will apply to Shaebia and Woyane.

Current State of Affairs

Eritrea: a *Language* based state

When we speak of history, we are not speaking of social history, cultural, economic or religious history of Ethiopia. We are referring to our political history via revolutionary path.

What is history? I would like to quote a famous slogan of history from And Ethiopia Radio "ታሪክ ምስክር ነው ኢትዮጵያ አንድ ናት!!! What kind of history, A'ND Ethiopia? That kind of slogan has helped Shaebia and Woyane to claim their base on languages and ethnic respectively. We should not use the same language that failed us while MIESON was within the power base of the DERG. Even Shaleka Dawit, a once Dergist has abandoned this slogan though with no remorse.

The stand against each other of shaleka Dawit and comrade Ayalsew is from military point of view. That of Shalleka is from the point of the DERG and that of Ayalsew is from EPRA (Ethiopian People's Revolutionary Army).

As far as military is concerned, the EPLF defeated the ELF army, the TPLF has defeated the EPRA (Ethiopian People's Revolutionary Army.) Militarily overall – the DERG has lost its military power although with all the resources of Ethiopia at his disposal, should have defeated any organization in war. Menghistu and his cronies were not aware of People's War.

In Ethiopia or Eritrea, it is somewhat stupid to talk about military power. How can we as (Eritreans and Ethiopians) boast about military prowess, when we don't produce bombs, guns, or tanks to talk? We manufactured no hardware to boast about. We buy them from foreign countries with hard currency – hard currency that comes from the labor and sweat of Eritreans and Ethiopians. So it is better to ask what was the motive for the people to fight or sacrifice life, money or hard labor. The soft powers of Aethiopians are much stronger than the hard ware stuff.

"Eritrean Independence: Is it worth all the sacrifice?" Written by Yosief Ghebrehiwot and posted on July 16, 2009 has stirred arguments and counter arguments. The argument of Yosief and Saleh does not seem to touch base for Yosief asks the wrong question and Saleh responds with a wrong answer. Why don't they let the experts speak from their expertise? If Mr. Saleh and Yosief want to touch base with their readers – let us hear from them about politics of government– power base. Is there a power base in Eritrea apart from the one-man show or do you have an alternative? Readers want to listen!!! As far as answering Yosief's question, we may soon hear or read a Cost-Benefit Analysis (quantified in figures) about Eritrean Independence.

As to the language based state of Eritrea's formation, it is totally wrong. Eritrea with nine languages!!! This is not only untrue, but the basis for independence is totally wrong. ዓላም መሊእ ዓሰርተ ሕጀስ ትኽይድ አላ ናብ ዓሰርተው ሐዋ

Ethiopia: an Ethnic based nation

They call us Orthodox Christians for nothing. Orthodox is attached to Nature. Of course every other thing or history has origin. Having Arts developed socially, economically, politically and culturally in Aethiopia at a high end of scale, it was transformed to Europe and Asia as a science and further developed in America to become Technology – the application of science.

Now what? As human beings continue to travel to live on Mars or the Moon, it is necessary to go back and revisit the origins of Arts or Natural societies with symbols and written languages, where socially, culturally, and philosophically they can be observed "live".

I have written articles on the problem that challenge us all and suggested some provocative alternative solutions for the leaders of Eritrea and Ethiopia.

What is the problem then? It is the land and the language problem. Or is it?

The leader of Eritrea sticks to a land question while that of Ethiopia dwells on language differences. Both are wrong, there is neither shortage of land nor desire for language differences.

Aethiopia: Political based nation-state

There is an old adage, which says "political science without history has no root; history without political science has no fruit." To make myself clear as far as politics is concerned, politics at its best will perform the followings:

1. Politics can preserve peace
2. Politics can protect human rights
3. Politics can advance economic well being
4. Politics can encourage excellence in arts and sciences and
5. Politics can change or remove the governments of Ethiopia and Eritrea

At its worst, politics can do the followings:

1. Creates tyranny
2. Encourages war
3. Cause economic ruin
4. Bring barbarism and
5. Destroy or silence the losing side of the struggle for power

Politics is a civilizing activity when it is at its best. But in our case, it was not and still is not a game. If politics were a process, within or among political communities, there would have been a platform where public values would be articulated, debated and prescribed.

In EPRP's politics the stakes involve the following five choices in the order of priorities

1. Life or death
2. Freedom or fear
3. Peace or war
4. Order or disorder
5. Prosperity or poverty

The above five factors operate in reverse order for Woyane and Shaebia, life or death comes at the bottom while at the top of their agenda comes prosperity or poverty.

Concluding Remarks

Another shot at coup d'etat መፈንቅለ መንግሥት *or continuing the ongoing Eway Revolution?*

It seems that the elections of 2010 as scheduled in Ethiopia and 2011 (as rumor has it) in Eritrea of unknown type of election gave a boost up for all the pundits and advocates participating in these seemingly unpopular elections. By the way, election is a small part of DEMOCRACIA.

Of all the nations that have passed through the three types of revolutionary path, <u>*coup d'etat,*</u> <u>*insurrection*</u> and <u>*guerrilla warfare*</u> simultaneously should not easily succumb to merely elections. (See Solutions with DEBTERAW).

We have witnessed these with COPWE, we have seen this with Ginbot 7 and we are going to see more of the same. Many developing nations dwell on Election Day and ended up in disaster. Aethiopians should expect more than mere elections.

It is in the areas of

1. Land Issues in lieu of Feudalism
2. Governance in lieu of Bureaucracy
3. Free Market in lieu of Imperialism

That the journalists or the truth seekers update their stories about Ethiopia or Eritrea.

First things first though, we all should collaborate in order to force Shaebia and Woyane leaders to meet the following demands.

- Locating the whereabouts of prisons and prisoners
- Releasing all political prisoners
- Allowing free speech, free press and free assembly

We are basically a civilian society with no uniform. The uniformed men of the DERG destroyed us; the guerrilla military are posed to silence us. It is in this context that we should or should not ally with either the leaders of Eritrea or Ethiopia. There should not be an alliance for some individuals or groups" convenience. We should be in the business of saving

Humanity (HC) from dictatorship and tyranny. That is the weakest link of all dictatorships.

TRUTH WILL PREVAIL
Happy Meskerem for New Season and Year
For comments and questions: woldetewolde@yahoo.com

PROPOSAL

These are the political truth that should be accepted in order to move forward.

Consider the letter E and the number 3 coming together as Ethiopia = 8 = Erithrea = ኢትዮጵያ

CALL ME BY MY NAME:

Seeking Solutions with Debteraw, XXI

Wolde Tewolde, alias Obo Arada

Shawl December 13, 2007

> *"If a more likeable human being than DEBTERAW is currently around EPRP, I haven't found him or her."*
>
> *–Anonymous*

A WEEK of celebration on the occasion of the 2nd Anniversary of Debteraw's Website
A DAY of appreciation for DTSGM's work
A GENERATION of struggle by EPRP members

The event was sponsored by Assimba.org and FINOTE orgs. (Both radio and print). For those who missed the occasion, I recommend them to visit the archives. For those who have participated, I would like to thank and encourage all individuals and groups who testified for the figure father of EPRP – aka DTSGM to continue not only to demand for his whereabouts but also to continue to follow his path of struggle.

The event became a process for the Immortalized of Debteraw and according to the numerous testimonies it is summed up as follows:

Debteraw was admired by many people for his convictions and a love for his country, Ethiopia, his skills as a communicator, his understanding of himself and his honesty. It seems that he was incapable of dishonesty.

But above all, everyone and everybody admired Debteraw's ability to relate to people. Outwardly Debteraw looks shy but was able to connect with any one, be it a professor, a proletariat, a patriarch or member of a press. Debteraw basically liked people whether rich or poor, with Title or not Title.

But more importantly Debteraw connected with the people closer to him. He truly cared about the people in his organization of EPRP. As far as he is concerned, he treated everybody the same whether from the Politbureau, CC or ordinary member.

In short, Debteraw has solid relationships because everyone liked being around Debteraw because he loved people and connected with them. Debteraw understood that relationships were the glue that held his EPRP members together – the more solid the relationship, the more cohesive EPRP would

Be. More importantly Debu believe in people before they have proved themselves. He sees the best in people to have faith in themselves.

I woke up on Sunday morning, a day of mediation, at exactly 4:30 AM Washington Eastern time. Here is what has been relayed to me from Debteraw's voice.

"On my 2nd day of website anniversary- my current domicile- you seem to be lost in the maze of talks. I used to talk to you in Words i.e. verbal, then I used to send you a WRITTEN WORD i.e. WR and I also occasionally contacted you spiritually. There was no problem then. What has happened to you when it comes to join the pal talkers? They were all individual friends chatting in my current address. They call it D'H'RE Ge'TS website (maybe a misnomer). It is a different form of C and S. (conspiracy and secrecy). But it is OK. You are in ELECTRONIC digital SYSTEM, just smile."

The voice continued to say, **"Go to the mountain of AASSIMBA. Tell to the mountain about ⁰ and tell everybody and everyone to say my name as . ÖÖçç ìì̀.**

Did you listen to my real voice in FINOTE DEMOCRACIA? I can see you are still struggling to decipher the letter B so as to put the letter E in focus but I am still dealing with the letter F, F and F in

order to give it a third leg. Of course, you understand what I mean?"
With that sememen, Debteraw is gone.

My own reflections
I woke up in real time and reflected on the following:

What am I? Who am I?
When did I come? Where am I going? And
Why ME? May be for posterity – alias WARSAI.

Why me: Or more particularly because I am possessed by the data and access of the Regions from A-Z (T).

1. National resource *from ARUSSI*
2. Border cooperation from BALE
3. Energy from ERITREA
4. God's Bridge from GEMUGOFA
5. Water from GODJAM
6. Government from GONDER
7. Unity fr o m HARARGHE
8. Rainfall fr o m ILLUBABOR
9. Coffee from KEFFA
10. Secrecy & Conspiracy from SHEWA
11. Security from SIDAMO
12. Wisdom fro m WOLLO
13. Soil from WOLLEGA
14. Trade from TIGRAI

What: I am War, Revolution and Terror (WRT)
Who: Born in Eritrea, raised in Agame Awraja, educated in Addis Ababa and have worked all over Ethiopia and currently residing in America. What is my identity? Can anyone tell me or put a label on me, please?
When: From the time of HENOK (descendant of Adam & Eve)
Where: From AAssab port to RAS Dashen i.e. AAGMELAGO

So where is the land of Peace and Democracy? Nowhere in Ethiopia as you can see from the above resource and data analysis. Practically all organizations and political parties cry for Peace and Democracy. Do they know that EPRP has been crying for these two words since its inception? EPRP members and its supporters have been literally and figuratively were massacred for asking for PEACE in Eritrea and DEMOCRACIA in Ethiopia. Nobody listened and nobody seems to learn from EPRP either. Is it not a shame not to learn from the experience and history of EPRP?

LESSONS TO BE LEARNED FROM DEBTERAW

PAST	**PRESENT**
Discipline	Respect
Integrity	Shared Experience
Responsibility	Trust
Self-Respect and	Reciprocity and
Team work	Mutual enjoyment
In Short (DIRST)	(RSTRM)

CONCLUSION

Debteraw's website is getting passionate. Passion is the difference between doing a job and being a professional. The passion for Debteraw's website is the difference between liking DTSGM as a person and claiming him as READ for EPRP and as national hero for Ethiopia and Eritrea.

Special thanks for Debteraw Team. Let the light for Truth is ignited in your Website beginning on Christmas and spreading throughout via other websites for the sake of EPRP.

For comments and questions: woldetewolde@yahoo.com

CALL ME BY MY NAME: Solutions with Debteraw, XXII

Wolde Tewolde alias Obo Arada Shawl

January 13, 2008

EPRP believes that when the time comes, the youth will come or inquire about EPRP. One such inquiry has come from the following individual.

EPRP'S DECLARED PROGRAMS

1. Replacement of the military by the provisional popular government
2. Recognition of basic democratic rights
3. Political prisoners should be released
4. Eritrean question must be resolved peacefully and democratically
5. Peasants must be armed
6. Economic demands must be fulfilled and
7. Ethiopia must be free from foreign domination

EPRP'S DECLARED CONCLUSION

Only a popular and democratic government could give Ethiopians and Eritreans a chance to unite and survive. That had been the goal of the popular movement, which was betrayed by the intervention of the military. The soldiers did not relinquish power as they have initially promised (see "confession" a book in Amharic written by Tesfaye Lema).

Woyane did not hand over power to the elected Kinjit groups. And there is no guarantee that from now on, that EPRDF will hand over if they loose in the coming elections.

Power of the people comes only if and when the seven points in the declared programs presented by EPRP comes to fruition. Although these were written and demanded a long time ago, these declared programs are still valid, after all DEMOCRACIA – the organ of EPRP warned us all by writing in its first issue ALEBABSEW BIYARSU BE'AREM YIMELSU – what goes around will come around.

MY RESPONSE: 3 points of clarification for all young adults of Ethiopia and Eritrea

1. **Peasants should be armed,** as asked by Arhuse A. should be answered in conjunction with the 2nd question i.e. recognition of democratic rights and the 4th question i.e. the Eritrean question must be resolved peacefully and democratically.

The 2nd and 4th questions/demands

The second demand is a very crucial issue for a lot of Ethiopian intellectuals.

The issue of Eritrea was taken as solvable by "peaceful and democratic" means. What does democratic mean, anyway?

In the language of EPRP it means that the MEANS justifies the ENDS unlike EPLF's, TPLF's and many others who follow the Machiavellian principle YETM F'CHEW DuKqtun Amchew equivalent to the END justifies the MEANS.

Saying it differently, there is a huge difference between "might is right versus right is might".

EPLO's struggle started with 'might is right' background

EPRP's struggle was based on the concept of 'right is might'. In order to put things more clearly, EPRP's 2nd and the 5th political demands coincides with the Bill of Rights of 1st and 2nd of the USA.

The Bill of Rights is the first ten amendments to the United States Constitution. Among the enumerated rights are those that guarantee

Freedom of Speech, Press and Religion; The People's right to keep and bear arms

The right to bear arms refers to the concept that individuals and/or governments have a right to weapons. Mostly this right is often presented in the context of military service and the broader right of self-defense. In USA, the term "bear arms" is a matter of recent dispute and continuing political debate.

Armed Struggle versus peasants should be armed

By the time EPLO, the precursor of EPRP was launched, the struggle for "right is might" was no more accepted. On the one hand, the nationalists, ethnicists and progressives stand on one side of the equation "might is right." It was proper to take arms against the Monarchy, the Nobility and the Church who refused to change the status quo of oppression and exploitation, but when the collapse of the Monarchy was imminent to collapse and the Eway Revolution was set in motion, the slogan of EPRP became "right is might" was reverted to its natural place as a priority calling itself as DEMOCRACIA –in name and in substance.

It is obvious that EPRP has continued to defend itself by any means necessary including and up to armed struggle, as the DERG and its cohorts declared that their government would embrace all the demands of EPRP except the first demand which asks for a provisional popular government. EPRP challenged the DERG in written form explaining as follows: "There is no way that 120,000 members, will bring an iota of positive change to Ethiopia let alone 120." With this belief EPRP defended its political position and worked for the demise of the military regime.

And so EPRP continued to educate the peasants and to defend itself unabated until the TPLF possibly with the blessing of EPLF and the Sudanese government launched an offensive campaign to destroy EPRP's nucleus army when they marched into Addis Ababa in 1991. It is to be noted that EPRA was not a fighting army. It was supposed to be a Revolutionary army "AN'Qi"- a liberator of the mind of Ethiopians and Eritreans.

Once the Eway Revolution was set in motion, 'might as right' was over. EPRP has demanded to the Ethiopian and Eritrean fighters to follow the concept of 'right is might' and it is still continues to this day.

Zeru and Berhane- long time comrades were for the armed struggle. Berhane despite his intellectual capacity and preparation to be Che Guevara of Ethiopia was captured in a cave. I have met his captor and it seems to me that true to Che Guevara's betrayal by his own people, it was similar to Berhane Redda's moment of capture. Zeru Kihshen died without speaking out his thoughts or admitting his mistakes. Zeru was instrumental in recruiting young adults from the United States of America to go to the war zones at home while Berhane had led the EPLO into Assimba Mountain in order to start the Long March that is still ONGOING by Debteraw and his comrades.

The idea of right is might or the means justifies the ends comes mainly by Walleligne and Debteraw Tsegaye. Unlike the false pretense by the TPLF that Wallelegne is a war like hero is false and unhistorical. The idea of self-determination including cession was hinged on the means of the Eway Revolution. In our case, the 5th program was meant to resist government tyranny especially in Insurrection theory.

Of all the things that EPRP has been condemned for is the use and the abuse of Ethiopian and Eritrean youth. Actually this accusation does not normally come from the once upon a time youth or the current youth of Ethiopia themselves. Most of the allegations emanates from outsiders who have no knowledge of EPRP's style of workings or from those who deliberately wants to distort the facts in order discourage the youth from joining EPRP. I have experienced this with my own daughter.

Actually, EPRP does not encourage the youth to join any political Party until they feel comfortable to do so. The old generation of EPRP has to take the responsibility of explaining why the E-way revolution was necessary and correct. I believe this recruitment policy is the best of all policies carried out by EPRP.

2. **_The three layers of EPRP leadership_** Political, Organizational and Ideological (POI) PAC = party + army+ community

The nature of a political organization of EPLO was described as

> *"An organization with a minimum political organization to distinguish it from a military organization such as the ELF, and to emphasize the importance of its political role."*

Kiflu continued to write

> *"This characterization was based on the assumption that the revolutionary activists who emerged out of the student movement, with the necessary tools and guidance, would be able to provide leadership*

*to the struggle. 'This therefore means that there must be just enough number of revolutionary cadres who are **ideologically clear**, **politically mature** and **organizationally trained**.... before the People's War is launched'"(Kiflu: The Generation P: 80 emphasis is mine)*

On collective leadership Kiflu wrote "Berhane, the current General Secretary of the organization, was not comfortable with the changes made. In one of the central committee meetings, he stated that since he was elected by the 1ˢᵗ congress, he would hand over his post only to another congress. The CC ignored the personal aspects of the issue and focused only on structural changes that it felt were obstacles to the internal democracy of an organization."(Kiflue: The Generation P: 237)

The point I am trying to tell is how democracy works within the members of EPRP and to indicate only the bare elements of complex issues of politics, ideology and organization.

It was not simple and it is not going to be either. The following relationships were not rhetorical and shallow but persuasive. EPRP's fountain is the youth as the old will leave footprint, but we should remember that the old is not going to give up what they have built for nothing. There should not be confrontation when handing over the legacy of its work to the youth. What is my name? Call me by my name. Respect and Trust is my name.

Political Leadership (current plus past)

Students' and professional associations with many civic and business communities

Labaders' : Mother Teachers' : Berhanu Ijigu Workers :Marcos Hagos Youth: Tito Hiruy (Babile) Professionals: Wogofa

Organs: websites, pal talks, radios, TVs and publications

Organizational Leadership Current: Fassika Bellette Past: Kiflu Tadesse

Organ: DEMOCRACIA

Ideological leadership Current: Iyassou Alemayehu Past: Tesfaye Debessai Organ: Red star

The Army of EPRP

B and **M** member of a nucleus army died and were kept secret because EPRP was still on a journey. The Trust of sacrifice is still intact within the IFs. What if (Iyasou and Fassika become dictators? What if the Ifs become rich? What about the ifs surrender their principles? What about if they suddenly run their personal lives? Is it reason enough to betray the party of Debteraw Tsegey especially when he is held incommunicado?

Mersha Yoseph was wounded in the Marathon struggle of EPRP and I believe figuratively he is still in the leadership of the army that would fight the TPLF until justice and democracy prevails.

The implications of all these is that EPRP was not based not only in name, organizational structure but also in motion, time and space laden with principles and core values for Ethiopia. EPRP has no other name with or without adjectives other than its own name with its management and leadership intact.

3. Debteraw's culture and faith is calling us for an action. Let us free him to free Ethiopia

So far, as I have been describing Debteraw Tsegaye as a role model for REVOLUTION, EDUCATION, ART and Democracy (READ) in Ethiopia and Eritrea.

Let me give you some hints as why Debteraw's implication is vital Debteraw strongly believed in the culture of **unity in diversity of Ethiopia** via DEMOCRACIA

Debteraw strongly believed in the viability of modern and traditional education Debteraw inspired hundreds of thousands to believe in the Ethiopian KINET (art) Debteraw is languishing in prison in order to promote justice for all for all Ethiopians regardless of nationalities, ethnicities or ideologies and

Debteraw is a well-known Ethiopian scholar who believed in VIVE LA DIFFERANCE in religion, in social, economic and political reconstruction known as the Eway Revolution.

When I write about Debteraw's reflection in CULTURE as in FAITH, they were not empty words and phrases they are real and natural.

I don't advise anybody to see the party of EPRP with a perspective of individual personalities. There were hundreds of intelligent and some with gifted minds but failed because of lack of experience. EPRP should be seen in wholeness. I know that Kiflu Tadesse has used not only individual personalities but also used their ethnic background as if it mattered to EPRP's organizational structure. His way of writing or labeling even to his own personality was not appreciated. It was wrong to put it that way and it was disservice to EPRP's policy.

Finally let me give you an example why I say Debteraw's freedom will free all Ethiopians and Eritreans. Debteraw is one of the TS'EN'HATE MUHUR AKAL, which means that he has the concept, the theory and the application and for that many intellectuals in Haile Sellassie University did not like him as he used to challenge them to think conceptually, theoretically and practically. A clear example would be professor Mesfin W. Mariam. When Mesfin Wolde Mariam became a Human Rights chairman, and while he was touring the Netherlands, he was approached by a certain individual and asked him as to what had happened to Debteraw's whereabouts. The professor replied that he did not know anybody by Debteraw Tsegaye G. Medhin. It was an act of revenge pure and simple. Can we say that Ethiopia will be free if our professors and doctors do not dare to protect individuals regardless of their personal grudge? That bothers me very much especially when somebody in authority or power replies in this manner. Does this bother young adults? Please, comment.

Can we be our individual selves without fear or apology to witness that the culture and faith of Debteraw will free us all?

For comments and criticism: woldetewolde@yahoo.com

BREACHING TRUSTS OF CULTURE AND UNDERSTANDING

CALL ME BY MY NAME:

Solutions with Debteraw, XXIII

Obo Arada Shawl alias Wolde Tewolde -

February 13, 2008

The crocodiles are dead
The Animals are imprisoned
The Oak is still burning
Badme and Assab are in non-negotiating
EPDJ and TPLF live by your name
Let us give EPRP a break so as to stay in its true name!

BREACHING TRUSTS OF CULTURE AND UNDERSTANDING

A change is an essence of life. An attitude change is much needed. Practically everyday, we change our clothes, shoes, and take shower (personally I don't) food and so on and so forth.

When we were young, we think differently, when we are old, we cannot think in the old way. We should grow old and be mature. In what way, one might ask?

History and Culture are our main references for survival, stability and unity. However, as elites we do not distinguish between history (by the way there are hundreds of history types) and culture (of course there are many cultures.) Our political history is full of errors. Our cultural history is not documented. Our revolutionary history is being discarded. So how can we trust one another and understand each other? It is a tough call.

As for me, the **followers** of king Minliks I & II, Tewodros, Yohannes are the real hindrance to progress and understanding. These kings have done their useful work. Their history is done. It is no use to follow their ideas of holding to and transferring of power. If reference is needed for stability, take the case of Jesus the Great who ruled Ethiopia in 1704 when the stability of the country was at its peak. It was after his death that the local lords became stronger. We should all remember that we had kings and kingdoms without *maps and demarcation.*

The point I am trying to make is that if we want change as we did in the 1960s and 1970, then we have to abide by all rules and regulations that govern human beings. For almost fifty years, I have heard the same slogans and intrigues from our elites. Don't we have the capacity to learn? Don't we read maps, least directions? When I was in high school, there were some seventy countries, now there are over two hundred countries. When I used to travel from Addis Ababa to Asmara, it used to take me three weeks, now it takes a day and a half. Can't we see this? I see in our community a lot of people (including me) carrying cell phones, for what? Is it not for communication unless we have different meanings for communication?

What is going on with our lecturers (including those who are on radio talk show) and writers? Is anybody listening to what they are lecturing or any one reading to what they are writing. I leave this for them to answer. I demand them to heed to John Adams, 1765 that wrote as "let us dare to read, think, speak and write."

Notwithstanding these elites, the general populace of E-countries have already the answers for the journalistic questions of what, who, where and when long time ago thanks to people like Debteraw. What the EE-peoples are asking now is the Socratic question of Why and How. Debteraw has fought and still struggling to do that by showering questions of why and how even to his captors.

Politics demand that some truths cannot be told. In hindsight our politics was a cheap piece of instant wisdom. We had operated on passion at the exclusion of intelligence. We should have done both then and do it now.

We need the intellectual firepower from our professors and PhDs to those of us who want to preserve it and pass it on. My partial inquiry is provided in the following paragraphs.

However, unlike the current American primary election that is based on personalities our own struggle is based on issues. Let us examine a group of individuals who were part and parcel of the progressive movements of Ethiopia.

ISSUES AND PERSONALITIES

BADME: Border demarcation as disturbing news by DR. YACOB H. MARIAM
ASSAB: Natural outlet to the Sea by NEGUSSAY AYELE, Ethiopian scholar

A lawyer and a Politician (YHM & NA)

The old guards of Haile Selassie I University Muhuran's reasoning concerning the port of Assab and Eritrea is as follows: -

"Assab in the hands of Eritrea will always be a menace to peace for Ethiopia as well as for Eritrea itself. Nobody can deny that Eritrean struggle for secession from the day of its inception has enjoyed material and diplomatic support of we know who, without whose support the secessions would have been a pipe dream. It is not farfetched to think that piper may one day feel that she has to be paid, embroiling the Horn of African in the Arab-Israeli conflict. In addition, since Eritrea has absolutely no use for the Port of Assab, it may pass it over to enemies of Ethiopia, providing yet another opportunity for Assab to become a flash point for conflict. I can also not imagine that any future generation of Ethiopians will ever acquiesce to Eritrean annexation of Assab and let itself be asphyxiated. These statements should be construed as pleas for banishing war from our region. We Ethiopians want to live with our neighbors in peace and good neighborliness, particularly with Eritreans with whom we are inextricably intertwined for the better or worse- a relationship that could be developed for mutual benefit. The Eritrean and Ethiopian politicians who in my view could not see beyond the tip of their noses elected for separation of a people, which should never have been torn asunder. Though we do not know the wherever they are. Nonetheless, we cannot afford to allow ourselves to be

landlocked and condemned to perpetual poverty and approbation and entrust our security to even our kin, if we can help it.

The ball is on the Eritrean court. For us Ethiopians, access to the sea and the rights of the Red Sea Afars hold the key to the bliss that may await Ethiopia and Eritrea. The Eritreans we hope will understand the emotion, sense of anxiety the loss of Assab spells among Ethiopians, and we hope they will have the foresight and the maturity to see to it that this useless piece of property for Eritrea, yet a life-line for Ethiopia, will forever be a wedge of hostility between these two sisterly African nations. There are myriad peaceful ways of incorporating Assab with Ethiopia, which are equitable, fair and just to all parties concerned. What is needed is goodwill on the largest recently landlocked country and yet the closest to sea anywhere in the world, has an access to the sea as it did for several millennia."

"No Ethiopian issue in recent memory has galvanized the otherwise fractious Ethiopian intellectual with such unprecedented unanimity" (www.Ethiomedia.com 11/26/2007)

The above two professors at the height of the Ethiopian Student Movements, were supporters of the impending Eway Revolution. In fact when the Monarchy ended its life, both individuals had joined organizations in order to promote their interests (personal or public). I believe both were seeking for political solutions between Ethiopia and Eritrea. When they could not deliver the political solution, they have resorted to the economics of transportation. What do they know about economics of transport? If they do we want them to teach us. As far as I know, Assab is not useful for transport outlet for Ethiopia. And, Badme is not a cause for disturbing demarcation.

Consider this

Badme = Bad Me (I am no good)
Asab = As AB (I am the father)
A BA (bachelor of Arts) is adequate to understand the culture of Ethiopia and Eritrea least the condition of a village and an artificial port.

I am so sorry that such fine professors in their own fields of study have sensationalized the case of Badme and Assab. I can understand why

UNMEE and MI (Melese and Isayas) sensationalize and internationalize the village and the outlet, but not when these enlightened and one time Revolutionaries. I would ask these professors to re-examine their assertion of "useless piece of property for Eritrea, yet a life-line for Ethiopia." Talks are cheap as they say. Your one time colleague Debteraw has a solution for your concerns. It is called AAGMELAGO (see Call me by my name: a small talk with Debteraw, part I). You wrote, "There are myriad peaceful ways of incorporating Assab with Ethiopia". Please name one.

WEBSITES OF DEBTERAW & ASSIMBA

A call for Movement: Eliminating the twin tyrants, by Mesfin Araya, PhD
Helter Skelter, Topsy Truvy, by Hama Tuma, A Revolutionary writer
The self-less generation (middle aged guards) of Haile Sellassie I University, a.k.a. Tsinhate

Muhuran's reasoning for the ills of Ethiopia and Eritrea are described as follows:

The student movements have created revolutionaries and nationalists. As professor Endrias Eshete wrote, "the irrationals have done their useful work, it is for the rational to carry on" I believe these so-called rational are now carrying the duty of educating the young mind of Ethiopian students, carrying out the diplomatic programs in the USA and conducting business in the name of free market in Ethiopia. It is an anomaly that those who created them are out of the country, dead or imprisoned.

Mesfin Araya, on the one hand, has written an open letter calling for the need for resolving the ensuing problems of the Horn Africa by demanding removal of the twin tyrants again without telling us why and how to do it. Definitely, there is no progress but the process has been going on since professor Mesfin played a role in Haile Sellassie I University Campus. What has happened to the Revolutionaries? Or what has happened to their idea of unity, stability and prosperity? Were there flaws in their ideology of Philosophy, Religion or Politics? Or was the methodology of struggle was wrong? Why did everyone as the professor has indicated that everyone and everybody have returned safely into his/

her mother's "womb"? Can the professor distinguish between dictatorship and tyranny?

Or alternatively, do our intellectuals know that the entire system of global economy or the digital era have created havoc in our region? I wish all the professors could come together to form a Think Tank to solve the perceived problems of Ethiopia and Eritrea or what he call the "Horn of Africa." I wish they could call me by my name? What is my name?

My own way of explanation is simple and straight foreword in that there is a switch of role models. Robin Hood is replacing Che Guevara. Reverend Martin Luther is replacing Malcolm X. Makonnen Bishaw is replacing Tilahun Gizaw and son on and so forth.

Hama Tuma, on the other hand, in his article of Helter and Skelter, Topsy Turvy, vividly explored the questions of what, who, where and the when questions without the why and the how questions. Here is what he wrote: -

> *"The victims always do the dying, the killers thrive. It is not a fair world. Tell me another story please."*

I will tell you this. ELF (Equality, Liberty and Fraternity), the story of the French Revolution has been and is being copied in Toto by our organic and inorganic intellectuals.

Hama Tuma presented 38 statistical figures concerning the status of the whole world including USA.

However, in America, unlike that of France, our struggle is for Life, Liberty and the pursuit of Happiness (LLH). Without statistics, can we choose between these two concepts? As an example, take the case of Jerome Keviel who embezzled US$7.2 billion or Euro $4.9 billion for our discussion. Mr. Jerome is becoming movie hero for the whole world including perhaps for Melese). In France, they say he is "Mis a pied". In America, we say, "you're fired".

Is this an aberration or what? Tell me more Mr. Hama!

Mr. Hama Tuma! Who says the world is fair? Are we not struggling to bring another story? There is no fraternity and no equality in America. There is only liberty. That is our common denominator with you guys over there in Europe.

In general people don't vote based on issues. They vote based on judgment and character. I believe it is true with the May election in Ethiopia. Most of the candidates have poor judgment and character.

Mr. Hama continues to write, "People with short memories have messed it all up. Yesterday's criminal can be feted as today's hero without a pip of an apology or a mea culpa from them. The new persists and spreads. No wonder many people are confused and mediocrity has ascended to the throne." I agree completely on this one. Here is what should be done.

On one hand, while on the process of changing everyday we may make mistakes, if we do, in religious lexicon, we have to REPENT or say MEA CULPA and move on to a new direction or position. Being stubborn is ignorance; arrogance offends not only God but also humans.

While on the other hand, if we make mistakes in our political belief systems or strategies be it military or propaganda, we have to admit and REGRET and say sorry.

Both requests are acceptable by both the Almighty and the Mighty.

In Ethiopia or Eritrea, there are no role models. Before the Revolution, there were the apostles, prophets, evangelist, priests and teachers. After the Revolution, there were only comrades (a good name became sour). Among the civilian population, there were mostly titles, which we labeled feudal. On hindsight, they may be useful. Now, we have Doctors and professors. It is for this reason that I ask the "organic intellectuals" to be role models.

In Ethiopia, we have to remember that Debteras are the role model for social justice. EPRP's Debteraw is a scholar and a model for both Ethiopia and Eritrea. We are not asking to memorialize Debteraw, we are asking for immortalizing him and his works. That is the task of all the progressive elements of Ethiopia and Eritrea.

I am wondering if these educated veterans of the Haile Sellasie era as prudent and cautious politicians as Negusse Ayele and Mesfin Araya, as bold and blunt Revolutionaries as Hama Tuma and Yacob H. Mariam, have a common culture and understanding towards Eritreans and Ethiopians. If not, we have to look for other serious relationships in familial, personal, religious and historical phenomena, in lieu of political revolution.

Freud's famous case studies that seek to come up with an explanation for what happened could be a starting point.

Reading the Bush Tragedy by Jacob Weisber may help us to understand our own dilemma. It is about a plane crash with a black box that can help explain what brought the White House down in flames. A black box of ours with serious relationships is in order. Laboratory and diary can be our stepping-stone for our educators and revolutionary leaders to teach and lead us.

EPRP's DEMOCRACIA

And then there is confusion when we see DEMOCRACIA in the name of EPRP in two websites. Apparently both seems the same outwardly but inwardly, they have deep differences in unresolved issues of Eritrea. For how many years can we use the case of Eritrea and Eritreans as an issue to be resolved? Eritrea and Eritreans have not changed since Gherhi (Adam), along with Dinkinesh (Eve) the father of humanity has been created and I do not believe they will change. In fact the world is going to change into their way of life. It seems to me that some ex-EPRP leadership assumes that by using DEMOCRACIA, which was and is the mouthpiece of EPRP can become automatically the heir of EPRP. DEMOCRACIA was not and is not the mouthpiece of some individuals but the mouthpiece of all its members, associate members and supporters. It should be identified with those held incommunicado and with those who sacrificed their lives for the sake of all Ethiopians. Above all it should be under one banner and leadership.

There is something about the word "Democracies" with the letter D: D for divide, divorce, doubt, drug, and dirt. So many words with a D are on our lips as in depression, debt, debauchery, dyslexia, dementia, and dysfunction
For us Defeat and Deny are important word concepts. Let us compare and contrast the case of Ethiopia and Eritrea using the following ten criteria: -

- Elimination of Corruption
- Crime Reduction
- Protection of private property
- Reduction of Taxes
- Enforcement of Contracts
- Supporting the Rule of Law

- Encouraging Savings and Investment
- Educate their population
- Become self-sufficient in food production
- Stopping fight with neighbors

The above analysis may help to evaluate the current situation in Ethiopia and Eritrea. This is a choice to make for non-political individuals. Just to give them a hint, Estonia and Ireland are examples where creating it is creating not by buying but wealth.

The interest of EPRP, I believe is to challenge the governments of EPDJ of Isayas and the TPLF of Melees do not think that EPRP neither challenge the ownership of Assab nor the demarcation of Badme. It was not and should not be an issue for EPRP.

Consider these:

The Tsinhate Muhuran Akals of the Haile Sellassie I University were hoping to continue to implement the following: -

Representatives = Rs of EPRP (animals)
Senators + Ss of EPRP known as (crocodiles)

Decipher the letter B and spin the letter E and be whatever you want to be.

- Bellette *(excellence)*
- Berhanu *(enlightment)*
- Beyene *(justice prevails)*
- Bereket *(blessing)*
- Bekele *(planting seeds)*

Call me by my name: what is my name?

CONCLUSION

The Long March of experience in the Eway Revolution and the bitter lesson of Badme war do not seem to sink in our head least in our soul. Have we learned to decipher the alphabet of English? If so we have just not progressing. It seems that we have not grasped the letter A and still we have not been able to decipher the letter **B.**

If there is no BDT (building democratic tradition), we have to BBC (building bridges for communication). Liberty is promoting virtues and excellence. Liberty is in Europe and USA and we should have it for all Ethiopians and Eritreans regardless where they live.

Let us have a common call.

CALL ME BY MY NAME:

Solutions with Debteraw, XXVII

Obo Arada Shawl alias Wolde Tewolde -

May 13, 2008

Politics is about Addition
Revolution is about Division
Cession is about Subtraction
Nationalism is about Multiplication
EPRP is about Addition and Division

On Meeting

I normally do not attend public meetings especially if I sensed hidden agendas and time bomb. I do not quite understand why hidden agendas will help for advancement or cooperation. Most of the time, on the one hand, while the educated class or elites of Ethiopia practices hidden agendas, on the other hand, the uneducated class of Ethiopians prefers time bomb. What I meant by "time bomb" is that they hold grudge against those who have different opinions for them opinions are not separated from facts and truth. As a result, they wait patiently until their organization or groups or tribes gain control and ready to attack. This is what I call a time bomb, which will blow up in time of adversity. Most Abyssinians belong to this vengeance system. But the educated classes all cling to its hidden agendas when they are short of alternative solutions and lack of freedom.

Let me be an apologist for a moment for EPRP's hidden agendas and time bomb. Many opponents of EPRP claim that EPRP practice hidden agendas and wait for time bomb. But this is not true. It seems true because politics is about controlling the message. While EPRP was struggling to bring change for all Ethiopians, the people who were in power were using the propaganda (Yabiyen Ekek wede Emye L'kk) of hidden agendas and time bomb propaganda against EPRP. The fact of the matter is that EPRP's addition via politics and division via Eway Revolution is difficult for many folks to grasp.

Some years back, a personal friend of mine invited me to attend a public meeting of EPRP that was held at 1610 16th street, in Washington DC. The meeting place was a church called "Unification Church." EPRP getting unified in religious terms! Wow. I did not attend the meeting to analyze EPRP in terms of religion, but here I was inside a church watching a heated presentation about EPRP's quo vadis (from where to where) and its future struggle.

Starting with the seating arrangement of the EPRP leadership in the open was a bit strange for me. Normally, the collective leadership is conceptualized in a circular table but this one the seating arrangement was *hierarchal*. Five leadership members sitting in a row and behind them in raised platform two veterans, a patriot and a heroine. This was my first image of collective leadership in a holy alliance. Right there and then, I did not take it to be a political or an organizational meeting. For my self, I perceived the meeting from a religious point of view. Here is why.

On the first row was sitting Ato Iyassu whom I considered as an Apostle
On the second row was seated Ato Mersha whom I considered as a Prophet
On the third row was seated Ato Fassika whom I considered as an Evangelist
On the fourth row was seated Dr. Getachew whom I considered as a Reverend
On the fifth row was seated Dr. Mesfin whom I considered as a Teacher

The main reason why I labeled them as I did was simply not only because of their sitting arrangements and the fact that they were in a church but also because their presentation and analysis of the Ethiopian situation. I have told them in person about my labeling of course, jokingly.

On Religion

Religion is recognition on the part of man of some higher unseen power as having control of his destiny, and as being entitled to worship, obedience and reverence (WOR). Much of traditional organized religion is of the nature, Debteraw used to argue. Debu used to indicate that the tragedy of all religions is that they violate the principles of freedom as soon as they become mass organizations controlled by an ecclesiastical bureaucracy.

The worst thing is that many people have character structures, which are authoritarian and therefore easily fall prey to the large religious organizations. When such people join the church, for instance, they become a part of a great authoritarian structure. They feel that they too now possess the strength of the authority, which in turn gives them a sense of security, even if at the expense of their own integrity.

In authoritarian religion God is a symbol of power and force, whereas in humanistic religion God is a symbol of man's own powers. The individual who is attracted to the first symbol and internalizes it may find a tentative kind of psychological security, but he will never be an individuated person, a whole mature adult. For genuine maturity a person must embrace humanistic religion.

Debteraw's faith-love-hope (see call me by my name XII.). A humanistic religion is centered around man and his strength. Man must develop his power of reason in order to understand himself, his relationship to his fellow men and his position in the Universe with God. He must recognize the truth, both with regard to his limitations and his potentialities.

I know Debteraw has developed his powers of love for others as well as for himself and experience the solidarity of all living beings. Debteraw has principles and norms to guide him in his aims. Debteraw's argument is to achieving the greatest strength, not the greatest powerlessness. He says that virtue is self-realization, not obedience.

In Debteraw's Ethiopia religion was united as far as loving humanity but separate in structural operation.

> Dr. Tesfaye Debessay was Catholic Christian
> Debteraw Tsegey is an Orthodox Christian
> Engineer Osman was a Muslim
> Berhane Meskel Redda was an atheist
> Many other leaders of EPRP were Protestants.

This collective leadership used to respect not only their own religions but also their friends religions including their organizational and geographical set up. After all, every one and every body in EPRP must embrace all religions.

The Tesfayes can have a center in Vatican if they want to
The Debteras can have their center at Axum if they desire to
The Osmans can have their center in Mecca if they prefer to
The Berhane Meskels can have the "Communist Party' as their center if they choose to

The Protestants can embrace the corporate world if they can handle it. By the way, I believe that the current Ethiopian situational crisis have emanated from the corporate religion.

On Conclusion

Notwithstanding about my labeling, what did the collective leadership say during the five-hour meetings?

The Apostle summarized that EPRP is going from "Struggle to struggle" (Ke'Tigle wede Tigle). The Prophet's emphasis on EPRP as losing ground.

The Evangelist revealed that words of EPRP is spreading all over the world

The Reverend disclosed about his student presidency during the downfall of the Monarchy of Ethiopia.

The Teacher pleaded to call back all ex EPRP members.

As democracy is only relevant when a group of people want to make decisions collectively for the group, the existence of a group is vital, but issues of its size and composition can raise problems for the success of democracy. Relations within the group are important. When the group is seen as a collective, as a cohesive whole, then decision making will be different from cases where the group is seen as an aggregation of individuals. Reflecting back to what was going on during this important meeting, we should have asked the collective leadership the following questions:

- Who can put an issue on the agenda?
- Who can suggest alternatives?
- Was there informed debate on the issue?

- Who decides on the options?
- Are the decisions that are made followed?

Now what has happened? Two of the five or seven collective leadership have withdrawn or walked away from the main stream of EPRP. I can see that the prophet could not predict the future of EPRP and the Reverend could not feed members of EPRP not only physically but also mentally. What a tragedy!

For comments and criticism: woldetewolde@yahoo.com

This entry was posted on 15. May 2008 at 00:22 and is filed under Articles. You can follow any responses to this entry through the RSS 2.0 feed. You can leave a response or trackback from your own site.

CALL ME BY MY NAME:

Solutions with Debteraw, XXVIII

Obo Arada Shawl alias Wolde Tewolde

June 3, 2008

About nine months ago, I wrote an article about Dignity and Pride in relation to EPRP. (See call me by my name: XVIII). Now it seems to me that Ethiopians are giving up hope of restoring dignity and pride by not paying a simple price known as RESPECT to oneself and other. For there is not Me without You in our community.

Why do Ethiopians campaign for Obama? Is it because he is from a neighboring country of Kenya? Why do the Eritreans do not campaign for Clinton for I know the majority of them are campaigning for Obama? Mrs. Clinton has at least visited their country, Eritrea. I believe most Eritreans are male chauvinists. What ever the reason is, I do not see why their hopes is being shattered. The following examples will illustrate my points of departure.

Long time ago, while Blacks were allowed to sit in the back of the buses, it is said that an Ethiopian boarded the bus and the driver told him to take a seat in the in the back. The Ethiopian passenger told the driver that he is an Ethiopian. The driver asked the passengers where Ethiopia is. The passengers suggested that Ethiopia may be somewhere in the state of Florida. The driver said to the Ethiopian passenger, "You see, move and sit in the back."

My daughter while she was in elementary school, all her friends were African-American, while walking in the streets of Washington, many Ethiopian passersby ask her whether she was an Ethiopian and were curious why she was going with Black girls? And her friends used to ask her what they were asking and she simply told them "are you an Ethiopian?" and her friends quipped "what a stupid question!" One day she confronted me with the question of whether we are black or white. I told her to visualize her uncles and aunts who came from the same womb but some of whom physically black and some look like white and so to make things better for her, I emphatically told her we are neither white nor black. She said to me at the time "it made a lot of sense". I do not know about now. She is grown up. She has her own explanations and preferences. I think she is campaigning for Obama following the Ethiopian crowd.

It is a common knowledge that Emperor Haile Sellassies while visiting the United States of America in the 1960s, a journalist asked him, "are you the first Negro to come to the White House?" And the Emperor said, "I am not Negro." And the journalist continued, by saying then you are white, and the Emperor said, "No I am not white." But the propagandists continued to inculcate hatred among Ethiopians and African-Americans by harping on one section of the Emperor's i.e. "I am not black."

So what now? Have we learned our lessons? How do we learn and from whom?

There are two ways of learning, one by reading books and the other by experience. Experience is the best but it is inconceivable and so the easiest and convenient is learning through books. Today, I want to quote two individuals who were supposed to have learned through reading books. These are Professor Mesfin Wolde Mariam and Robele Ababya. Professor Mesfin in „Ethiopia from where to where" as quoted in www.abbaymedia.com defined "ETHIOPIAWINET" in seventeen red written words all of which do not explain any concrete things. They are all abstract terminology. As a geographer, he should at least define it in terms of location if not in politics. Does the professor understand what politics is? Does he understand what science is or for that matter does he has some grasps of technology? I am still puzzled what he knows or where he is from? No Arts, No Science and No Technology. It is a disaster not only for him and his students (if he is still teaching?) but also for many of his followers.

The other quotable person is also from abbaymedia.com posted on March 26th, 2008. Mr. Robele attempts to discredit the Ethiopian Revolution in direct contradiction with the Professor Mesfin. "The copycats made a mess of applying the works of Marx to the socio-economic conditions of technologically, scientifically and industrially backward

Ethiopia." Mr. Robele seem to tease Ethiopians that "Land to the tiller" was a passion. According to him it was an empty slogan. Shouldn't he recognize the DERG's proclamation of land to the tiller, 10 hectares was enough for Mr. Robele!!!

In addition Mr. Robele misunderstood the nature of the Eway Revolution. He thinks like most ordinary people that the Revolution was a one-day event. He continued to argue, "In the aftermath of the revolution, various political orientations emerged including copycats of the works of Marx, Engel, Lenin, Stalin, Mao et al." What about EPRP? Was it a copycat? Did you know anything about EPRP at the time of the so-called revolution? If the revolution of the Derg was real and beneficial to all Ethiopians including you, why do you think EPRP had opposed? I am sure you do not know the answer. I have no doubt that your knowledge of Revolution is limited. You have repeated what was said as is (in written form at that), all the wrong allegations labeled against EPRP by the Dergists and their cronies. Here is what you repeated like a parrot "The onset of white terror led to red terror. That was a horrendous political mistake of the EPRP (old) leadership in firing the first bullet to kill their opponents. The other blunder is that they argued that the Eritrean problem is a colonial question and should be resolved in that context. During the invasion by Siad Barre, their cadres in the battlefield actively opposed Ethiopian forces fighting to repulse the aggressor in the Ogaden. It was heart-breaking to see the exodus of Ethiopians in the Ogaden for safety in the north of Ethiopia." What a Papa Gallo person you are! After thirty something, you do not know. Where are you now? What is your name? Do you live by your name? Why do you mud slug the name of Ababya?

What is worst, you seem to be joyous about the split of EPRP. It is about a split beyond your comprehension. It is not about make it or break it like you think. It is about process of Democracia'w way of struggle. In EPRP, there is no old or new, it was the same and it is the same EPRP. Give up hope of splitting the Party for it was founded on solid grounder like the obelisk of Axum which stood for three thousand years, or like that Fassil Ginb, the Lalibela church or the Wall of Harrar which stood hundred of years. EPRP, whether you like it or not, it is psychologically, physiologically, philosophically and politically is grounded. Robele conclude by saying "they are now politically bankrupt. The split is welcome. Good luck to EPRP (d)!" What a wishful thinking!!!

In conclusion, what I wrote on www.Debteraw.com call me by my name, XVIII is a good outlook for Ethiopians and EPRP opponents. The article explains the relationships of EPRP Party-Army-Community. An Ethiopian Integrity, Trust and Dignity are illustrated through the eyes of an observer. Call this Ethiopiawinet if you like.

Finally, I would like to remind the professor and the Robele that Debteraw Tsegaye was not and is not a phony man. He is held against his will in INCOMMINCADO in Woyene's hidden Prison. As a person, Debteraw was not a bad person for both of you. I do not think you have a quarrel with that assessment but I am of the opinion that both of you are coward towards „learned Ethiopian men". Debtera's and his colleagues are not copycat men but creative, bold and generous in every aspect. Please, be advised that you do not have to be a parrot and arrogant individuals. The professor wants to cover up his weakness through the Ethiopian flag of red, yellow and green, and Mr. Robele has written his article under a map of the Horn of Africa. What is this? Have they switched professions? A Flag and a Map, the very beginning of a scout boy.

Let it be clear to everybody and everyone that Debteraw was not hiding either under the guise of flag like the professor or fighting under the map just like Mr. Robele in order to explain what Ethiopiawinet meant. Debteraw and his party of EPRP have lived in Integrity, Trust and Dignity since the 1970s so as to demonstrate the value of ETHIOPIAWINET or call it by any other name.

For criticism and comments: woldetewolde@yahoo.com

This entry was posted on 4. June 2008 at 00:45 and is filed under Articles. You can follow any responses to this entry through the RSS 2.0 feed. You can skip to the end and leave a response. Pinging is currently not allowed.

CALL ME BY MY NAME:

Solutions with DEBTERAW, XXIX

Obo Arada Shawl alias Wolde Tewolde

June 13, 2008

There is the Natural Way

And there is the Artificial Way

There is the Wrong Way
And there is the EWAY Ethiopia

Introduction

On Saturday morning, June 7, 2008, there was a race – a race not for power, not for time or for revenge but a race for a CURE (Breast Cancer). The winner was ABYOT ABEBE. He stood 1st out of the 40, 000 participants. What a name! He must have been born during the Ethiopian Revolution. Deciphering his name tells me that the Eway Revolution is still blooming as he won the race for cure to bring peace and prosperity for Ethiopia.

Nowadays, it seems to me that there is a race to cure Ethiopia and Eritrea from poverty, disease and from sell out for disintegration. To me there was no poverty in Ethiopia and Eritrea. The truth of the matter was such that *philosophy of poverty* in Ethiopia and *poverty of philosophy* in Eritrea had reigned for centuries. However, after the war of 1998-2000, between Eritreans and the government of EPRDF, the reverse became the truth. That is to say that the Ethiopians are forced to resort to the poverty of philosophy and the Eritreans to the philosophy of poverty. What a paradox!

What about disease? What about societal disintegration? These are issues that could not be analyzed individually. Personally, I dare not guess let alone to analyze about these issues.

Various professional Institutions and Organizations should come together to study and delve into these matters.

The purpose of this article is to inquire and to resolve the confusion that is being perpetuated by EPRP collective leadership in the hope that the experience of EPRP is not wasted as a resource of Ethiopia. The greatest untold story of EPRP is the under performance of its leadership. After many decades for democratic struggle, EPRP collective leaders should have been the role models of Ethiopia for many organizations and groups that aspire to follow EPRP's style of leadership.

Collective Leadership

Some folks might misunderstand me on my advocacy for the concept of collective leadership. In a simple term, it is a style of participants sitting arrangement around a circular (round) table. To the naked eye, no one can detect "who is the boss". The boss is the one who can convince and who can see eye to eye. This style of leadership would have been a panacea for all of us. It is precisely why EPRP has and is paying a heavy price to practice and implement this style of leadership for it is contrary to the medieval culture of ruling style.

My mission as "Obo Arada Shawl" is not rhetorical but on record and not mere mobilizations but rather persuasion. I want to raise dialogue and conversations about substantive issues. Instead of dwelling on substantive issues, people are dwelling on petty differences of opinion and not facts or truth. There is a clear demarcation between opinion and facts inasmuch as there is a clear difference between facts and truth. Two names, two emblems, two radio broadcasts and two publications of DEMOCRACIAs will definitely confuse not only personalities but also the issues of Ethiopia and Eritrea. The Obo factor (democracy), the Arada factor (conspiracy) and the Shawl factor (arrogance) should be considered in the path of struggle at least for the survival of "AEthiopia".

What is right and what is wrong among EPRP's collective leadership? In the recent past,

- Hama Tuma led the Department of Education (Ye'Nkat Guday)
- Samuel Alemayehu (now deceased) has led the Organizational Department (Aderaj)
- Mohammed Jemal has led the Department of financial Empowerment (Astataki)
- Fisseha Assefa has led the Department of Management style (Tebaki)
- Yoseph Nigatu has led the Department of Co-Ordination (Meri)

In addition to the above, Tsegeye G. Medhin alias DEBTERAW, Yishak Debretsion, Amha Bellette and Sitotaw Hussien who were captured alive are still held incommunicado somewhere in the Terror zone of Tigrai.

Members and supporters expect these leaders and others to use their collective energies toward what **EPRP is for instead of what EPRP is against.** On this score, the Zematches (followers) and the Azmatches (leaders) have trusted one another for 33 years on end. But after the 33rd years of struggle, things have begun to change especially among the collective leadership. Why?

Although I don't have all the answers to the beginning of leadership faltering, I sensed what might befall on some personalities of the collective leadership's psychic. On the 33rd anniversary of EPRP that was held in Georgia Ave, in Washington DC, there was a rare case of display of EPRP's presence For the first time in my whole life, I have seen DEMOCRACIA openly displayed on a table as if it is a menu. What a show it was!!! In fact, I examined the publication for its authenticity. Fortunately, it was deciphered as true and correct. The audience was full of diversified people including prominent journalists and official from the DERG era.

According to my readings and recollections, there were also musicians represent ting the Monarchy by Telela Kebede, the Military Derg by Maritu and the EPRDF by Solomon Tekalegne.

EPRP did not have singers on the stage, only a group of troupe singing "LE ZEMENAT". The only vibrant individual speaker for the occasion was Tesfaye Debessay's daughter. She was young who seem to be inspired by her deceased father DR. Tesfaye of EPRP leadership. It was a pity that she did not even know what her father was teaching at the university. Shouldn't we teach our children the true history of EPRP? I am the first one to be blamed for this state of affairs.

Trust:

Given the entire struggle for the **Eway Revolution** to change Ethiopia's political system, would you confuse your own members? Instead of spirited rivalry, a long time revolutionary by the name of Mersha Yoseph along with a man who parked from the Revolutionary struggle for a long period of time have created confusion among many supporters of EPRP. I do not appreciate this lack of trust; in fact, it almost hurt my feelings and the feeling of many Ethiopians and Eritreans. In the past, it used to be character assassination but this time; there is no such thing because everything is clear and simple. It is about stand and value. My point is to bring substance back into the struggle not individual connection. Relationship is all about trust.

There were people like Kifle Tadesse who believed that because they have been attending a conference and as all of them are dead but one, he thought that the party of EPRP is dead and buried or alternatively he is the one who should lead in any other way including working with the Woyanes.

Then there were people like Tamrat Lyne, Getachew Jebessa and Teffera Waluwa who formed a splinter group. Again it is all about trust. I remember when I used to ask questions about who the fighters or liberators roaming around the environs of Lalibela, Danghla, Dabat, Debarik and so on and so forth. The peasants used to tell me that they could not differentiate between them for they greet them in Tigrigna and Amharic. There was no education there. It was all gimmicks. That was a matter of trust.

Then there were individuals like Kebede Essatu and Yoseph Tesfaye who believed that they were the leaders of EPRP and so on and so forth. But the true of the matter is that none of them are or were still true

Power:

EPRP's leadership emanates from the members willingness to follow. How do they know that the leadership is in the right track? Or do members know the leadership in person? Were there overall national conferences for all members of EPRP? There was no way for all EPRP members, delegates, super delegates could come together for their true struggle for political CHANGE was arduous and tumultuous. Regardless of their ethnic background, race and religion, EPRP members and supporters operate based on TRUST alone. Nothing less nothing more!!!

Planning:

How do members and supporters, then know whether they have leaders and followers? Historically, the best glue for all of EPRP members and supporters was to see through the stated goals and objectives – One Flag, One Fidel and Many Freedoms (See call me by my name, XXVI). And where can they find how EPRP is operating? There were many publications to follow though, but the most important media for EPRP was DEMOCRACIA. Everything that was being written and documented in DEMOCARCIA was true and authentic. Practically everyone's and everybody of EPRP members and supporters ideas and concerns and issues were being incorporated in the Publication. That means that the struggle being waged was the concern of all Ethiopians. What about now? Whom do Ethiopians follow? Or for what they stand for? Nowadays, there is the Internet, radios and newspapers. The Internet and the radio waves are plenty and sometimes create confusion instead of creativity and clarity for problem solving.

Conclusion

Let everyone pull out magnifying glasses and examine EPRP more closely. We need to pay closer attention to the omitted details. We need to reinsert our values and talents into interdependent EPRP where they belong. The little invisible things are after our best clues – the betrayal, the disinformation, the sabotage and the mistrust should be forgiven but not forgotten. Much of the damage inflicted upon EPRP was quite invisible to the laymen. It is too easy to ignore problems until they slap us in the face. Only a few factions' problems have slapped EPRP in the face, at least in earnest. Many more are gathering the strength to do the process of learning to see the Truth. While on the other hand, the penalties for political education is that some lives could suffer alone in the past wounds, in the current shallow politics and in global social fashion.

Ignorance is a regular visitor in the life cycle of EPRP, in all decades, (seasons), at all place, it arrives to play an annoying, unpredictable role. The ignorance of yesterday's walk away is not the ignorance of the lazy or the slow. It is the ignorance of the decent, motivated intellect that is honestly and legitimately overwhelmed. Yet in the end, their decisions need to be made legitimate and truthful.

For comments and critics woldetewolde@yahoo.com

CALL ME BY MY NAME:

Solutions with DEBTERAW, XXIX

Obo Arada Shawl alias Wolde Tewolde

June 13, 2008

There is the Natural Way

And there is the Artificial Way

There is the Wrong Way
And there is the EWAY Ethiopia

Introduction

On Saturday morning, June 7, 2008, there was a race – a race not for power, not for time or for revenge but a race for a CURE (Breast Cancer). The winner was ABYOT ABEBE. He stood 1st out of the 40, 000 participants. What a name! He must have been born during the Ethiopian Revolution. Deciphering his name tells me that the Eway Revolution is still blooming as he won the race for cure to bring peace and prosperity for Ethiopia.

Nowadays, it seems to me that there is a race to cure Ethiopia and Eritrea from poverty, disease and from sell out for disintegration. To me there was no poverty in Ethiopia and Eritrea. The truth of the matter was such that *philosophy of poverty* in Ethiopia and *poverty of philosophy in Eritrea had reigned for centuries.* However, after the war of 1998-2000, between Eritreans and the government of EPRDF, the reverse became the truth. That is to say that the Ethiopians are forced to resort to the poverty of philosophy and the Eritreans to the philosophy of poverty. What a paradox!

What about disease? What about societal disintegration? These are issues that could not be analyzed individually. Personally, I dare not guess let alone to analyze about these issues.

Various professional Institutions and Organizations should come together to study and delve into these matters.

The purpose of this article is to inquire and to resolve the confusion that is being perpetuated by EPRP collective leadership in the hope that the experience of EPRP is not wasted as a resource of Ethiopia. The greatest untold story of EPRP is the under performance of its leadership. After many decades for democratic struggle, EPRP collective leaders should have been the role models of Ethiopia for many organizations and groups that aspire to follow EPRP's style of leadership.

Collective Leadership

Some folks might misunderstand me on my advocacy for the concept of collective leadership. In a simple term, it is a style of participants sitting arrangement around a circular (round) table. To the naked eye, no one can detect "who is the boss". The boss is the one who can convince and who can see eye to eye. This style of leadership would have been a panacea for all of us. It is precisely why EPRP has and is paying a heavy price to practice and implement this style of leadership for it is contrary to the medieval culture of ruling style.

My mission as "Obo Arada Shawl" is not rhetorical but on record and not mere mobilizations but rather persuasion. I want to raise dialogue and conversations about substantive issues. Instead of dwelling on substantive issues, people are dwelling on petty differences of opinion and not facts or truth. There is a clear demarcation between opinion and facts inasmuch as there is a clear difference between facts and truth. Two names, two emblems, two radio broadcasts and two publications of DEMOCRACIAs will definitely confuse not only personalities but also the issues of Ethiopia and Eritrea. The Obo factor (democracy), the Arada factor (conspiracy) and the Shawl factor (arrogance) should be considered in the path of struggle at least for the survival of "AEthiopia".

What is right and what is wrong among EPRP's collective leadership? In the recent past,

- Hama Tuma led the Department of Education (Ye'Nkat Guday)
- Samuel Alemayehu (now deceased) has led the Organizational Department (Aderaj)
- Mohammed Jemal has led the Department of financial Empowerment (Astataki)
- Fisseha Assefa has led the Department of Management style (Tebaki)
- Yoseph Nigatu has led the Department of Co-Ordination (Meri)

In addition to the above, Tsegeye G. Medhin alias DEBTERAW, Yishak Debretsion, Amha Bellette and Sitotaw Hussien who were captured alive are still held incommunicado somewhere in the Terror zone of Tigrai.

Members and supporters expect these leaders and others to use their collective energies toward what **EPRP is for instead of what EPRP is against.** On this score, the Zematches (followers) and the Azmatches (leaders) have trusted one another for 33 years on end. But after the 33rd years of struggle, things have begun to change especially among the collective leadership. Why?

Although I don't have all the answers to the beginning of leadership faltering, I sensed what might befall on some personalities of the collective leadership's psychic. On the 33rd anniversary of EPRP that was held in Georgia Ave, in Washington DC, there was a rare case of display of EPRP's presence For the first time in my whole life, I have seen DEMOCRACIA openly displayed on a table as if it is a menu. What a show it was!!! In fact, I examined the publication for its authenticity. Fortunately, it was deciphered as true and correct. The audience was full of diversified people including prominent journalists and official from the DERG era.

According to my readings and recollections, there were also musicians represent ting the Monarchy by Telela Kebede, the Military Derg by Maritu and the EPRDF by Solomon Tekalegne.

EPRP did not have singers on the stage, only a group of troupe singing "LE ZEMENAT". The only vibrant individual speaker for the occasion was Tesfaye Debessay's daughter. She was young who seem to be inspired by her deceased father DR. Tesfaye of EPRP leadership. It was a pity that she did not even know what her father was teaching at the university. Shouldn't we teach our children the true history of EPRP? I am the first one to be blamed for this state of affairs.

Trust:

Given the entire struggle for the **Eway Revolution** to change Ethiopia's political system, would you confuse your own members? Instead of spirited rivalry, a long time revolutionary by the name of Mersha Yoseph along with a man who parked from the Revolutionary struggle for a long period of time have created confusion among many supporters of EPRP. I do not appreciate this lack of trust; in fact, it almost hurt my feelings and the feeling of many Ethiopians and Eritreans. In the past, it used to be character assassination but this time; there is no such thing because everything is clear and simple. It is about stand and value. My point is to bring substance back into the struggle not individual connection. Relationship is all about trust.

There were people like Kifle Tadesse who believed that because they have been attending a conference and as all of them are dead but one, he thought that the party of EPRP is dead and buried or alternatively he is the one who should lead in any other way including working with the Woyanes.

Then there were people like Tamrat Lyne, Getachew Jebessa and Teffera Waluwa who formed a splinter group. Again it is all about trust. I remember when I used to ask questions about who the fighters or liberators roaming around the environs of Lalibela, Danghla, Dabat, Debarik and so on and so forth. The peasants used to tell me that they could not differentiate between them for they greet them in Tigrigna and Amharic. There was no education there. It was all gimmicks. That was a matter of trust.

Then there were individuals like Kebede Essatu and Yoseph Tesfaye who believed that they were the leaders of EPRP and so on and so forth. But the true of the matter is that none of them are or were still true

Power:

EPRP's leadership emanates from the members willingness to follow. How do they know that the leadership is in the right track? Or do members know the leadership in person? Were there overall national conferences for all members of EPRP? There was no way for all EPRP members, delegates, super delegates could come together for their true struggle for political CHANGE was arduous and tumultuous. Regardless of their ethnic background, race and religion, EPRP members and supporters operate based on TRUST alone. Nothing less nothing more!!!

Planning:

How do members and supporters, then know whether they have leaders and followers? Historically, the best glue for all of EPRP members and supporters was to see through the stated goals and objectives – One Flag, One Fidel and Many Freedoms (See call me by my name, XXVI). And where can they find how EPRP is operating? There were many publications to follow though, but the most important media for EPRP was DEMOCRACIA. Everything that was being written and documented in DEMOCARCIA was true and authentic. Practically everyone's and everybody of EPRP members and supporters ideas and concerns and issues were being incorporated in the Publication. That means that the struggle being waged was the concern of all Ethiopians. What about now? Whom do Ethiopians follow? Or for what they stand for? Nowadays, there is the Internet, radios and newspapers. The Internet and the radio waves are plenty and sometimes create confusion instead of creativity and clarity for problem solving.

Conclusion

Let everyone pull out magnifying glasses and examine EPRP more closely. We need to pay closer attention to the omitted details. We need to reinsert our values and talents into interdependent EPRP where they belong. The little invisible things are after our best clues – the betrayal, the disinformation, the sabotage and the mistrust should be forgiven but not forgotten. Much of the damage inflicted upon EPRP was quite invisible to the laymen. It is too easy to ignore problems until they slap us in the face. Only a few factions' problems have slapped EPRP in the face, at least in earnest. Many more are gathering the strength to do the process of learning to see the Truth. While on the other hand, the penalties for political education is that some lives could suffer alone in the past wounds, in the current shallow politics and in global social fashion.

Ignorance is a regular visitor in the life cycle of EPRP, in all decades, (seasons), at all place, it arrives to play an annoying, unpredictable role. The ignorance of yesterday's walk away is not the ignorance of the lazy or the slow. It is the ignorance of the decent, motivated intellect that is honestly and legitimately overwhelmed. Yet in the end, their decisions need to be made legitimate and truthful.

For comments and criticism: woldetewolde@yahoo.com

SOLUTIONS WITH DEBTERAW, A commentary on the "Art of death"

Obo Arada Shawl

May 11, 2009

መህይሙ ማነው?
ምሁሩ ማነው?
ጽንሐተ ፀጋየስ ምንድን ነው?
አርቲስት ይሞታል፤ ኪነት ግና አትሞትም

What is Art? What is Artist?

Frankly speaking, I am not enchanted to memorialize the death of a singer (albeit famous) as to memorialize the death of victims of "Red Terror". In Washington, DC, on the same day and at the same time, it is reported that only 50 people have attended in memory for the death of victims of the "Red Terror" that was presented by Ali Hussein from Canada whereas there were a thousand attendees for the memory of Tilahun Gessese's death. What is the art of death? Is it related with God or Life? Although we are neither sure to touch God nor to pinpoint Life, we are certain about death.

I hate to write on a subject I do not know, but on this one on the "art of death", I need to express my opinion –that of the Art and Artist - although not a professional level but on a cultural basis.

Yemane Baria

This man died in Asmara on December 1997 and hundred thousand Eritreans buried him. It was reported that his burial ceremony was larger than WWM (woldeab wolde mariam), who is considered to be the "father of the Eritrean separation" from Ethiopia. It was puzzling why a singer was given the highest death ceremony. The explanation is as follows:

Yemane Baria (I don't know his last name) was neither a talented vocalist nor a musician. But he composes his own lyrics. My question was, how did he become popular without voice and instruments, after all there are many singers with ghost composers behind them but were not or are not famous like him. The answer rests on something else.

Yemane blended love songs with political matters. In this case, the Eritrean population had embraced Yemene's music despite his deficiency in **Auditory Arts.** In other words, Yemane packages the feelings and thoughts of ordinary people and had presented it back to them. That was and still should be the art of politics. Politics after all is a relationship between a singer (in the name of ሓፋሽ) and the government in power.

Another factor that was much superior to the above elements of his popularity was the fact that Yeman Baria owned nothing. Whatever material or financial he earns from his music, he used to give it back to the poor or to whoever needs help. That by itself is the hallmark of Eritrean cultural struggle. Yemane lived for the people and died for the people. And I believe, that thousands have attended his burial ceremony to say goodbye to their own inner "Art of Death". The Auditory Art or lack of it has died with Yemane.

The Eritrean people became voiceless and powerless - ብከያያን አዘራርባ

Yemane's touching song as far as I am concerned was that "what is the solution now? እሞ

ሕጂ'ድኣ እንታይ ይገበር has remained unanswered.

Tilahun Gessese

In sharp contrast toYemane Baria, Tilahun was a singer par excellence. Tilahun's song was targeted to the elites of Ethiopia. I believe that Tilahun neither composed his songs nor did he play musical instruments. Nevertheless, he was popular among all Eathiopians. Why was he popular, one may ask? The answer may lie in his **Visual Art.**

Tilahun Gessesse may not have been a political man but his composers were definitely revolutionaries of the time. To prove this sentence, let me narrate two stories.

On one occasion, that is, during the coming of the DERG, Tilahun had a song which runs like this. "Beyond the revolution, I can see a bright hope" ከአብዮቱ በስተ ጀርባ ይታየኛል ብሩህ ተስፋ, and EPRP members and associates were quickly dismissing Tilahun's false premise. It was very true that Tilahun's lyrics came from the Ethiopian elites and those of EPRP's supporters voice of dissent came from the leaders of EPRP. And so the struggle for hope against hope continued until the downfall of the DERG.

On another occasion, while we were sitting in a coffee shop, Ato Berhanu – normally considered as a distributor of "wisdom" entered the coffee shop with the intention of selling a book entitled "the Generation": a history of EPRP by Kiflu Tadesse. The book-distributor did presented the book to Tesfaye Lemma for purchase to which Ato Tesfaye Lemma rejected the idea of reading a book about EPRP. I asked Artist Tesfaye, whether Tilahun Gessesse was a member of EPRP? He snatched the book from Berhanu and found out that Tilahun's name was mentioned in a political context. Ato Tesfaye Lemma bought the book and he came back on the third day as happy as he can be. Later on I found out that the man behind Tilahun was Tesfaye himself. I believe that Art has a snowball effect. For this reason, it was no surprise that hundreds of thousands had attended the burial ceremony that was held for Tilahun Gessesse. Even if Tilahun was not a revolutionary per se to speak directly to the Power that be, he has indirectly contributed to the Eway Revolution albeit to the elite class not to the broad masses.

Tsegaye G. Medhin (DEBTERAW)

Performing Art is a combination of Auditory and Visual or it is an Art by itself. DEBTERAW belongs to this category of Art. Alternatively, DEBTERAW even though he is from an elitist class, he speaks the language of the people, he empathies with the people and he gives them back their true cultural identity. Above all DEBTERAW speaks to Absolute Power regardless. DEBTERAW owned nothing of material but he gave everything political, philosophical and spiritual to everyone and everybody. He calls such act as ኪነት የሕዝብ ናት not the "art of death". DEBTERAW highly believes in CREATIVITY as opposed to carbon copy.

Conclusion

What is the difference between honoring a normal death and a victimized death? I have witnessed heroic deaths. I have also seen cowardly deaths. But they all are deaths or are they really? Apart from going to Heaven or to Hell, there is a criterion to judge by the way the deceased should be evaluated. I believe that death for some, it is _heroism_ and for others it is _patriotism_. Yemane's Art belongs to heroism while that of Tilahun reflects of patriotism.

Of course, it is anybody's guess about DEBTERAW; it is both heroism and patriotism.

Tilahun may have had at heart - songs about *Love-Family-Friendship*, while that of DEBTERAW and Bariaw is about *Liberty-Unity-Justice.*

Of course, the triangle of love-family-friendship for DEBTERAW precedes the triangle of LUJ (liberty-unity-justice). It is a big CHOICE WE ALL SHOULD MAKE. At this junction of Eathiopian history, we cannot go back talking about sexuality, false unity and fake friendship. Instead let us dwell on liberty, unity and justice for all.

TRUTH WILL PREVAIL
For comments and questions: woldetewolde@yahoo.com

PS:

I have witnessed a party celebration for the dead. Three days of music with traditional dancing was carried out in Metekel Awraja, in Godjam among the Shankala people. Without my calculated intention, I landed among the celebrating population. Children were suckling and dancing at the same time, naked men and women compete for show. Some sit while others walk but all dance to the tune of the oncoming music that seems to come from nowhere.

I had asked the occasion for the celebration. I was very much in shock when they told me it was because a certain lady had died. I was puzzled why an entire community dances instead of mourning. Would you not ask the question I asked? Of course, you would.

The answer lies in the marital status of the deceased. If the deceased has children, he is parted with pomp and drink, if without children; the community burns the village and relocates. What a wonderful act of "Art of death?"

Should we mourn for Tilahun with twelve children, for Yemane with six children or for DEBTERAW with no children? The answer lies within each one of us.

SOLUTIONS WITH DEBTERAW, III:

Call me by my Name, Address and Task

Obo Arada Shawl

(January 5, 2008)

The Eway Revolution is about

- *Dealing with the failure of the Monarchy's Constitution*
- *Showing the failure of the DERG's revolution*
- *Telling the truth about TPLF's anti-democracy and*
- *Pointing out the failure of EPLF's search for justice*

The United States of Aethiopia, which will come in 2013, should dispel the "sea of doubt" among the traders (such as TPLF), territory lovers (such as EPLF, OLF) and the ideologists (such as EPRP). The current problems of mistrust, lie and cheat will be halted when the Eway Revolution is revealed.

Education and Religion

Historically, the three wise men brought Gold, Incense and Murk to the Son of God, Jesus Christ. According to some historians, gold was obtained from Israel, murk from Persia and incense from Ethiopia. The significance of these three products is obvious in today's world.

The Society of Jesus popularly known as the Jesuits were organized some 470 years ago. This Society branched to Ethiopia, first to Teferri Makonnen School and later on moved to Addis Ababa University. Though the Jesuit's teaching require the promotion of justice, its member vow of poverty, chastity and obedience. On that basis, the first of the alumni Ethiopian graduates wanted to serve the State and the Church but not the public.

After graduation, it was very unfortunate that the alumni in Ethiopia were not encouraged to be organized. Instead, they were under watchful eye of the government. The alumni association was for the most part was run by one man under the name of Samuel Alemayehu not to be confused with the Revolutionary Samuel Alemayehu. The history of these two individuals' course of action has contributed much to the current situations in Aethiopia. However, my intention is not to compare the Samuel Alemayehu's contribution to the Great Society of ours. Instead, let me quote the following

In 1960, there were about one thousand students at the University College of Addis Ababa (UCAA), less than fifty of who were women. Political attitudes were not yet formed and student concerns were introverted and parochial, focusing mainly on conditions in the college. The major conflict concerned the Jesuit administration and their pedagogical methods based on their experience in running elementary and secondary schools in Ethiopia. These methods were applied with minimum adaptation to the university. Student indignation was fueled by many trivial and humiliating restrictions, such as the rules forbidding dancing and whistling on campus. Issues of autonomy for the student council and freedom of expression for the student publication, News and Views were of particular concern. The Dean of Students kept the student council under a tight reign. All material published by News and Views had to be approved by a faculty advisor. Kiflu Tadesse, "the generation", P: 35

Once the students have left the schools, the outside world also views them with suspicion and jealousy. The majority of the graduates became complacent as the government was the sole employer and those who stood for principles and beliefs have been labeled as anti-Ethiopian. In addition, the majority of high school students did not have the opportunity to continue education. The students had to fail of necessity the High School Leaving Certificate (ESLC). In such a dire condition, it was obvious that the failure of the education program (championed by the Emperor) had helped in the collapse of the Monarch, Haile Sellassie I.

Suffice to say that alumni reunions or forming alumni associations were difficult during Haile Sellasie time. (An alumnus or alumna is ether someone who has attended the school, a former student of a school or someone who has graduated). Alumni reunions are popular events at many institutions organized by alumni associations and are often social occasions for fundraising. The absence of these associations, I believe is behind every problem of past and current. The absence of SEA (freedom of speech, expression and assembly) should be considered in our daily menu.

In other words, it is no wonder that the Revolution was based on the failure of the Education system and its aftermath. The hope and aspirations of graduates and high school students were dashed.

The two elements i.e. the graduates and high school students have succeeded to penetrate the Ethiopian workers to get organized on clandestine basis. According to the literature and other country experiences of Revolution, the proletariat led by CELU (Confederation of Ethiopian workers Union) was embarked to lead the Revolution with alliance of the peasants of Ethiopia.

The failure of workers to lead the peasants has changed the Ethiopian reality and turned into an ugly bloodshed and personal feuds. As this aberration for leaders and followers occurs, The Monarchy and the Church have lost their source of power. Nevertheless, the remnants are still clinging to revive their power base. How far they can go, it is anybody guesses.

My present priority is to dwell on the fate of DEBTERAW who has left the Monastery but retained his faith that would have incorporated a family, and above all he would seek social justice for all Aethiopians without learning from the Jesuits. DEBTERAW wanted to bring social justice through the secular means of politics. DEBTERAW'S personal belief of God or Devil, or both or neither, I cannot testify. But what I know, he blew thousands of minds, touched millions hearts of Aethiopians. Today, I can hear that millions want spiritual journey by calling DEBTERAW as "heal me and touch me." After all what comes from the heart comes to the heart.

Politics and Revolution

Political changes came from two sources.

- First, The USAID in collaboration with the government of Ethiopia has funded scholarships for countries south of the Sahara.
- Second, the Neway brothers had carried out a coup d'etat to topple the 225 King of Ethiopia.

These two events encouraged college students to be political. The African students have come with political traditions to be open and aggressive towards their demands for campus privileges. Some conscious Ethiopian students began to meet in clandestine fashion. But the unconscious college students have noticed albeit uncritically how a powerful king with a heritage for over three thousand years (225 x 15) =3375 years of historical rule could be toppled by officers of his own bodyguard. It was an amazing phenomenon; a light at the end of the tunnel was begun to be seen.

Alternatively, which power of Influence was important to our current conditions? Was it the external factor that was brought by the Africans including the Eritreans who considered themselves as foreigners or was it an internal dynamic phenomenon that was brought and developed through these forty-nine years (1960-2009)?

The answer lies in either of us who were unborn and not interested in the past or in those who carried the internal dynamic Revolution in Ethiopia. Take your choice, the Obama way or the DEBTERAW way? That is, *Politics plus Change* or *Politics plus Revolution*. My choice is the DEBTERAW's way.

The DEBTERAW alias the Eway Aethiopian Revolution is an internal one that recognizes, the effort of Minilik's *modernity*, Yohannes's *religious belief*, Tewodros's *unity* of purpose, and Haile Sellasie's *education* program (not system). However, this does not mean that the way these kings carried out was democratic. It was autocratic simple and clear.

The Education Sector Review was a plan designed to stop the mass based education proposed by the Ethiopian government and opposed by the Ethiopian Teachers Association (ETA). The Eway Revolution was emerged to preserve and protect the positive aspects of modernity, belief and unity by reversing the education sector review. That was the last straw that broke the back of the mule so to speak, Haile Sellasie's system of government into history.

The methodology of bringing modernity, belief and unity via the education system as proposed by Ethiopian Teachers Association galvanized by DEBTERAW to all Ethiopians regardless of race, religion or class was and is via – DEMOCRACIA-

Once the student movement has exhausted its limit to

- Modernize the country
- Secularize the state
- Unite the country and
- To improvise the education system

The methodology applied to take political power in almost all Ethiopian Liberation Fronts was similar to each other – by armed protracted struggle. Their basis of claim, however, was radically different from one other. The end results are testimony to their objectives and operations.

- EPLF has waged protracted war on the basis of a "colonial theory"
- TPLF has waged and is still waging wars for power on the "theory of ethno-nationalism"
- EPRP is struggling for political power on the "theory of multinationals"
- OLF is waging war for democracy on the "theory of ethno-colonialism."
- Other recent comers are struggling on the basis on the "theory of unity."

A discussion on the merits and demerits of these theories should be a topic for solutions.

Concluding Remarks

Basically our community is divided into two camps, those who had supported the Ethiopian Revolution and those who regret that they have joined the Revolution. To those who had regretted to join the Eway Revolution, I have nothing to say except to read the following dialogue:

ልጅ፡ አባባ አብዮት ግዛልኝ
አባት፡ ምን ልታደርገው?
ልጅ፡ ላፈንዳው።

We all know what had happened in Ethiopia and among Ethiopians and hopefully what is going to happen in the future. Those who like to discredit the Eway Revolution had a kind of hope and child's mind as indicated in the above dialogue.

The struggles that were applied for societal change in Aethiopia are the following five tenets that I believe were used in the guidelines for revolution and counter- revolution.

- "The objective of war is to preserve oneself and annihilate the enemy" as preached by Mao Zedong and practiced by EPLF
- "The Chinese Communist Party claimed to power through its military arm, political power grows out of the barrel of the gun" as practiced by TPLF
- "We must emphasize politics. Our army is an army in the service of politics and politics must guide the military in its day-to-day work" as preached by Lin Piao and practiced by EPRP
- "A hundred victories in a hundred battles is not the best of the best; the best of the best is to subdue the enemy without having to fight," Chinese proverb as practiced by OLF
- "Let us demonstrate to the world and seize political power as has happened after the collapse of the Soviet Union as practiced by KINJIT

I believe our choice is clear.

TRUTH WILL PREVAIL
For comments and questions: woldetewolde@yahoo.com

CALL ME BY MY ADDRESS:

Solutions with DEBTERAW

Obo Arada Shawl alias Wolde Tewolde

MESKEREM 1, 2001 alias

September 11, 2008

Of Introduction

These days we are witnessing articles written by real names more than pen names. I hope it is a step foreword towards freedom of using one's given name. What is in a name? By now everybody and everyone in Ethiopia seems to decipher what his/her name means. Call me by my name is past due and so I move to "call me by my address".

History and Culture are the two culprits for most of our problems. What is history and what is culture? These are two fundamental questions to be answered by each and every one of us if our perceived problems of social, political and economic are to be resolved.

There are many histories and cultures (ሀc). I cannot discuss them here.

Today, on the beginning of our AEthiopian Millennium new year, I want to present personal histories of struggle (ገድል) of three individuals in the hope that their experience will lead to some lessons to be learned from their Education and Experience (EE).

Of Encounter

Forty years ago, to be exact forty-three years, the three of them met in college. All three of them had respect for Religion, for the Emperor and for Wealth. At the same time, they had fear of the Clergy, of the Government and of the

Rich. It was DEBTERAW, however, who revealed to them the secrets of the Clergy vs. religion: of the Emperor vs. his government and of the Aristocracy vs. the intelligentsias. In other words, these three individuals came face to face with *freedom of faith, political choice,* and *economic opportunity.*

Today, after 36 years, the three of them once again met in Washington, DC with their freedom of religion, political choice and economic opportunity in unison and intact. What a wonderful encounter! Many thanks to DEBTERAW TSEGEYE G. MEDHIN'S enlightened and mentoring.

The thing that surprised them most is that none of them has changed name in as much as the place they met. It was in a restaurant where the names of Addis Ababa communal communities are displayed on the walls of the restaurant. The hostess invited them to sit between WUBE SEFER and ERI BEKENTU! One of them said to himself, "am I still crying for nothing?" for he used to live in Eri Bekentu neighborhood.

As one of the trio has been recently to Addis Ababa, (the other two have never been either to Ethiopia or Eritrea since 1972), the two asked him whether these places of WUBE and IRI still carry the same names and same surroundings. He himself was surprised by their inquiries. He said, "People like you „developers" are outside the country, what do you expect?" he posed a rhetorical question. "Everything is in the same condition but with subdued people", he concluded.

Most people who have been to Addis Ababa remember that Wube Sefer and Eri Bekentu were full of vibrant people. Their colleague briefed them about the current Ethiopian practice of religion, politics and economic development in the country. "There is so much a sad story and history to tell to people in the Diaspora", he said. Could this be a result of their mentor DEBTERAW's prolonged imprisonment and disappearance?

Who knows? Call me by my address! Where am I?

Of Background

After graduation, all three were employed in the ministry of communication and transport authority (though all three graduated in economics with special emphasis in International trade). However, right after their employment, like most of their colleagues, these three individuals have been in the shadows of death since the DERG assumed political power.

Despite fear of the Clergy, the Emperor or the Bureaucracy, the majority of graduates of the 1970s have embarked upon the positive work of Minilik's Development Programs, Haile Sellasie's Education effort, Tewodros" concept of Unity and Yohannes's Religious beliefs. However, the Military and its mentors as well as the Nationalists rejected everything that these kings stood for and instead emulated foreign models of development.

But these three had quickly realized that the ministry they had joined, though critical, was in an infant stage. At the time, out of the population of Ethiopia, 95% of the passengers were using traditional mode of transport whereas over 90% of the goods and services were being transported by pack animals. This realization from their work place accompanied by their education and Debteraw's mentoring had convinced them to alleviate the Ethiopian transportation and communication system via Planning. It was in this area of planning that the then government of Ethiopia and subsequent regimes failed to convince these individuals to bring them to their side. Instead, these individuals have chosen a different path of struggle to bring change (the Eway Revolution led by EPRP).

Here is a review of their religious, political and economic values in concordance with the past and the future.

Of Religion

The history of AEthiopian religion is based on the symbol of the flag of red, yellow and green. This flag with a primary color was perceived as a bond between the Creator and the AEthiopians. Emperor Minilik II, had embraced it as a country national flag for Ethiopia. However, the narrow nationalists of Tigrai, the humble nationalists of Oromia and the arrogant nationalists of Hamasien have rejected this Flag of sacrifice, peace and prosperity. One has to look closely at what has been added to the current TPLF flag, to OLF flag and to Eritrean government flag. As far as color is concerned, there is no difference. The difference is that the leaders have their own design of stamp of passion to rule or desired to be. Their common factor is their enmity towards Emperor Minilik who adopted it as a national flag. Were the

Nationalists against the color of the flag or faith upon which the flag was based? I cannot tell. As far as I can decipher, it is not the color but the faith. If so, let them reveal their faith, whatever it is.

Minilik was not a fervent religious man. In fact when he was deep in economic and social development plans, there was opposition towards his implementation program. For example, he wanted to install telephone lines. There was stiff opposition, but just for implementation purposes, he threatened the pope that he was going to change his religion.

Of Politics

The system of government was the centerpiece for the Eway Revolution as proposed by EPRP. It is appropriate to quote Minilik's plea for establishing a modern system of government.

European government consuls have arrived in our country, Ethiopia. This is uncommon in our Ethiopian system of government. They cajole us by saying that without a rule of law, there cannot be a country worthy of a government. You also know that they want us to surrender to them. Even though Ethiopia had system of rules and regulations, in a few days, we will have new system of government based on Europeans, I have written rules upon which you will carry your duties and responsibilities without quarrels, without jealousy thereby fully cooperating to strengthen our government.

If we carry on to serve our people, it will be beneficial to our government and our country. No one will envy our country. Even though I have tried and tried tirelessly, without minister, council or consul, it is a one-man show resulting in discrediting my efforts.

Now with less sleep, less drinks, less love for money but more love for people, I hope you will accomplish the tasks I have assigned to you. In as much as I have trusted you, you should also appoint those whom you trust, those who don't love money, those who do not abuse the poor but really can help them.

As far as money is concerned, I will give you salary so that you will never solicit money from the poor except the required tax.

> If you go beyond the rules of love set and exploit the poor, I will have to hate you. You will be abused. In the name of your Soul, the Bible and the Cross-, you will be excommunicated.
> **(Atse Minilik II, Paulos Gnogno, and P: 360)**

And so Minilik in the spirit of implementation for his programs, he had appointed ministers in the following ministries appointed in order of their importance.

1. አፈ ንጉስ (Afe Nigus) For ministry of Justice
2. ፊት አውራሪ (Fit Awrari) For ministry of Defense
3. ጸሃፊ ትእዛዝ (Tsehafe Tazaz) For ministry of Pen
4. በጅሮንድ (Bejrond) For Finance and Home affairs
5. ሊቀ መካስ (Like Meqas) For ministry of Interior
6. ነጋድራስ (Negadras) For the ministry of Trade & Foreign Affairs
7. ከንቲባ (Kentiba) For the ministry of Agriculture

The current regimes of Shaebia and Woyane don't understand the power of _justice_ and _food_ in the way Minilik understood it. What a travesty!

Of Economics

There is and was no economic thinking in Ethiopia. The current leaders of Ethiopia do not seem to differentiate between Needs and Wants, a basic premise for economic theory. Previously, they had the Albanian model of development and now they seem to be caught between the Chinese and American model of development.

Of Conclusions

The trio individuals has concluded that the TPLF/EPRDF government don't seem to embrace any works of Haile Sellassie I, Tewodros, Minilik or of Yohannes IV. They also, do not follow the Eway Revolution of Ethiopia as spearheaded by EPRP. Instead they are operating in the footprints of the DERG. The DERG collapsed on its weight and this one is no exception. Without vision and planning (tools for development in political system, religious mechanism for love and peace and above all economic development) the regime of Zenawi cannot survive. It is predicted that it will collapse on 2013 Julian calendar and it is also predicted that Eritrea and Ethiopia will merge into one **E** on 2013 Gregorian calendar.

Happy New Year to all AEthiopians.
Let it be the beginning of our true Millennium
For comments and criticism: woldetewolde@yahoo.com

CALL ME BY MY NAME:

Solutions with Debteraw, XIV

Obo Arada Shawl alias Wolde Tewolde

March 13, 2008

Confused or Confuser

Am I confused or a confuser (no such word is found in the English Dictionary, though)? My pen name is Obo Arada Shawl, which signifies that I stand for Rural Ethiopia, inner cities of Addis Ababa and Asmara respectively but my real name is Wolde Tewolde. Am I creating some confusion for my readers? If there is, please let me know as our given Names signify something of value.

In my previous article, actually it was a commentary on professor Mesfin Wolde Mariam who might intentionally or unintentionally lived in a confused environment or smart enough to confuse others during our lifetime. In the past, I had attempted to save Ethiopians from confusion made by a prominent Poet, deceitful geography professor and by an emotional journalist in Diaspora. I have always believed since years back that three professions (personalities) namely of Arts, Geography and Journalism can create distortion on any Ethiopian realities.

MWM (Geographer)

I do not want to go on answering the twenty questions posed to professor MWM by EthioLion.com. Besides, no one asked me to do so despite my plea. However, since the professor cannot stop meddling in the affairs of innocent Ethiopian/Eritrean lives, we have to continue to reveal and disgrace his personality a la mode of CC (combat & challenge) and TT

(Tagel & Tateq) style of struggle. CC was the name of the publication of EPRP whereas TT belonged to MEISON's. Both style of struggle were anemic to MWM. He likes Yaz & Leqeq despite his pretension as a leftist professor. When the EthioLion editor pleaded with the professor as to when to get off from the Ethiopian peoples" back, I responded that he would never do that until he finds out his DNA. When I wrote that comment I did not mean his DNA in order to find out his paternity or his criminality record. I was trying merely to locate his space in life, namely his political geography.

Now, true to my prediction, he wrote an article on Obama (see Abbaymedia.com). He labeled Obama's presidential race as a spirit. What kind of a spirit, one may ask? This kind of jumping into conclusion is what harmed our people and country. I am sure this is another blunder by the professor to be seen in the near future.

Every time there is a wind of change or a hope for change professor MWM jumps and make some serious mistakes including some irreparable damages. For instance, the professor had joined a panel of eleven PhD holders that was formed to demarcate the Ethiopian polity under the DERG. He also joined the group of so-called independent Ethiopians who went to London to witness the surrender of the Ethiopian government to EPLF/TPLF/OLF. This time, the professor had joined with three PhD holders and three Masters. One can go on listing his calculated or erratic activities. What I do not understand is why many Ethiopian intellectuals follow his example instead following the right people regardless of their titles. Call me by my name. What is my name? (Girzmatch, Kegnazmatch, etc. etc.)

I do not know whether it is true or not, but one simple explanation of the professor's attitude of character and personality is given like this.

- In his professional field, at a certain time during a proposed meeting of some local Amhara officials to be held somewhere in rural Shewa village, they did not know the location of the village and so MWM was summoned by the Emperor Haile Sellasie I in order to locate the meeting place and so the professor true to his geography knowledge pinpointed the village. From there on, the

Emperor reported to have said that „there is nothing that Mesfin does not know". Could this be a reason for his arrogance?
- In his family life, when asked why he wanted a divorce from his wife, it was circulated that he said, "Two husbands couldn't live in the same house". Let us hope that Mideksa has liberated him this time around.

Our Issue, Then

How do we handle our aspirations for Unity, Peace and Democracy? At the time when I met Debteraw, our communication was three dimensional, in religious terms (father-son-holy spirit), familial (husband-children-wife), governmental affairs (monarchy-church nobility), political (party-army-masses) and so on and so forth.

Specifically, Debteraw used to insist that the practical solution for bringing Unity-Democracy- Peace was through READ (Revolution-Education-Art-Democracia). For Debu and me the letters of A&E are one and the same (usage in pronunciation as first & fifth). However, their contents were fundamentally different from mine as AE = Arts and Education (he was excellent in Kinet and Education). For me, the letters of K& W were/are relevant as KW = Knowledge and Wisdom. Our common agreement for working together was based on Revolution and Democracia (RD). By the way every nation has progressed via Research and Development while ours was set on Revolution and Democratization.

Our Issue, Now

I do not want to go into detail as why each leader/professional, country/countries or global organizations aspire to indulge in Ethiopia or Eritrea. Suffice to indicate to my readers in a nutshell what is behind agendas of our time.

So what is our stand on these issues? What do we need to do? Let us discuss them.

On Domestic affairs

- Engineer Hailu for Costs
- Economist Berhanu for Benefits
- EPRDF/TPLF for confusion

On Foreign affairs

- USA for Strategic purpose of fighting Terrorism
- UNMEE for Employment
- AU/EU/China for Trade and Aid

Our Issue then and now

Domestic and foreign: Although all organizations, groups and individuals attempt to resolve the Ethiopian issues, they all do it in around about way. That is by switching places for the letters of U (unity), D (democracy) and P (peace). Changing names will not help to solve the problems of Ethiopia and Ethiopians. Prioritizing, yes.

EPRP for Unity, Democracia and Peace

For EPRP, it is not about prioritizing. It is about putting the three letters together. They have done this for four decades now. EPRP's main tasks as at yesterday, today and tomorrow were, are and will be as follows: -

- Visionary Solutions
- Fearless leadership and
- Timeless principles in
- Domestic and
- Foreign sectors.

What I wanted to bring to the attention to all my readers is that there is no Unity in Diversity as Debteraw has been fighting for a long time. We cannot go on using the same phrase or mission of Vive La Difference! I believe now that we have to bring <u>*Unity in Clarity*</u>. That is why I am asking intellectuals and other literate Ethiopians to expose their true nature in terms of Names, Symbol, Ritual and Values. Call me by my name? What is your name?

True to the nature of Debteraw Tsegeye's proposal for Ethiopia, I still insist to continue to dwell on the political solution based on Ethiopian History, Culture and DEMOCRACIA. He used to call this HCD. It is purely based on Ethiopian political History, Cultural and social/religious path (AAgmelago). To put it simply, let us see what has been said and presented to Ethiopians both at home and abroad.

EPRP is a unity of a political party, peace at the top of Red Mountain (<u>ASSIMBA.com & Assimba.Org</u>). Democracia in Eritrea and Ethiopia.

- *Let us share our experiences*
- *Let us write our shared experiences or perish as they say and*
- *Let us finish the Marathon of struggle with ADE*

When the war broke out between EPLF and TPLF and later agreed to settle their dispute through an arbitration but never materialized the agreement, but continue in disrupting the peoples" daily lives, I proposed in such a way that Europeans should settle in Zala Anbesa to administer them, to let America to settle in Assab so as to develop the Red Sea and to let the Chinese to let them to settle in Badme to develop agriculture. At the time, nobody heeded my call. What about now? I have now different types of proposal. Here it is.

For EPRP, Ethiopia is a **<u>Center</u>** for the Universe and Eritrea is a **<u>Key</u>** for the World.

It is about **CK. It is that simple.**

Proposal

The senator from Wisconsin, Russ Feingold described Ethiopia as demarcated/bounded by a failed state of Somalia, by an ethnic cleansing Kenya, by a genocidal Sudan and by an inaccessible authoritarian Eritrea. Of course, the senator forgot to add the country of Djoubiti. <u>It is inconceivable without D for our project of SEEDS country.</u>

For comments and criticism: woldetewolde@yahoo.com

The Eway Revolution: the missing points Solutions with spw of WDH

By Obo Arada Shawl

December 23, 2009

The spirit of Wallelign The process of Debteraw The writings of Hama Tuma have triggered respectively, to the downfall of the Monarchy, the military Dictatorship and to Ethnic Tyranny

Introduction

The politics of Eathiopia tend to pull in different directions. It is definitely three-dimensional class, the class of EPRDF led by TPLF, the class of EPLF led by EPDJ and all others with or without EPRP. The collective thoughts of Wallelign, DEBTERAW and Hama have predicted the end of nation states long before they began the struggle for change. Nowadays, the Nation State appears to be almost a nostalgic fiction. Take, for instance the State of Eritrea, or Tigrai state, for that matter, ten years ago, both TPLF and EPLF were fighting tooth and nail to become a nation state.

Recently, I have been reading a book entitled the "generals" by Eyob A. Endale (shambel) It is a book about how the Ethiopian generals attempted to overthrow one of their own military dictator, Colonel Menghistu Haile Mariam. Why on earth do the "generals" attempt a coup d"etat? This week, we are hearing about death sentences against coup plotters. I thought we have passed the stage of coup d"etats!

What was/is wrong with the elites of Eathiopians? Where do they learn their life lessons? Is it from their parents, peers or genes? Or is it something else? Perhaps, their education or training is alien to the Ethiopian masses. Where were these coup d"etat plotters during the Ethiopian Revolution and counter-revolution? I was not only surprised but also shocked to read about the way the generals died. No wonder, the so-called generals had to loose the war against EPLF and TPLF. They seem not to learn anything from the Eway Revolution.

The concept of self-determination by Wallellign Kassa Mokenen, the Eway Revolution as applied by DEBTERAW, Tsegeye G. M and the challenge of electoral politics by the writings of Hama Tuma are all - assets and heritage of EPRP. No one seems to deny that the experience and heritage of EPRP would come to be the *prime mover* of struggle in the context of Eathiopia.

In the entire struggle for power and politics in Eathiopia, notwithstanding with the above assertions, there are two missing points. First, it is the nature of the Eathiopian Revolution and second, it is about how the strategy and tactics for the Revolution were applied. In the first instance, the Eathiopian Revolution was about change of concepts and attitudes and not changing of personalities. In the second instance, the methodology applied was guerrilla warfare - የተሩዘመ ትግል - not coup d"etat - መፈንቅለ መንግሥት - or Insurrection - አመጽ -. Unless and otherwise, Eathiopian politicians are clear about these concepts, theories and applications, there will be no common ground to reach at a solution via *reconciliation or negotiation.*

For a good period of years, the Eathiopian politics will seem to pull along three-dimensional directions, i.e. Nationalism, Reaction or Revolution. In other words, Separation, Unification or Division. In actual fact, Eway Ethiopia has stepped into five dimensional directions, according to my mentor DEBTERAW. Let me briefly go over the missing points of departure.

The DERG military Factor: a power player

Although the DERG (comprised of 120 members) assumed political power without the generals of Ethiopia, nominally, they had placed personalities like generals Aman Andom and Teferi Bante, at least to lead them in name - hypocrisy.

On the one hand, it was true that the DERG's pronouncement was based on a revolution and not on reform. The DERG led by Colonel Menghistu had attempted to destroy, the ancien regime, to harass the Bureaucrats, and to become friendly with Moscow and Havana in order to oppose western countries political system of government. While on the other hand, the DERG's Politburo was mainly comprised of military men.

This means that the generals were part and parcels of the military rulers of Eathiopia another hypocrisy.

The "generals" have seen not only the movement of the guerrilla fighters but also, their organizational set up. It was a truism that the nationalists were embarked on a long struggle based on the peasant masses. From the DERG's side of movement and organizational structure, it was similar with a flavor of fear of the Dictator Colonel. What I don't understand is the "generals" attempt to overthrow the dictator without throwing him from the plane or putting him under house arrest. Besides, not only a coup d"etat was "massacre" considering the generals" power position. Why did they not learn from Menghistu's „slogan of massacre" ላምሳ ያሰቡንን ለቁርስ አደረግናቸው

Nevertheless, I am of the opinion that some of the military Eathiopian elites have learnt to accept a struggle for a democratic Eathiopia - a step in pentagonal dimension.

The "BEKAGN" and the "NOW" Generation Factor

This generation includes the victims of the DERG who were cheated by the military regime, particularly those students who were involved in Edget Behbret, those soldiers, marines, air forces or national guards; actually those who were promised by the DERG that it will return to its barracks once it has eliminated the ancient regime and its allies. Or alternatively, to those gullible Eathiopians who believed that Menghistu would fight until the last bullet to be used by him. Besides, this group includes those who were in prison or who saw deaths and mayhem within the "Revolution".

The second groups of "NOW" are those would not believe that "Ethiopia" had a glorious history of trade, religion, independence and civilization. Even if it had, this generation claims it is of no value. All they are interested is "quick cash". The amazing thing is that they don't know what cash is let alone money and finance. This generation is a product of EPRDF.

The Walleligne Factor: Concept of Self-determination

The Eritrean concept of struggle for Indepndence obviously was initiated in 1896 right after the Italian occupation. 65 years later, the Eritrean struggle formally started with an armed struggle.

Politically, the struggle took shape when the University students especially the radical students determined to solve the question of nations and nationalities. The university students" challenge against the administration, the professors and the subject matter became obsolete. The student body became followers of the radical student leaders.

As to the national question, many papers and discussions were presented but the most important article was written by WMK and it was presented on the occasion of freshman party. Later on, Walleligne's article was published in the popular student magazine of „struggle". The Ethiopian government newspapers condemned WMK's article on the national question. The Ethiopian University Students were also depicted as anti-Ethiopia. Wallellign was labeled as an agent of Imperialism as well as anti-Amhara.

However, both charges against Wallellign were absolutely false. Once the Ethiopian government propaganda machine lied about Wallellign and the student body, other news media continued to lie about WMK and the student body.

Despite TPLF and EPLF's distortion and damage of the question of nationality, WMK has sacrificed his life for the unity of Ethiopia via theory and application for he was Tsinhate Muhur Akal. The democratic nature of Wallellign will be honored when truth prevails.

Wallelign and his seven comrades* had attempted to hijack a plane and all killed but one by anti- hijackers. WMK and his comrades were not to kill or blow up themselves as in the current terrorists practice. They just wanted to scare the crew, the anti-hijackers and the passengers in that order. WMK and his team did not have the heart to kill but to sacrifice as their comrades in Assimba – shading blood if necessary – not in the name of the Eathiopians but in real terms. That event was a testimony for action.

As to the spirit of WMK, he was a highly motivated person and an honest thinker. He thought hard about the role of the ruling class. He knew that oppression (cultural and social) had created more damaging effect on the Eathiopian populace than exploitation (economic). WMK emphasized in his writings about the pretension of not only the Amharas but also even the Tigrians pretension of becoming Ethiopian with an "Amhara face".

I do not think it is fair to blame WMK for the cession of Eritrea and others that would follow. And we should blame the TPLF for perpetuating the concept of self-determination out of context. Even now, the TPLF are caught between the followers of WMK's article or becoming a wholesome Eathiopia. There is no creativity but copycat.

The DEBTERAW Factor: The Eway Revolution

DEBTERAW was prepared mentally, physically and emotionally to finish what was started – the Eway Revolution. He was not for coup d"etat; he was not for insurrection but for the long march of educating, organizing and arming the people of Eathiopia to empower them with information, knowledge and wisdom. DEMOCRACIA for DEBTERAW was a process not an end.

Articles on CALL ME BY NAME: a debate with DEBTERAW or Solutions with DEBTERAW should be revisited for grasping the essence of the Eway Revolution. They can be found on Debteraw.com Assimba. org Ethiox.com or by goggling on Goggle.

EPRP was the best political party fighting for the Ethiopian people. EPRP was a visionary political party for it saw the future and explained it in a new way

The Hama Tuma Factor: the struggle for Electoral politics

Hama Tuma is a prolific writer of Eathiopia as well as on African affairs. Since his early days of youth, he has been consistent with his ideology for combating against real or perceived enemies of Eathiopia and Africa.

EPRP was not well known for its political prowess or for its populist discontent, according to Hama's writings

A politically correct struggle was a lost struggle. Take the Badme war, take the generals" May coup d"etat, take the current article 39 in the constitution, and take Ginbot 7 Election or the coming election of 2010. They all depend on political correctness or in our parlance, feudal mentality.

However, it is time to reconsider EPRP's role in the current Eathiopian situations/conditions, as its enemies were ferocious to disrupt its mission and physically destroy its entity. EPRP can only win when its leaders talk head to head, when its army meets face to face, when its members communicate heart to heart and when the party regardless communicates with all Eathiopians soul to soul.

The most "dissenting generation" against EPRP have been those groups who became vengeful of events and circumstances. Such groups are those who really believed that Eathiopia was first in everything but was destroyed by those who were involved in one way or another in a "revolution" or socialism. Or alternatively, these are the groups who prefer to blame others but not themselves or rather who are scared to express their opinions in public but mostly involved in back biting. Hama Tuma's writing usually targets against such groups of hypocrites- አስመሳዮች - ፈሪዎችና ምንደኞች -

Conclusions

WMK has contributed a lot of ideas and thoughts for all Eathiopians to act whereas DEBTERAW's contribution is immensurable in terms of implementing the ideas and concepts of the Eway Revolution.

Hama Tuma's writing and exposition of opportunists and self-conceited Eathiopians along with their foreign masters have done incalculable damage to EPRP's image but an immense benefit and pride to the majority of Eathiopians.

If Eathiopians were to sacrifice lives and resources in the Eway Revolution, we must finish the war and the struggle to its conclusion. We must be committed to win and reach the goal.

In addition, EPRP's associates* its supporters should be educated and informed on EPRP's current mission and vision. Its leaders should lead, its army should defend, and its members would support. All these three units were supposed to sacrifice lives and resources. EPRP was not for political correctness. It was founded on correct political and democratic system to be instituted in their country Eathiopia.

TRUTH WILL PREVAIL

For comments and questions: woldetewolde@yahoo.com

www.ingramcontent.com/pod-product-compliance
Lightning Source LLC
Chambersburg PA
CBHW070606030426
42337CB00020B/3702